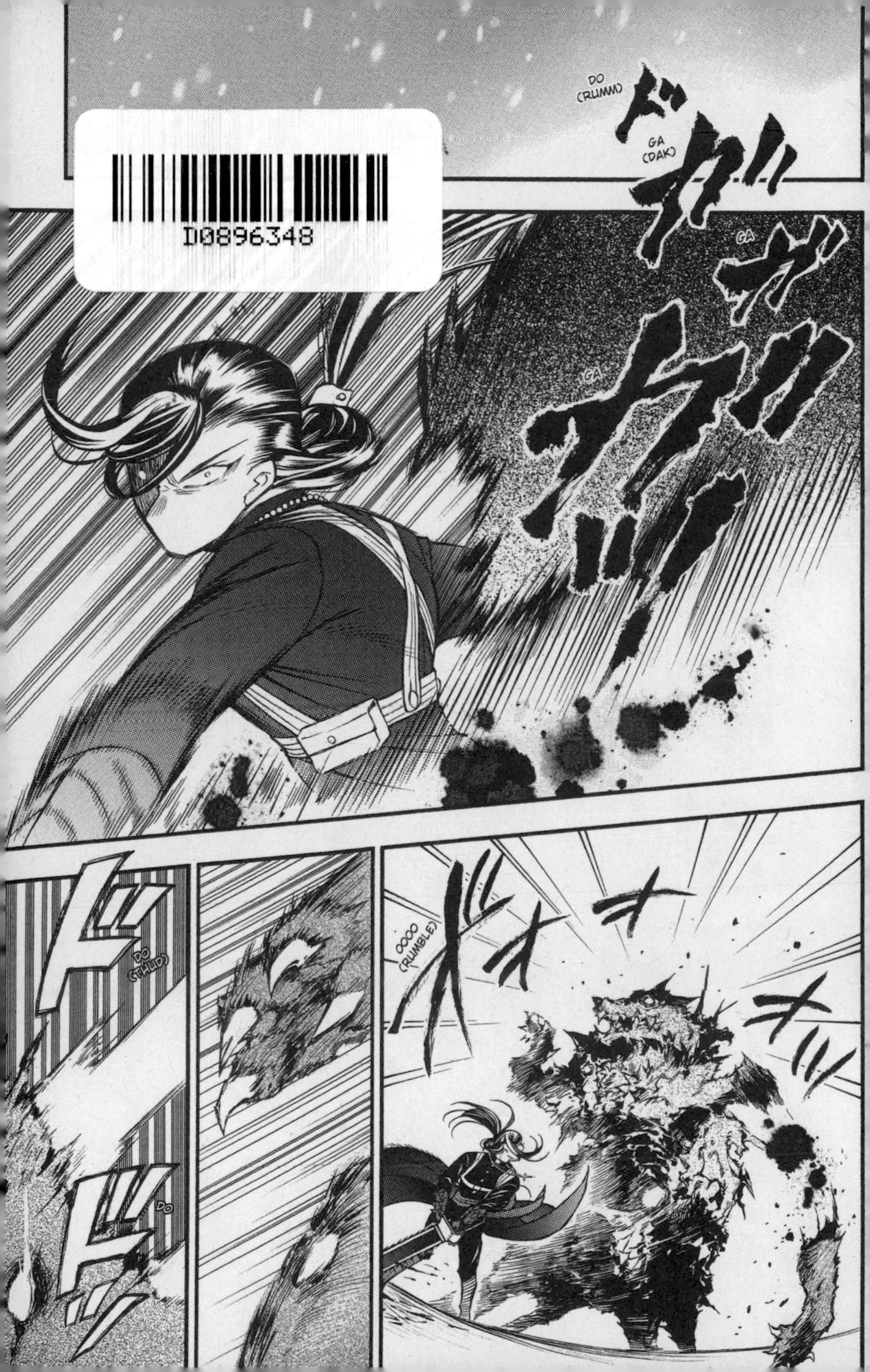
DO
(RUMM)
GA
(DAK)
GA
GA
OOOO
(RUMBLE)
DO
(THUD)
DO

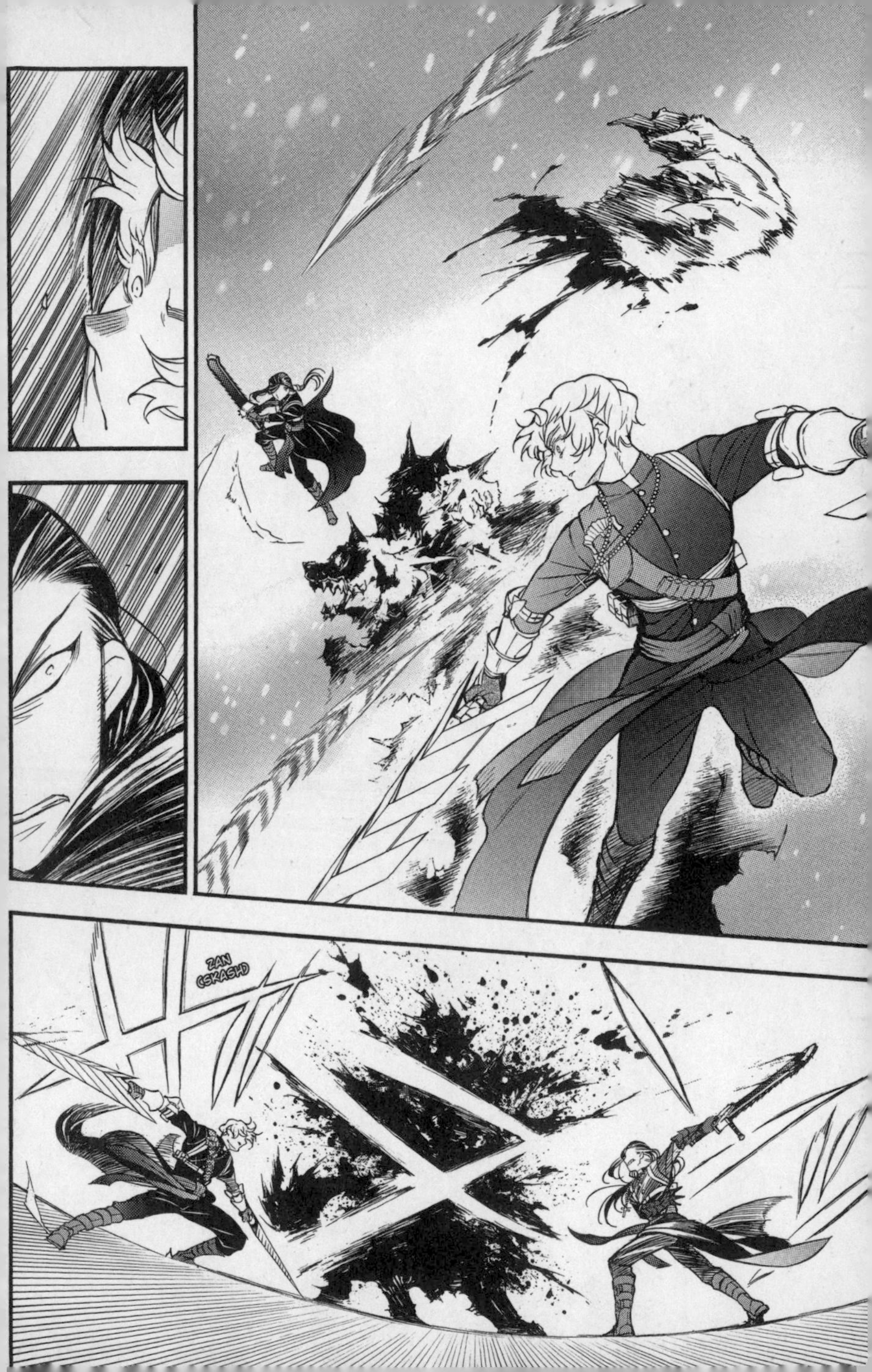
ZAN
(SKASH)

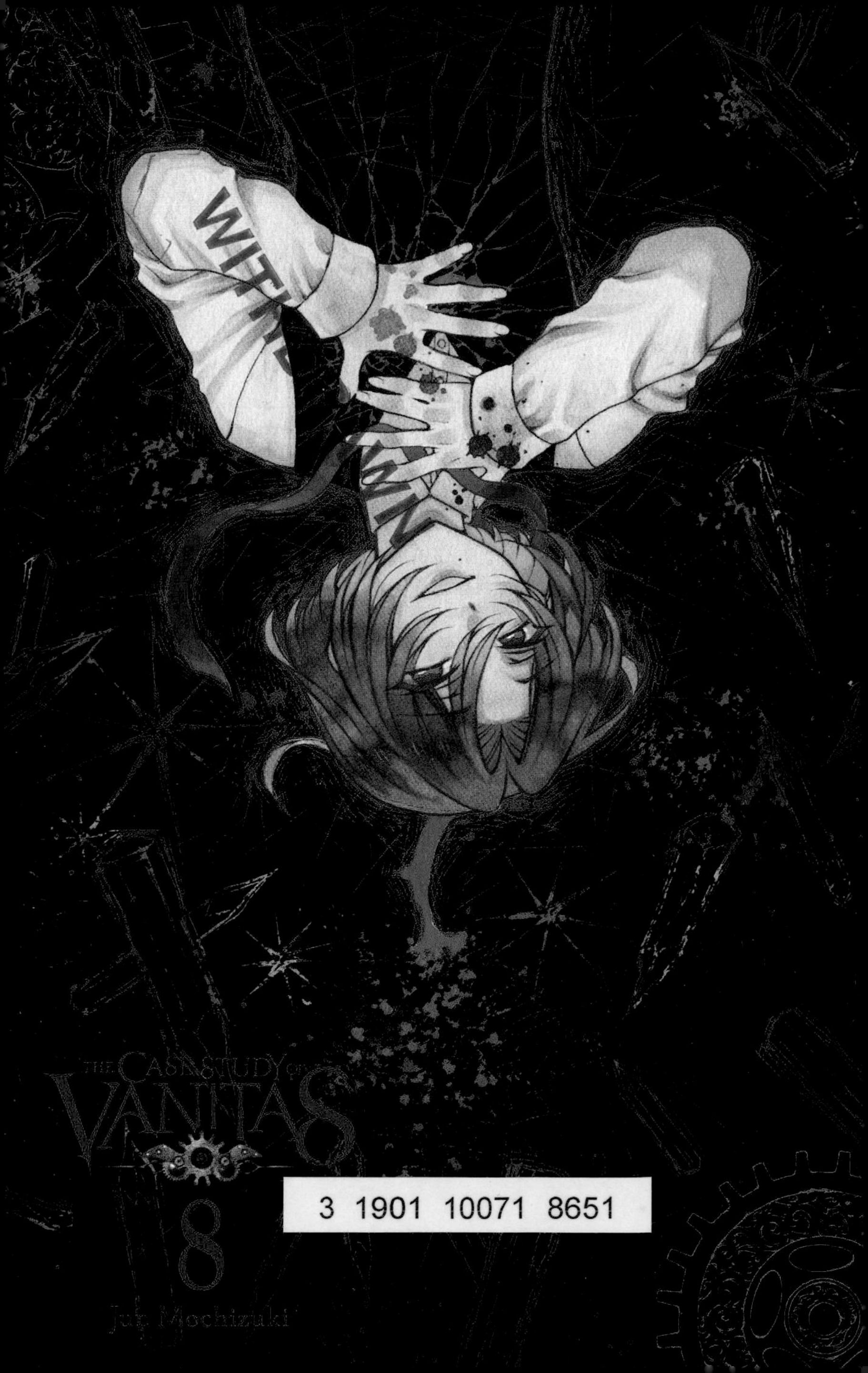
THE CASE STUDY OF
VANITAS
8
Jun Mochizuki

THE CASE STUDY OF
VANITAS 8

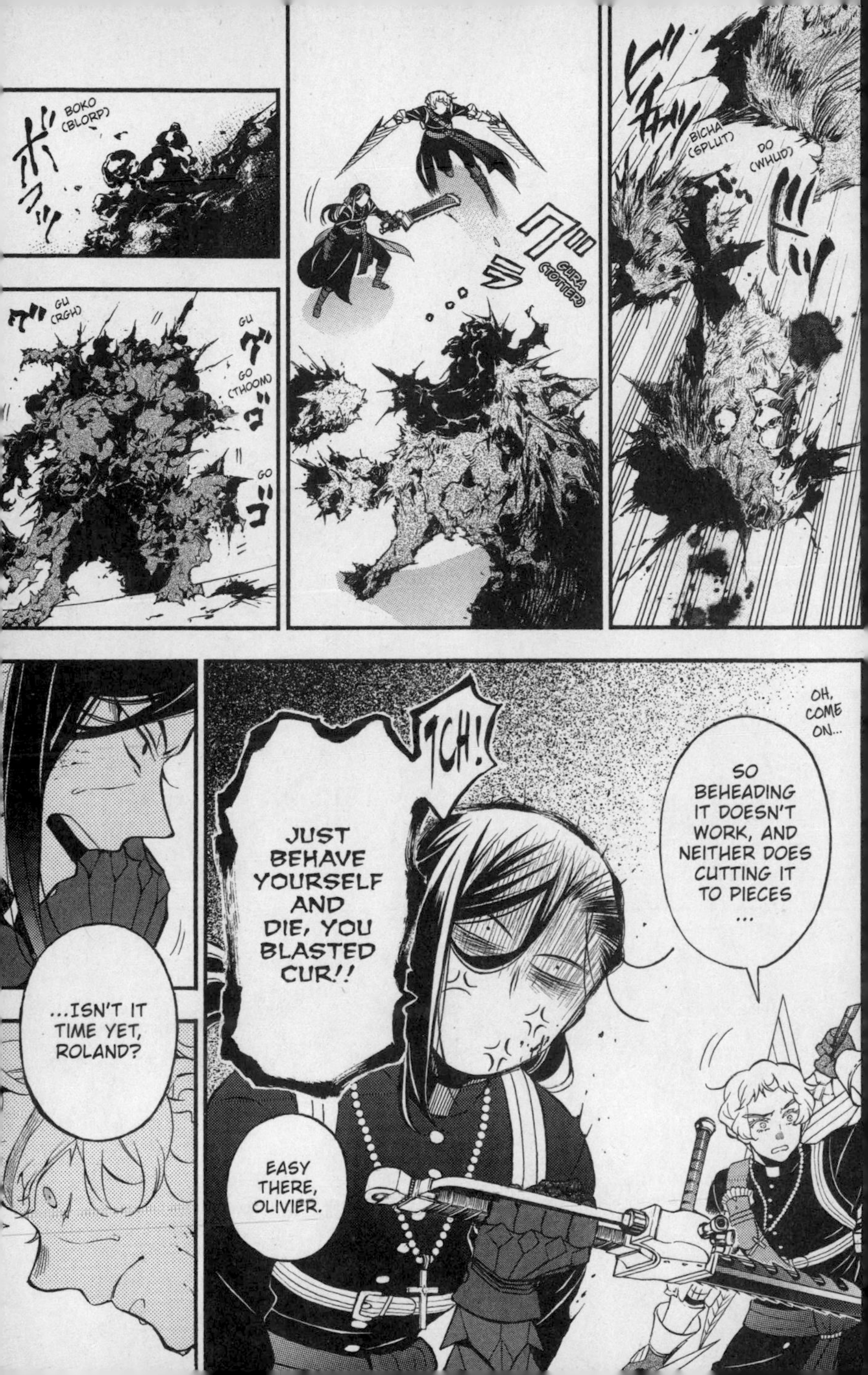
BICHA (SPLUT)
DO (WHUD)
GURA (TOTTER)
BOKO (BLORP)
GU (RGH)
GU
GO (THOOM)
GO
OH, COME ON...
SO BEHEADING IT DOESN'T WORK, AND NEITHER DOES CUTTING IT TO PIECES...
TCH!
JUST BEHAVE YOURSELF AND DIE, YOU BLASTED CUR!!
EASY THERE, OLIVIER.
...ISN'T IT TIME YET, ROLAND?

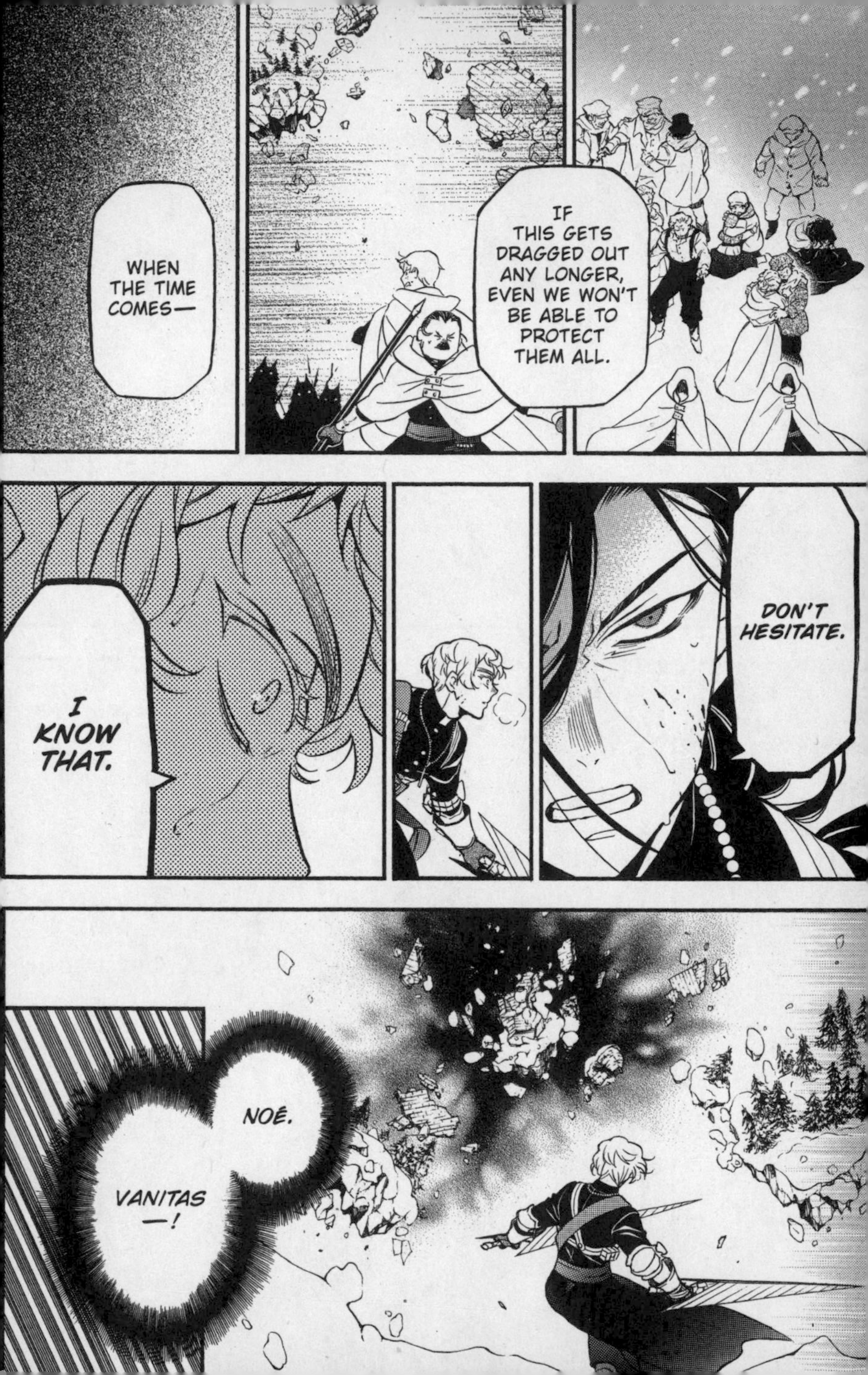
IF THIS GETS DRAGGED OUT ANY LONGER, EVEN WE WON'T BE ABLE TO PROTECT THEM ALL.
WHEN THE TIME COMES—
DON'T HESITATE.
I KNOW THAT.
NOÉ.
VANITAS—!

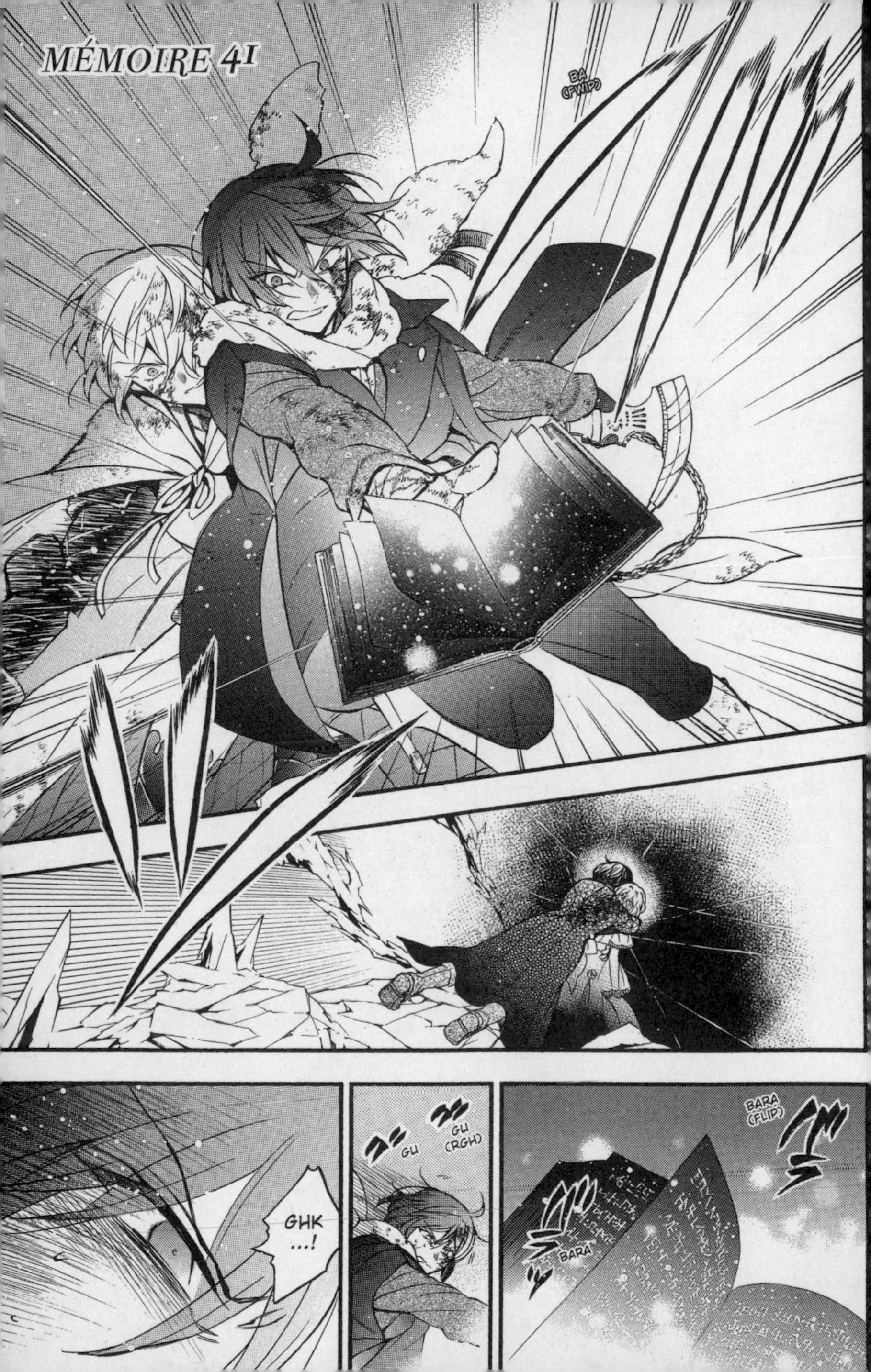
MÉMOIRE 41
BA (FWIP)
BARA (FLIP)
BARA
GU (RGH)
GU
GHK ...!

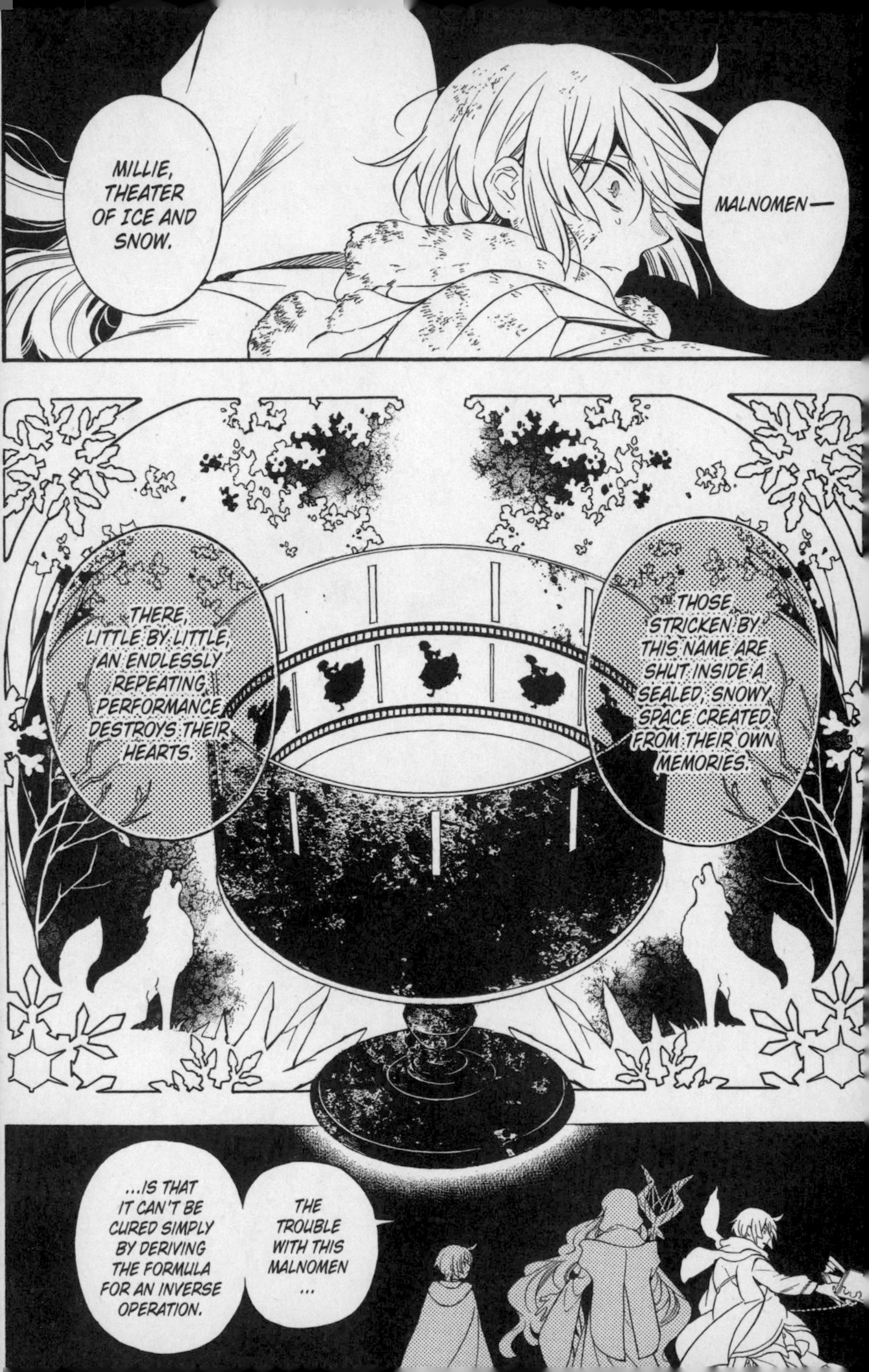
MALNOMEN—
MILLIE, THEATER OF ICE AND SNOW.
THOSE STRICKEN BY THIS NAME ARE SHUT INSIDE A SEALED, SNOWY SPACE CREATED FROM THEIR OWN MEMORIES.
THERE, LITTLE BY LITTLE, AN ENDLESSLY REPEATING PERFORMANCE DESTROYS THEIR HEARTS.
THE TROUBLE WITH THIS MALNOMEN ...
...IS THAT IT CAN'T BE CURED SIMPLY BY DERIVING THE FORMULA FOR AN INVERSE OPERATION.

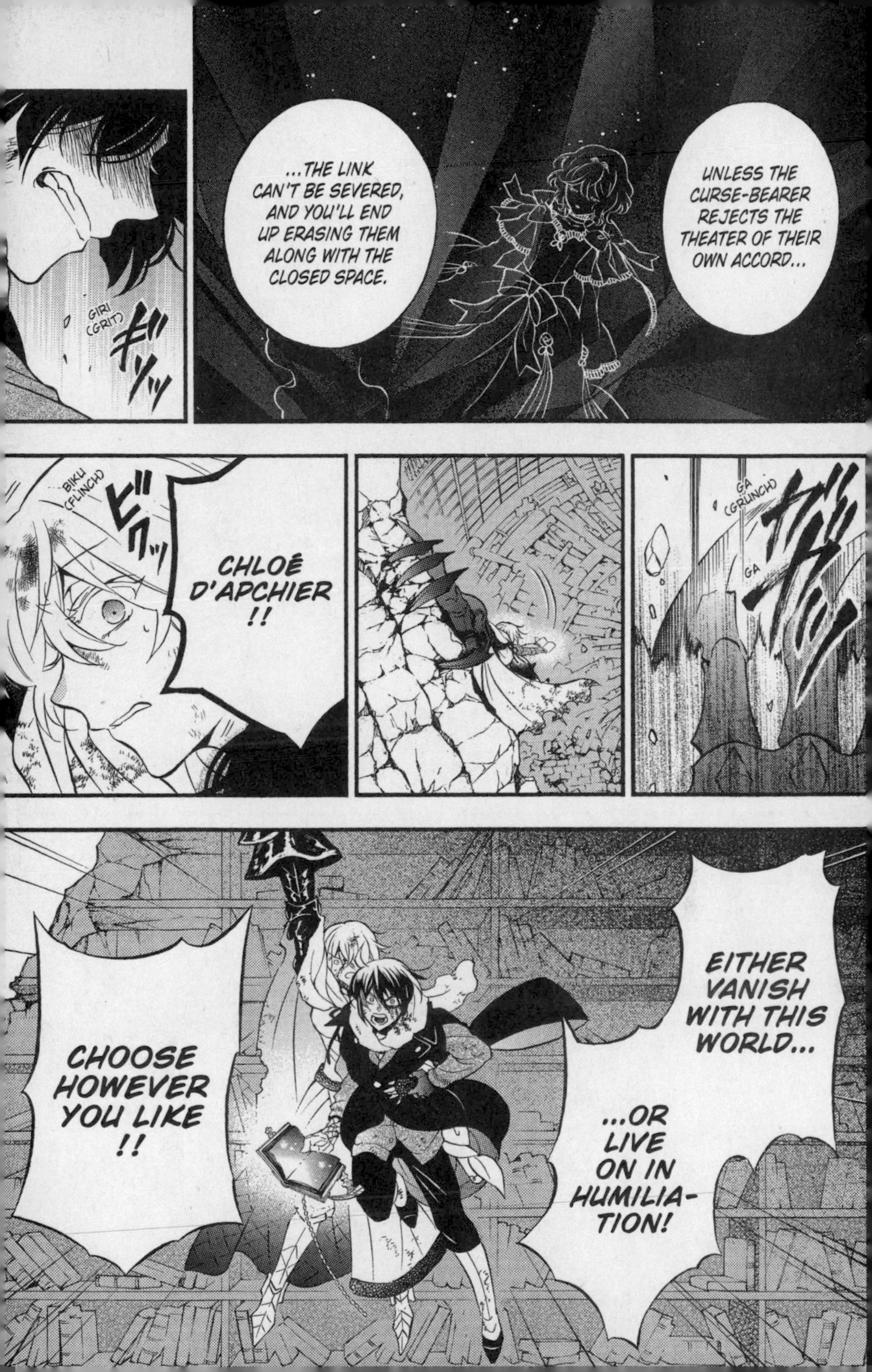
UNLESS THE CURSE-BEARER REJECTS THE THEATER OF THEIR OWN ACCORD...
...THE LINK CAN'T BE SEVERED, AND YOU'LL END UP ERASING THEM ALONG WITH THE CLOSED SPACE.
GIRI (GRIT)
GA (GRUNCH)
GA
BIKU (FLINCH)
CHLOÉ D'APCHIER !!
EITHER VANISH WITH THIS WORLD...
...OR LIVE ON IN HUMILIA-TION!
CHOOSE HOWEVER YOU LIKE !!

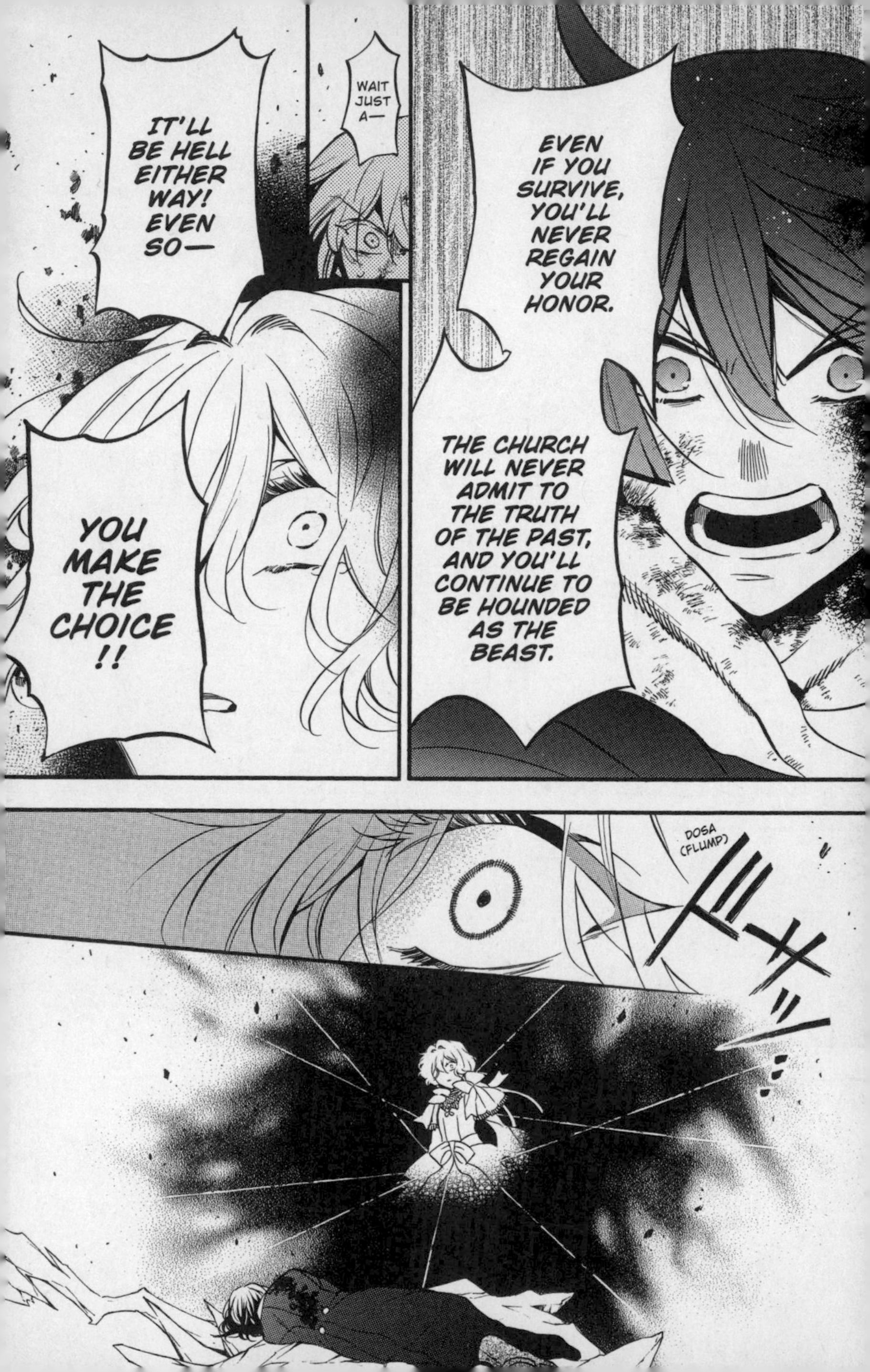
EVEN IF YOU SURVIVE, YOU'LL NEVER REGAIN YOUR HONOR.
THE CHURCH WILL NEVER ADMIT TO THE TRUTH OF THE PAST, AND YOU'LL CONTINUE TO BE HOUNDED AS THE BEAST.
WAIT JUST A—
IT'LL BE HELL EITHER WAY! EVEN SO—
YOU MAKE THE CHOICE !!
DOSA (FLUMP)

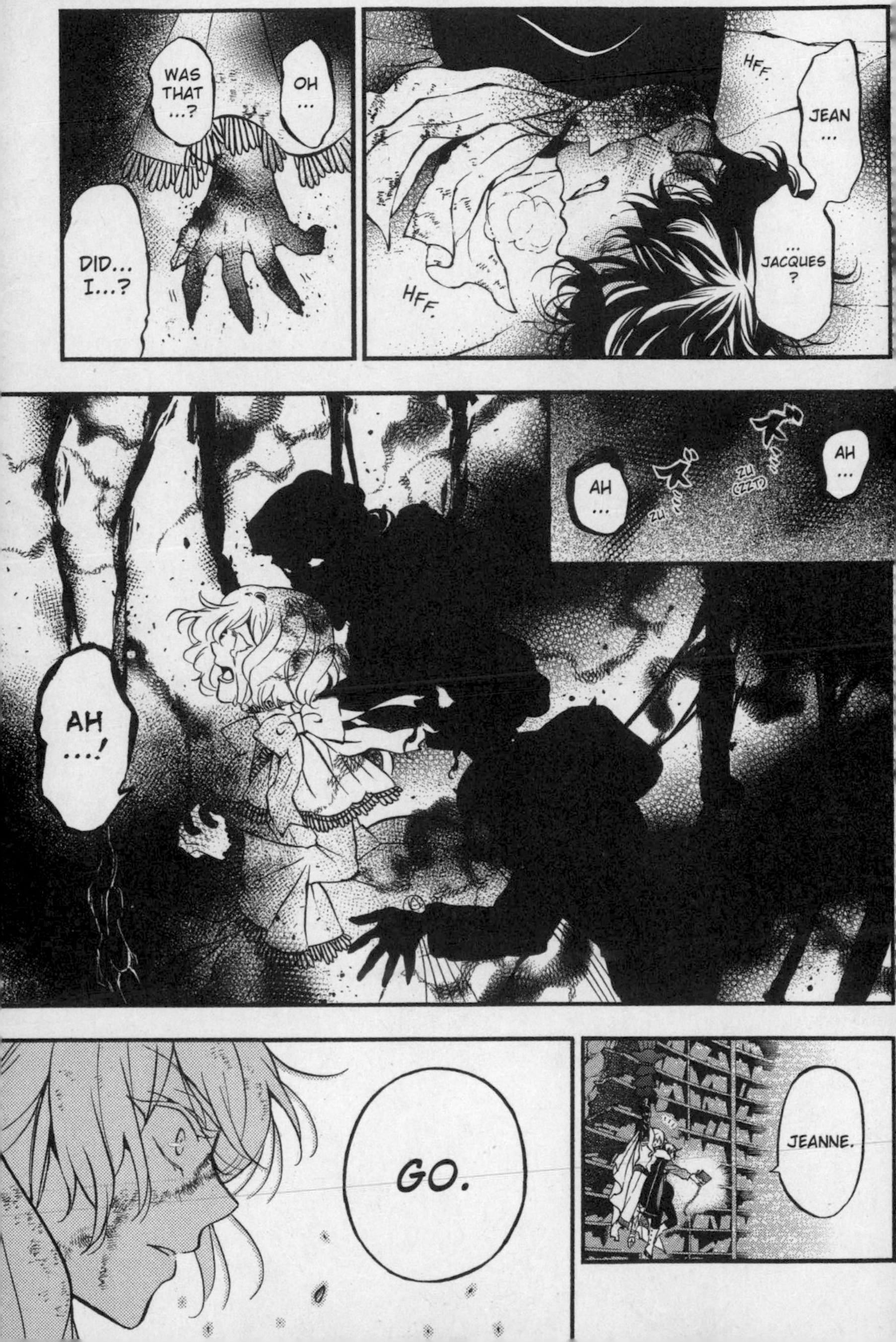
HFF.
JEAN ...
... JACQUES ?
HFF.
OH ...
WAS THAT ...?
DID... I...?
AH ...
ZU (ZZZT)
ZU
AH ...
AH ...!
JEANNE.
GO.

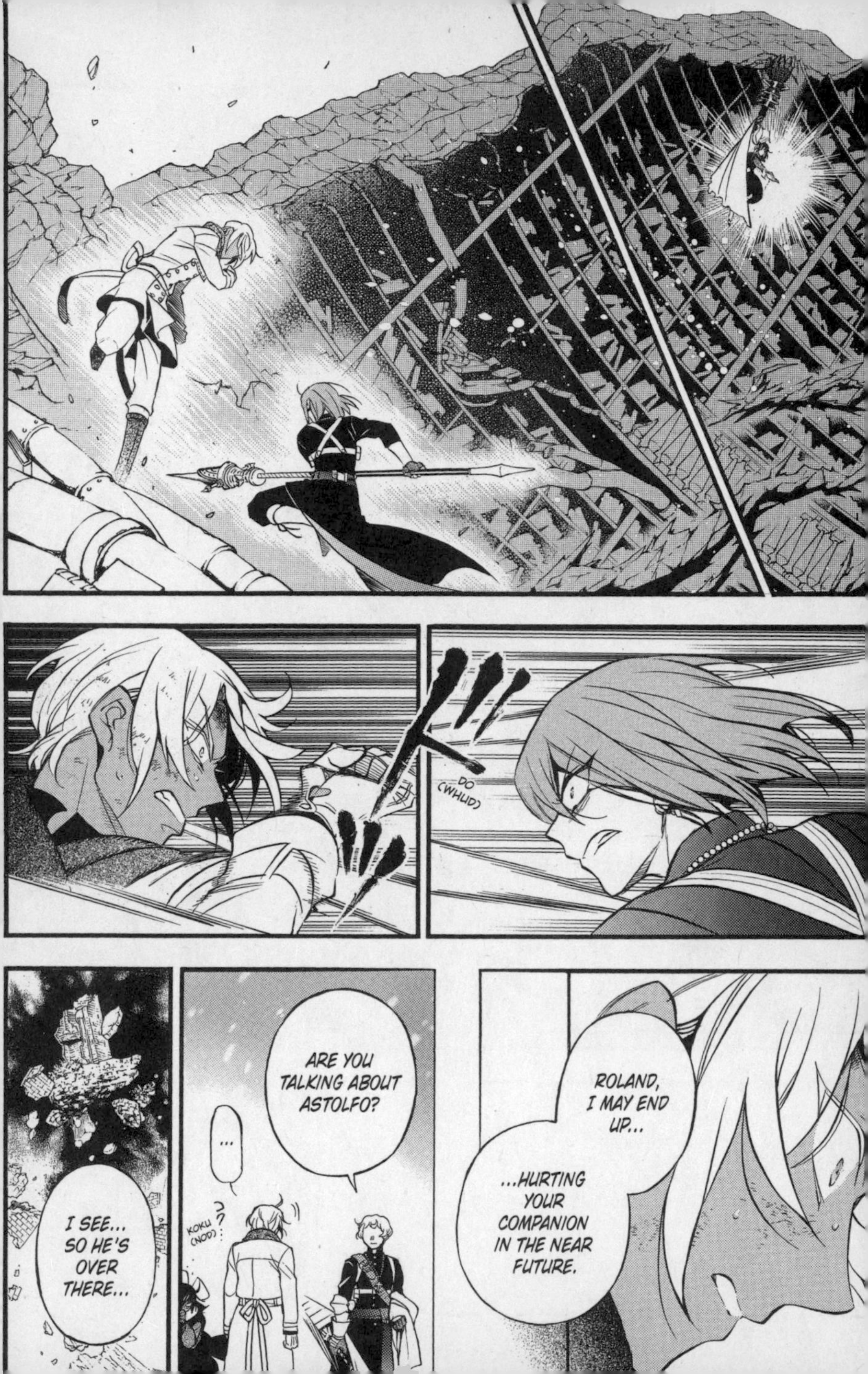
DO (WHUD)
ROLAND, I MAY END UP...
...HURTING YOUR COMPANION IN THE NEAR FUTURE.
ARE YOU TALKING ABOUT ASTOLFO?
...
KOKU (NOD)
?
I SEE... SO HE'S OVER THERE...

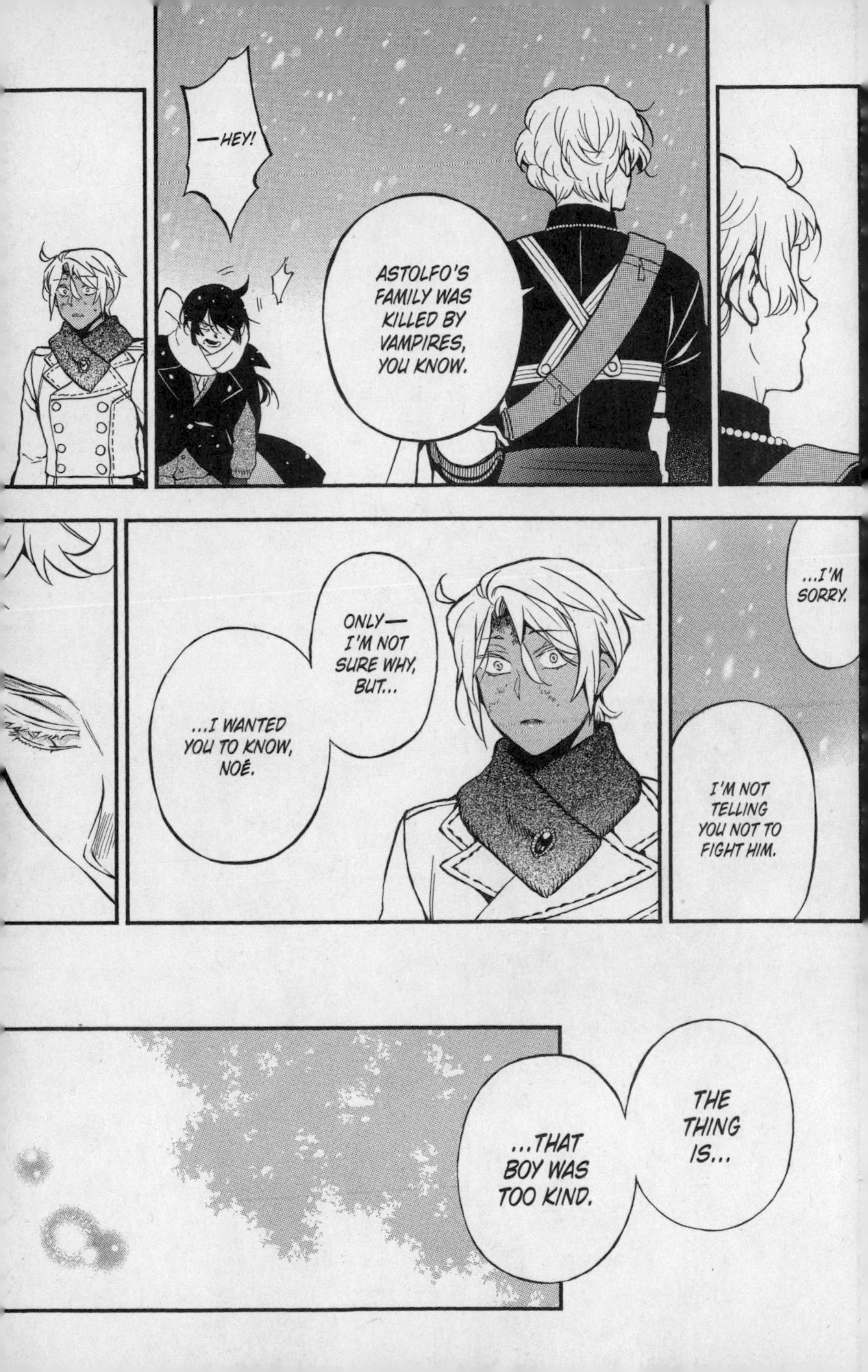
ASTOLFO'S FAMILY WAS KILLED BY VAMPIRES, YOU KNOW.
—HEY!
...I'M SORRY.
I'M NOT TELLING YOU NOT TO FIGHT HIM.
ONLY— I'M NOT SURE WHY, BUT...
...I WANTED YOU TO KNOW, NOÉ.
THE THING IS...
...THAT BOY WAS TOO KIND.

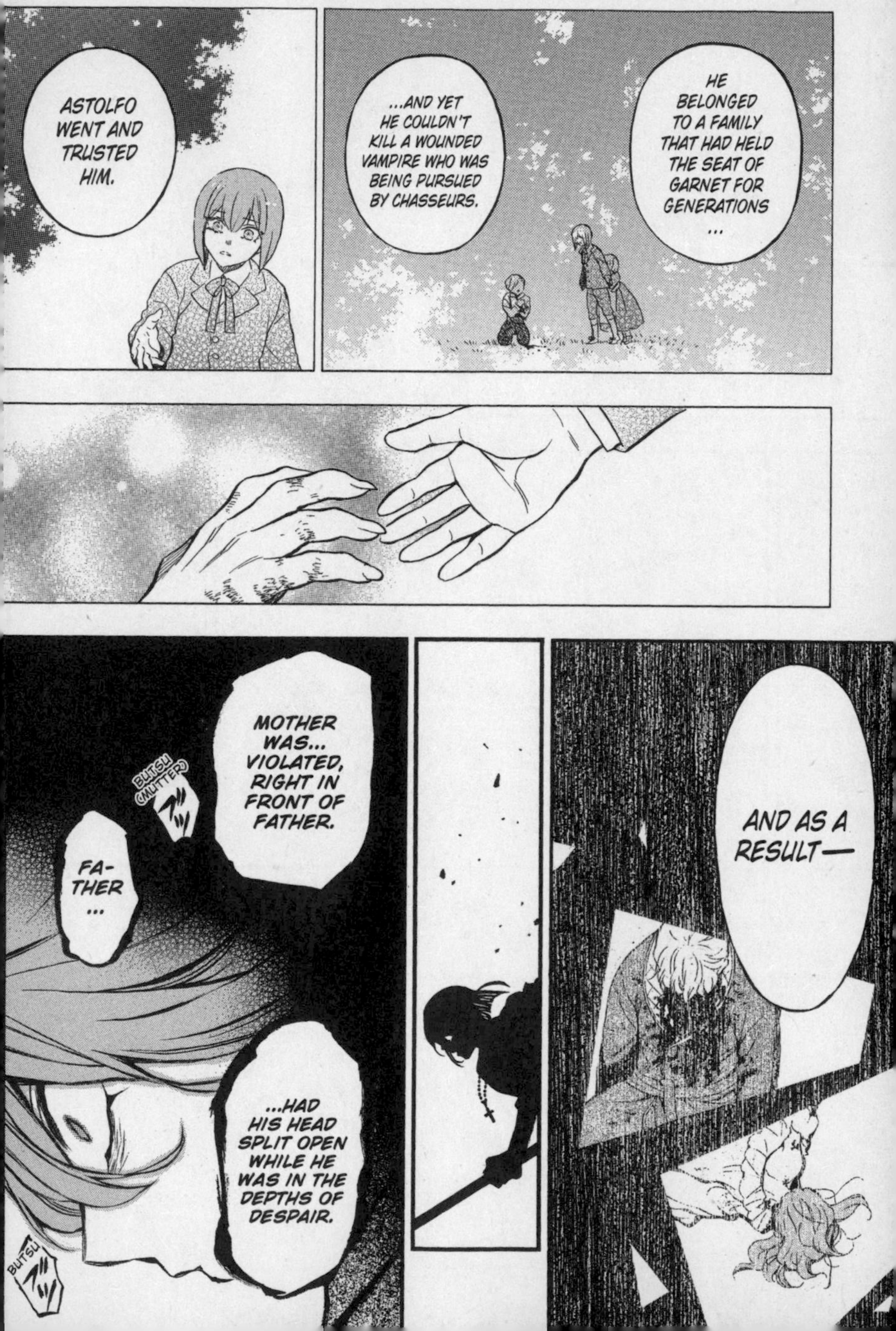
HE BELONGED TO A FAMILY THAT HAD HELD THE SEAT OF GARNET FOR GENERATIONS ...
...AND YET HE COULDN'T KILL A WOUNDED VAMPIRE WHO WAS BEING PURSUED BY CHASSEURS.
ASTOLFO WENT AND TRUSTED HIM.
AND AS A RESULT—
MOTHER WAS... VIOLATED, RIGHT IN FRONT OF FATHER.
BUTSU (MUTTER)
FA-THER ...
...HAD HIS HEAD SPLIT OPEN WHILE HE WAS IN THE DEPTHS OF DESPAIR.
BUTSU

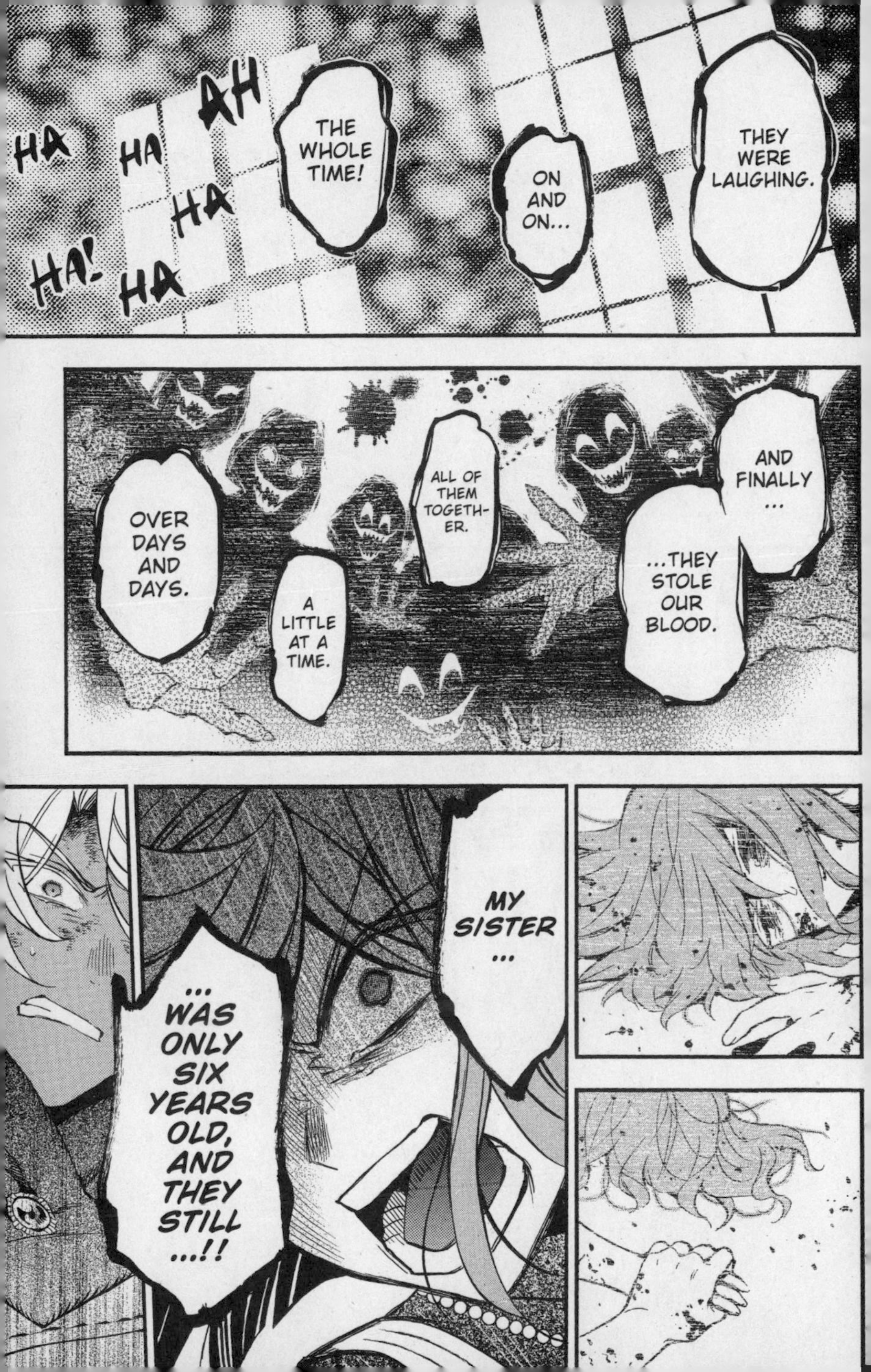
THEY WERE LAUGHING.
ON AND ON...
THE WHOLE TIME!
AH
HA
HA
HA
HA!
HA
AND FINALLY ...
...THEY STOLE OUR BLOOD.
ALL OF THEM TOGETH- ER.
OVER DAYS AND DAYS.
A LITTLE AT A TIME.
MY SISTER ...
... WAS ONLY SIX YEARS OLD, AND THEY STILL ...!!

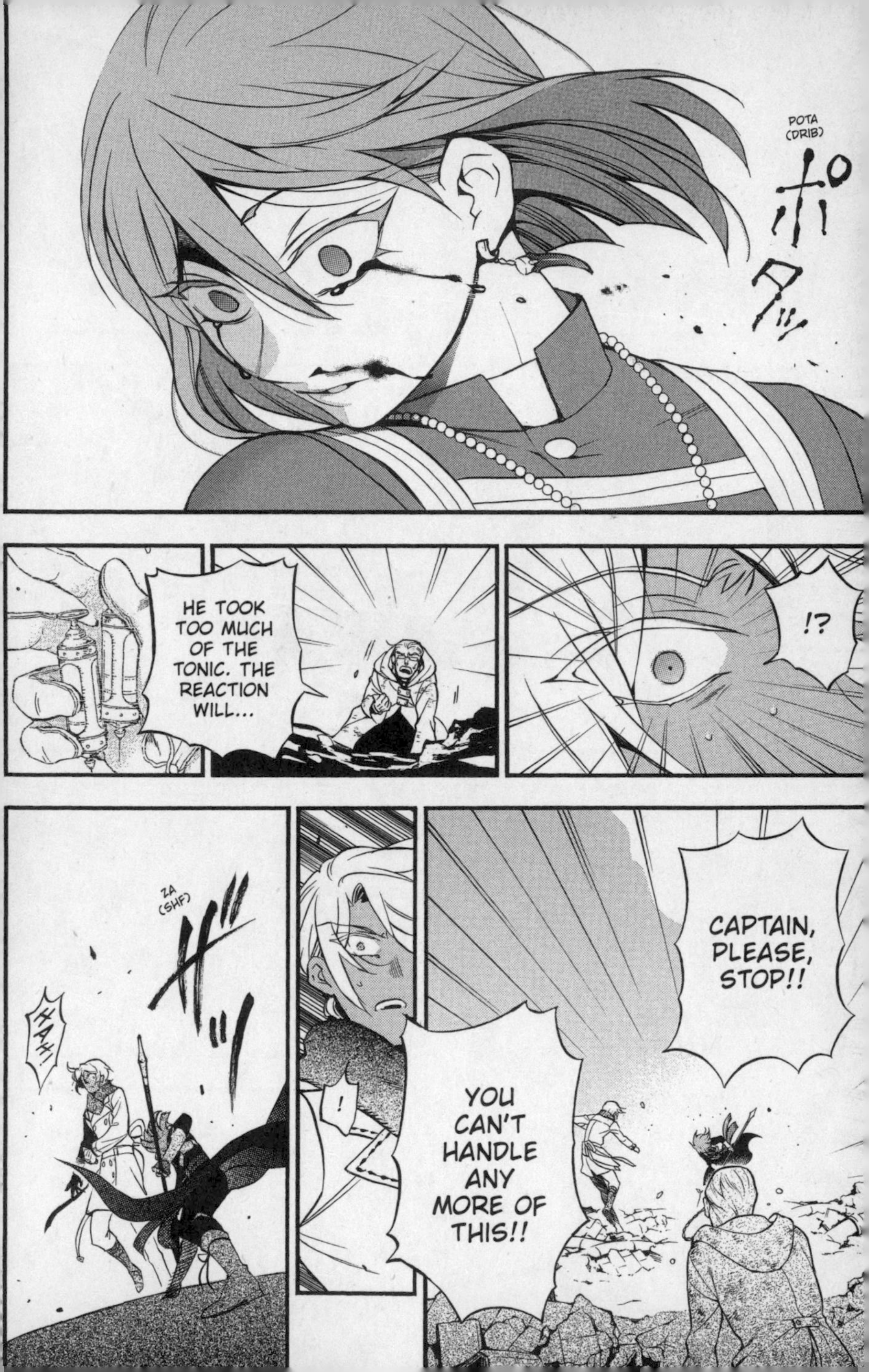
POTA
(DRIB)
ポタッ
!?
HE TOOK TOO MUCH OF THE TONIC. THE REACTION WILL...
CAPTAIN, PLEASE, STOP!!
YOU CAN'T HANDLE ANY MORE OF THIS!!
!
ZA
(SHF)
HAH!

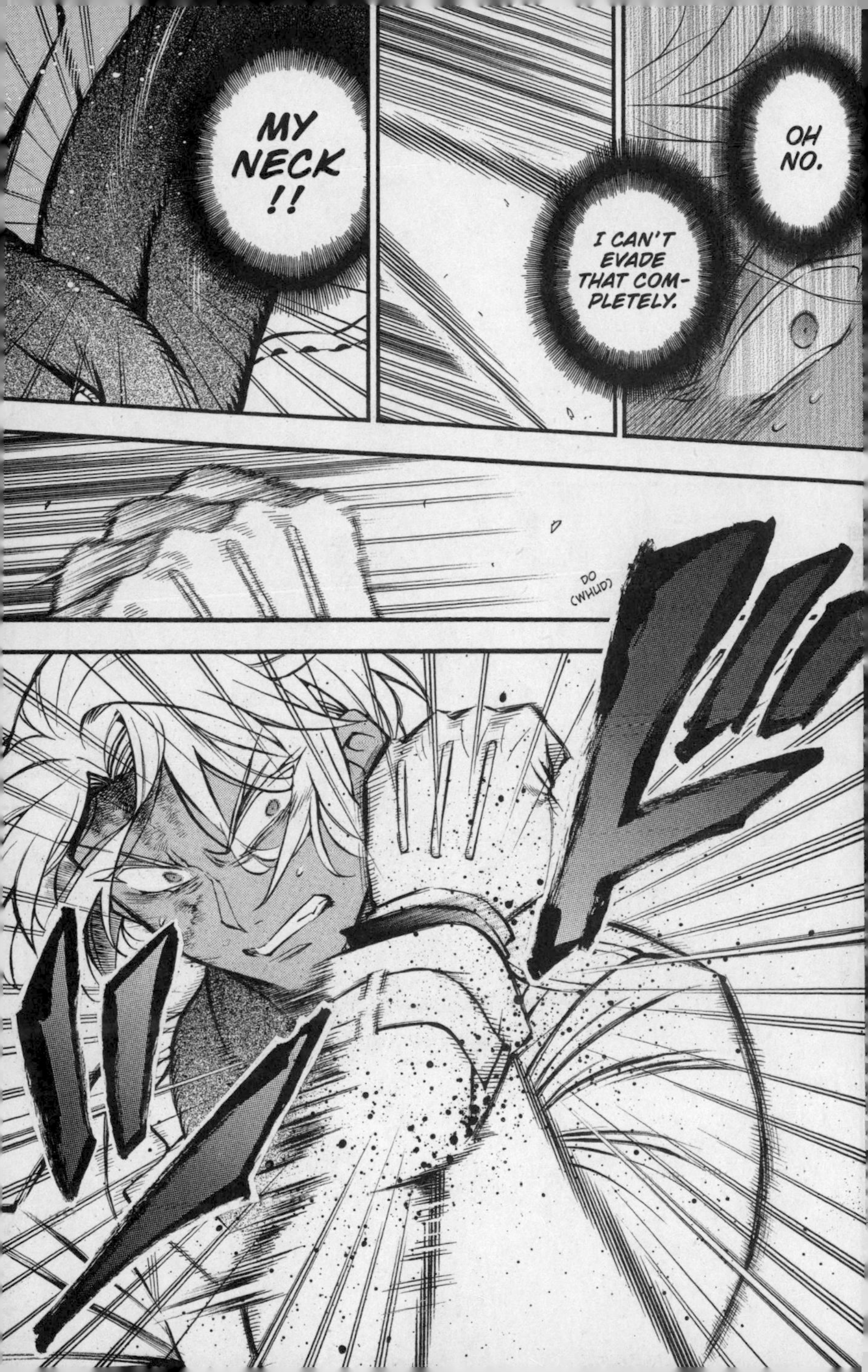
OH NO.
I CAN'T EVADE THAT COM-PLETELY.
MY NECK!!
DO (WHUD)

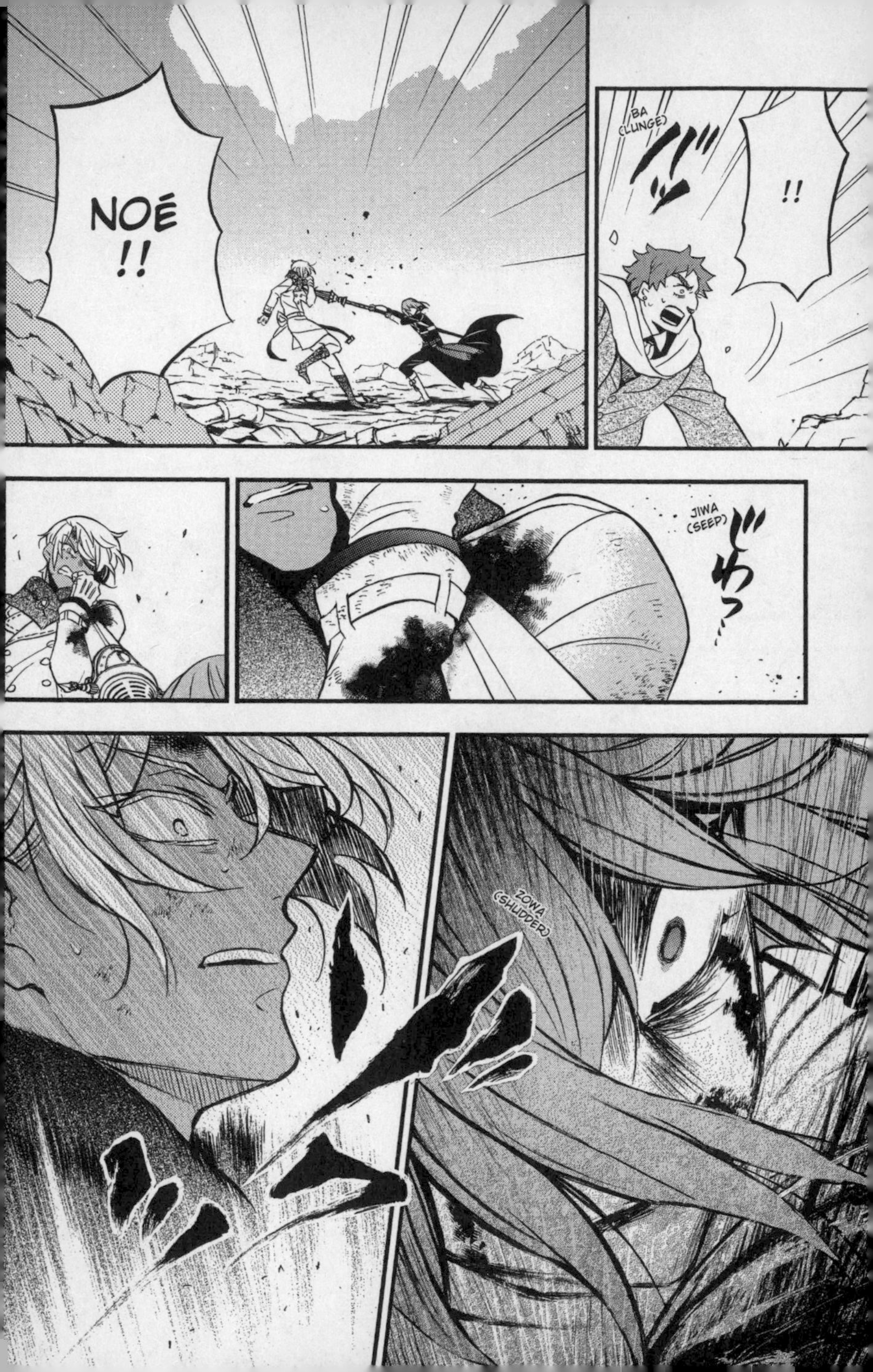
BA (LUNGE)
バッ
!!
NOÉ !!
JIWA (SEEP)
じわっ
ZOWA (SHUDDER)

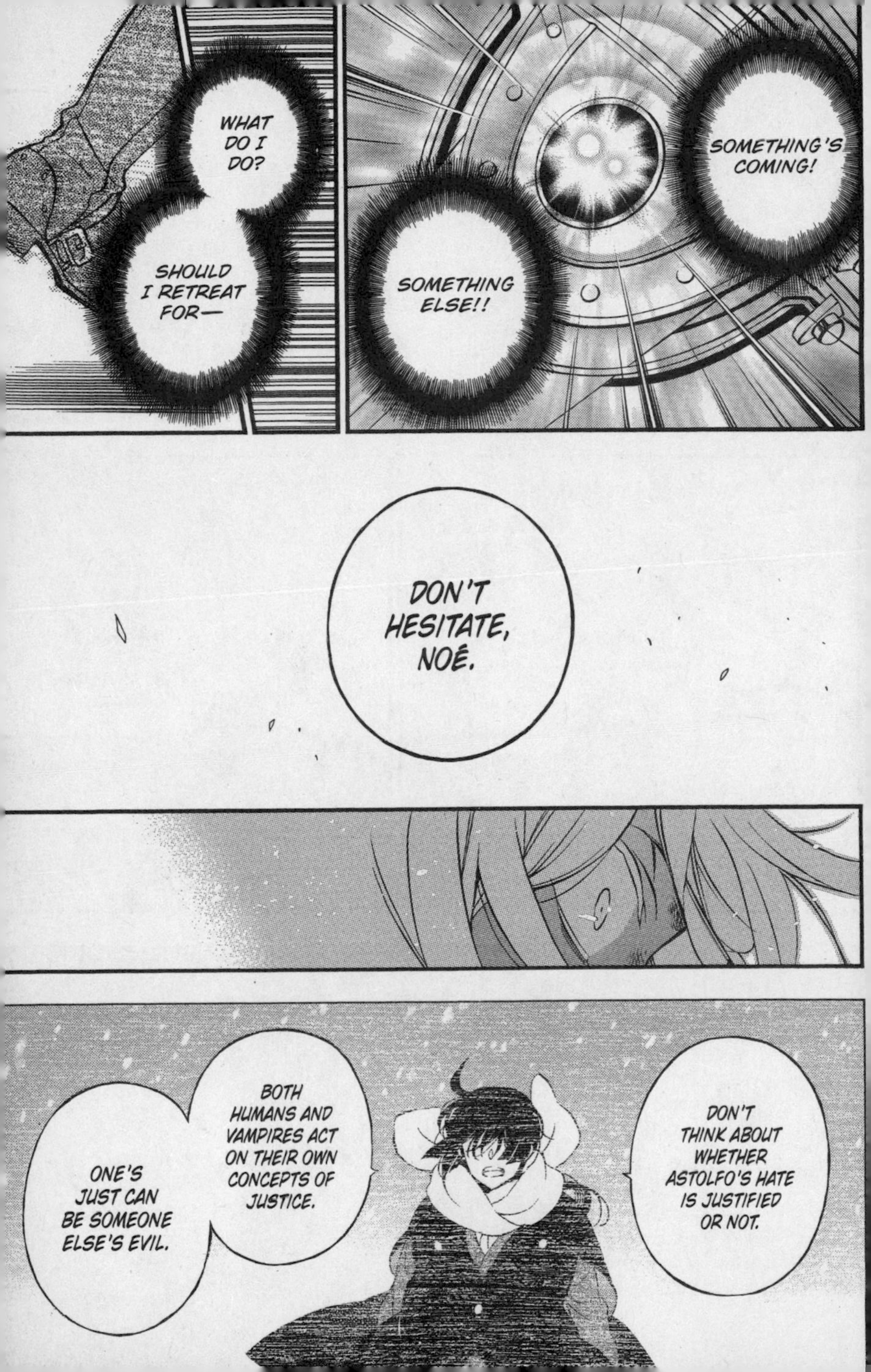
SOMETHING'S COMING!
SOMETHING ELSE!!
WHAT DO I DO?
SHOULD I RETREAT FOR—
DON'T HESITATE, NOÉ.
DON'T THINK ABOUT WHETHER ASTOLFO'S HATE IS JUSTIFIED OR NOT.
BOTH HUMANS AND VAMPIRES ACT ON THEIR OWN CONCEPTS OF JUSTICE.
ONE'S JUST CAN BE SOMEONE ELSE'S EVIL.

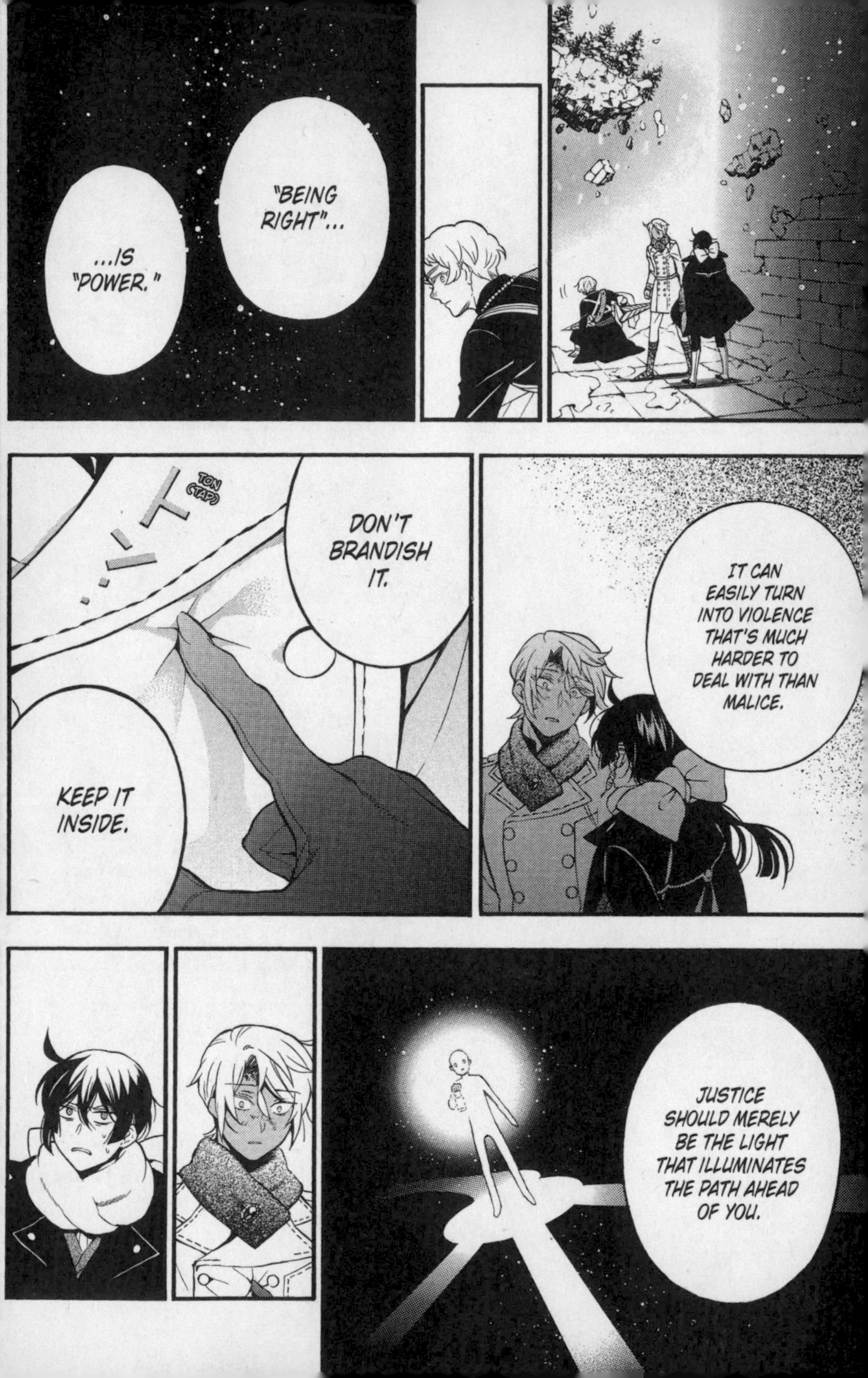
"BEING RIGHT"...
...IS "POWER."
IT CAN EASILY TURN INTO VIOLENCE THAT'S MUCH HARDER TO DEAL WITH THAN MALICE.
TON (TAP)
DON'T BRANDISH IT.
KEEP IT INSIDE.
JUSTICE SHOULD MERELY BE THE LIGHT THAT ILLUMINATES THE PATH AHEAD OF YOU.

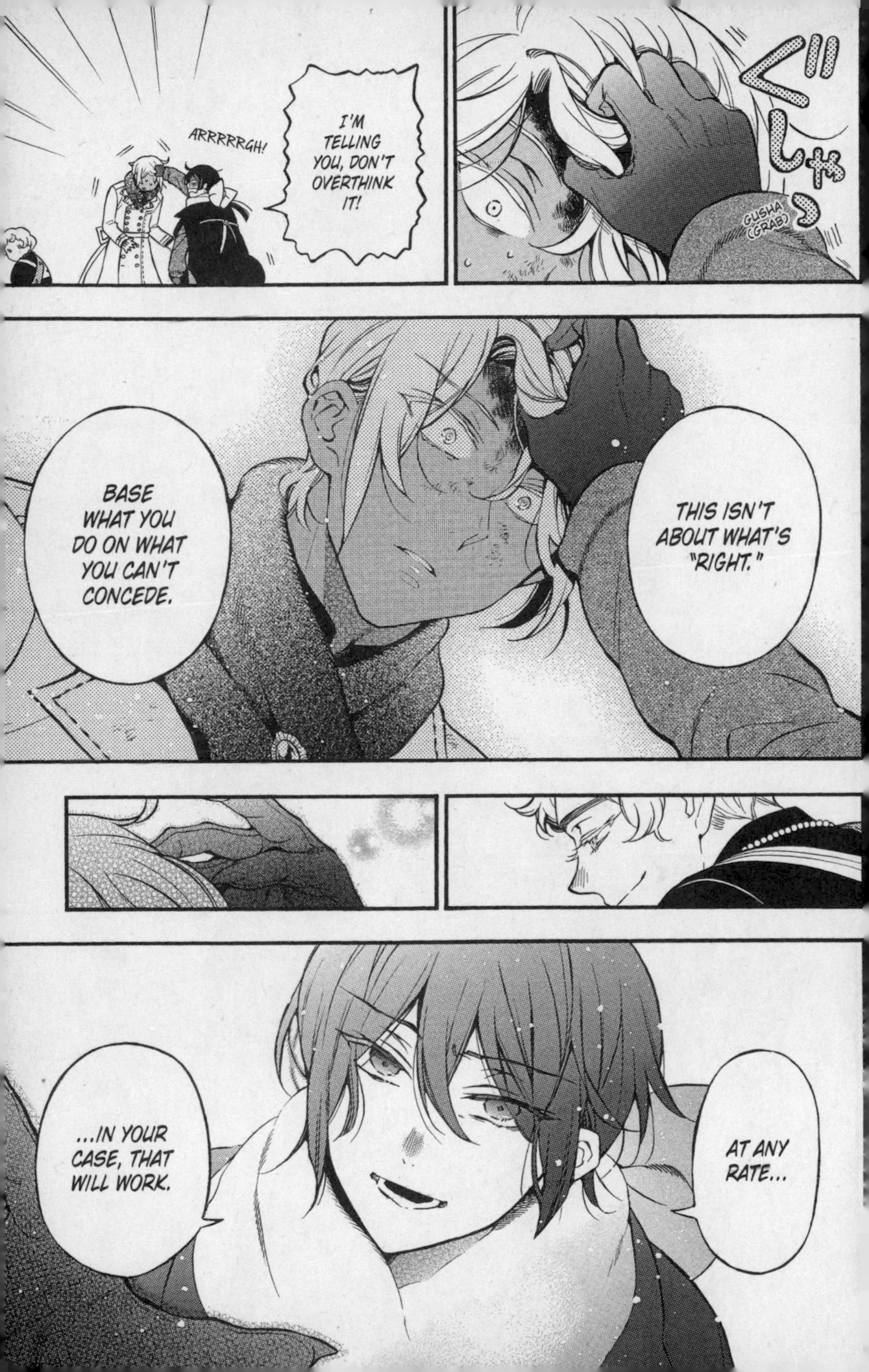
ぐしゃっ
GUSHA (GRAB)
I'M TELLING YOU, DON'T OVERTHINK IT!
ARRRRRGH!
THIS ISN'T ABOUT WHAT'S "RIGHT."
BASE WHAT YOU DO ON WHAT YOU CAN'T CONCEDE.
AT ANY RATE...
...IN YOUR CASE, THAT WILL WORK.

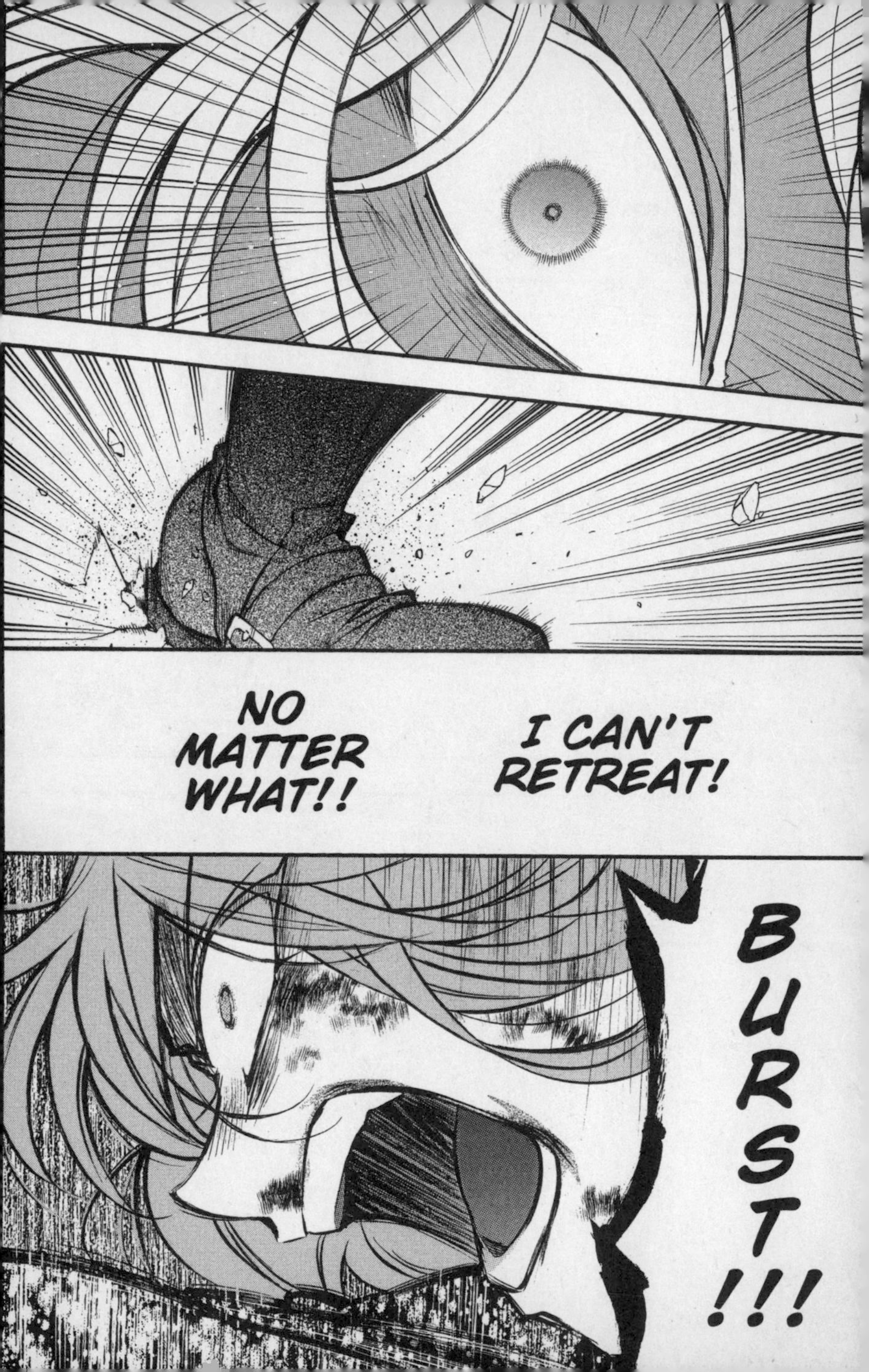
I CAN'T RETREAT!
NO MATTER WHAT!!
BURST!!!

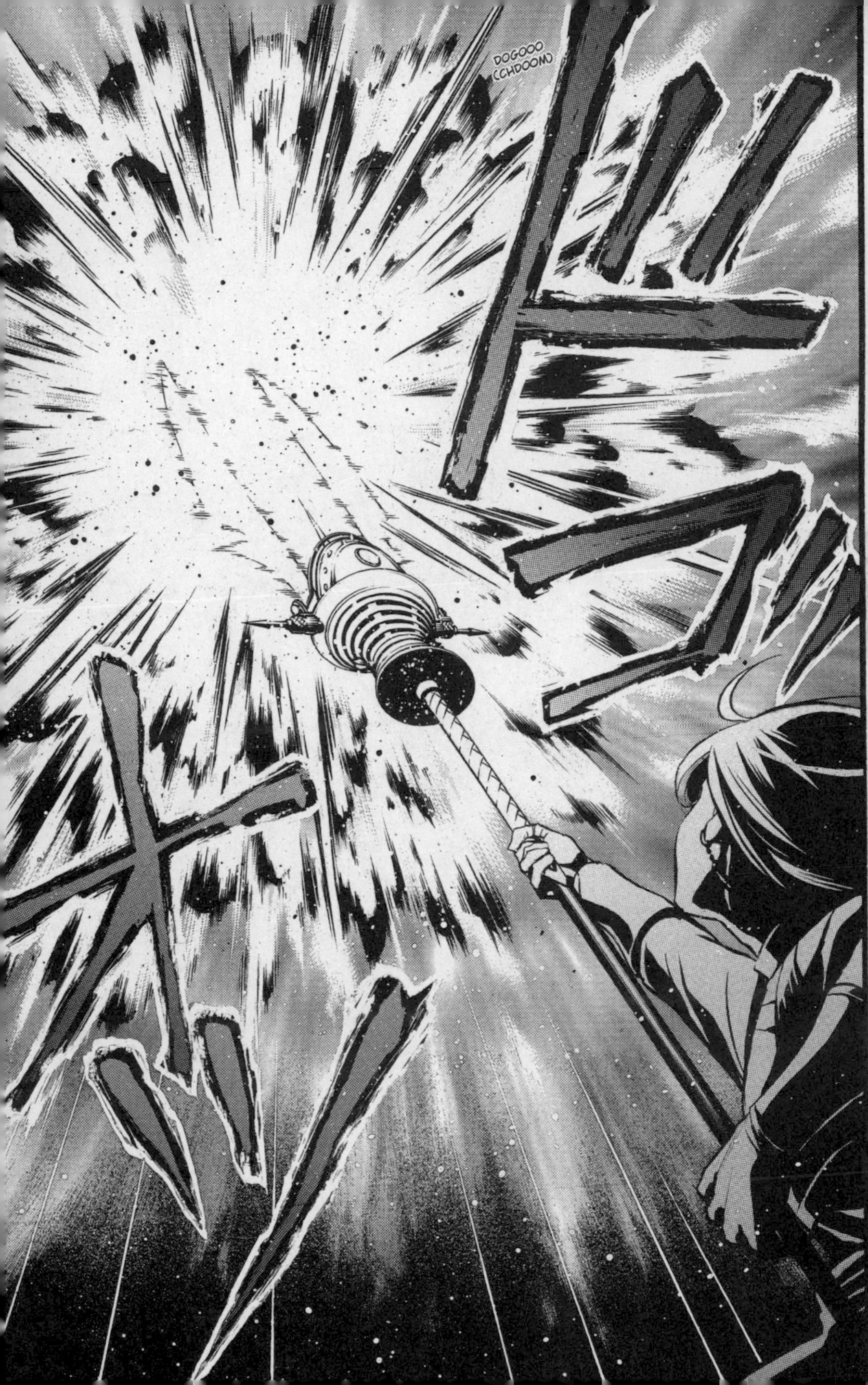
DOGOOO
(CHDOOM)

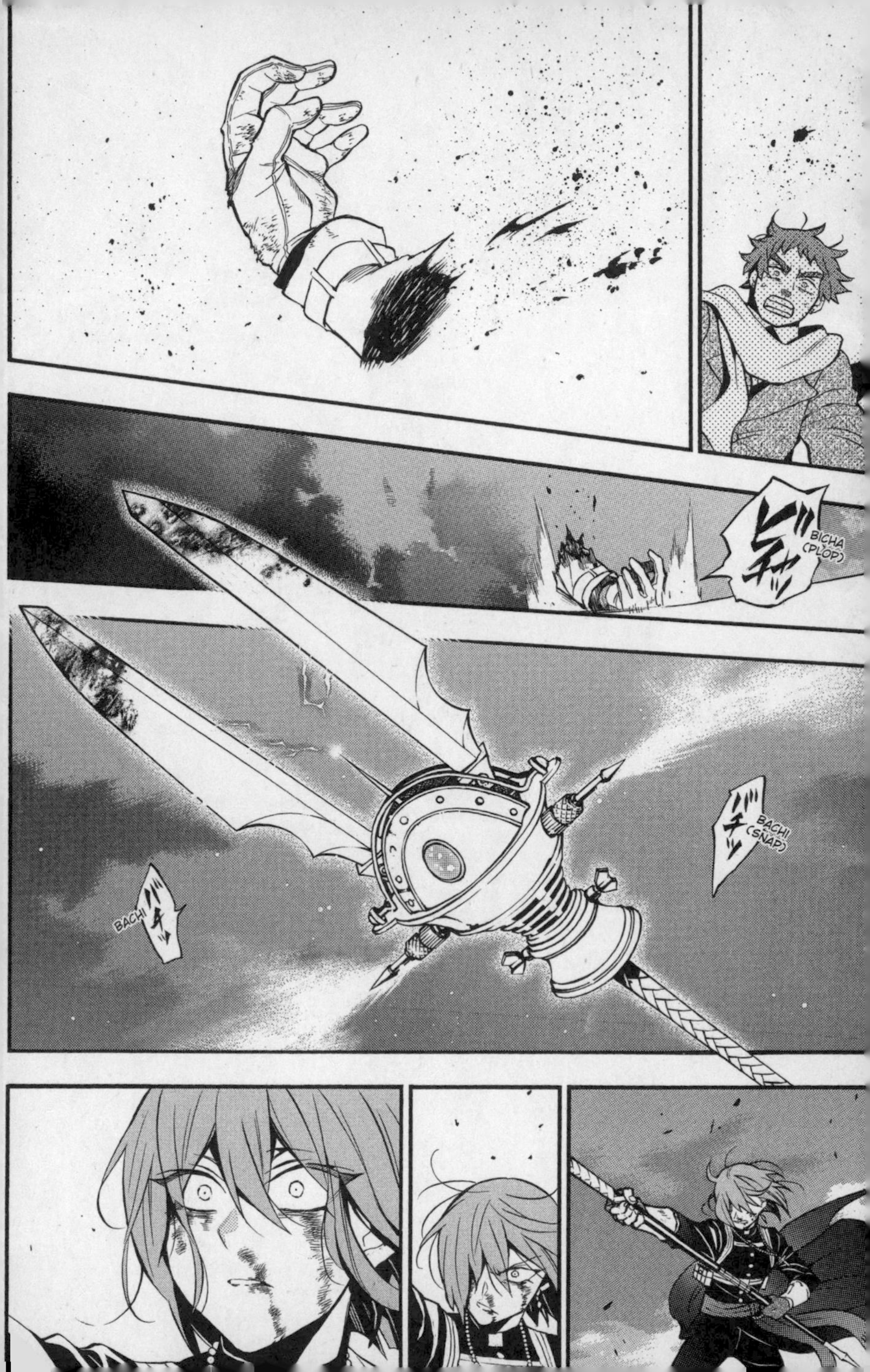

ビチャッ
BICHA (PLOP)
バチッ
BACHI (SNAP)
バチッ
BACHI

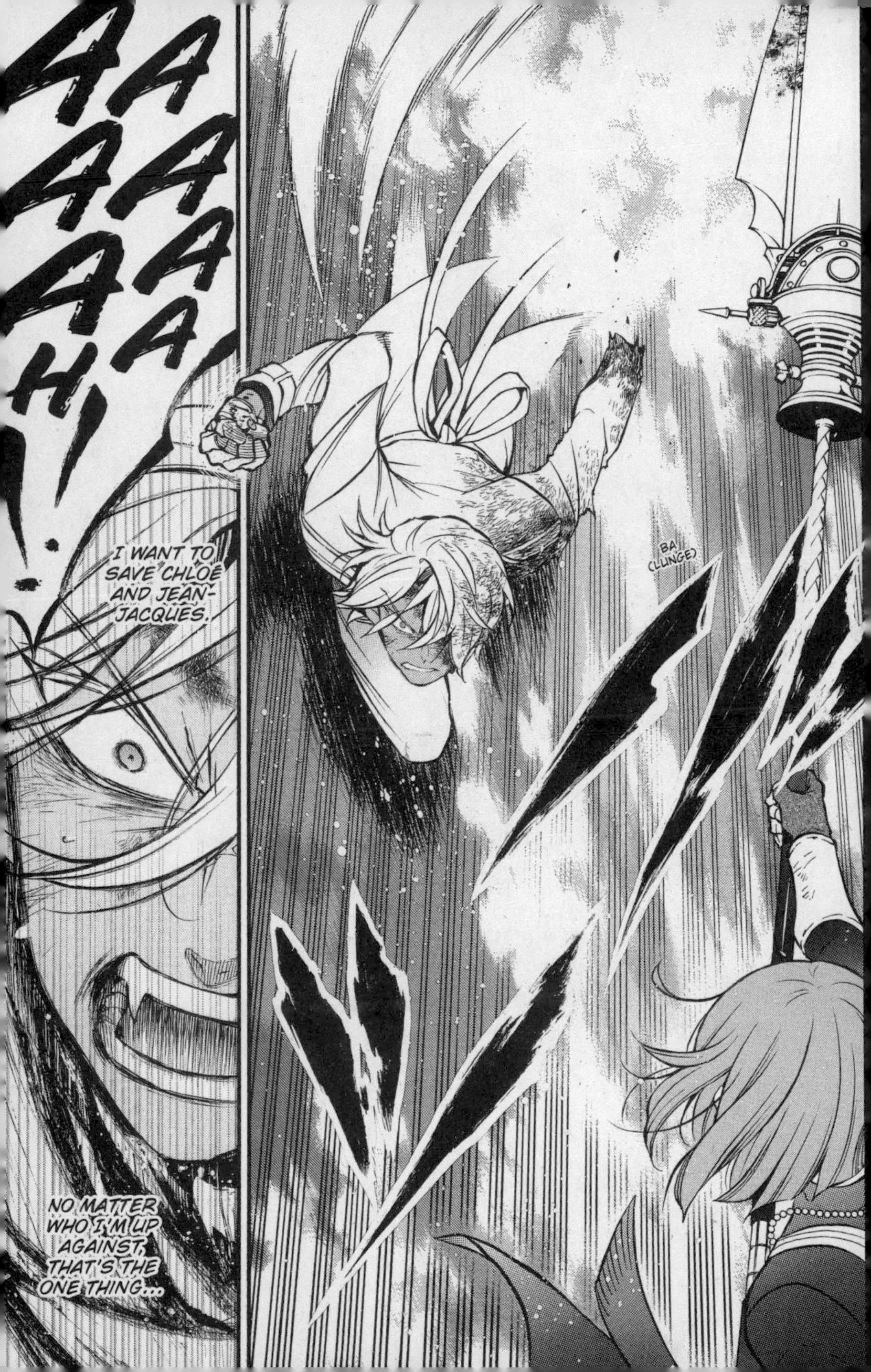
BA (LUNGE)
AAAAAAAAAH!
I WANT TO SAVE CHLOÉ AND JEAN-JACQUES.
NO MATTER WHO I'M UP AGAINST, THAT'S THE ONE THING...

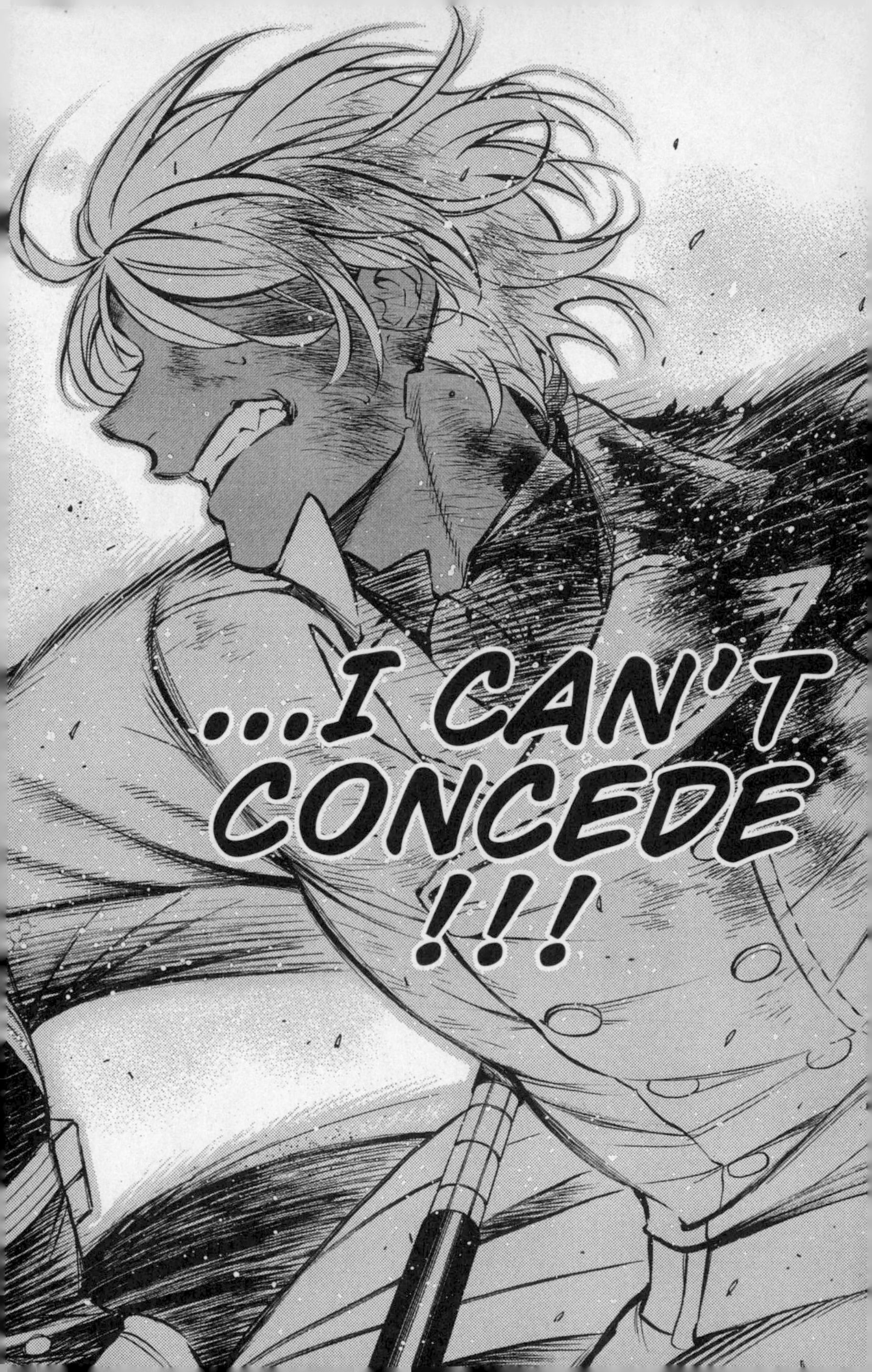
...I CAN'T CONCEDE!!!

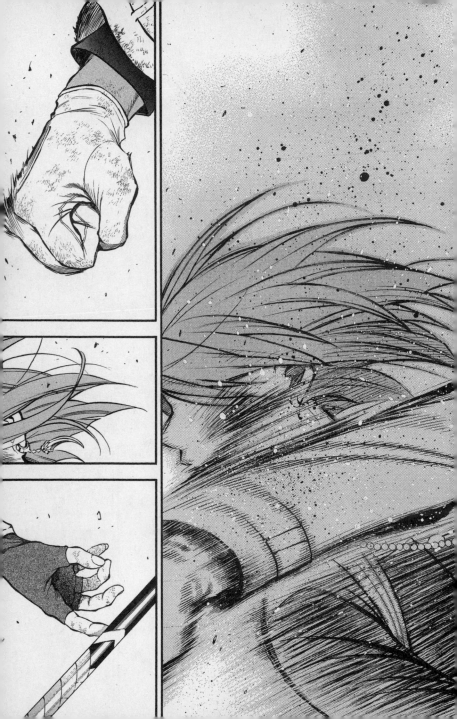

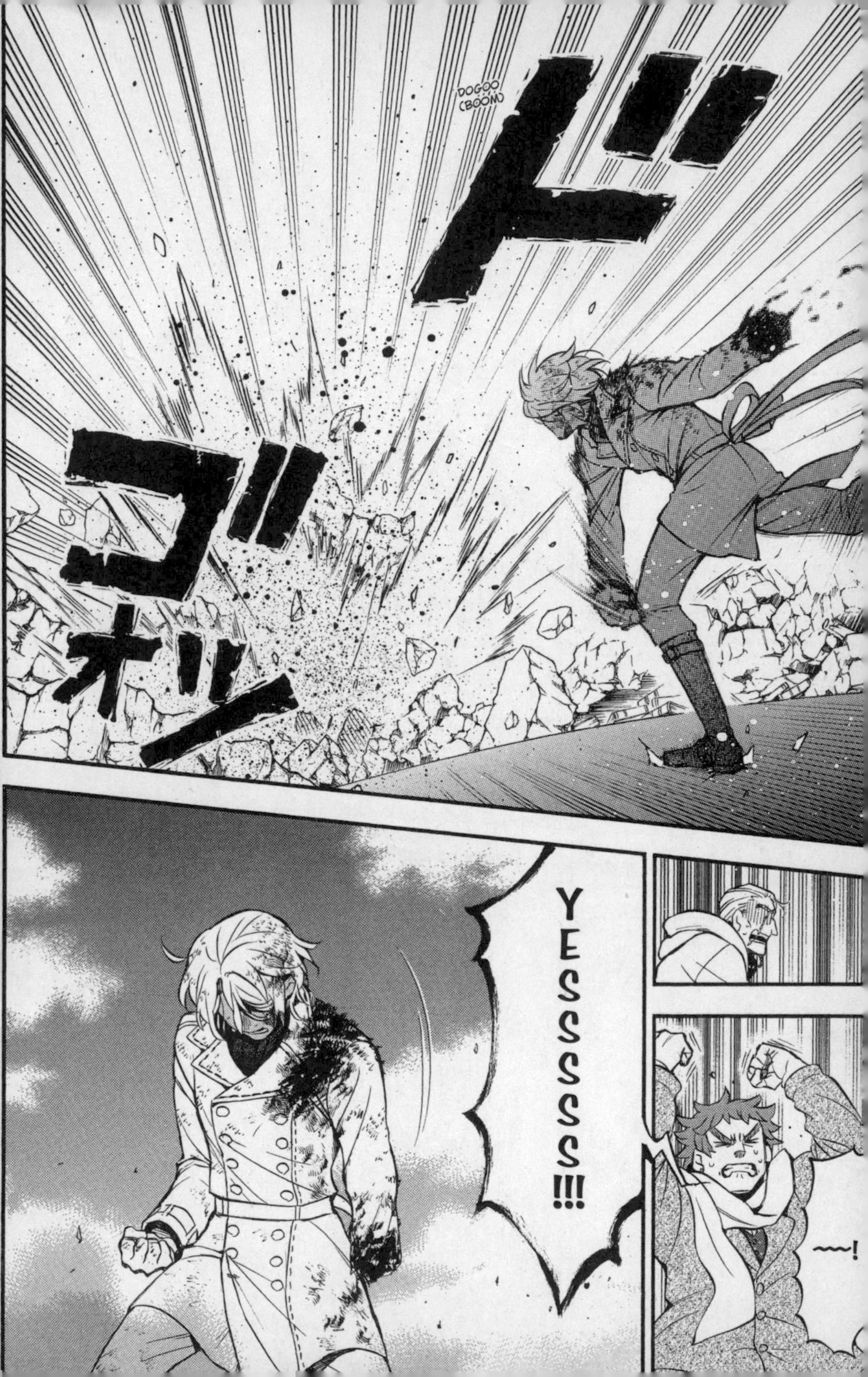
ドゴォッ
DOGOO (BOOM)
~~~!
YESSSSSS!!!
~~~

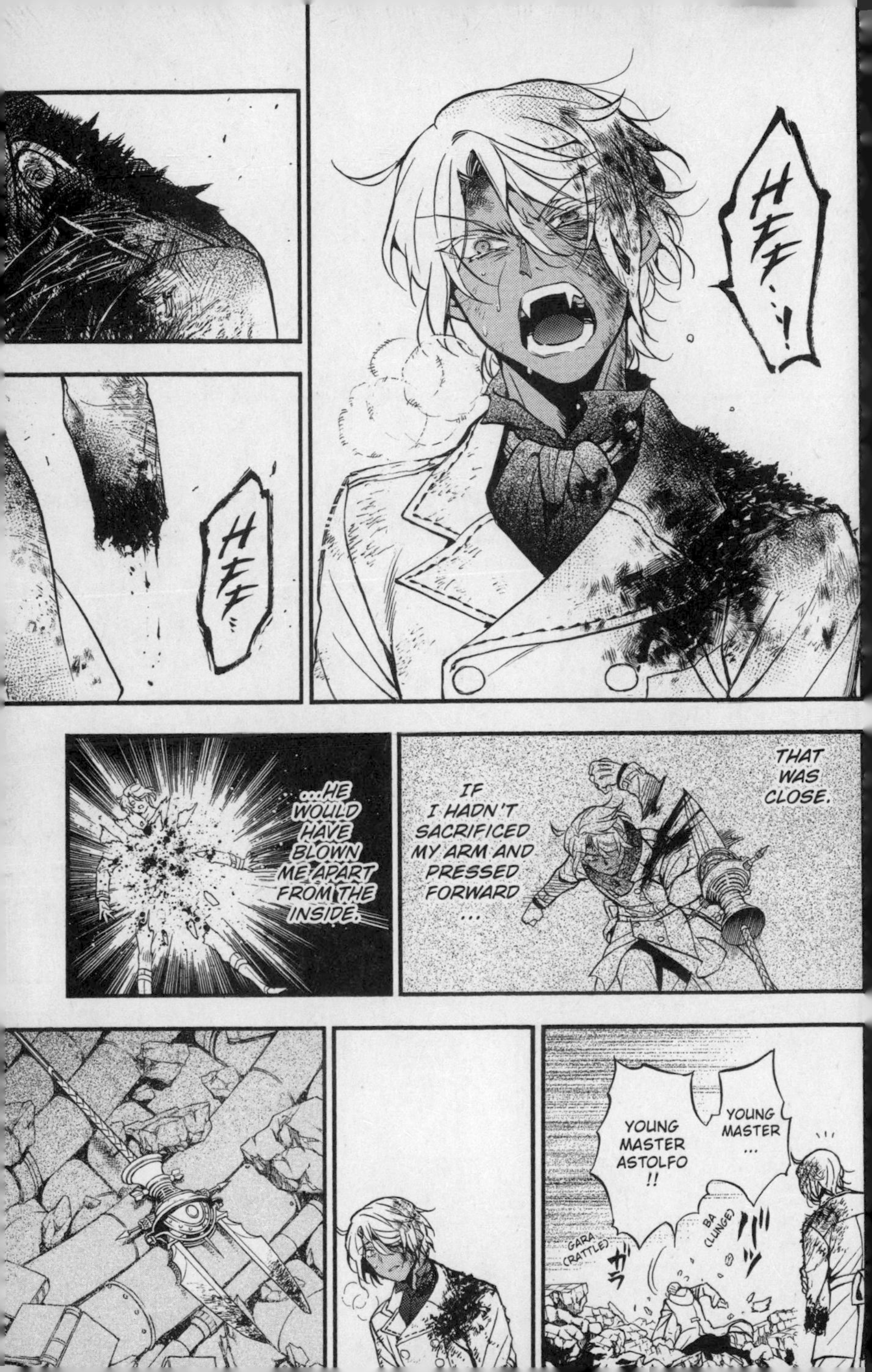
HEFF...!
HEFF
THAT WAS CLOSE.
IF I HADN'T SACRIFICED MY ARM AND PRESSED FORWARD...
...HE WOULD HAVE BLOWN ME APART FROM THE INSIDE.
YOUNG MASTER...
YOUNG MASTER ASTOLFO!!
BA (LUNGE)
GARA (RATTLE)

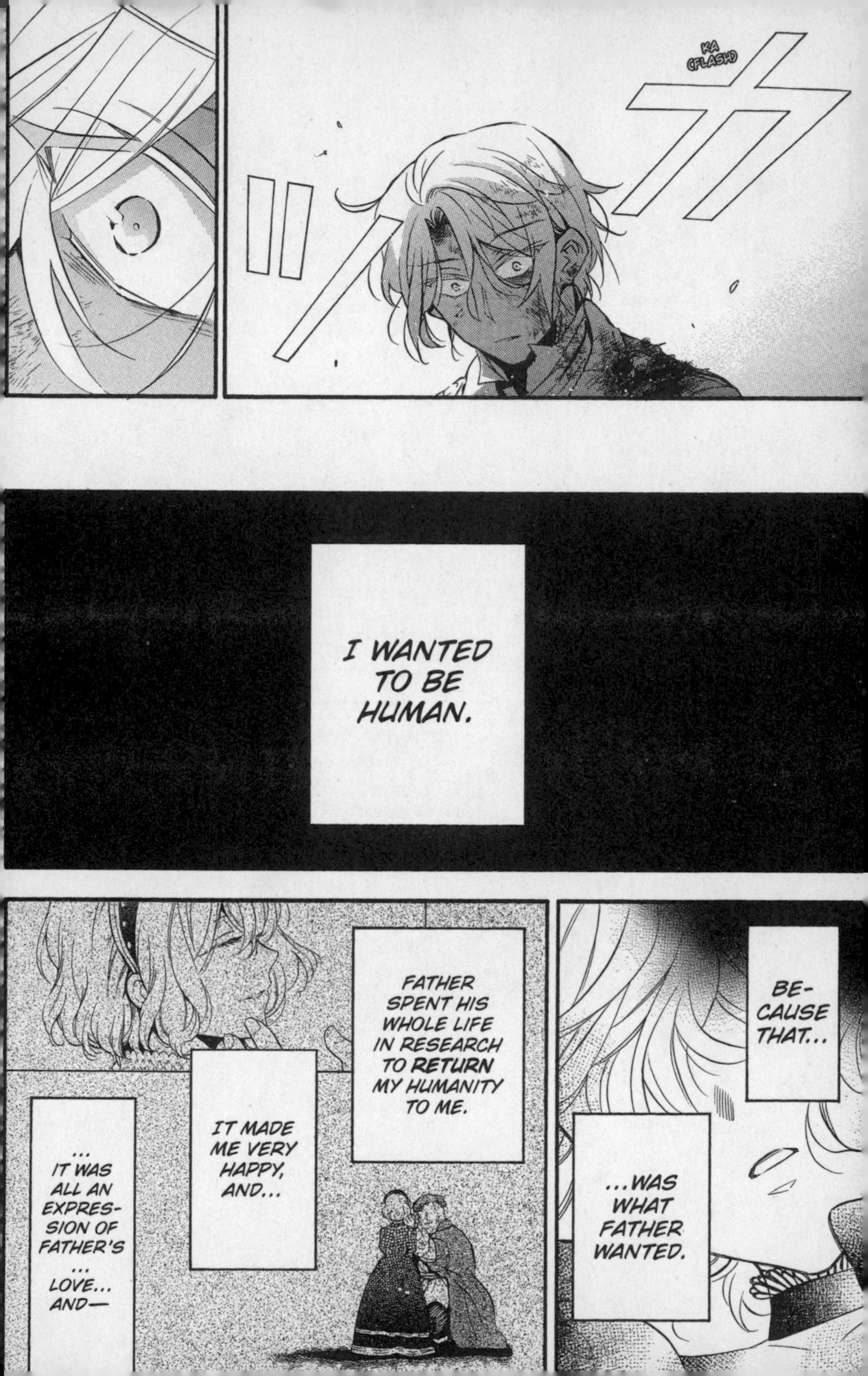
KA (FLASH)
I WANTED TO BE HUMAN.
BE-CAUSE THAT...
...WAS WHAT FATHER WANTED.
FATHER SPENT HIS WHOLE LIFE IN RESEARCH TO RETURN MY HUMANITY TO ME.
IT MADE ME VERY HAPPY, AND...
...IT WAS ALL AN EXPRES-SION OF FATHER'S ... LOVE... AND—

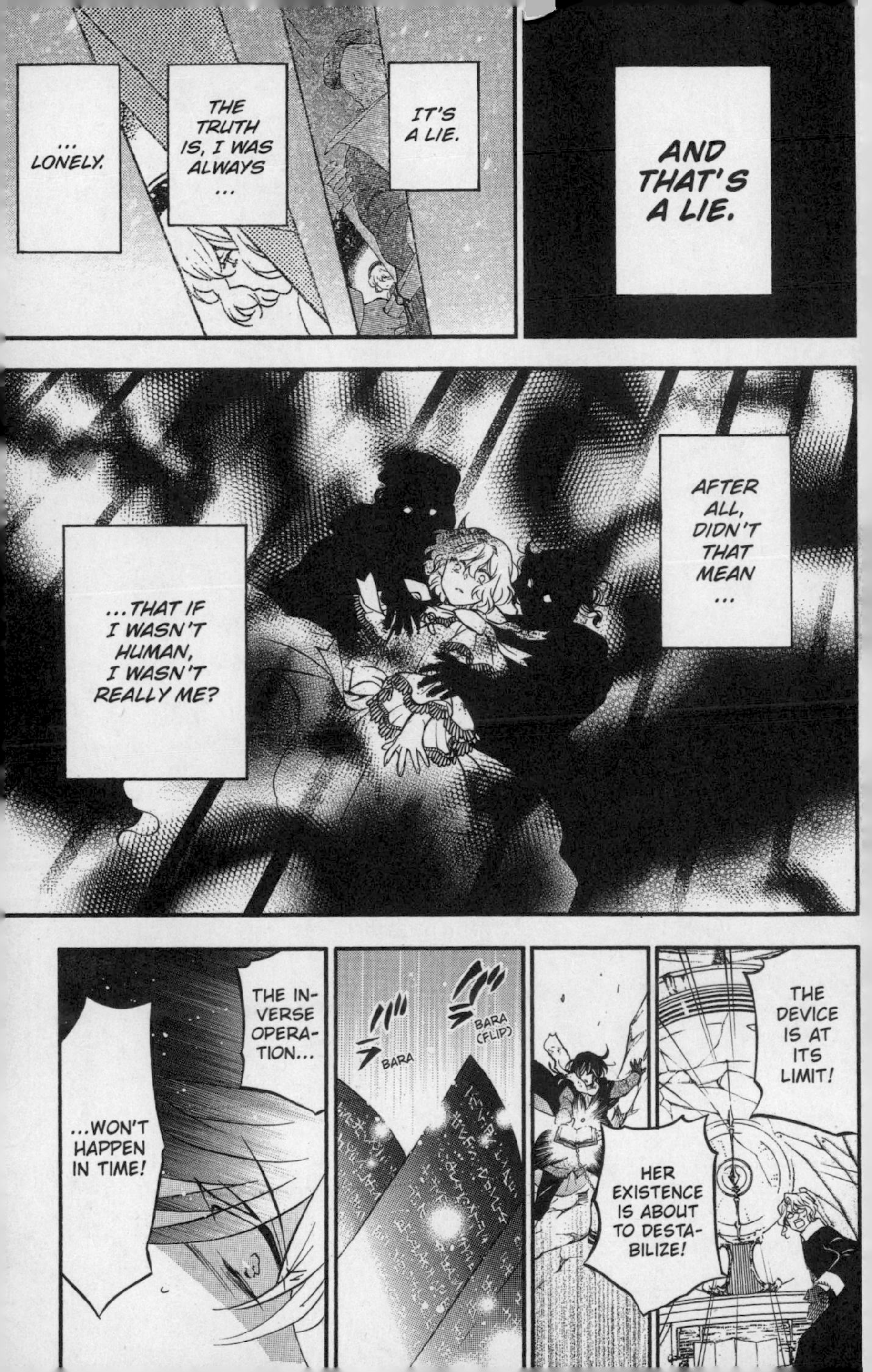
AND THAT'S A LIE.
IT'S A LIE.
THE TRUTH IS, I WAS ALWAYS ...
... LONELY.
AFTER ALL, DIDN'T THAT MEAN ...
...THAT IF I WASN'T HUMAN, I WASN'T REALLY ME?
THE DEVICE IS AT ITS LIMIT!
HER EXISTENCE IS ABOUT TO DESTABILIZE!
BARA (FLIP)
BARA
THE INVERSE OPERATION...
...WON'T HAPPEN IN TIME!

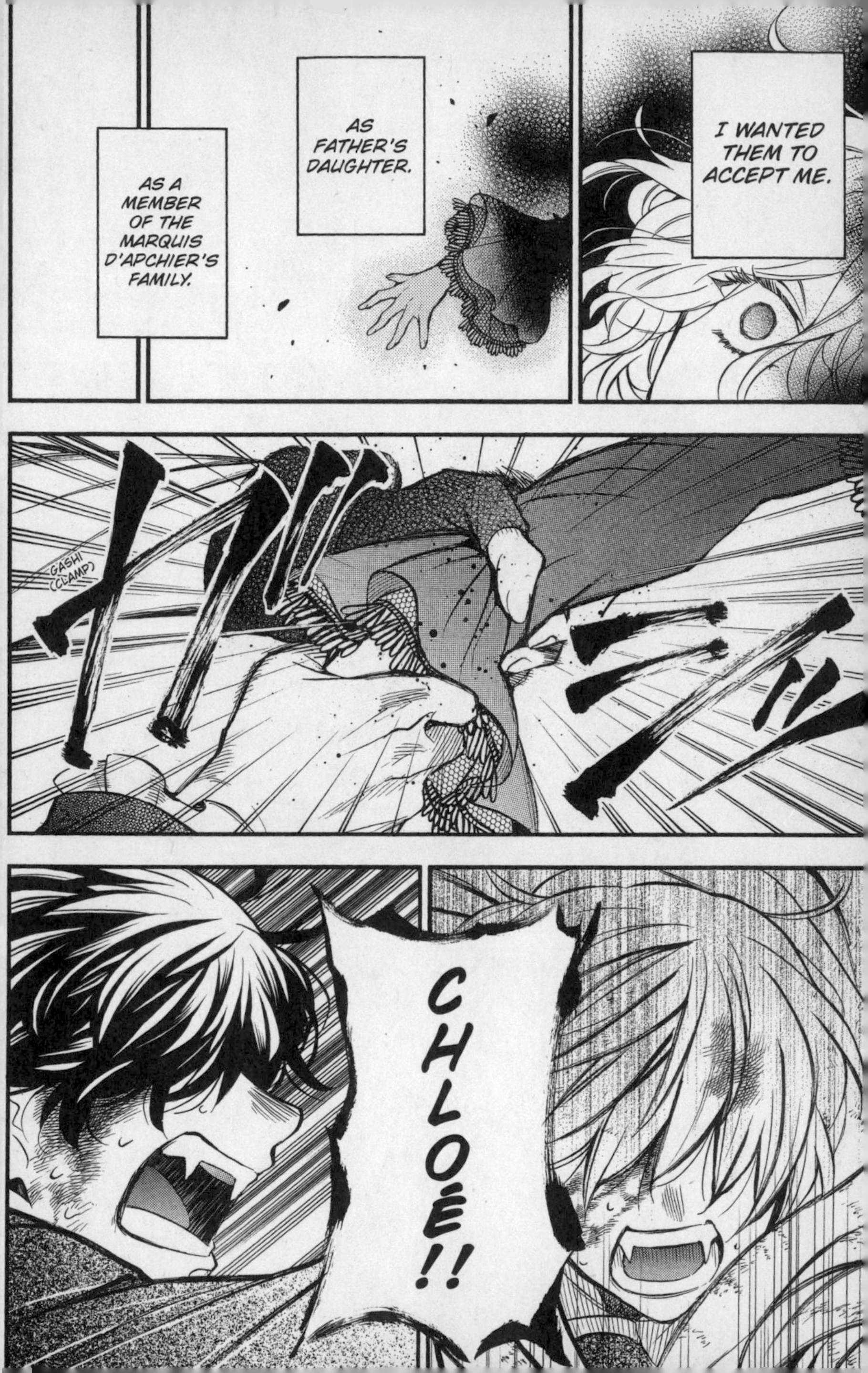
I WANTED THEM TO ACCEPT ME.
AS FATHER'S DAUGHTER.
AS A MEMBER OF THE MARQUIS D'APCHIER'S FAMILY.
GASHI (CLAMP)
CHLOÉ!!

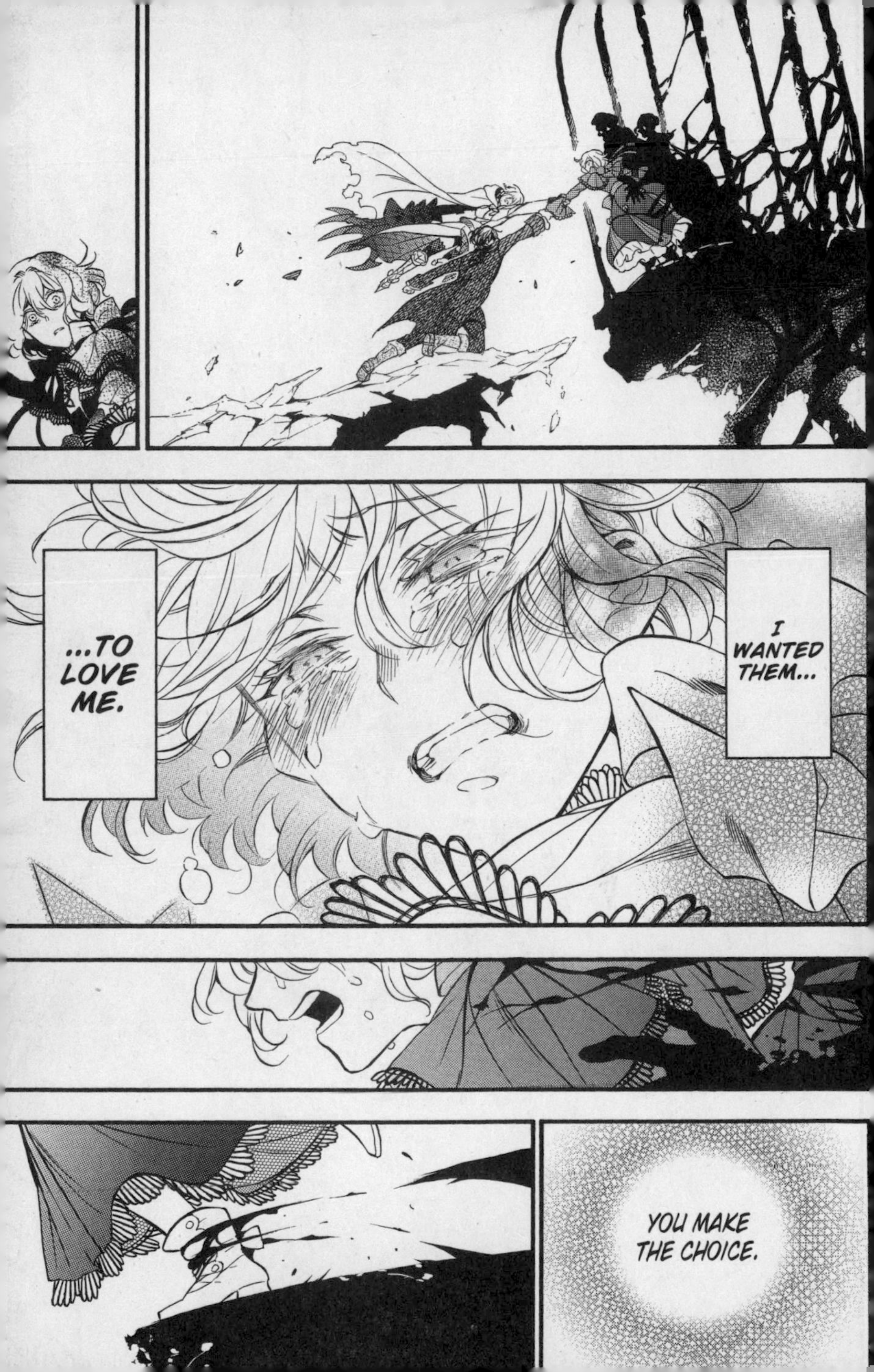
I WANTED THEM...
...TO LOVE ME.
YOU MAKE THE CHOICE.

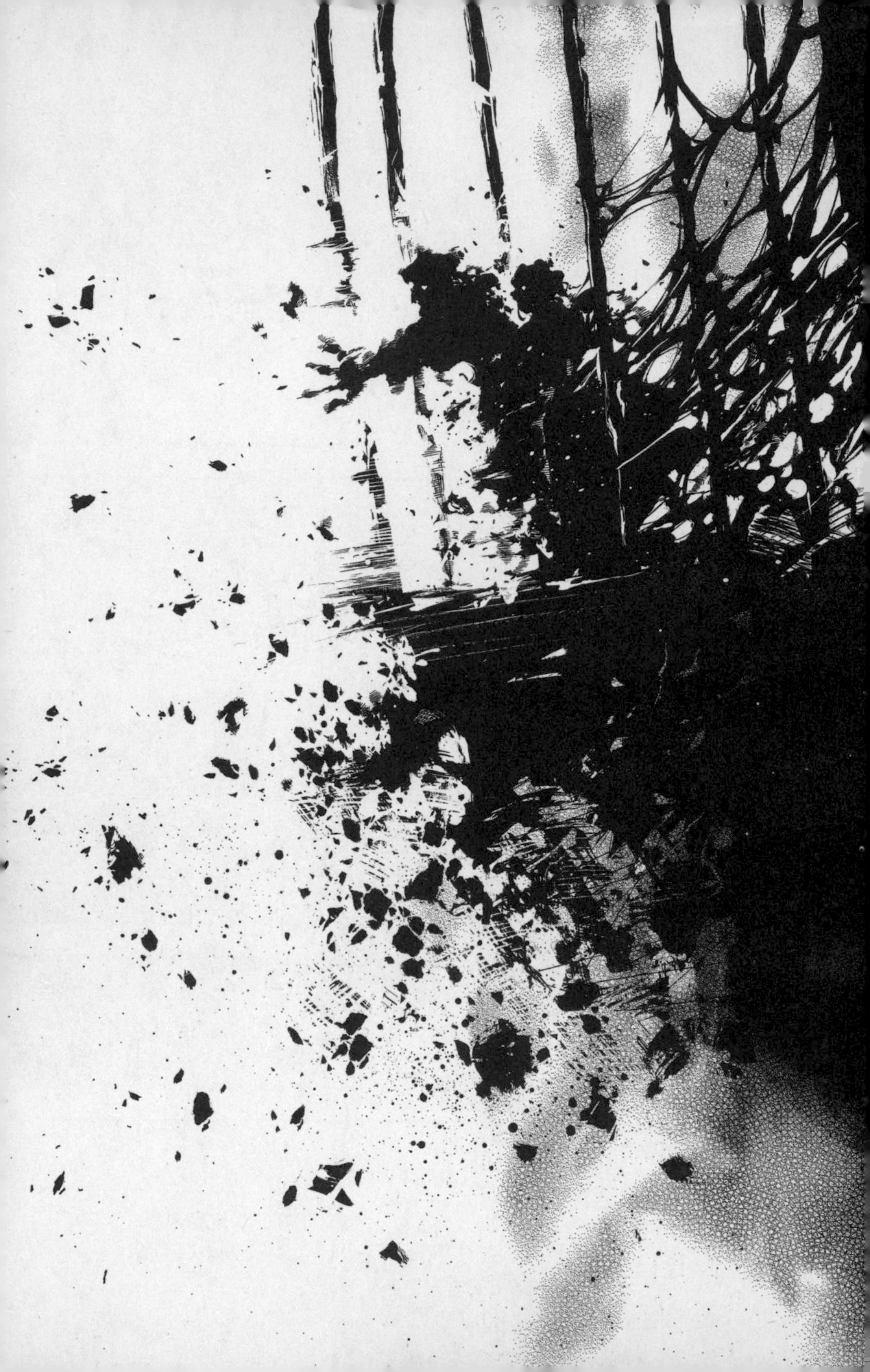

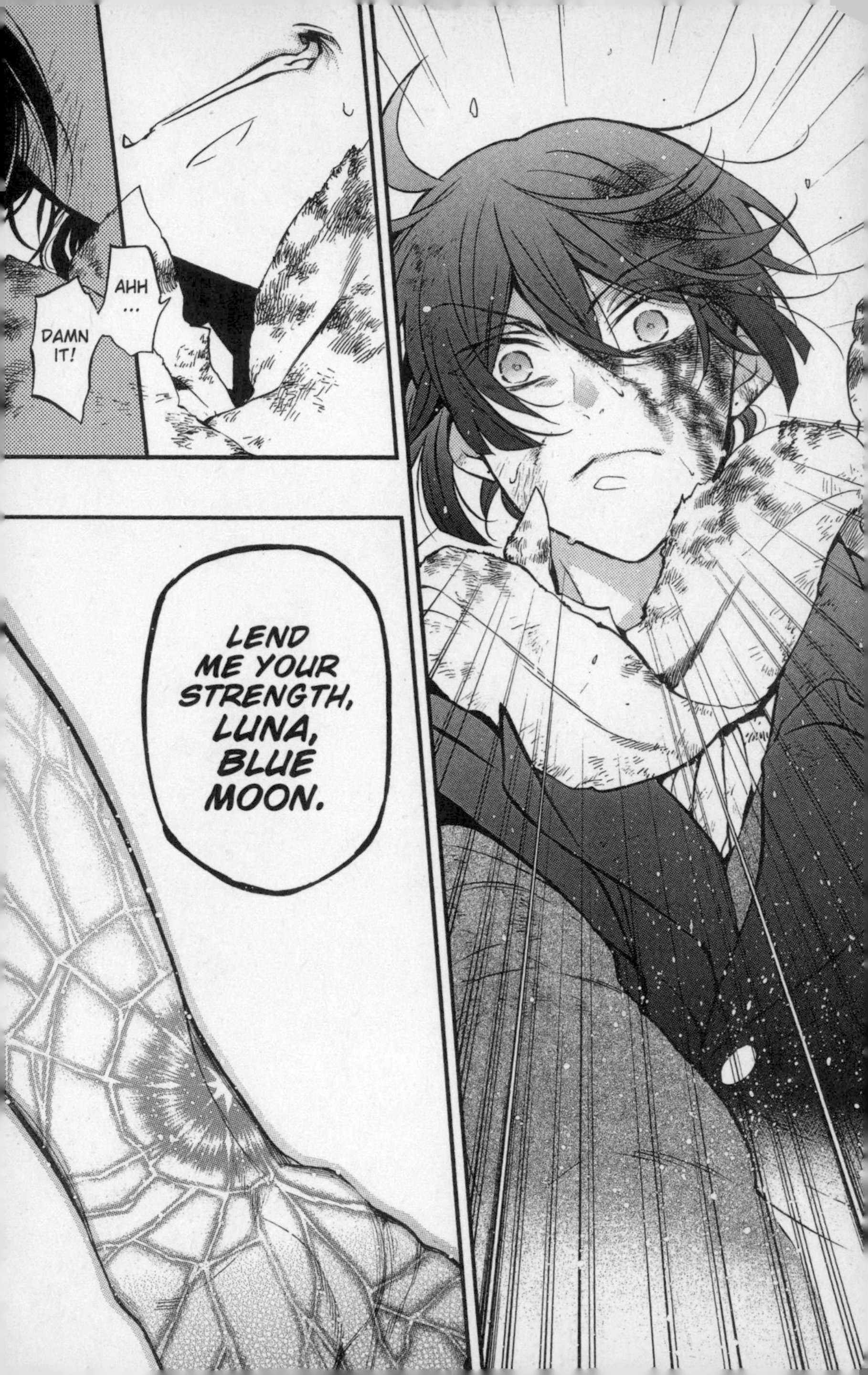
AHH...
DAMN IT!
LEND ME YOUR STRENGTH, LUNA, BLUE MOON.

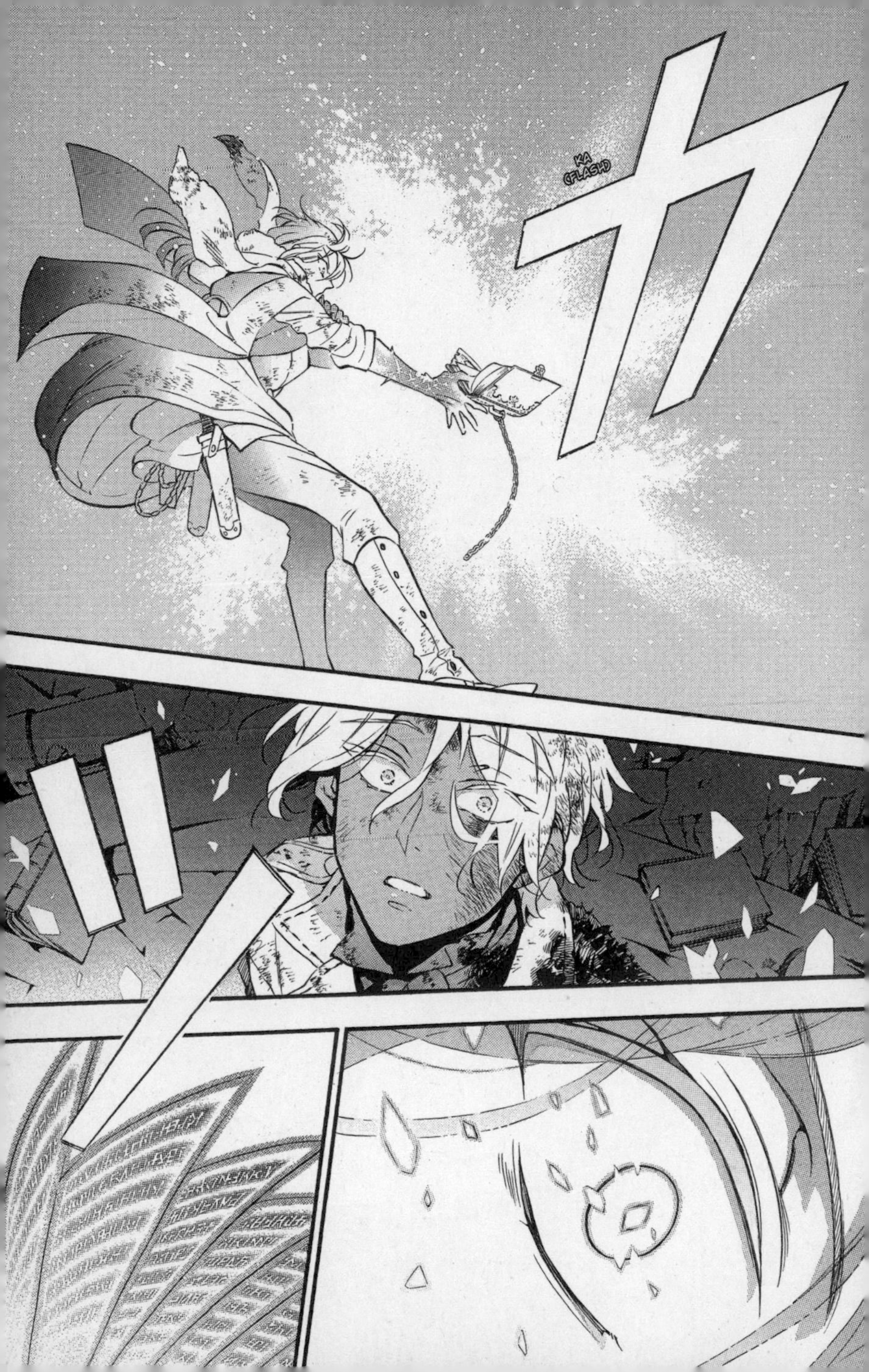
KA (FLASH)

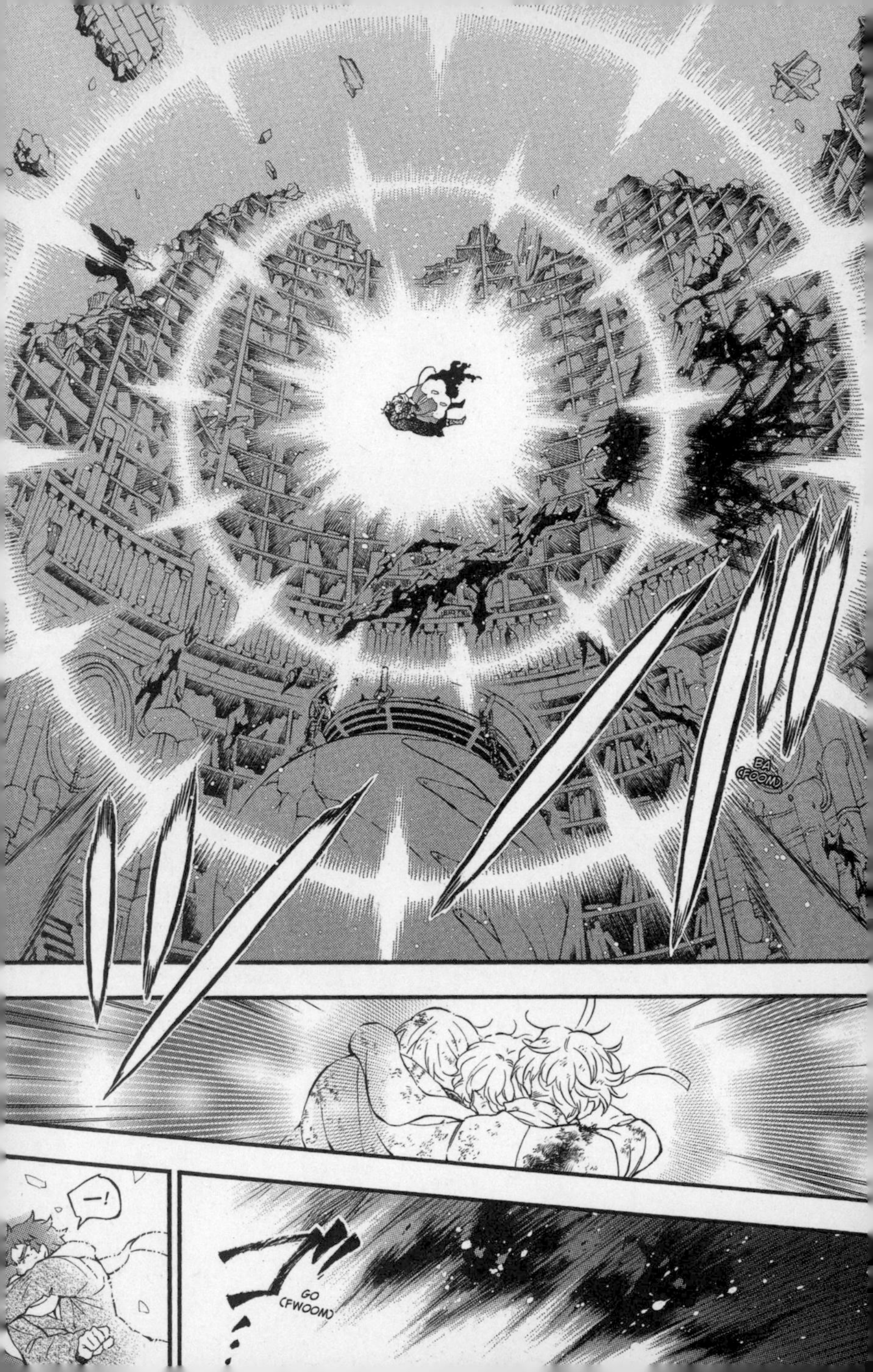
BA (FOOM)
GO (FWOOM)
—!

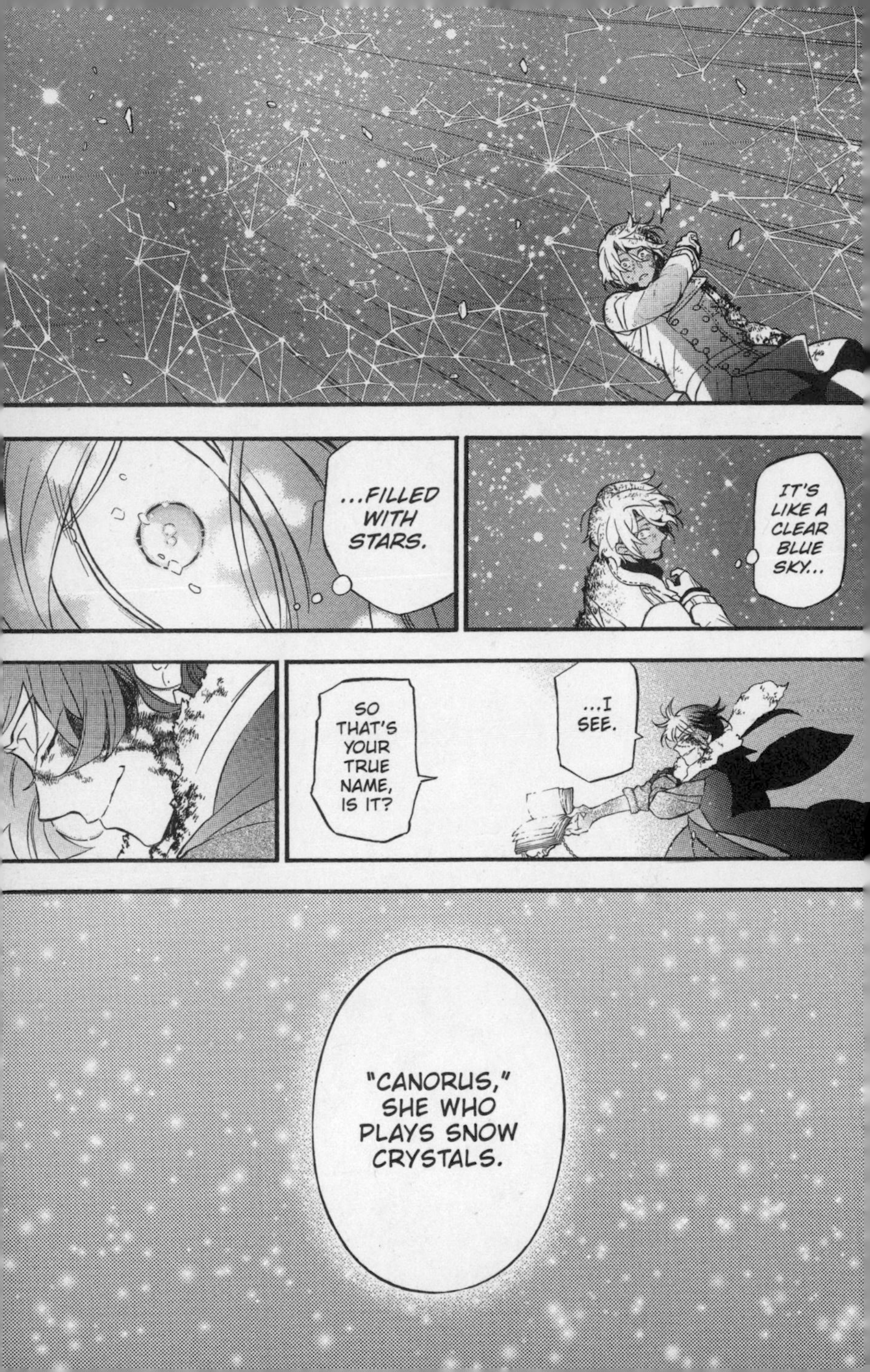
IT'S LIKE A CLEAR BLUE SKY...
...FILLED WITH STARS.
...I SEE.
SO THAT'S YOUR TRUE NAME, IS IT?
"CANORUS," SHE WHO PLAYS SNOW CRYSTALS.

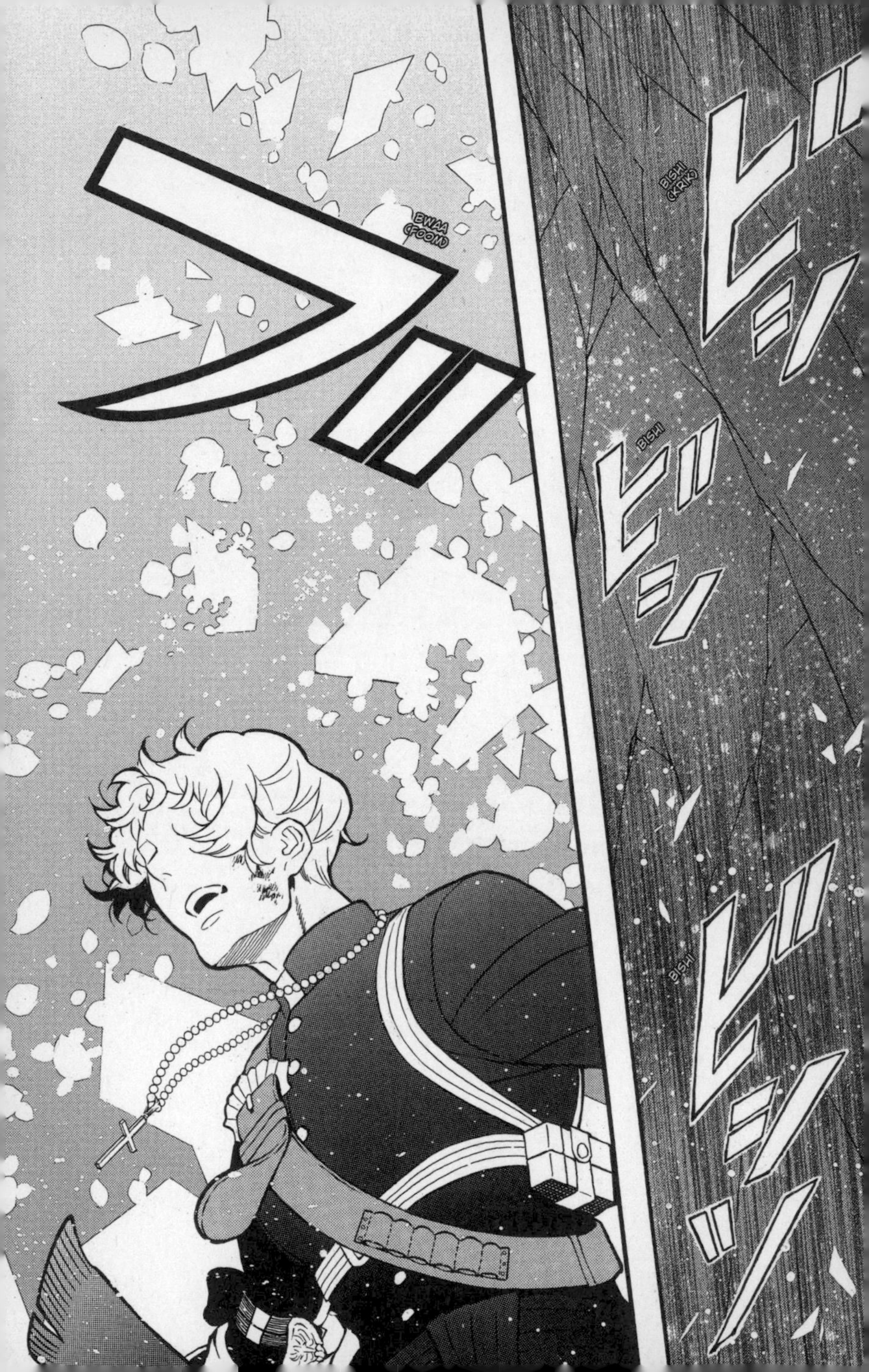
BISHI (KRIK)
BISHI
BISHI
BWAA (FOOM)

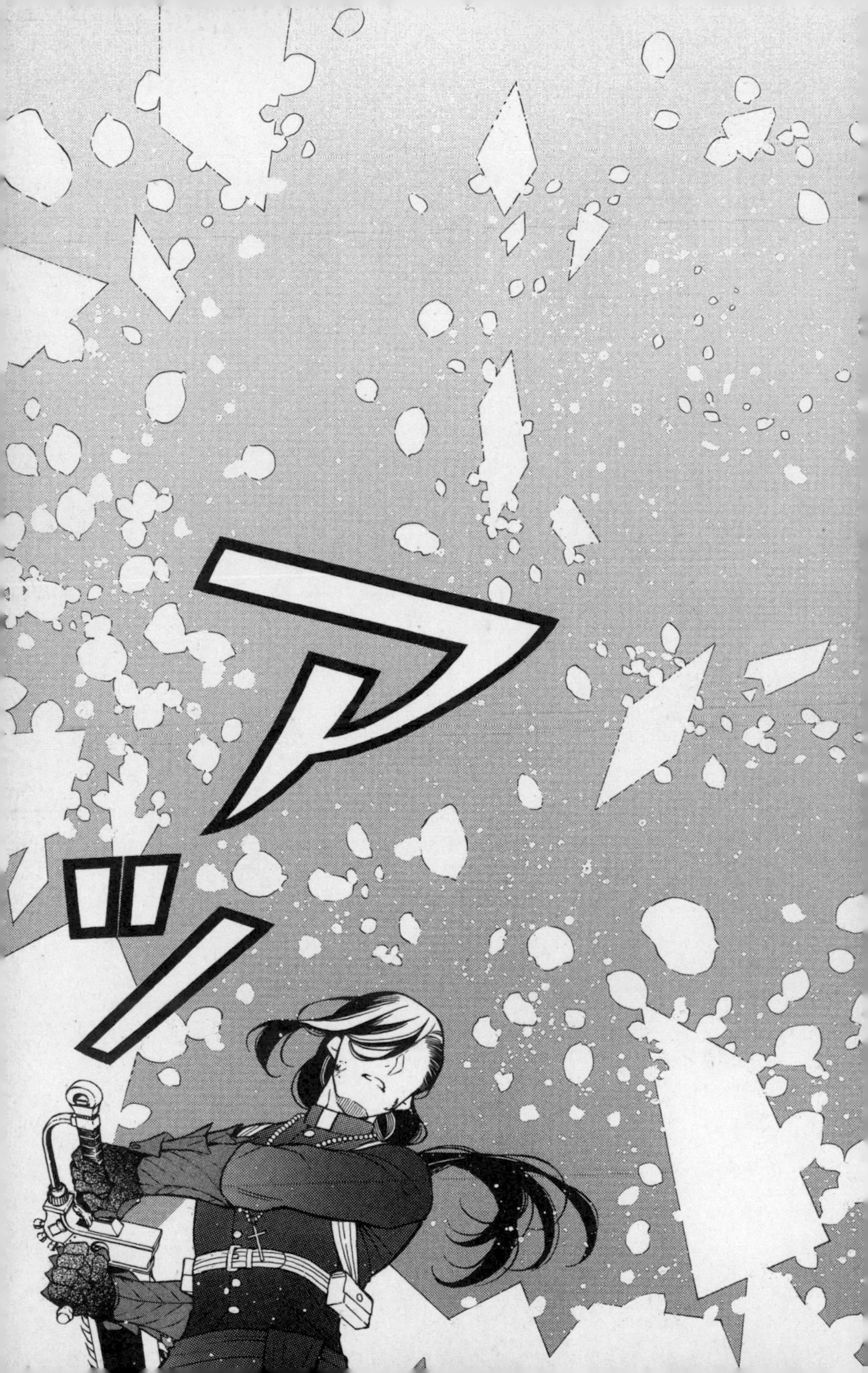
アッ

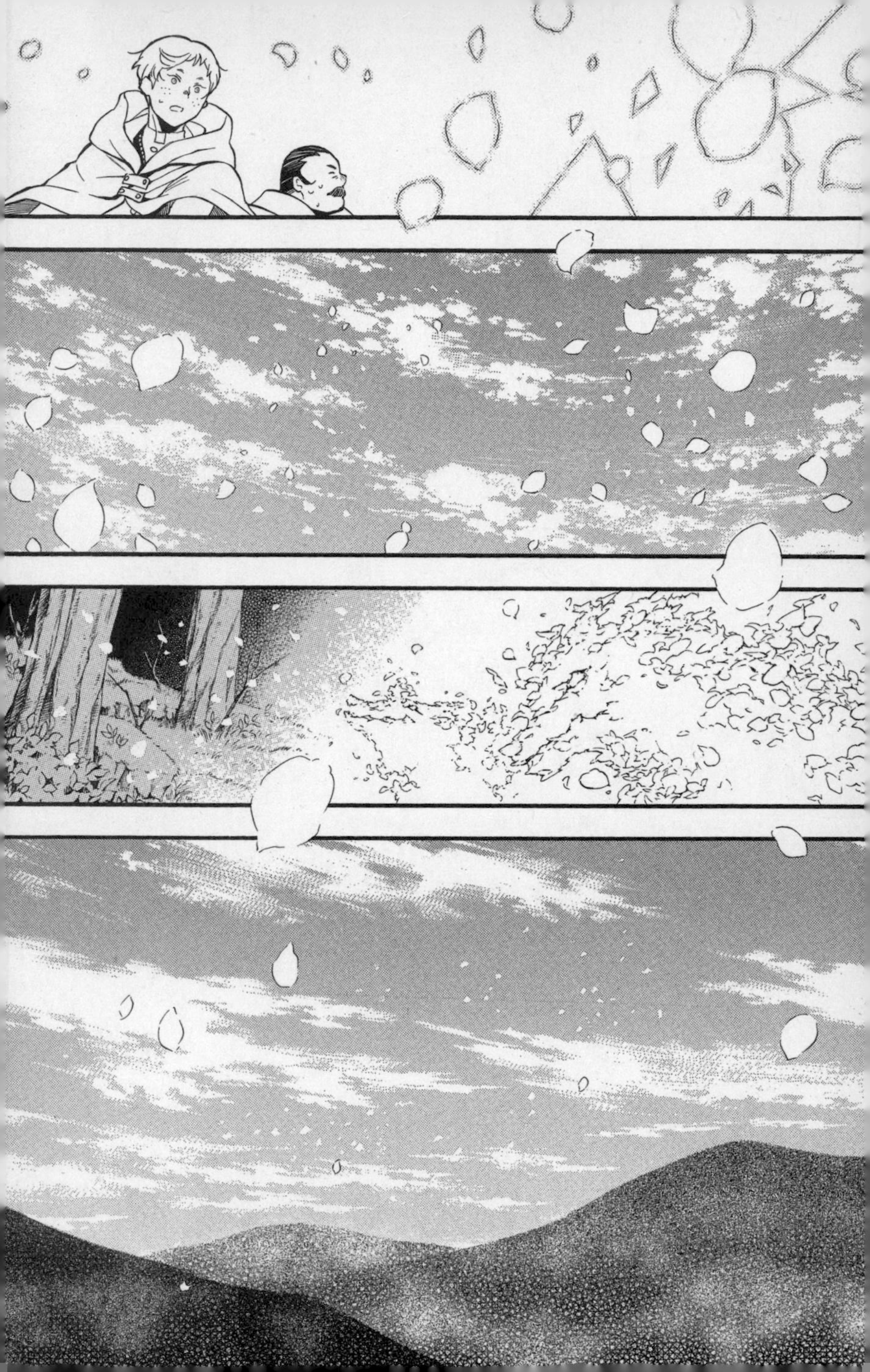

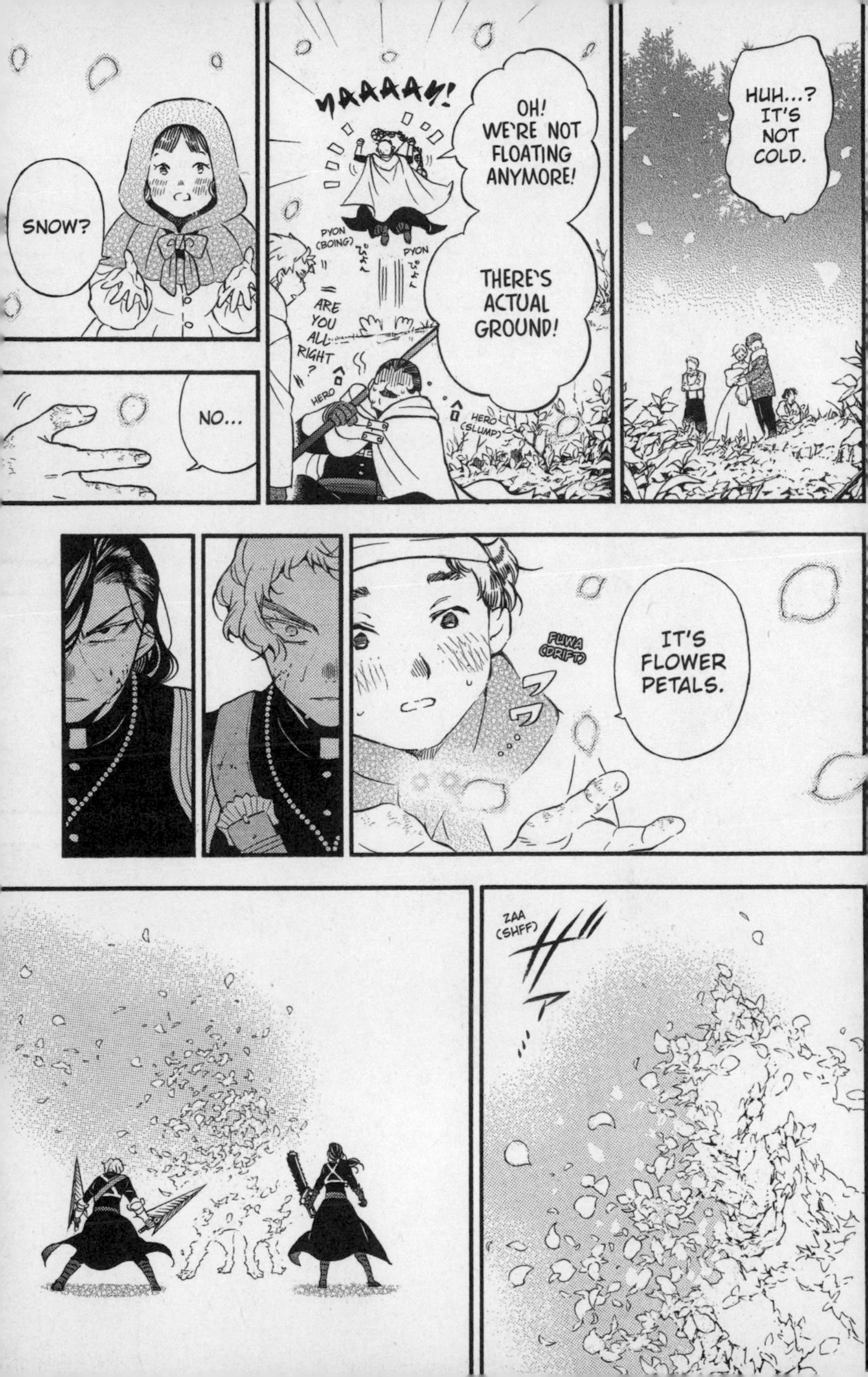
HUH...? IT'S NOT COLD.
YAAAAY!
OH! WE'RE NOT FLOATING ANYMORE!
THERE'S ACTUAL GROUND!
PYON (BOING)
PYON
ARE YOU ALL RIGHT?
HERO
HERO (SLUMP)
SNOW?
NO...
FUWA (DRIFT)
IT'S FLOWER PETALS.
ZAA (SHFF)

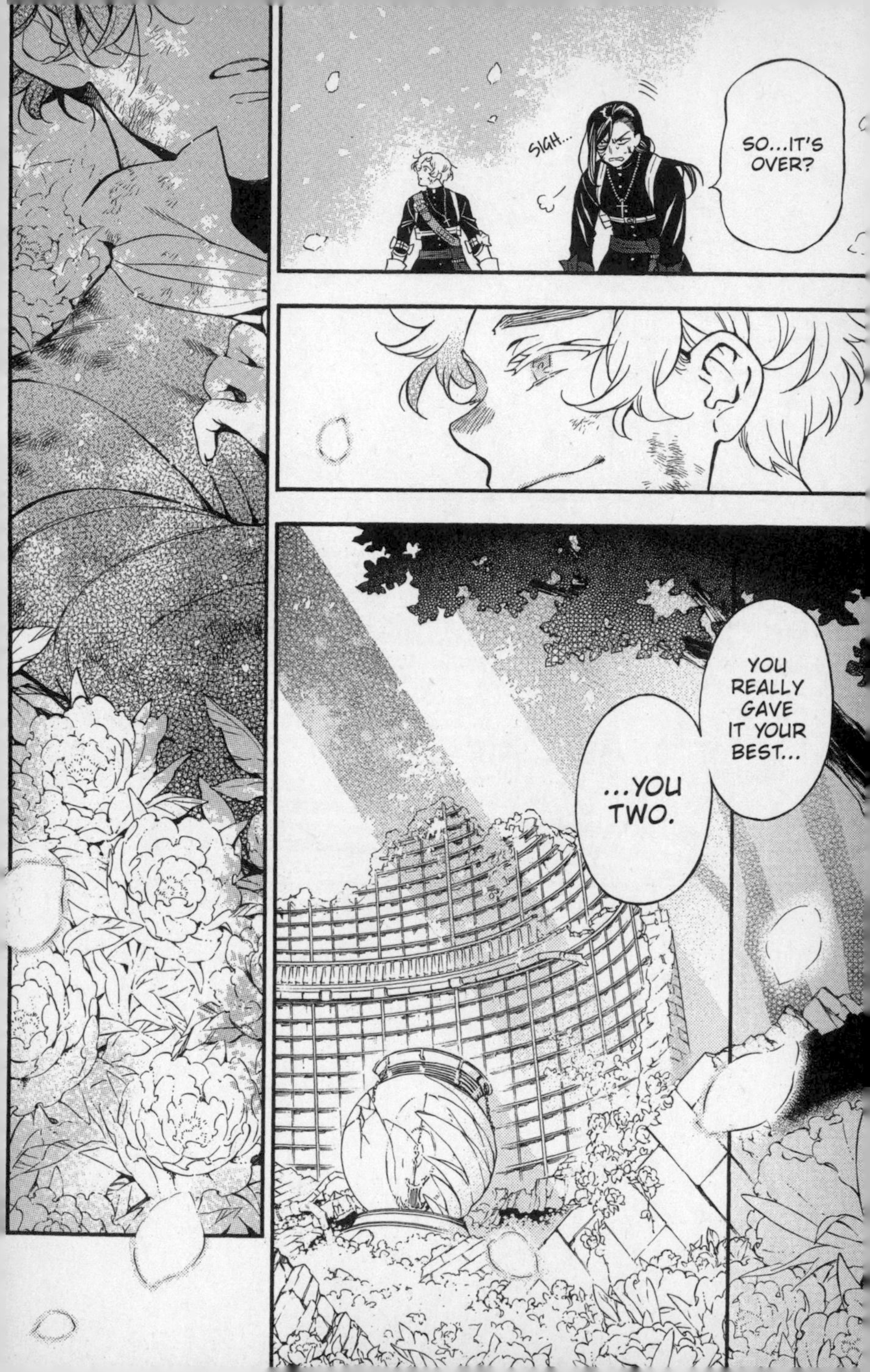
SO...IT'S OVER?
SIGH...
YOU REALLY GAVE IT YOUR BEST...
...YOU TWO.

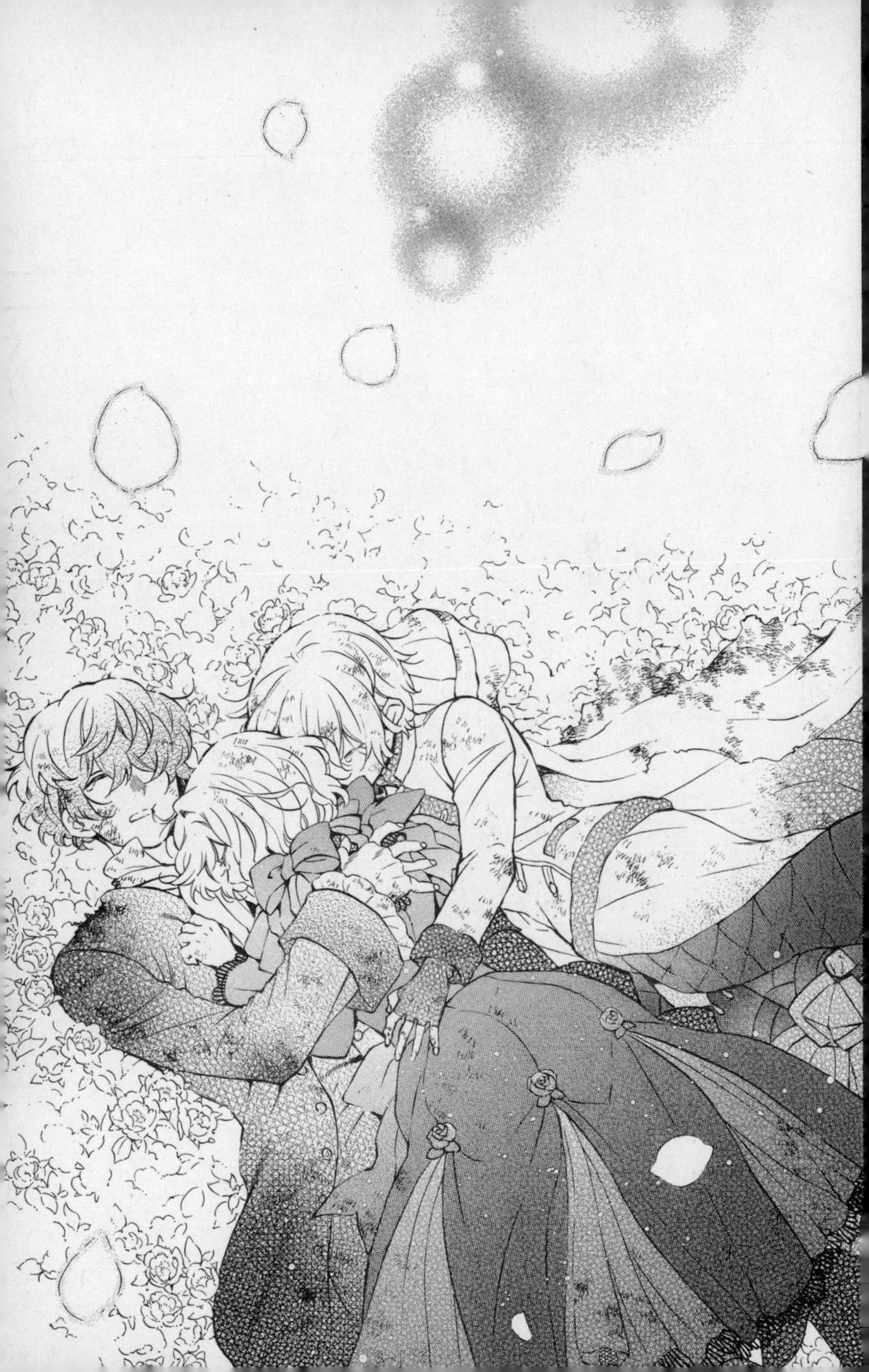

GÉVAUDAN ARC TRIVIA

JEAN-JACQUES'S
FATHER WAS A HUNTER
NAMED JEAN CHASTEL.
IN THE REAL-LIFE "BEAST
OF GÉVAUDAN" INCIDENT, HE
WAS A CHARACTER WITH A
DUBIOUS REPUTATION—WHILE
HE'S CREDITED WITH HAVING
KILLED THE "REAL" BEAST
AND PUTTING AN END TO
THE MATTER, HE WAS ALSO
SUSPECTED OF HAVING
TAMED AND TRAINED
THE BEAST IN THE
FIRST PLACE.

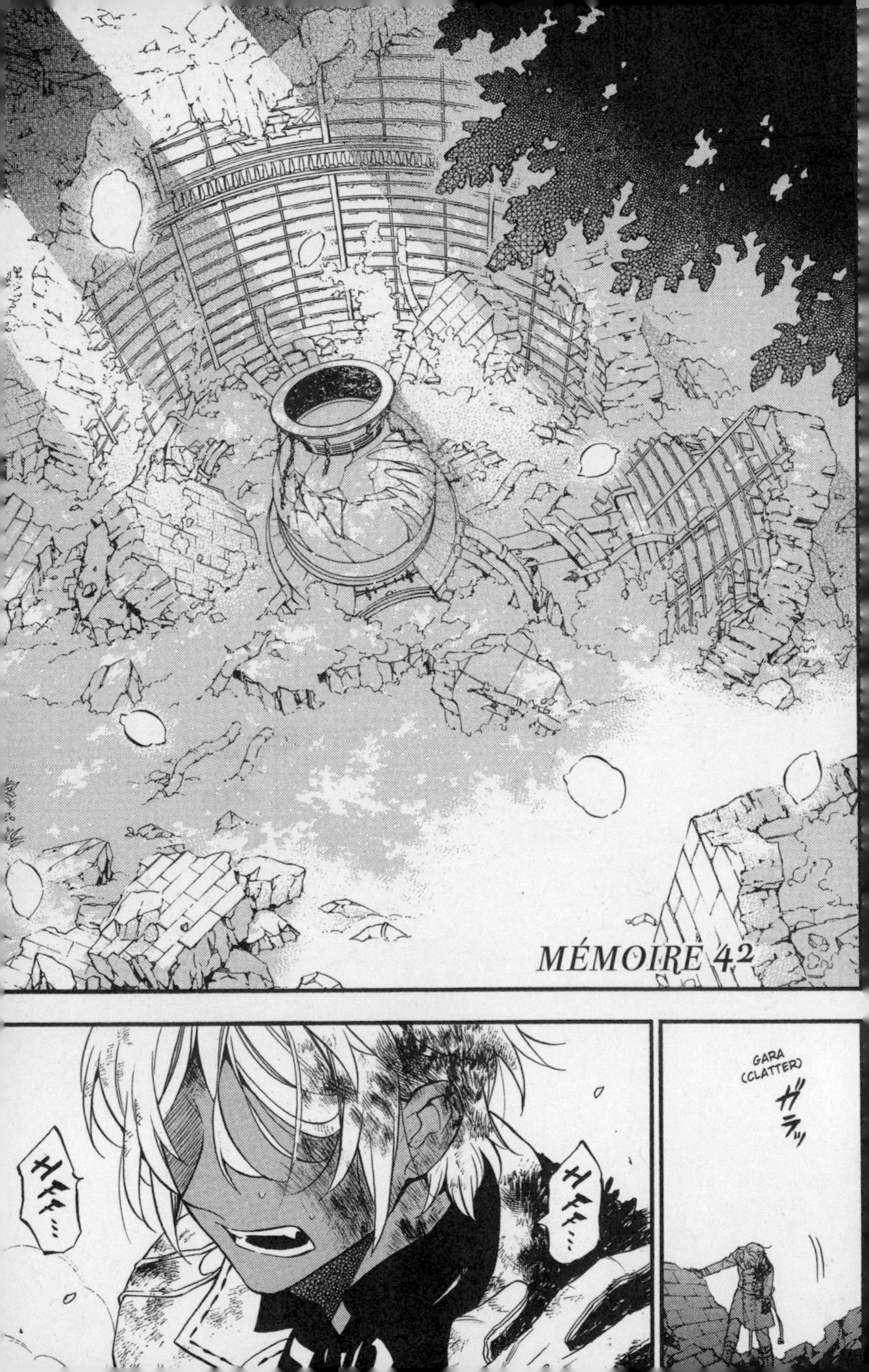
MÉMOIRE 42
GARA (CLATTER)
ガラッ
ハァァ…
ハァァ…

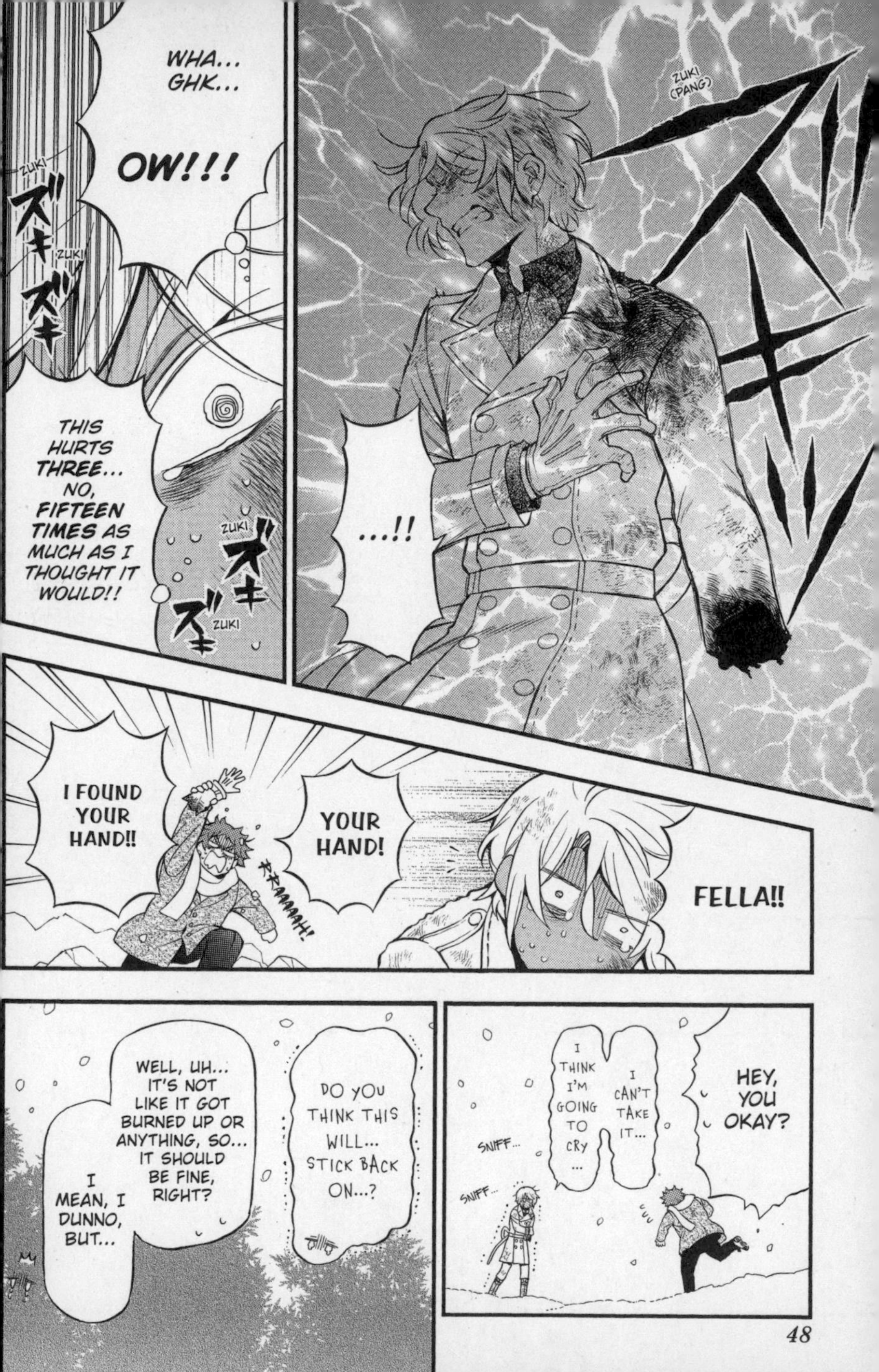
ZUKI (PANG)
...!!
WHA... GHK...
OW!!!
ZUKI
ZUKI
THIS HURTS THREE... NO, FIFTEEN TIMES AS MUCH AS I THOUGHT IT WOULD!!
ZUKI
ZUKI
FELLA!!
YOUR HAND!
I FOUND YOUR HAND!!
HEY, YOU OKAY?
I CAN'T TAKE IT...
I THINK I'M GOING TO CRY...
SNIFF...
SNIFF...
DO YOU THINK THIS WILL... STICK BACK ON...?
WELL, UH... IT'S NOT LIKE IT GOT BURNED UP OR ANYTHING, SO... IT SHOULD BE FINE, RIGHT?
I MEAN, I DUNNO, BUT...

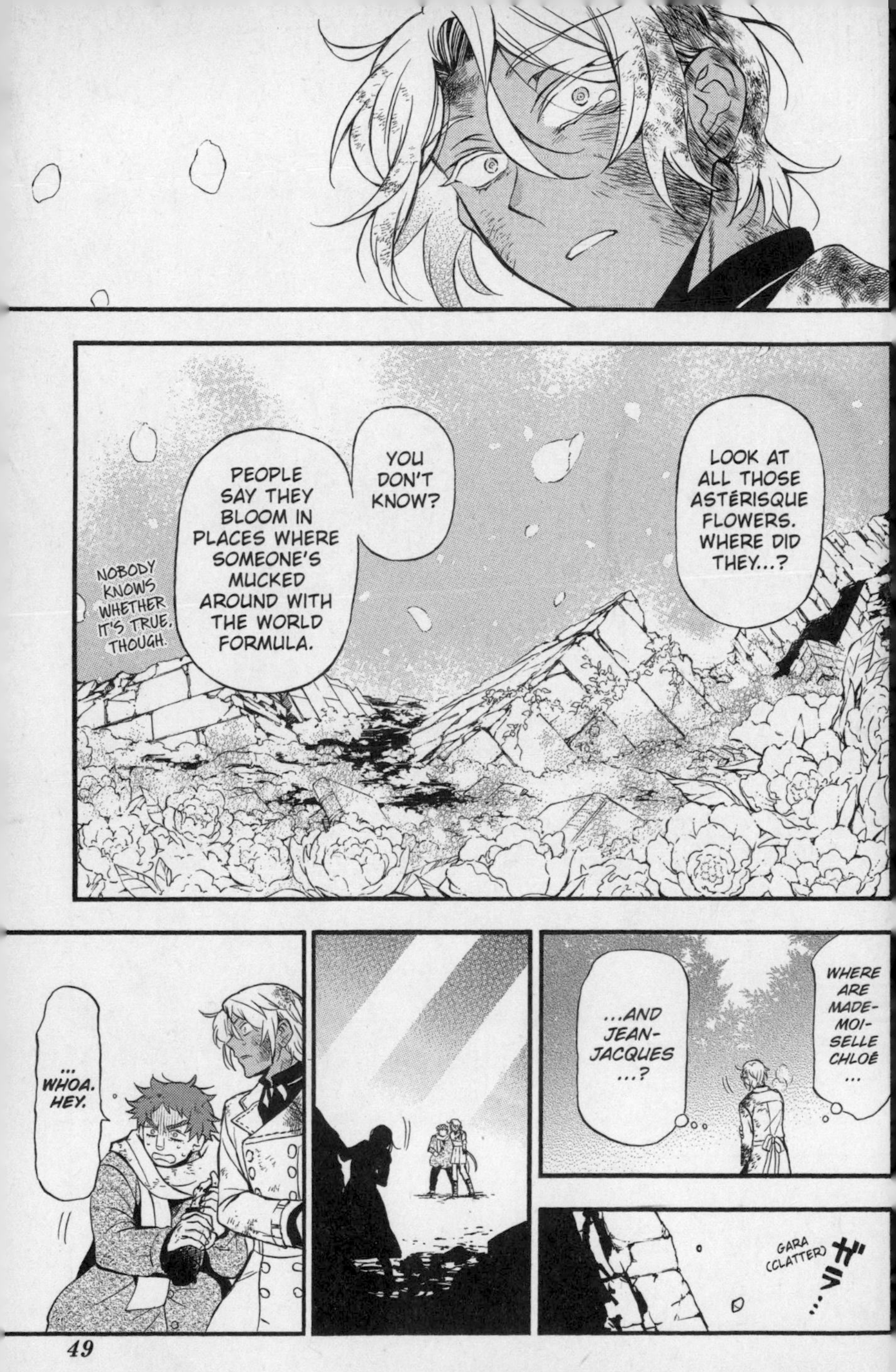
LOOK AT ALL THOSE ASTÉRISQUE FLOWERS. WHERE DID THEY...?
YOU DON'T KNOW?
PEOPLE SAY THEY BLOOM IN PLACES WHERE SOMEONE'S MUCKED AROUND WITH THE WORLD FORMULA.
NOBODY KNOWS WHETHER IT'S TRUE, THOUGH.
WHERE ARE MADE-MOI-SELLE CHLOÉ ...
...AND JEAN-JACQUES ...?
GARA (CLATTER)
...WHOA. HEY.

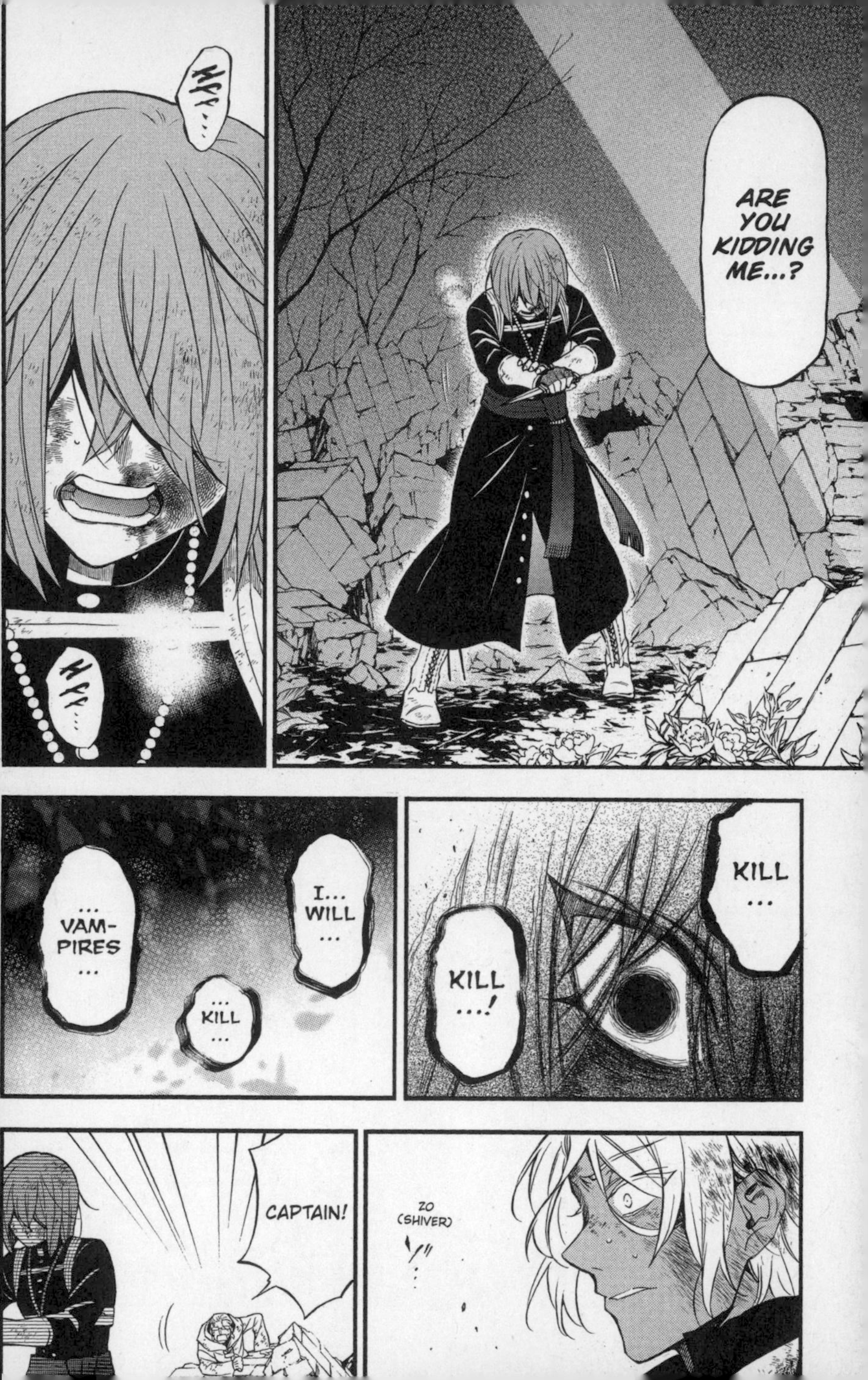
ARE YOU KIDDING ME...?
HFF...
HFF...
KILL ...
KILL ...!
I... WILL ...
... VAMPIRES ...
... KILL ...
ZO (SHIVER)
CAPTAIN!

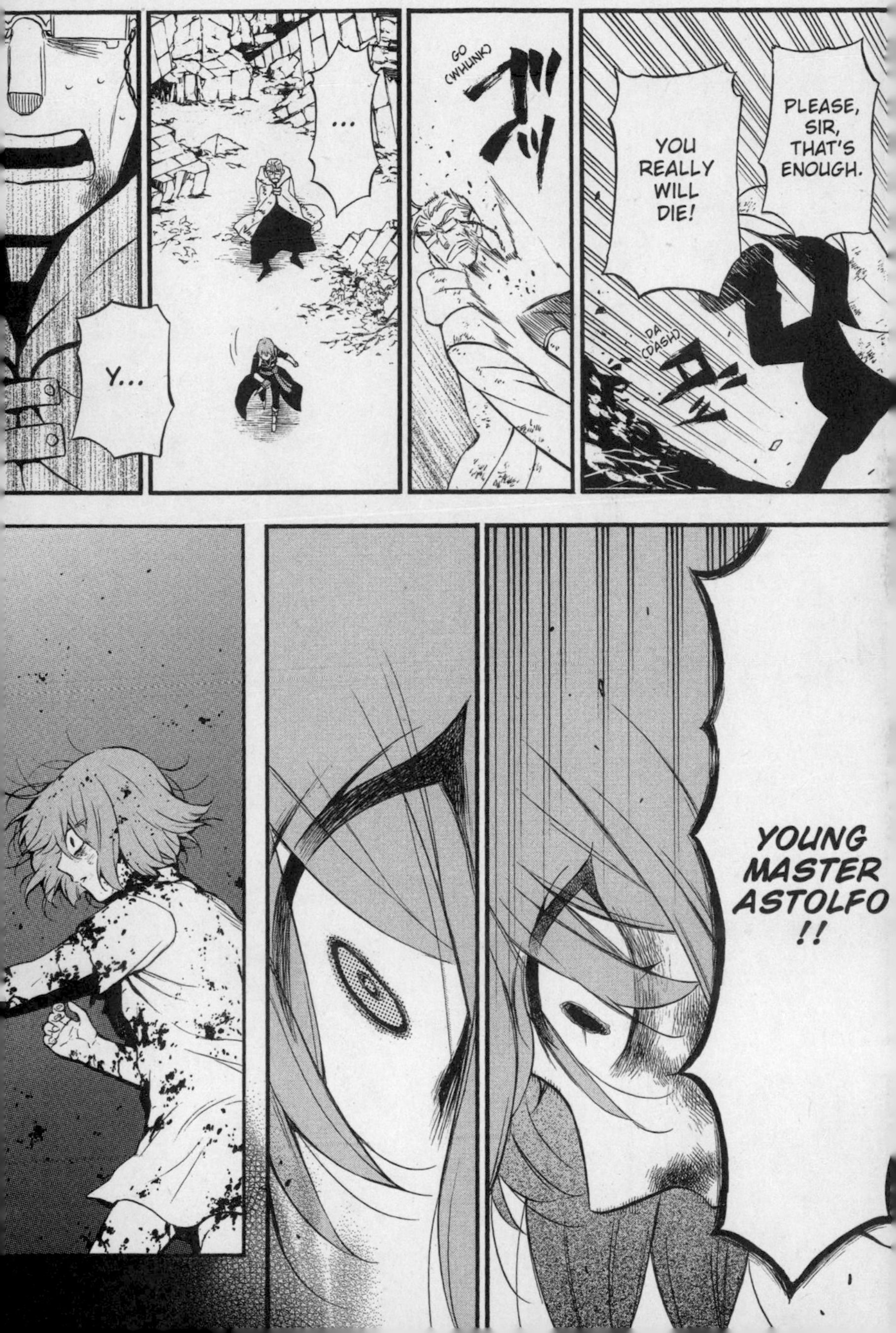
PLEASE, SIR, THAT'S ENOUGH.
YOU REALLY WILL DIE!
DA (DASH)
GO (WHUNK)
...
Y...
YOUNG MASTER ASTOLFO!!

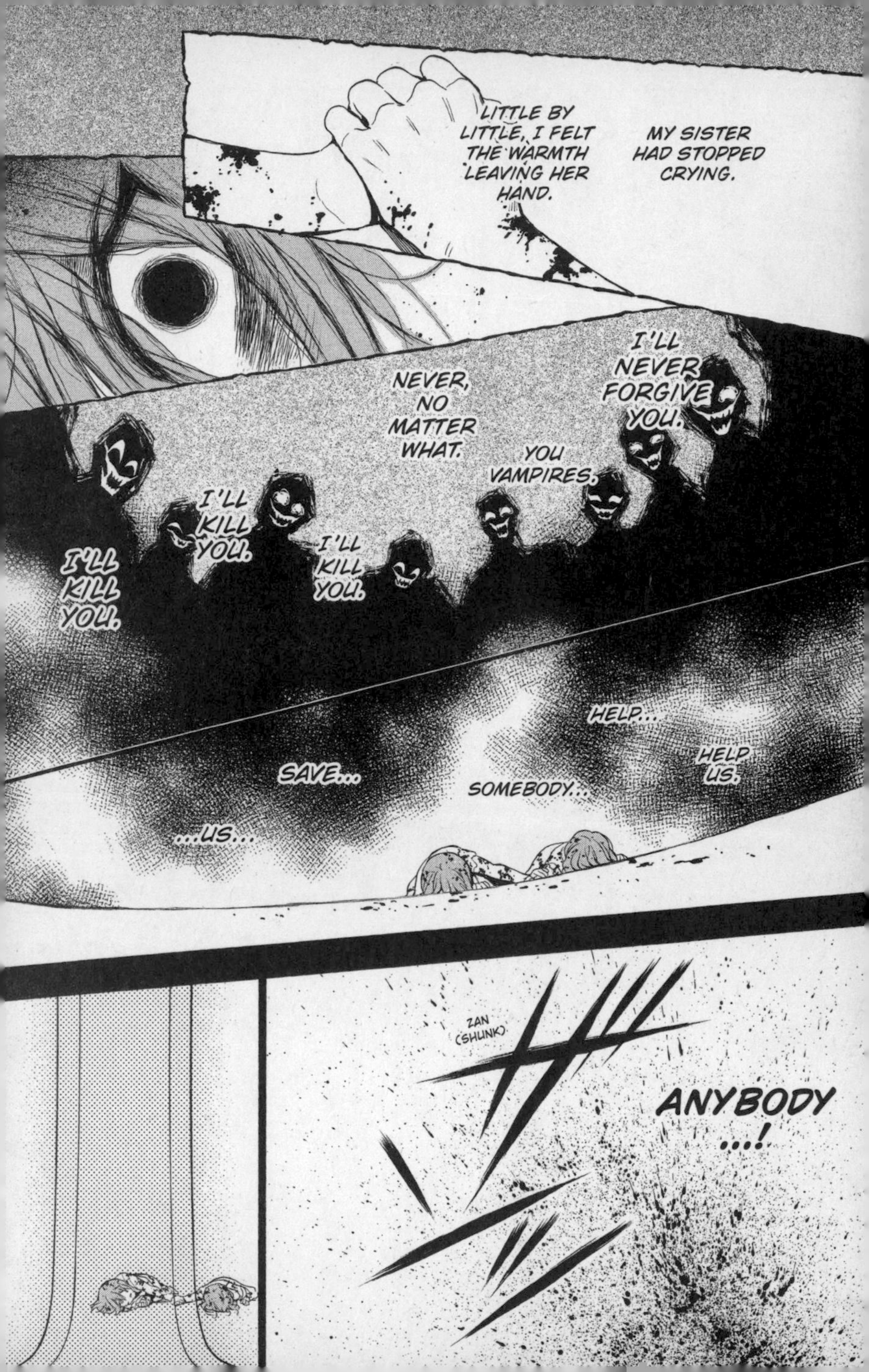
MY SISTER HAD STOPPED CRYING.
LITTLE BY LITTLE, I FELT THE WARMTH LEAVING HER HAND.
I'LL NEVER FORGIVE YOU.
YOU VAMPIRES.
NEVER, NO MATTER WHAT.
I'LL KILL YOU.
I'LL KILL YOU.
I'LL KILL YOU.
HELP US.
HELP...
SOMEBODY...
SAVE...
...US...
ANYBODY ...!
ZAN (SHUNK)

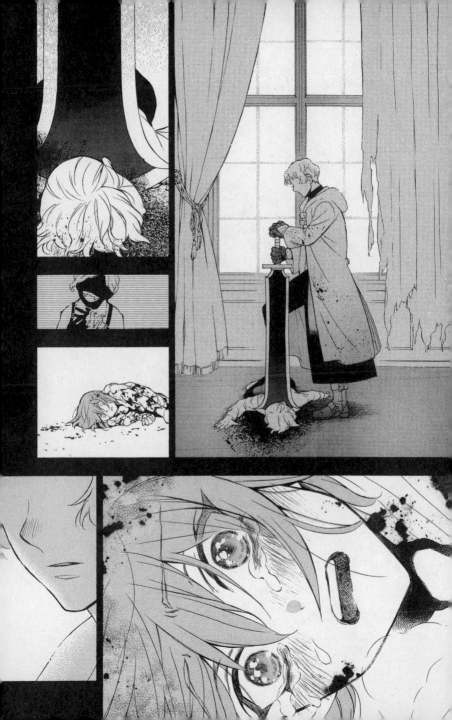

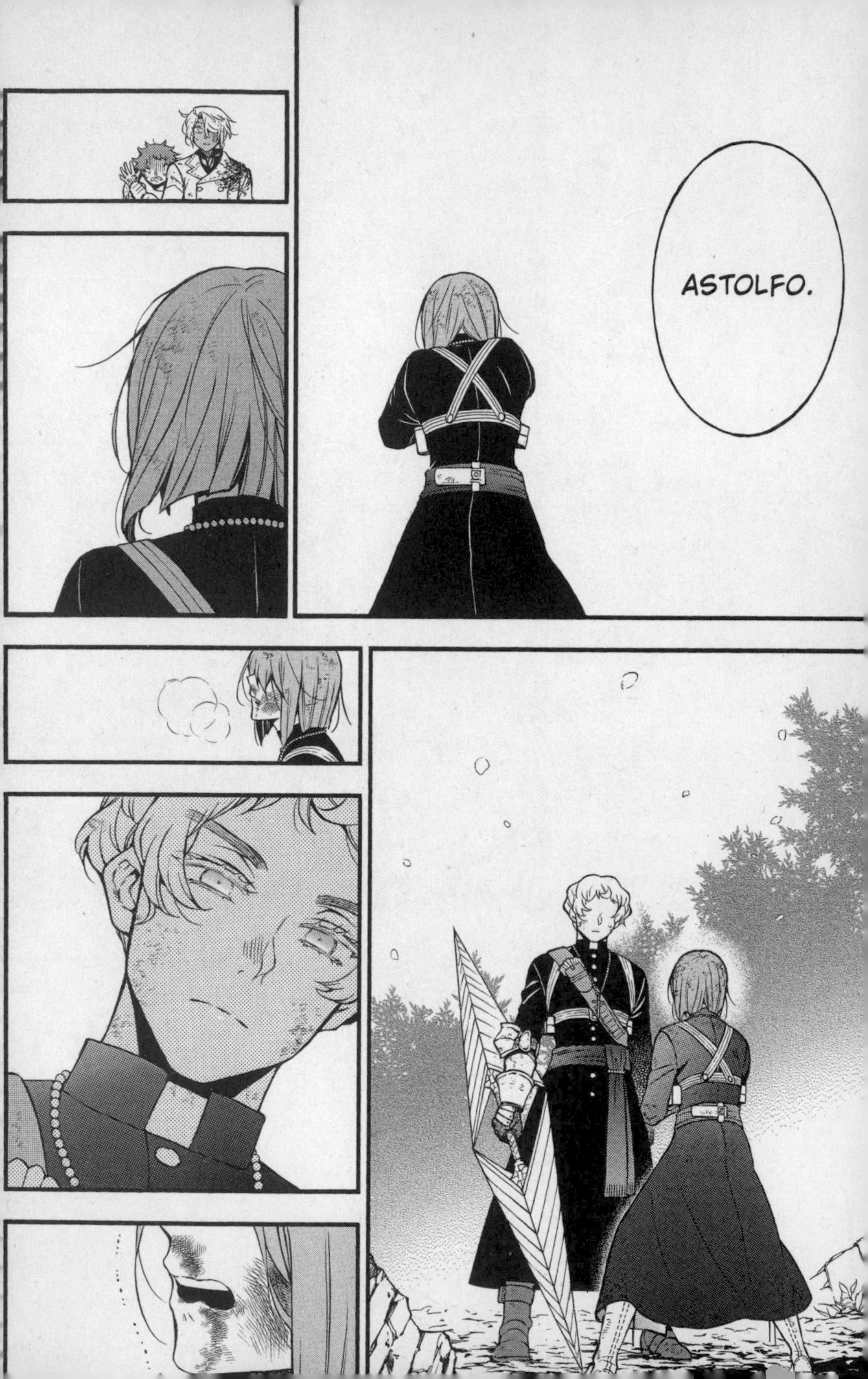
ASTOLFO.

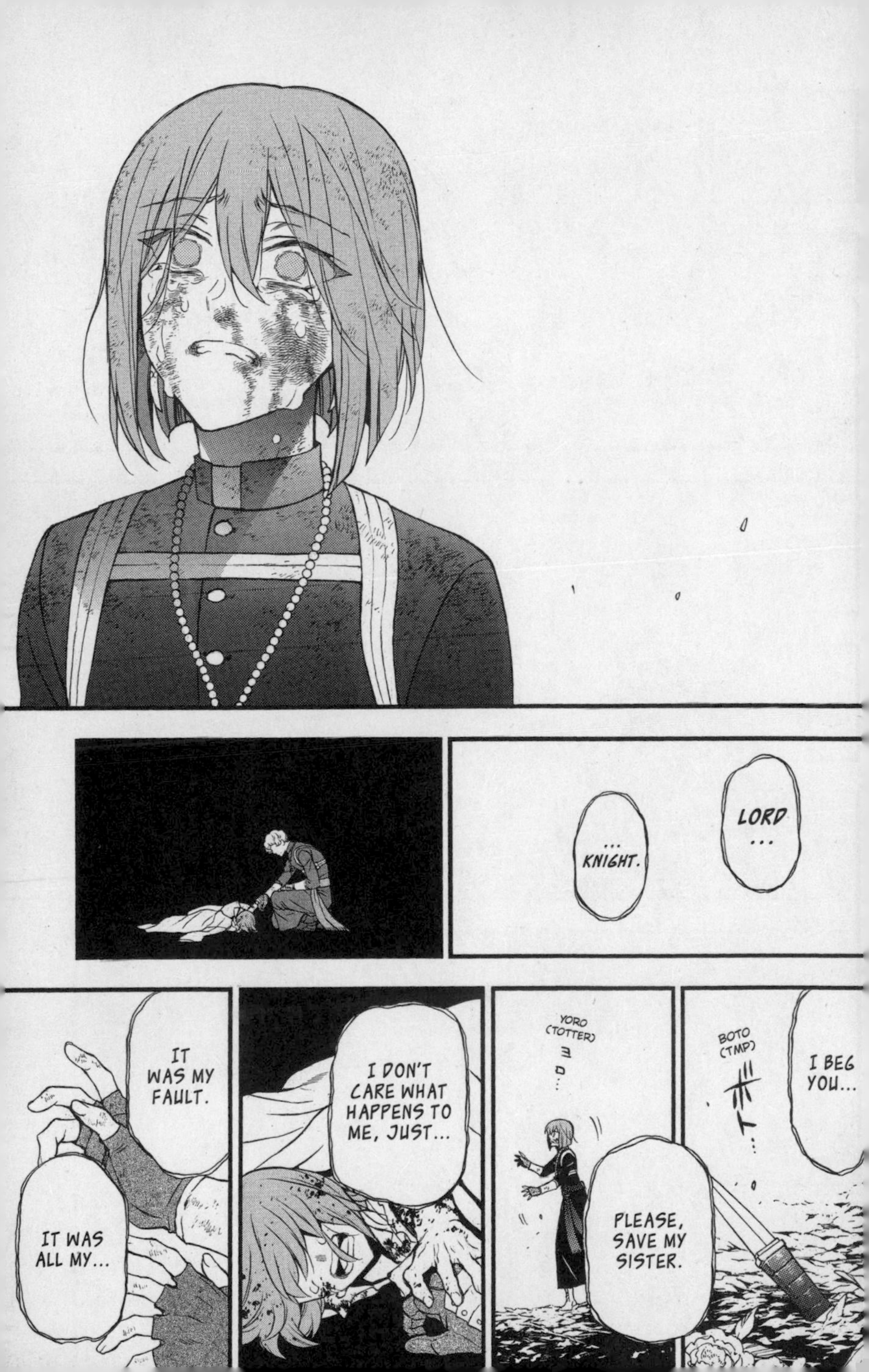
LORD...
...KNIGHT.
I BEG YOU...
BOTO (TMP)
ボト…
YORO (TOTTER)
ヨロ…
PLEASE, SAVE MY SISTER.
I DON'T CARE WHAT HAPPENS TO ME, JUST...
IT WAS MY FAULT.
IT WAS ALL MY...

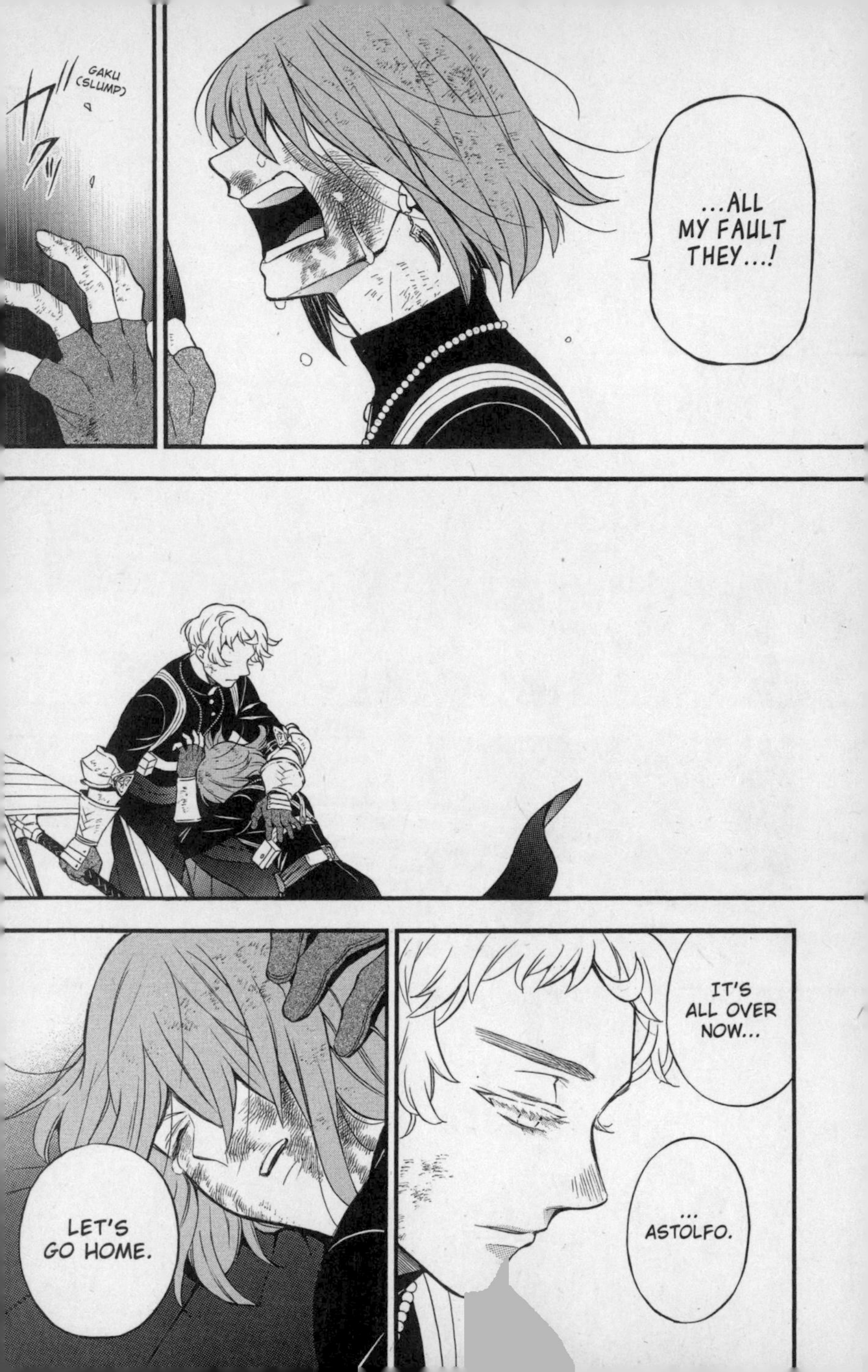
...ALL MY FAULT THEY...!
ガクッ
GAKU (SLUMP)
IT'S ALL OVER NOW...
... ASTOLFO.
LET'S GO HOME.

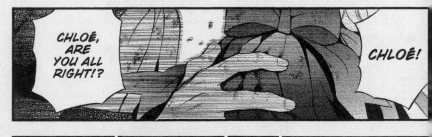

CHLOÉ, ARE YOU ALL RIGHT!?

CHLOÉ!

CHLOÉ ...?

ARE YOU HURT ANYWHERE?

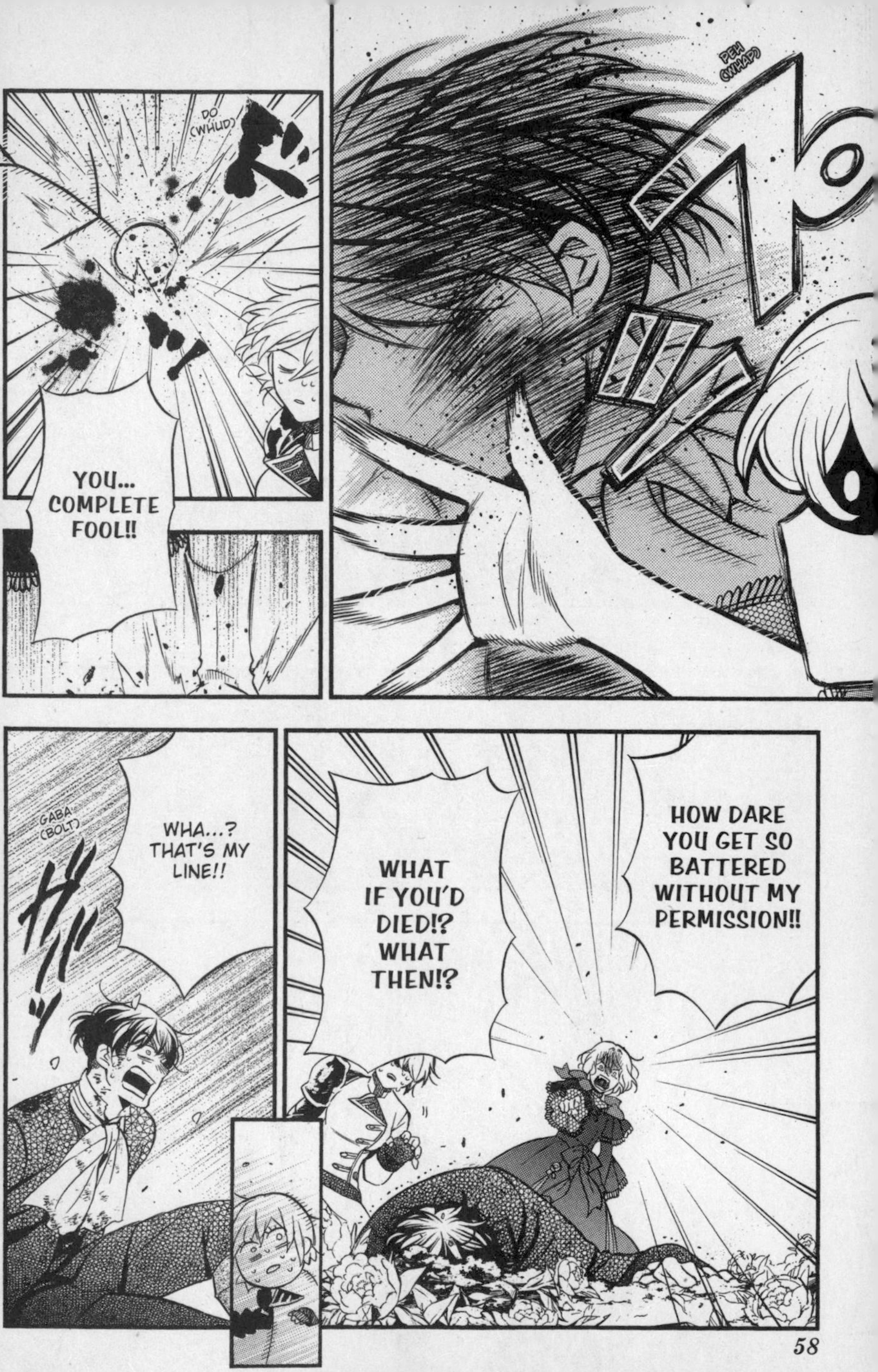
PEH (WHAP)
DO (WHUD)
YOU... COMPLETE FOOL!!
HOW DARE YOU GET SO BATTERED WITHOUT MY PERMISSION!!
WHAT IF YOU'D DIED!? WHAT THEN!?
GABA (BOLT)
WHA...? THAT'S MY LINE!!

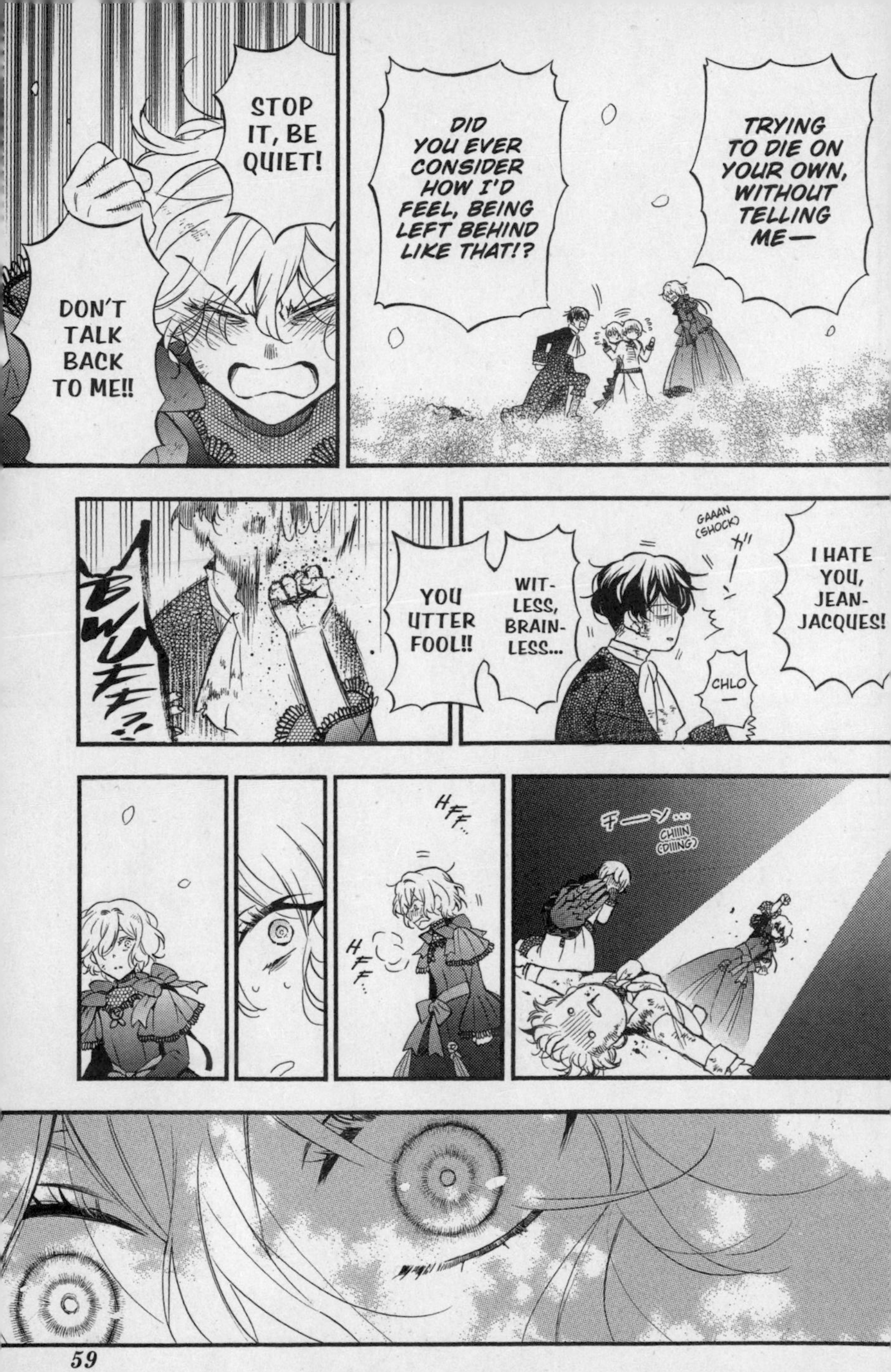
TRYING TO DIE ON YOUR OWN, WITHOUT TELLING ME—
DID YOU EVER CONSIDER HOW I'D FEEL, BEING LEFT BEHIND LIKE THAT!?
STOP IT, BE QUIET!
DON'T TALK BACK TO ME!!
I HATE YOU, JEAN-JACQUES!
GAAAN (SHOCK)
CHLO—
WIT-LESS, BRAIN-LESS...
YOU UTTER FOOL!!
BWUFFF?!
チーン… CHIIIN (DIIING)
HFF...
HFF...

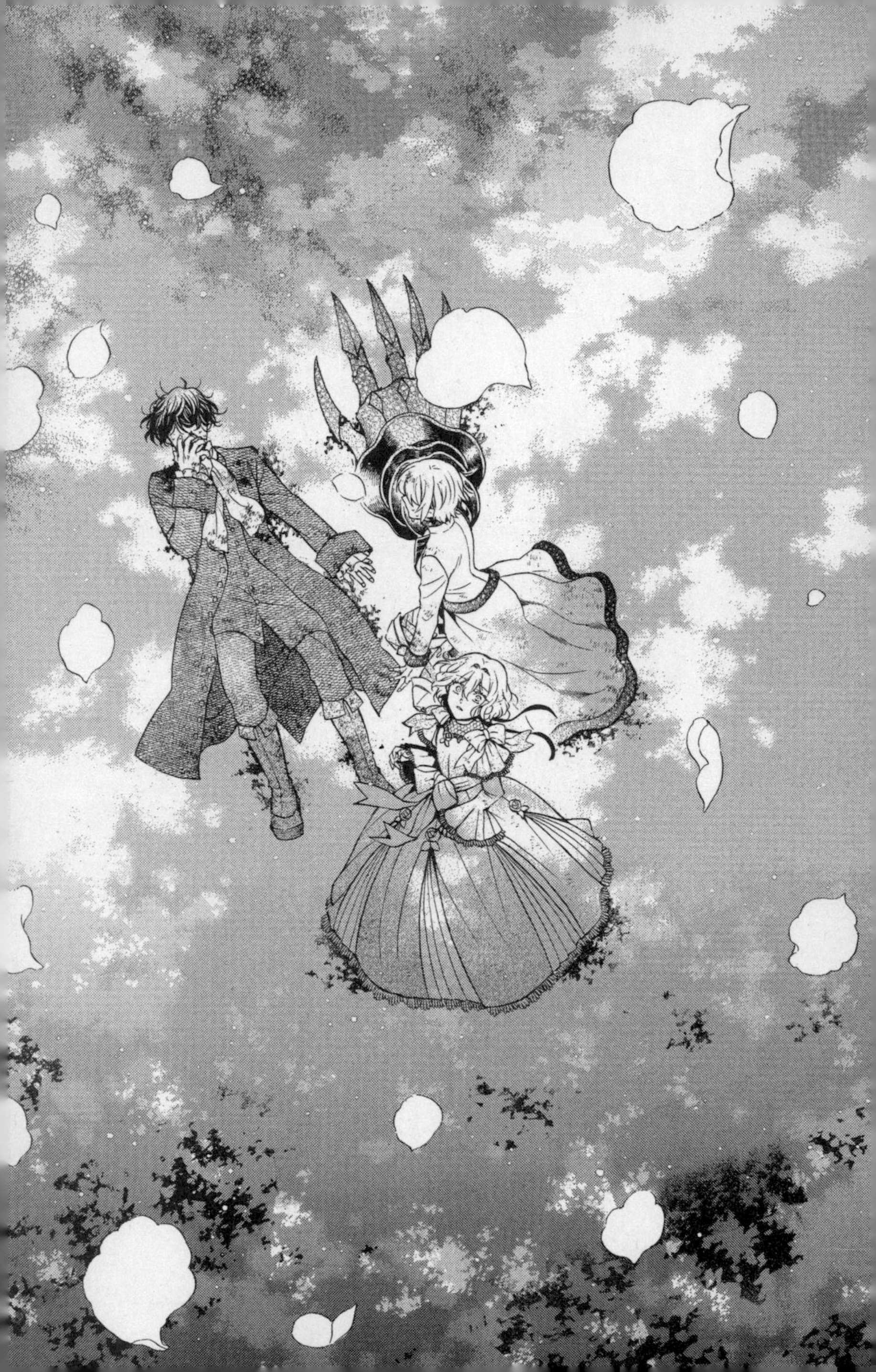

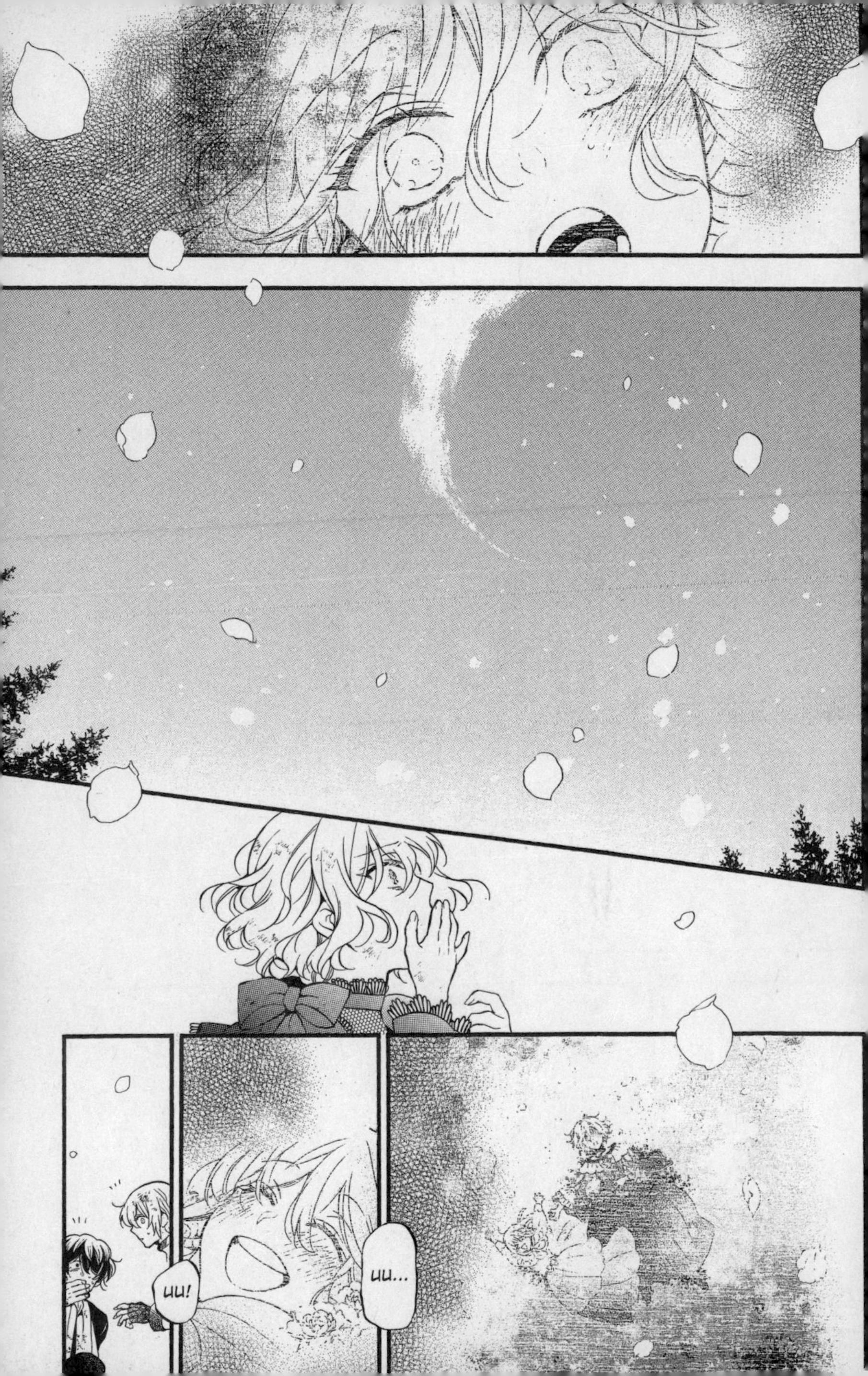
uu...
uu!

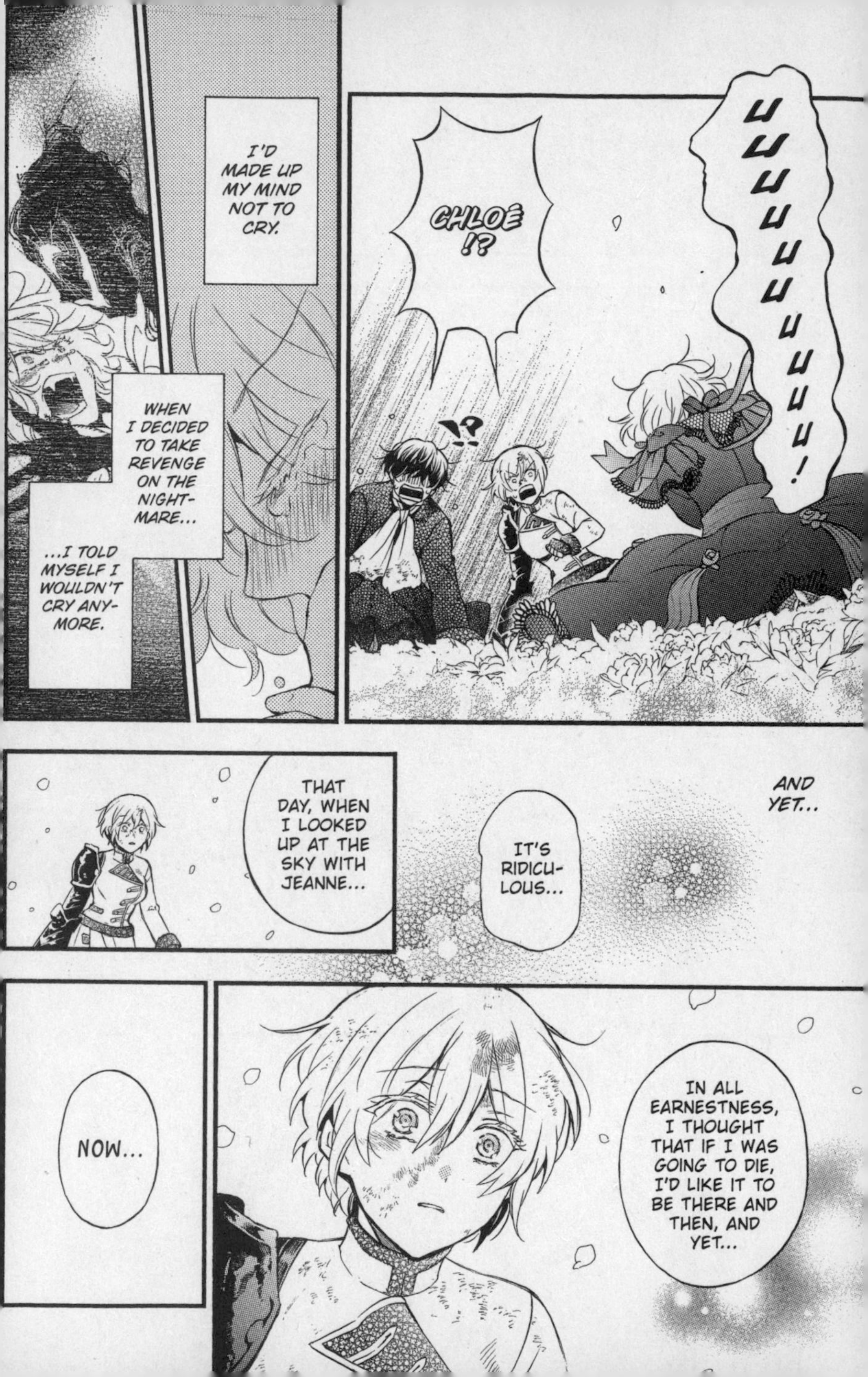
UUUUUUUUUU!
CHLOÉ!?
!?
I'D MADE UP MY MIND NOT TO CRY.
WHEN I DECIDED TO TAKE REVENGE ON THE NIGHT-MARE...
...I TOLD MYSELF I WOULDN'T CRY ANY-MORE.
AND YET...
IT'S RIDICU-LOUS...
THAT DAY, WHEN I LOOKED UP AT THE SKY WITH JEANNE...
IN ALL EARNESTNESS, I THOUGHT THAT IF I WAS GOING TO DIE, I'D LIKE IT TO BE THERE AND THEN, AND YET...
NOW...

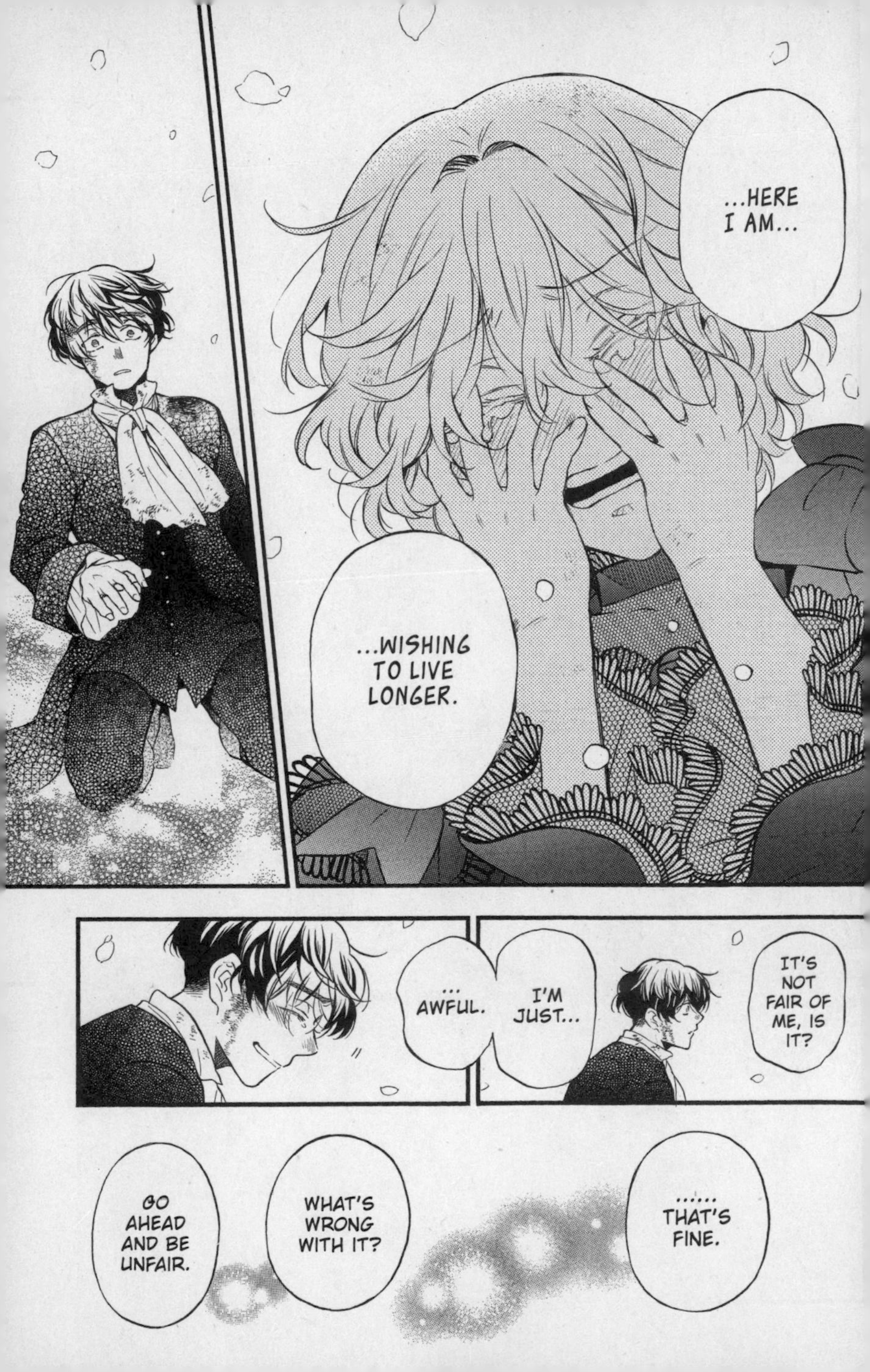
...HERE I AM...
...WISHING TO LIVE LONGER.
IT'S NOT FAIR OF ME, IS IT?
I'M JUST...
... AWFUL.
...... THAT'S FINE.
WHAT'S WRONG WITH IT?
GO AHEAD AND BE UNFAIR.

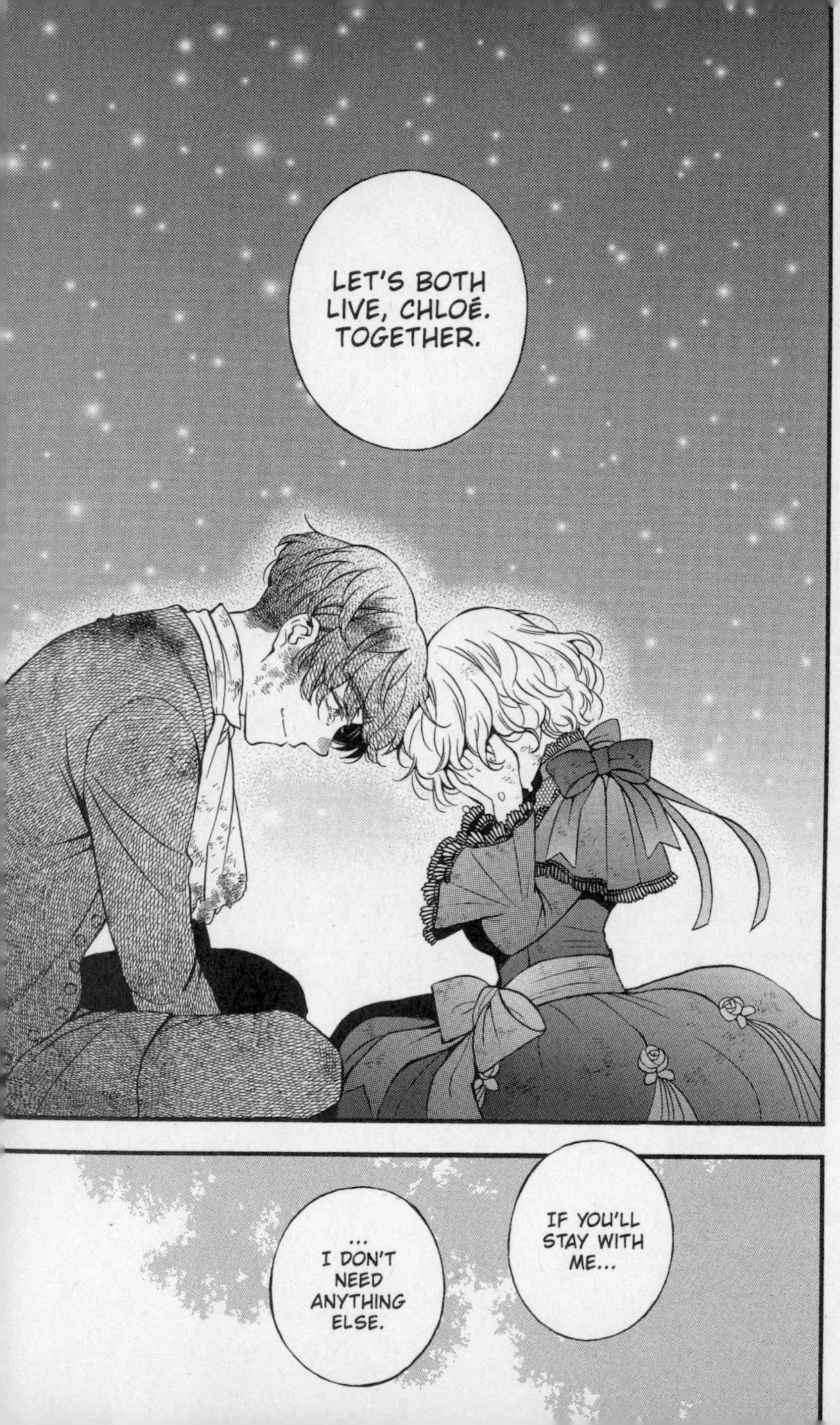
LET'S BOTH LIVE, CHLOÉ. TOGETHER.
IF YOU'LL STAY WITH ME...
... I DON'T NEED ANYTHING ELSE.

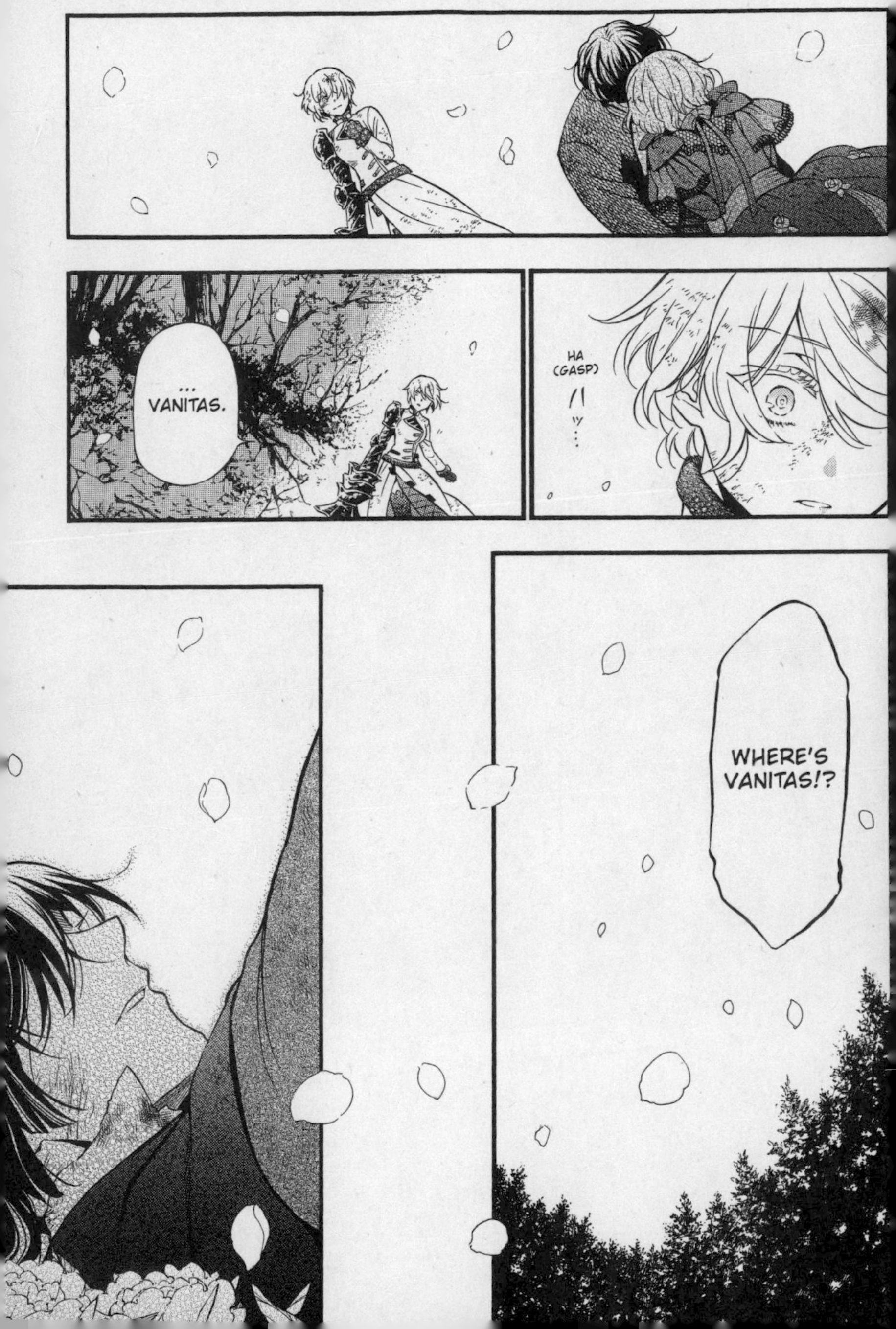
HA (GASP)
ハッ…
... VANITAS.
WHERE'S VANITAS!?

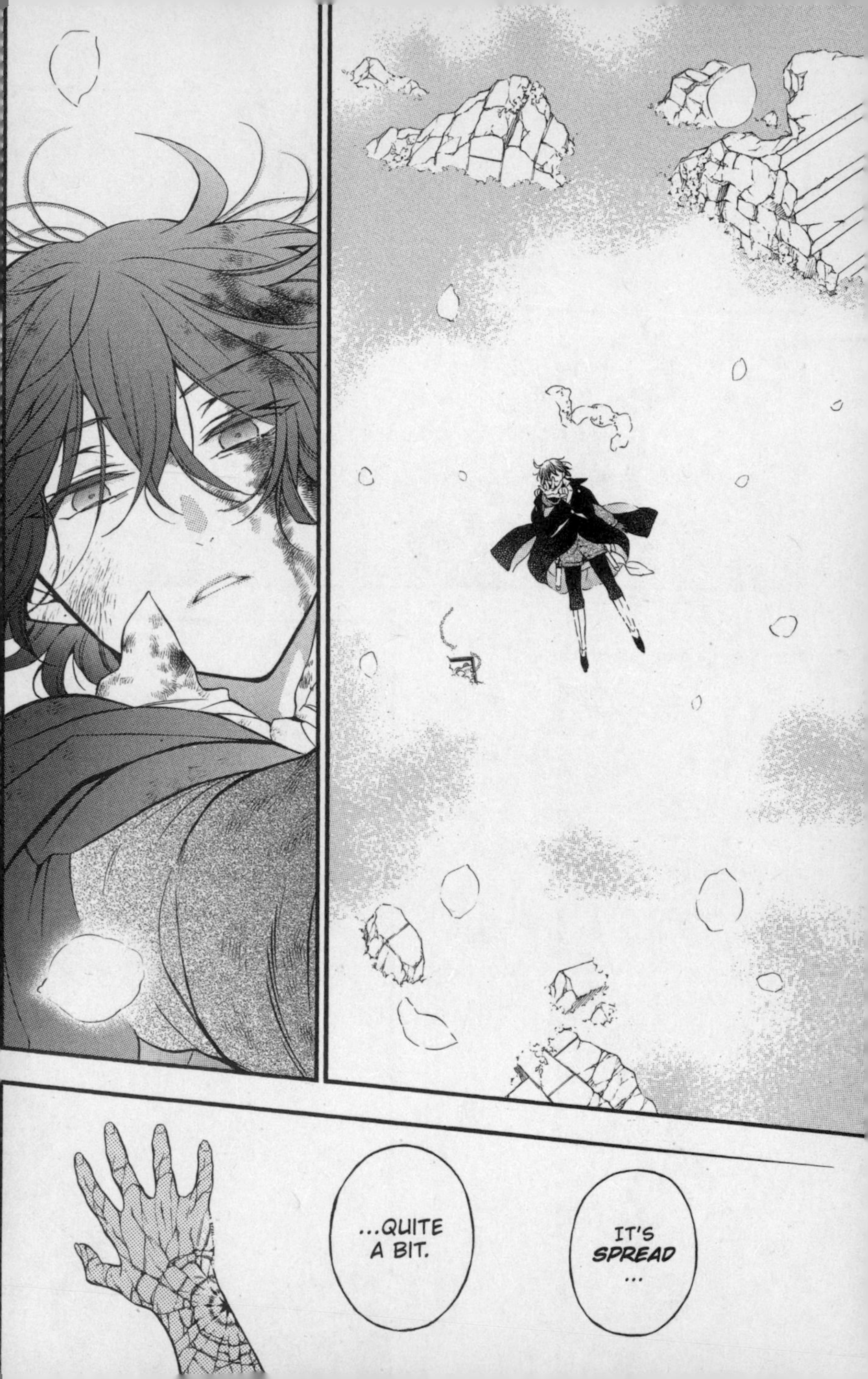
IT'S SPREAD ...
...QUITE A BIT.

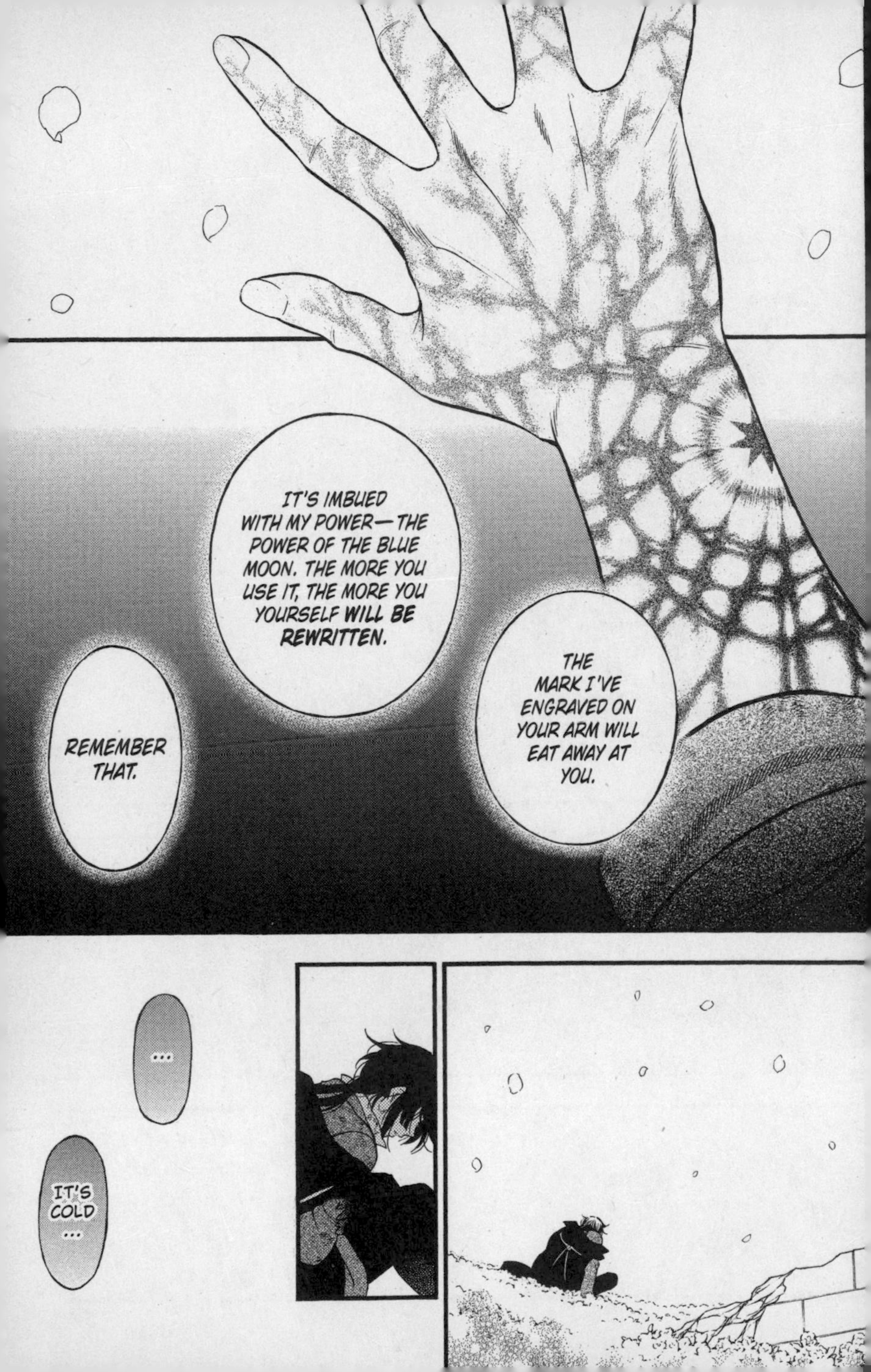
THE MARK I'VE ENGRAVED ON YOUR ARM WILL EAT AWAY AT YOU.
IT'S IMBUED WITH MY POWER—THE POWER OF THE BLUE MOON. THE MORE YOU USE IT, THE MORE YOU YOURSELF **WILL BE REWRITTEN.**
REMEMBER THAT.
...
IT'S COLD ...

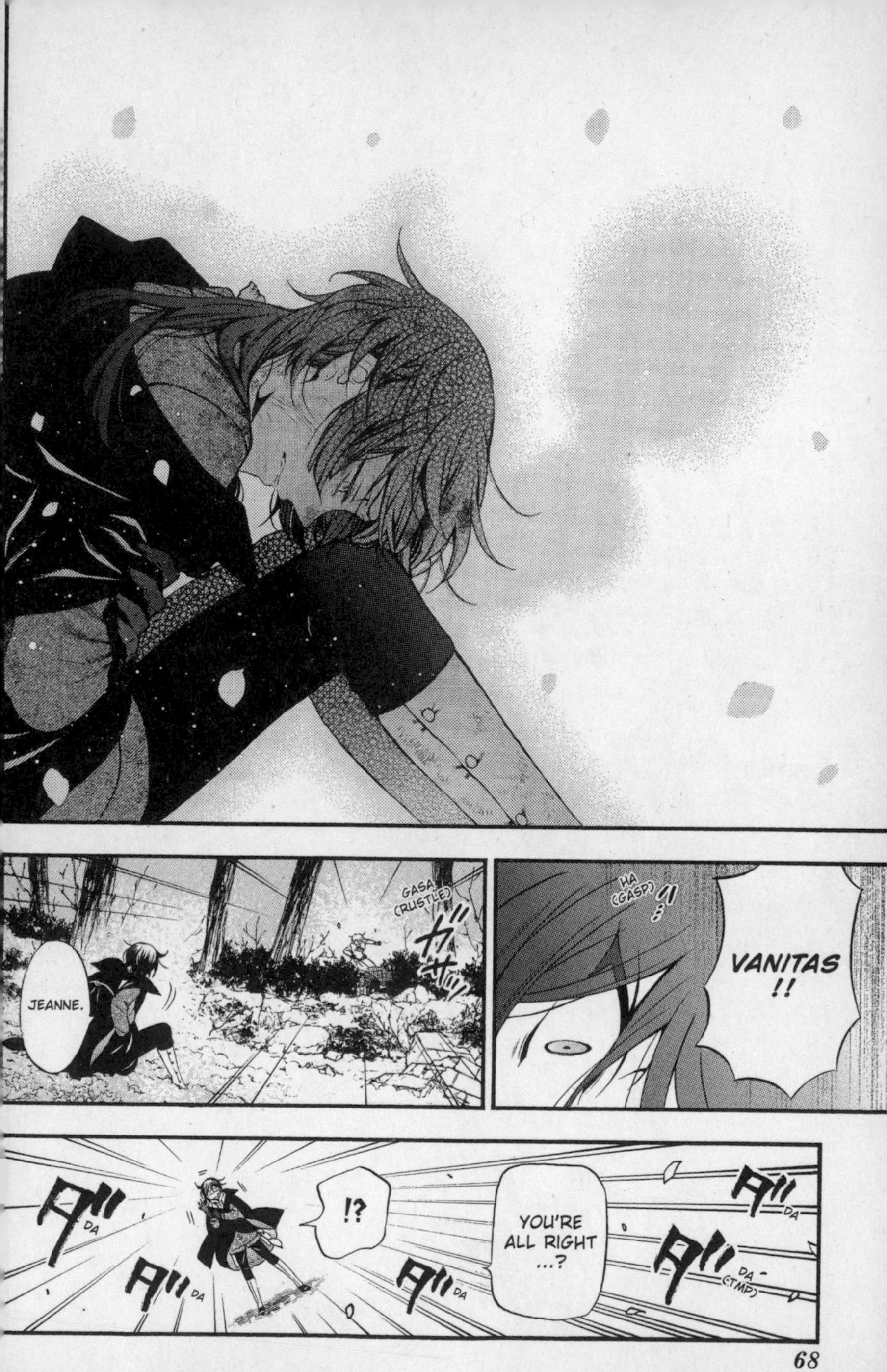
HA (GASP) !!...
VANITAS !!
GASA (RUSTLE)
JEANNE.
DA
DA (TMP)
YOU'RE ALL RIGHT ...?
DA
!?
DA
DA

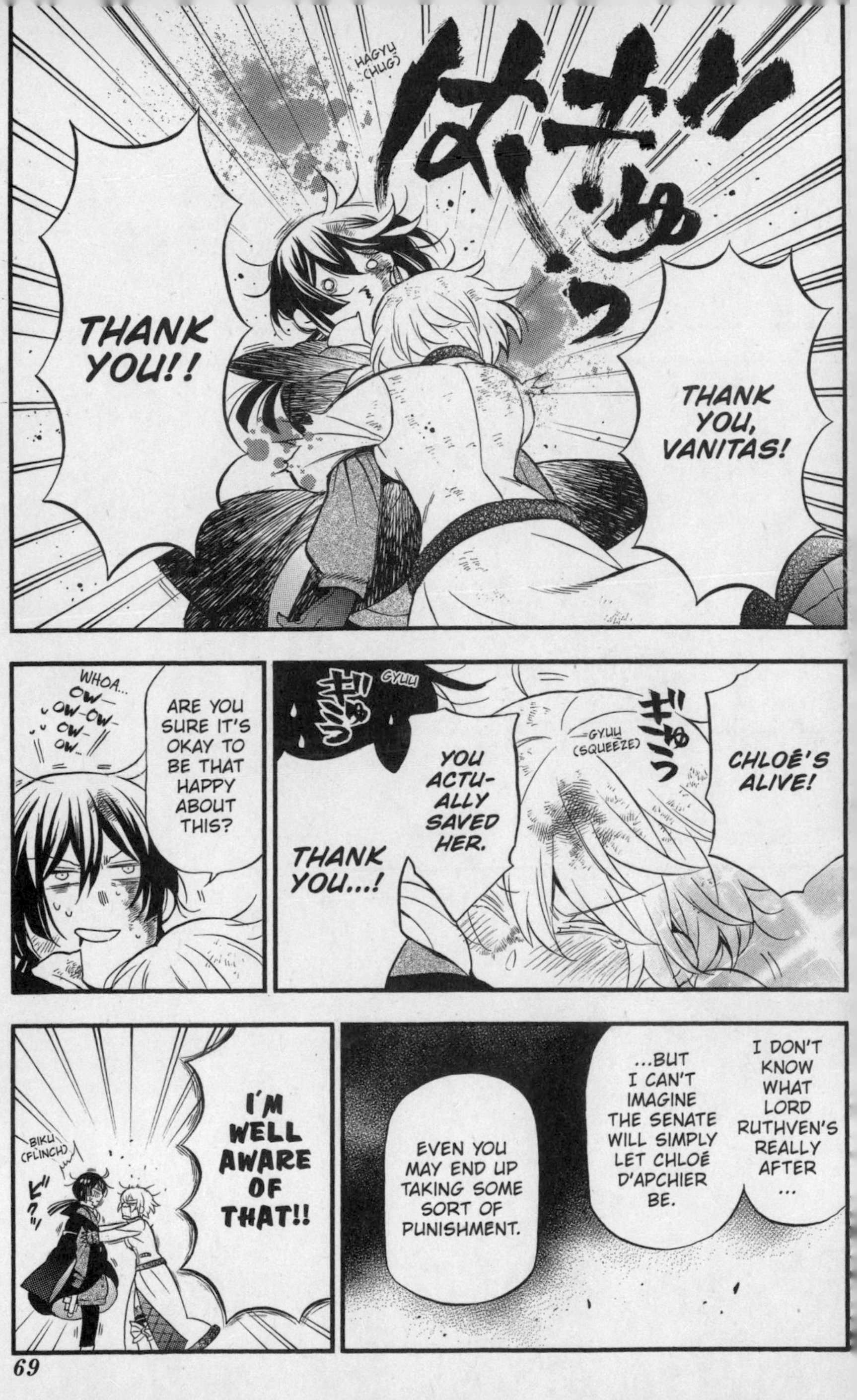
HAGYU (HUG)
THANK YOU, VANITAS!
THANK YOU!!
CHLOÉ'S ALIVE!
GYUU (SQUEEZE)
YOU ACTUALLY SAVED HER.
GYUU
THANK YOU...!
ARE YOU SURE IT'S OKAY TO BE THAT HAPPY ABOUT THIS?
WHOA... OW-OW-OW-OW-OW...
I DON'T KNOW WHAT LORD RUTHVEN'S REALLY AFTER...
...BUT I CAN'T IMAGINE THE SENATE WILL SIMPLY LET CHLOÉ D'APCHIER BE.
EVEN YOU MAY END UP TAKING SOME SORT OF PUNISHMENT.
I'M WELL AWARE OF THAT!!
BIKU (FLINCH)

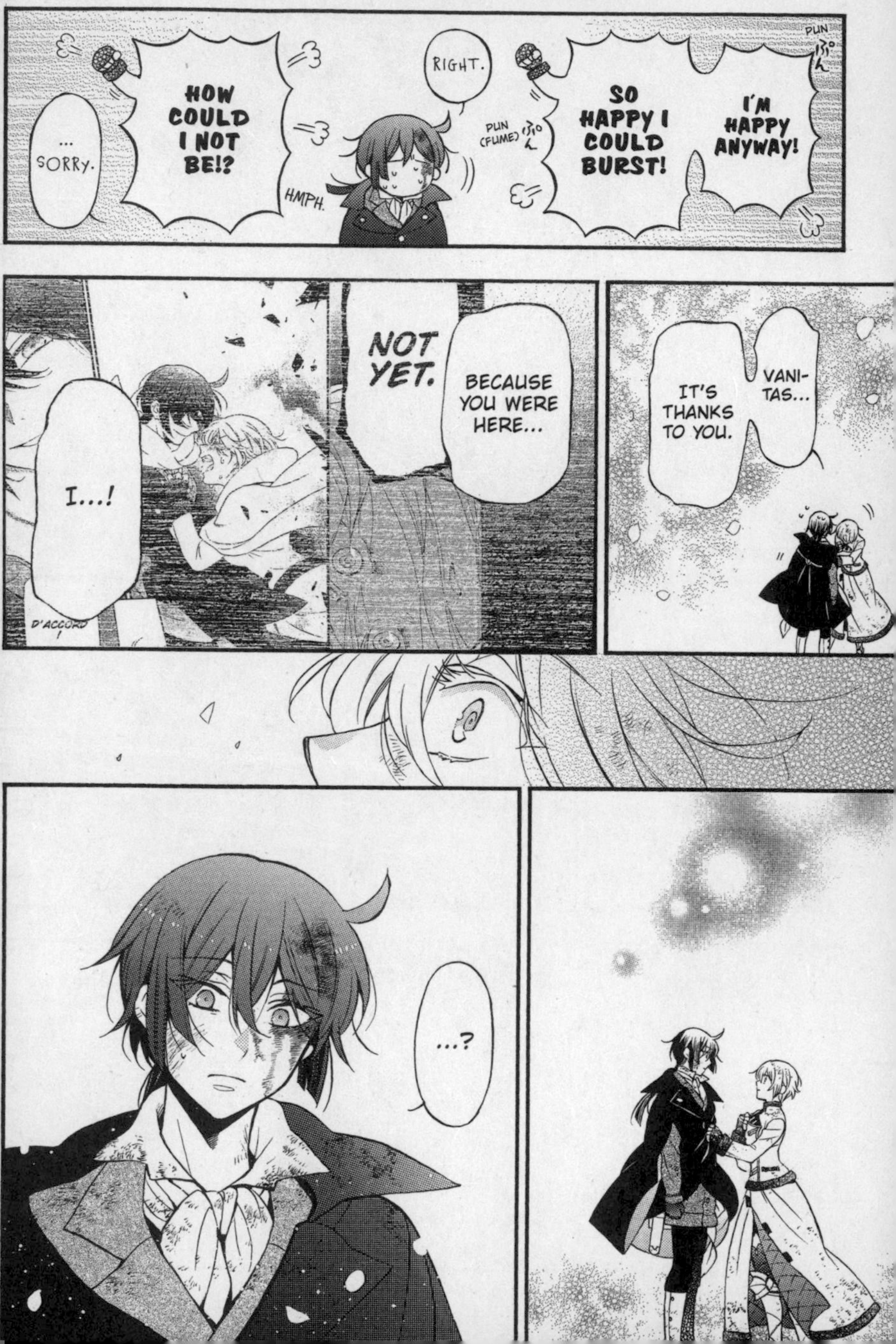
PUN ぷん
I'M HAPPY ANYWAY!
SO HAPPY I COULD BURST!
PUN (FUME) ぷん
RIGHT.
HMPH.
HOW COULD I NOT BE!?
... SORRY.
VANITAS...
IT'S THANKS TO YOU.
BECAUSE YOU WERE HERE...
NOT YET.
I...!
D'ACCORD!
...?

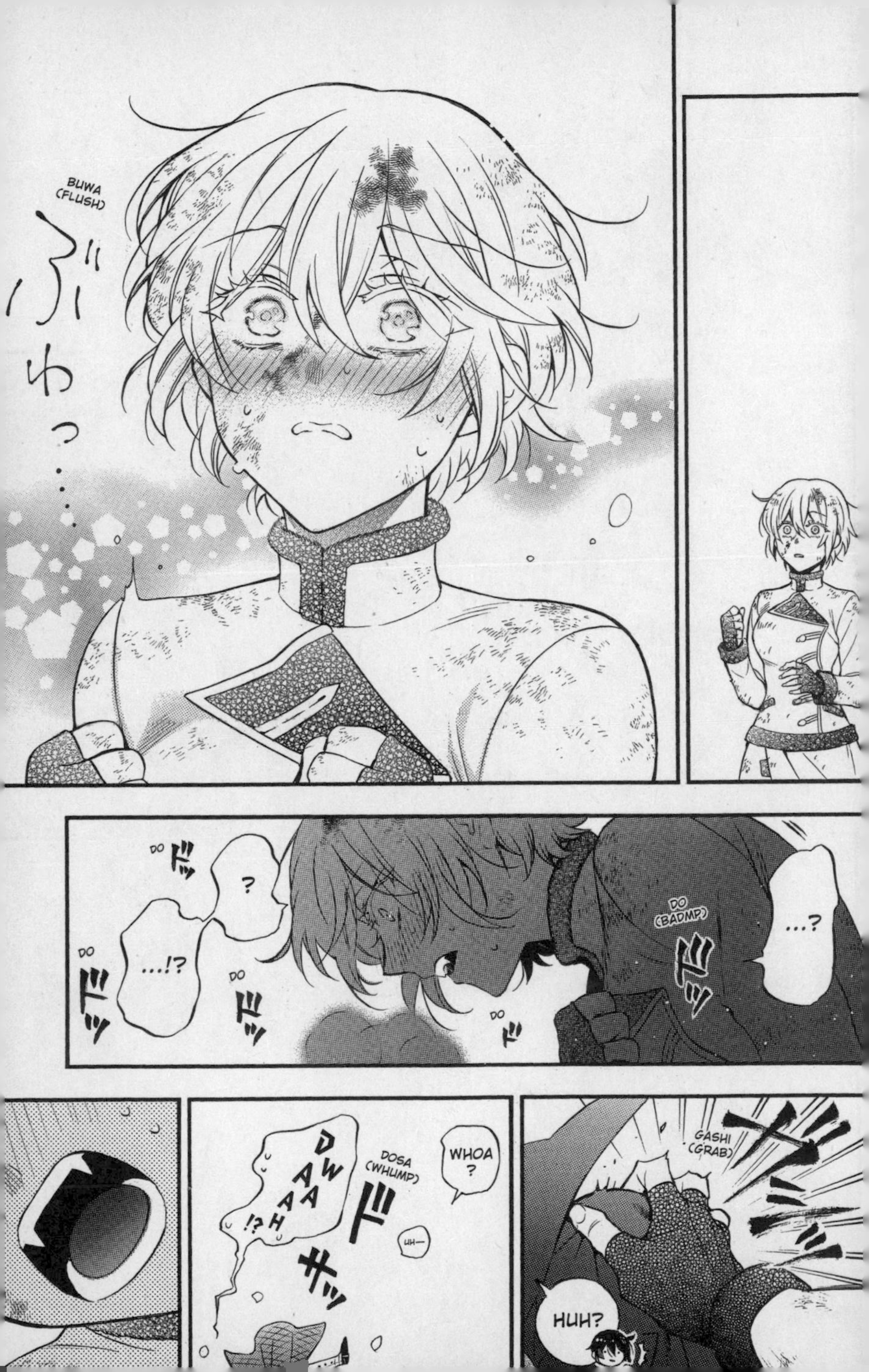
BUWA (FLUSH)
ぶわっ……
...?
DO (BADMP)
ドッ
DO
ド
DO
ドッ
?
...!?
DO
ドッ
GASHI (GRAB)
HUH?
WHOA ?
DOSA (WHUMP)
ドサッ
UH—
DWAAAH !?

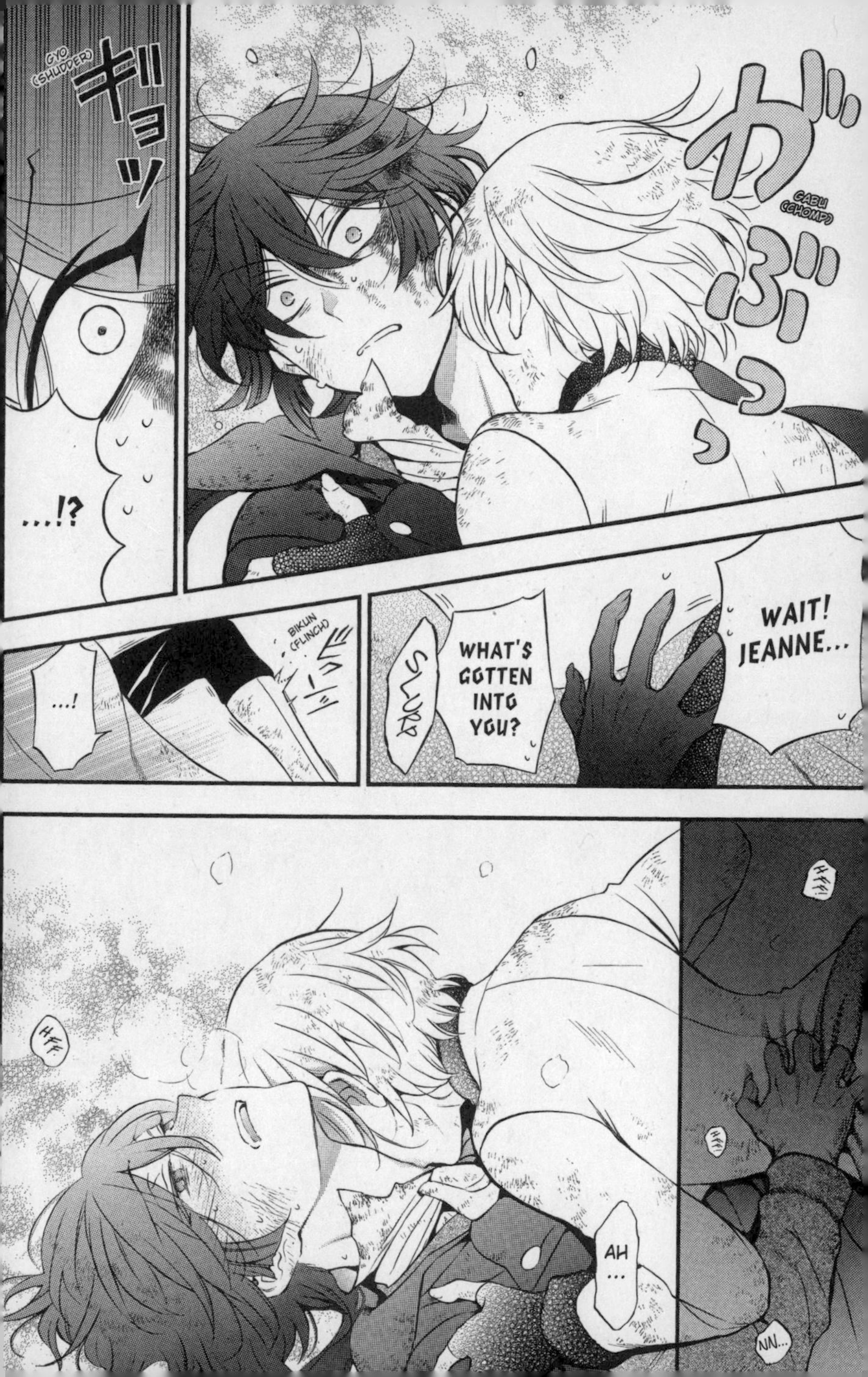
がぶっ
GABU (CHOMP)
ギョッ
GYO (SHUDDER)
...!?
WAIT! JEANNE...
WHAT'S GOTTEN INTO YOU?
SLURP
BIKUN (FLINCH)
...!
HFF!
HFF!
NN...
AH ...
HFF.

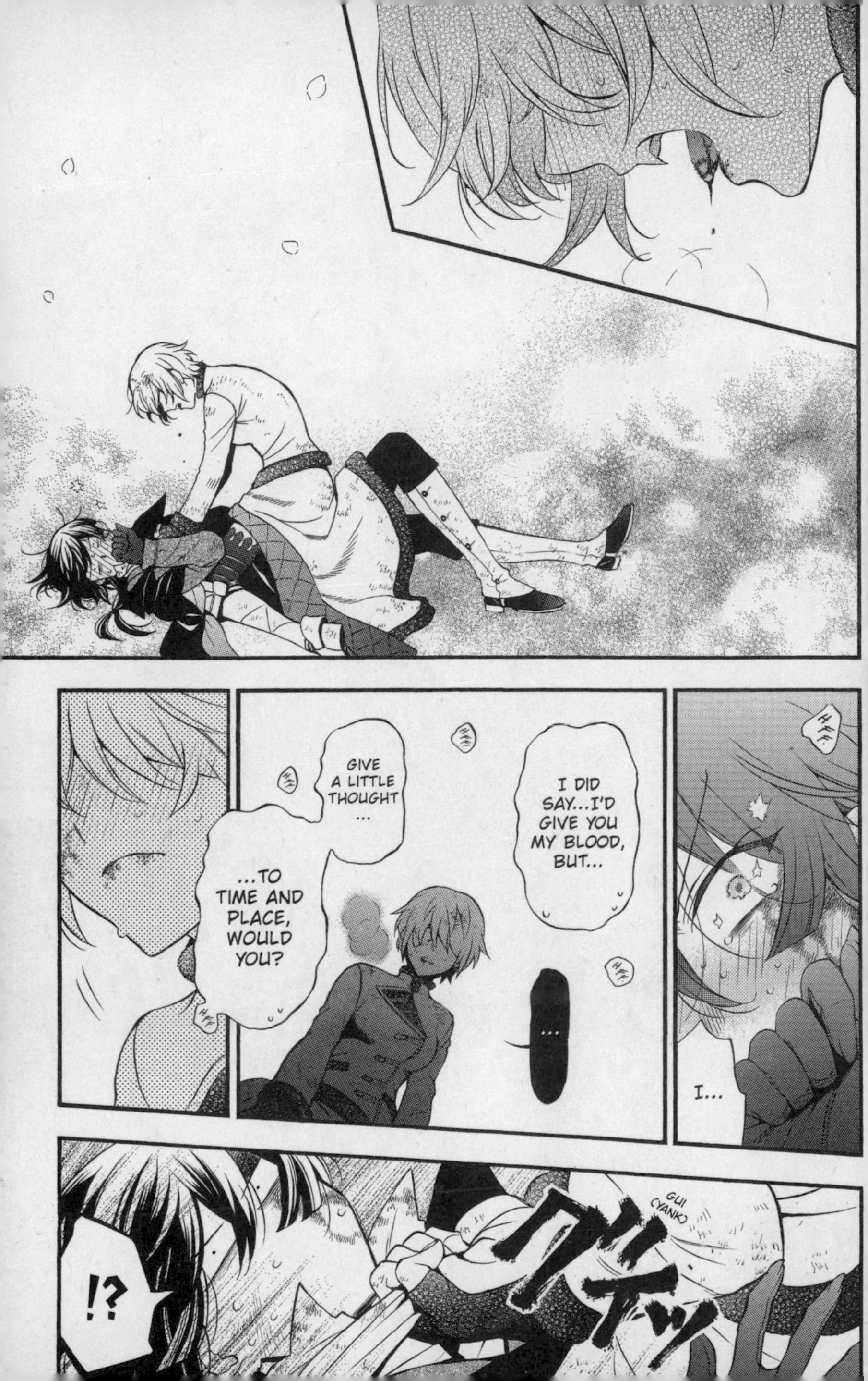
HFF
I...
I DID SAY...I'D GIVE YOU MY BLOOD, BUT...
GIVE A LITTLE THOUGHT...
...TO TIME AND PLACE, WOULD YOU?
...
HFF
GUI (YANK)
!?

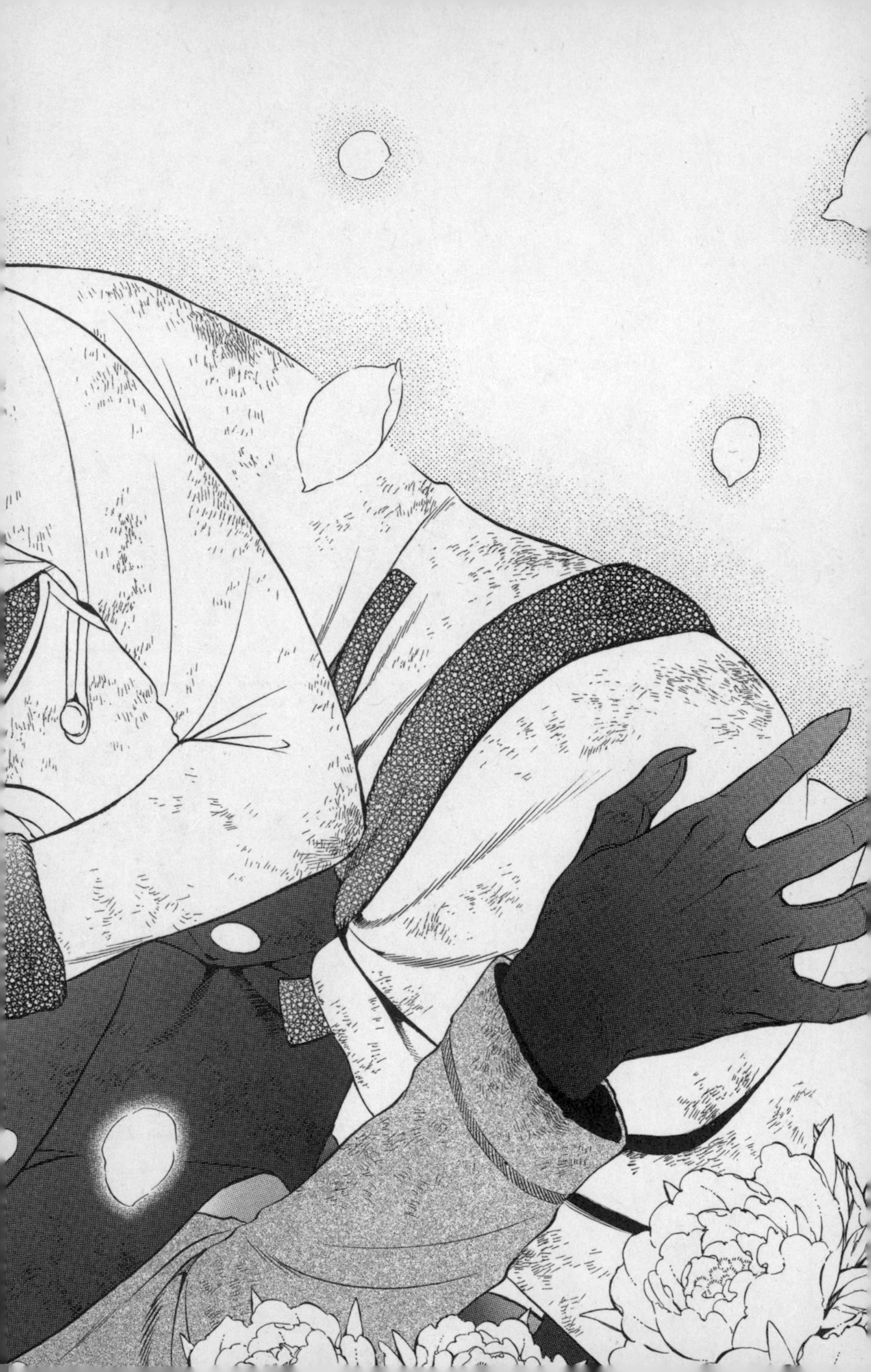

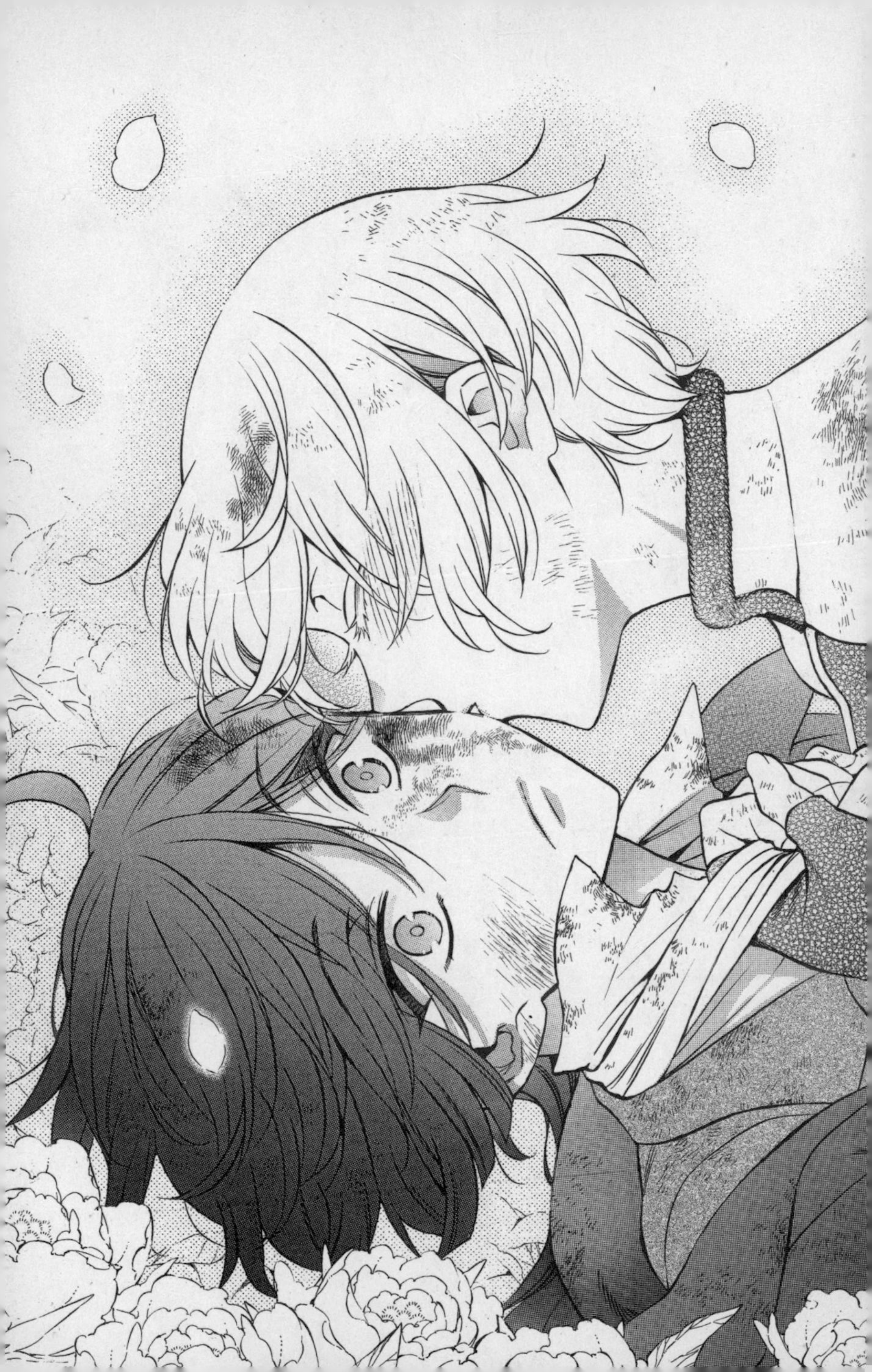

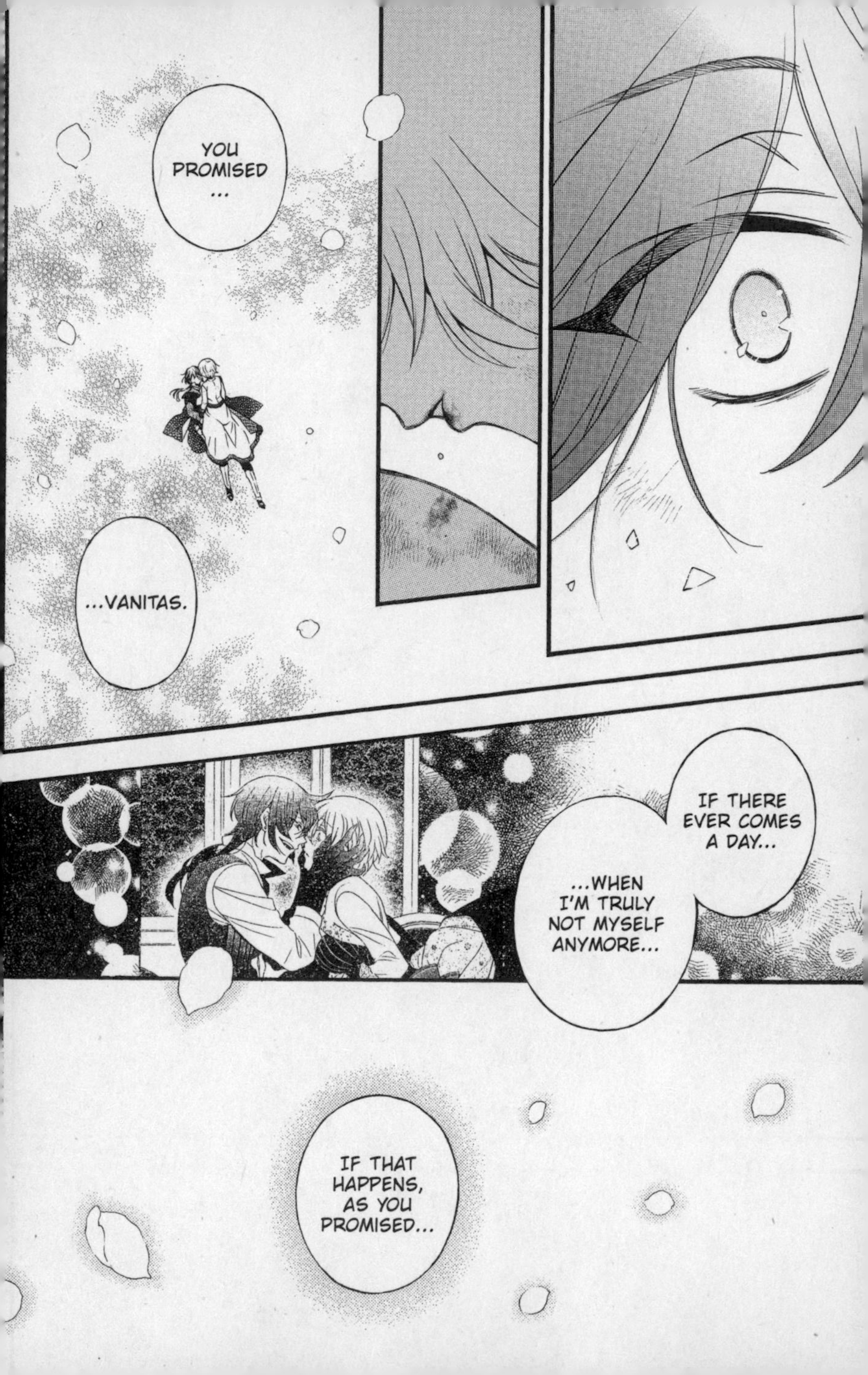
YOU PROMISED ...
...VANITAS.
IF THERE EVER COMES A DAY...
...WHEN I'M TRULY NOT MYSELF ANYMORE...
IF THAT HAPPENS, AS YOU PROMISED...

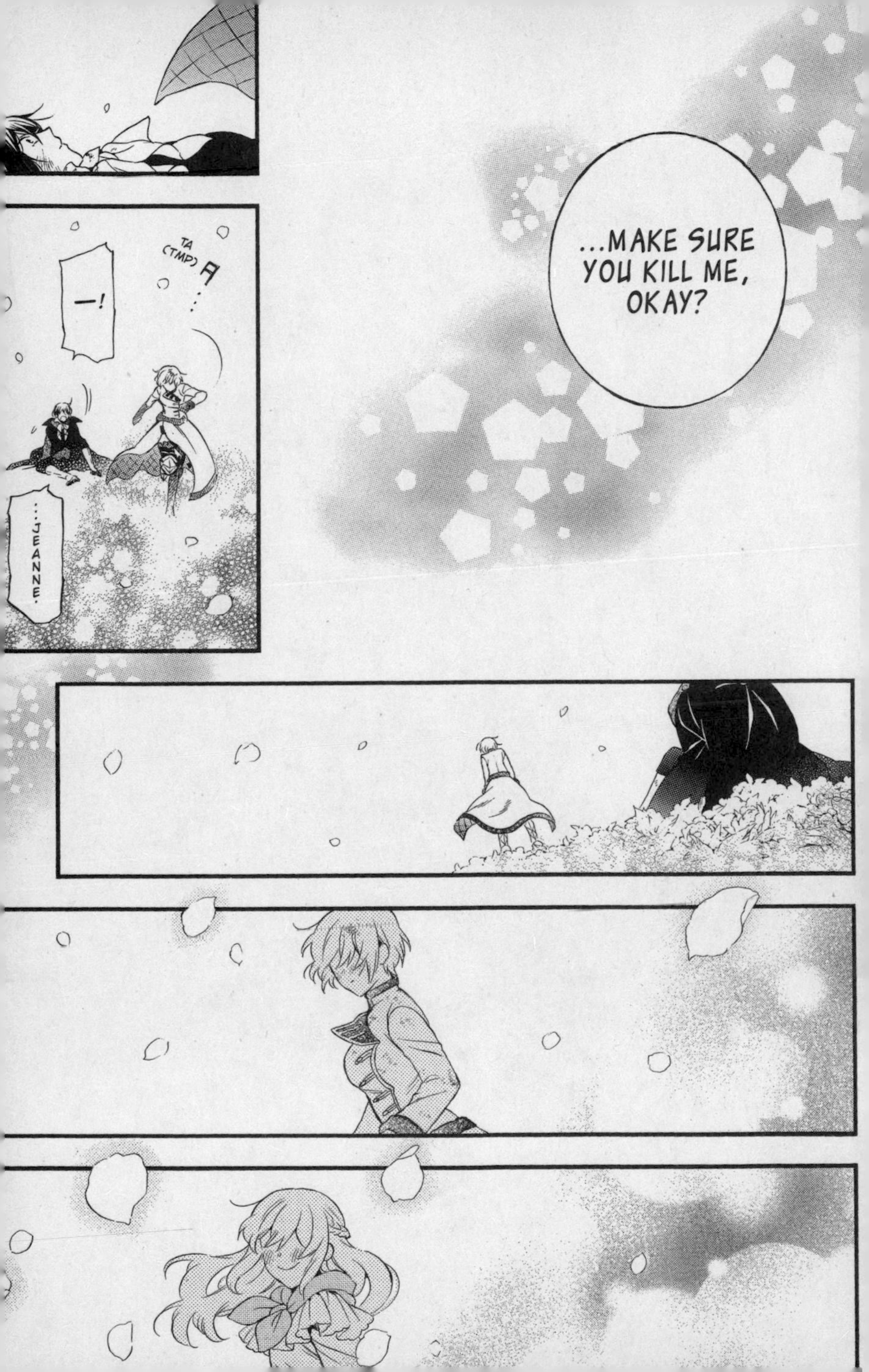
...MAKE SURE YOU KILL ME, OKAY?
TA (TMP)
—!
...JEANNE.

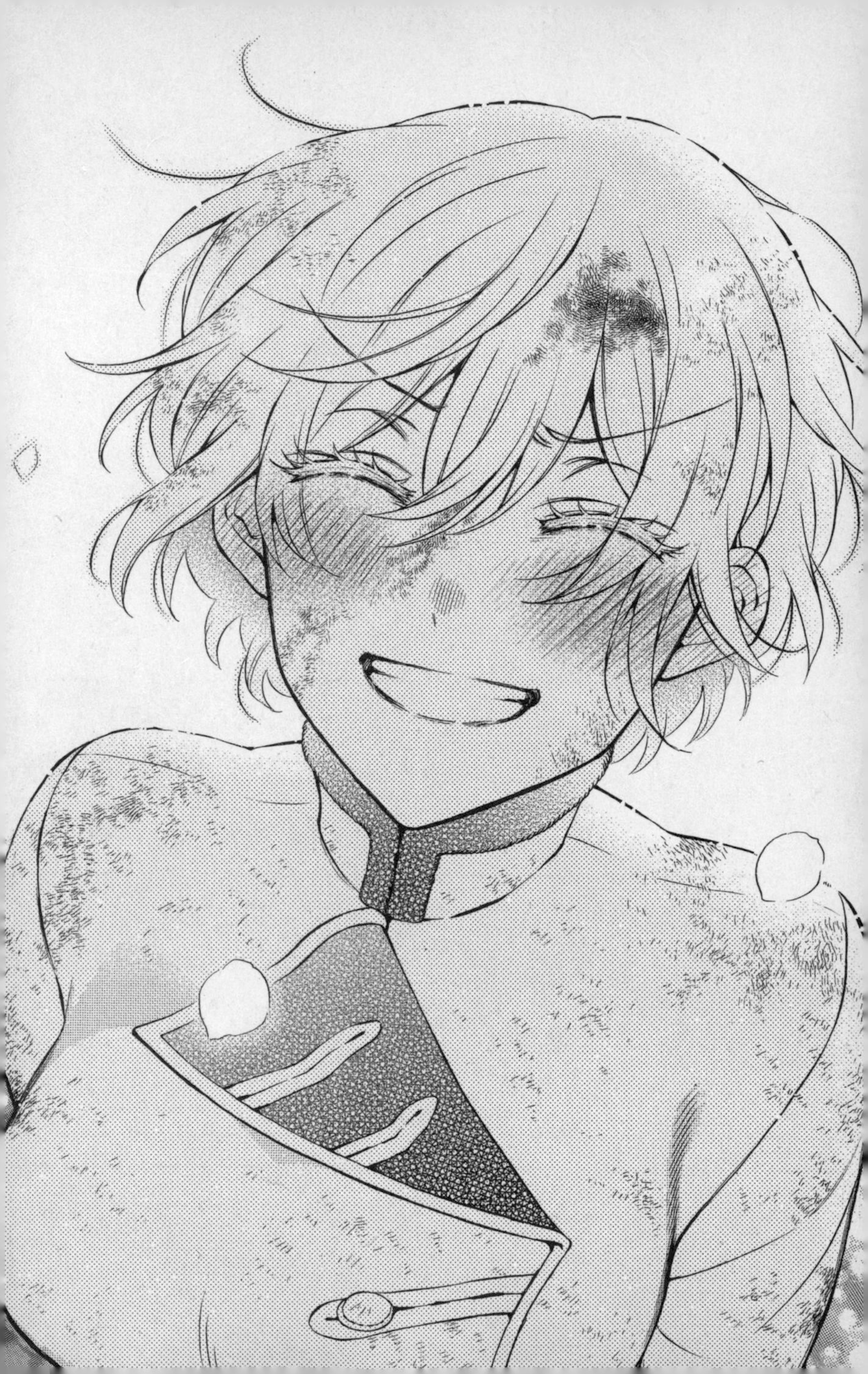

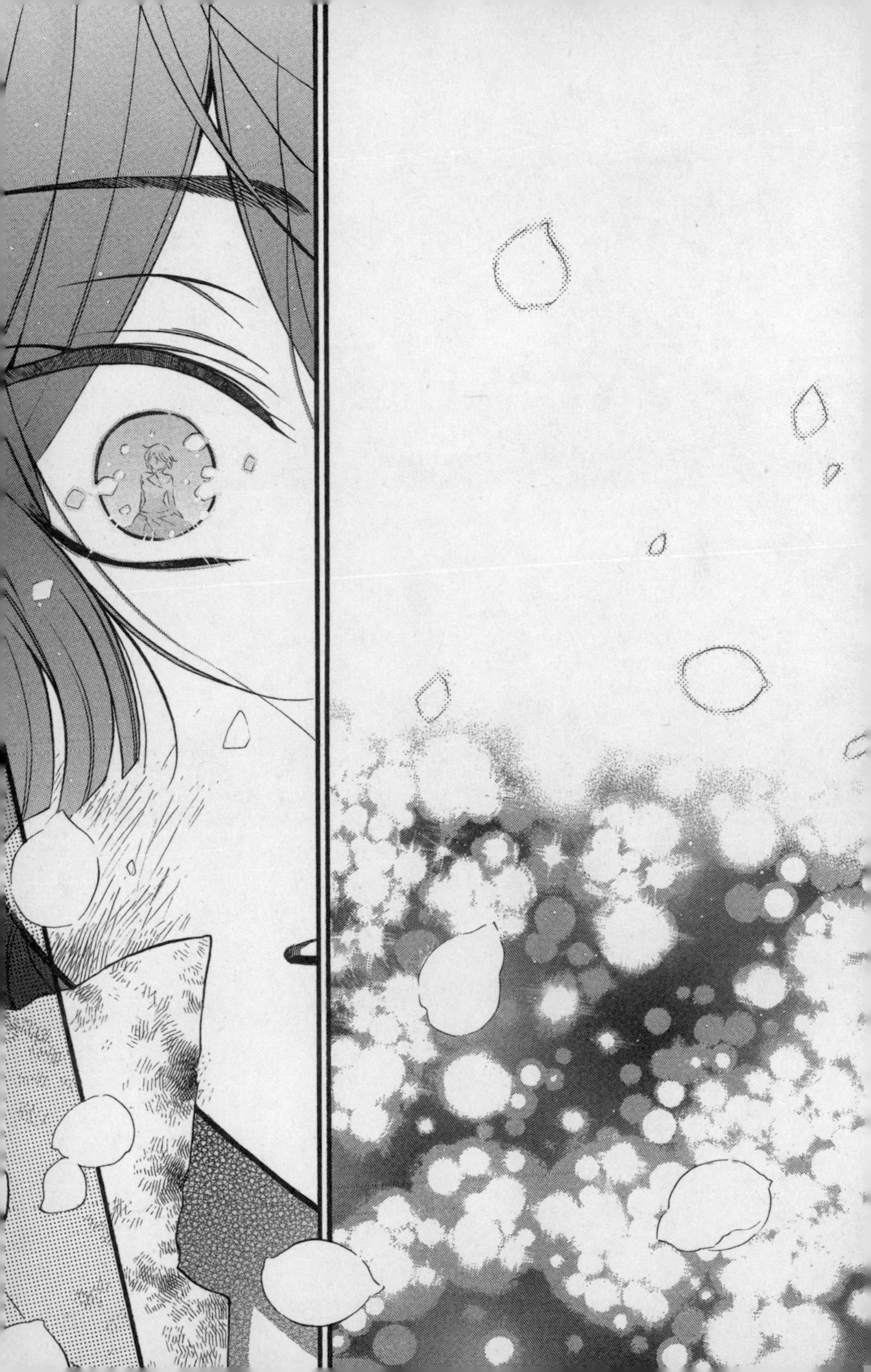

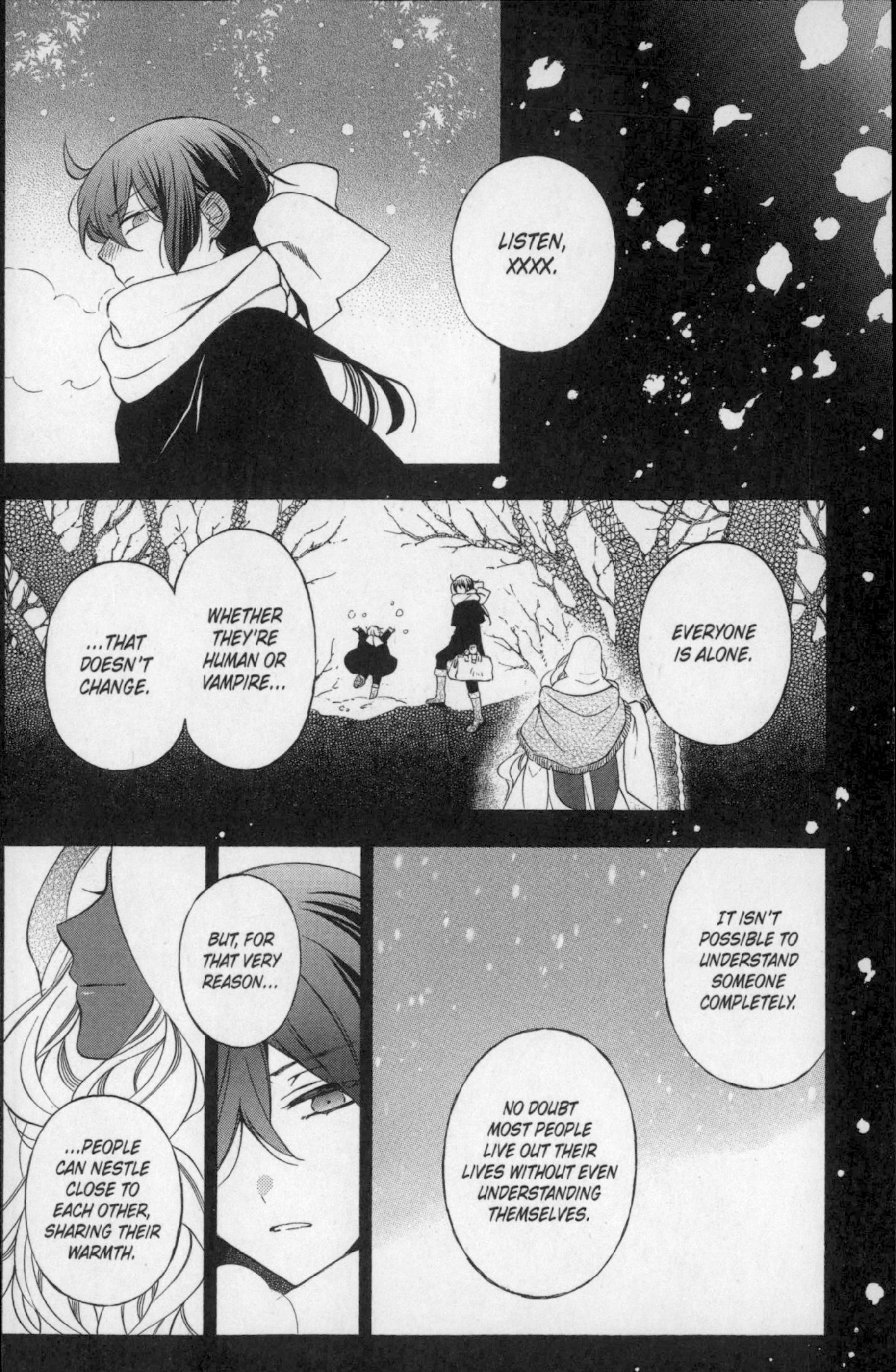
LISTEN, XXXX.
EVERYONE IS ALONE.
WHETHER THEY'RE HUMAN OR VAMPIRE...
...THAT DOESN'T CHANGE.
IT ISN'T POSSIBLE TO UNDERSTAND SOMEONE COMPLETELY.
NO DOUBT MOST PEOPLE LIVE OUT THEIR LIVES WITHOUT EVEN UNDERSTANDING THEMSELVES.
BUT, FOR THAT VERY REASON...
...PEOPLE CAN NESTLE CLOSE TO EACH OTHER, SHARING THEIR WARMTH.

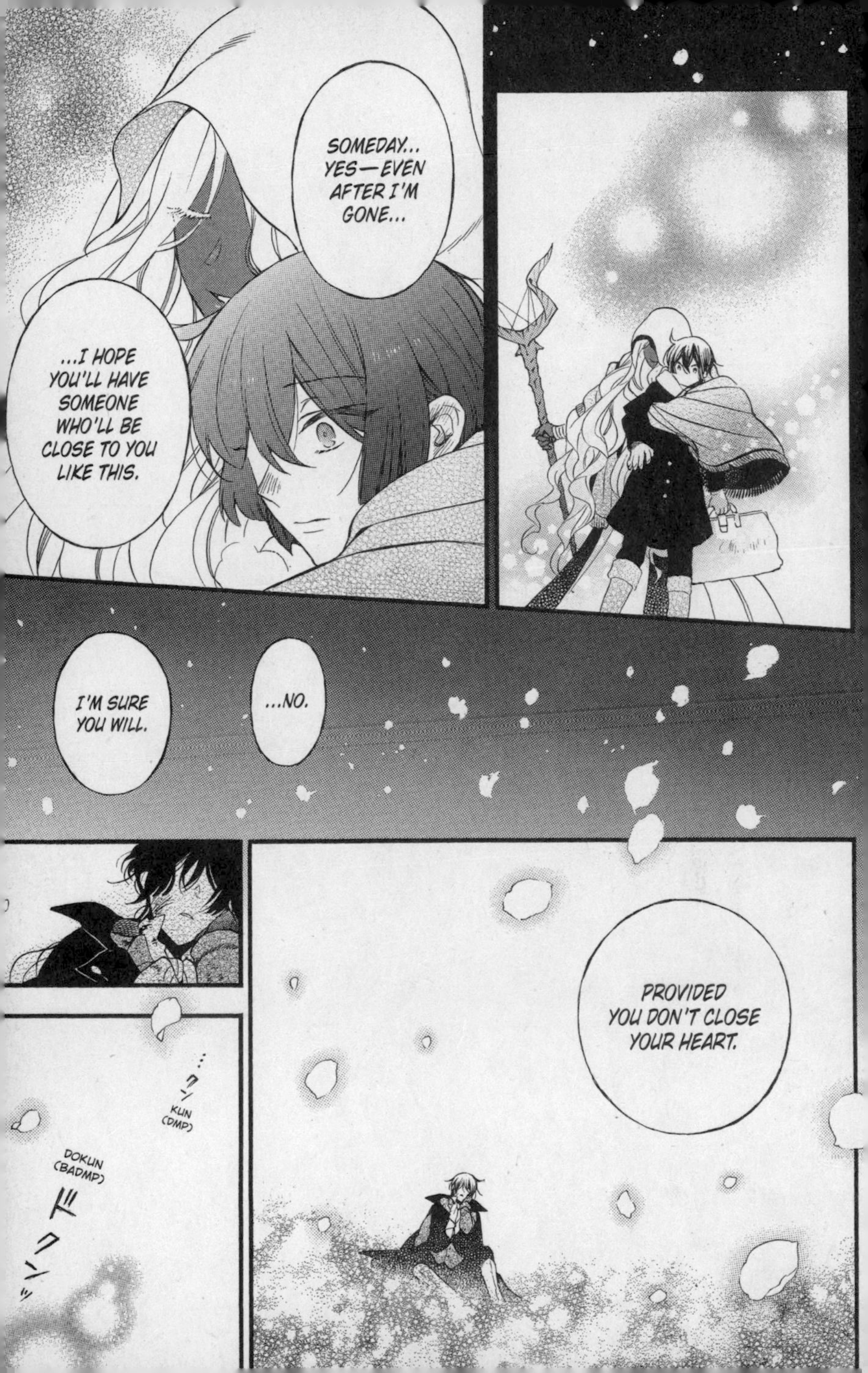
SOMEDAY... YES—EVEN AFTER I'M GONE...
...I HOPE YOU'LL HAVE SOMEONE WHO'LL BE CLOSE TO YOU LIKE THIS.
...NO.
I'M SURE YOU WILL.
PROVIDED YOU DON'T CLOSE YOUR HEART.
…クン
KUN (DMP)
ドクンッ
DOKUN (BADMP)

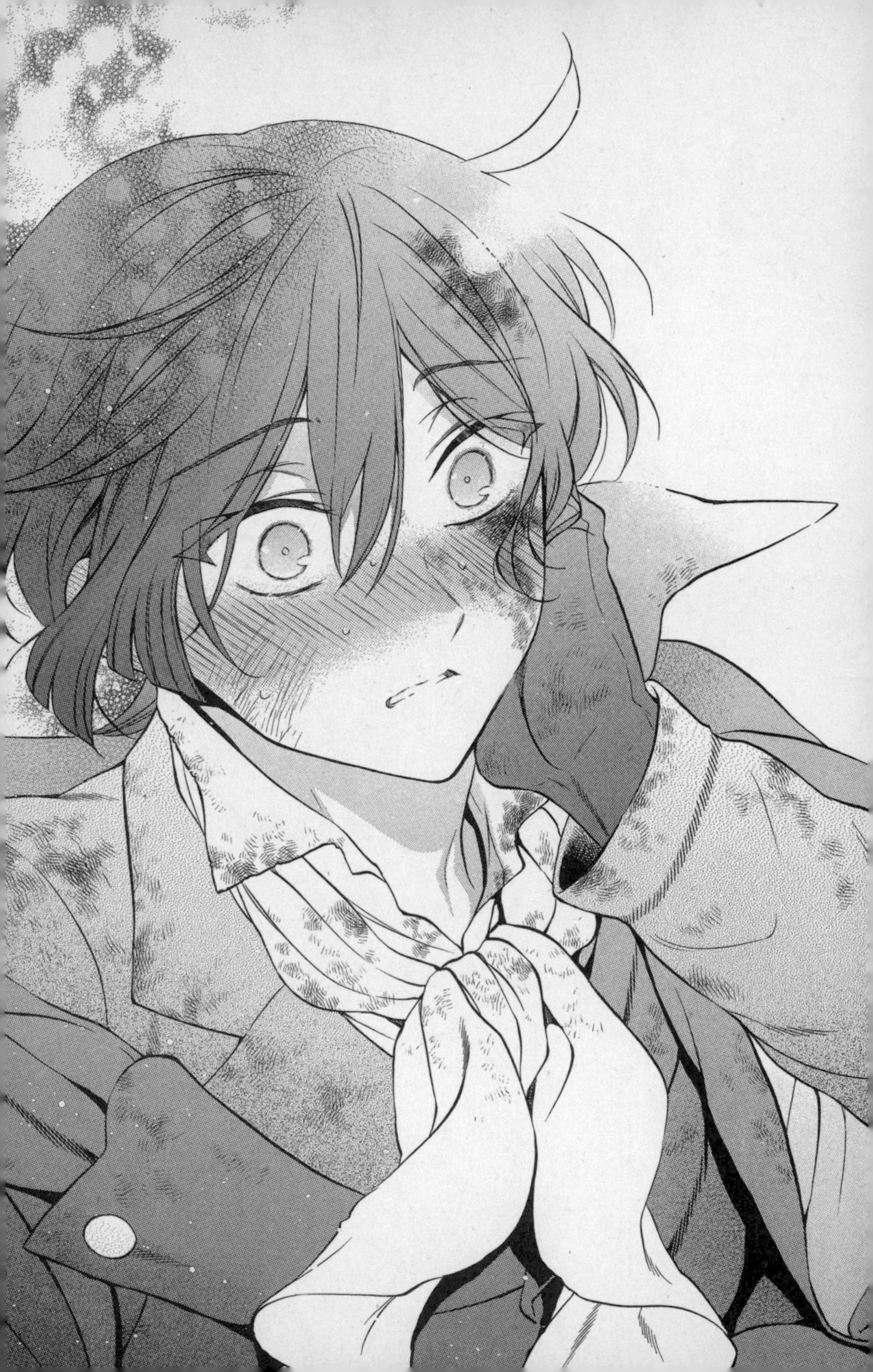

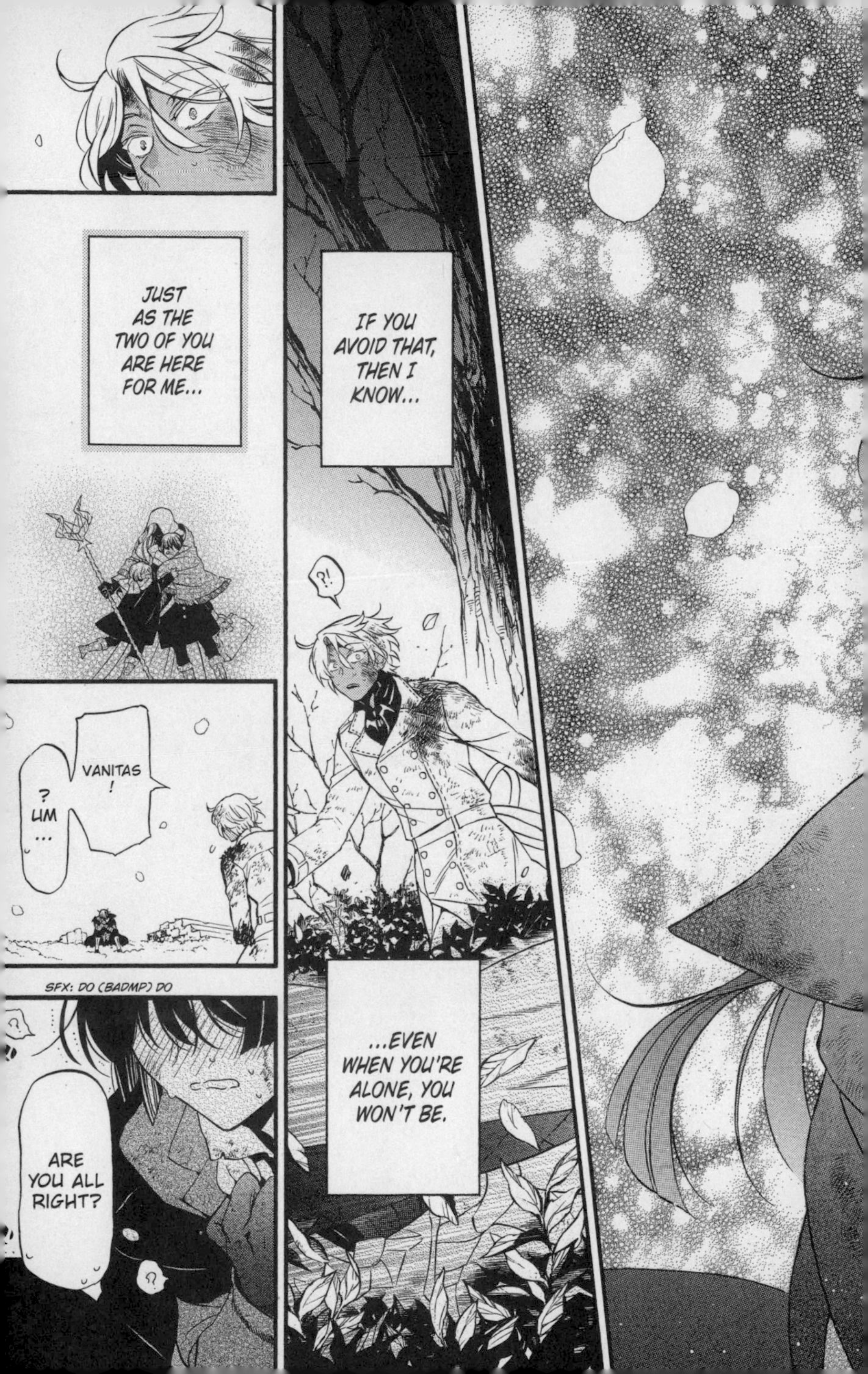
IF YOU AVOID THAT, THEN I KNOW...
?!
...EVEN WHEN YOU'RE ALONE, YOU WON'T BE.
JUST AS THE TWO OF YOU ARE HERE FOR ME...
VANITAS!
? UM...
SFX: DO (BADMP) DO
?
ARE YOU ALL RIGHT?
?

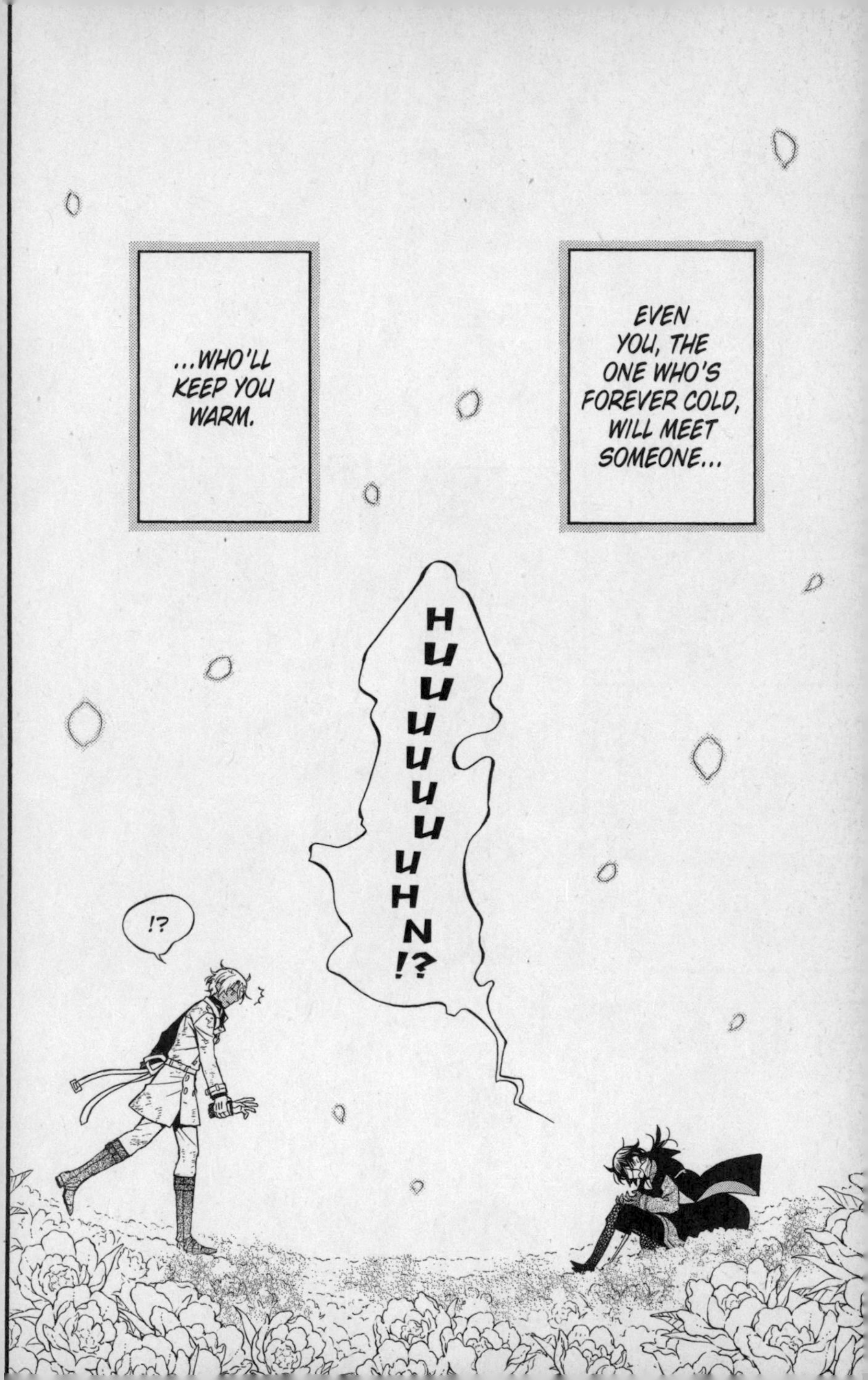
EVEN YOU, THE ONE WHO'S FOREVER COLD, WILL MEET SOMEONE...
...WHO'LL KEEP YOU WARM.
HUUUUUUHN!?
!?

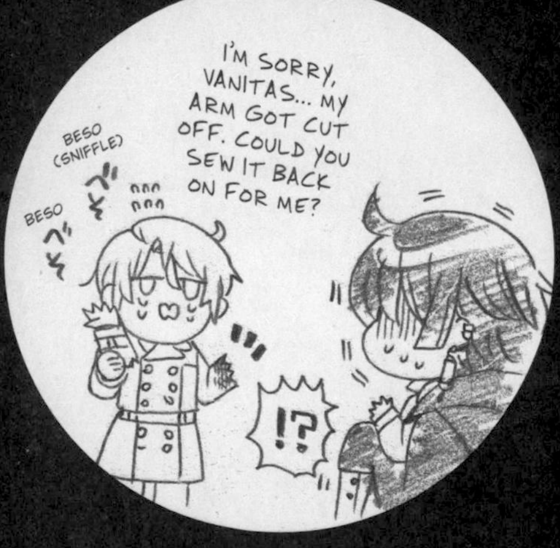
I'M SORRY, VANITAS... MY ARM GOT CUT OFF. COULD YOU SEW IT BACK ON FOR ME?
BESO (SNIFFLE)
BESO
!?

Les Mémoires de Vanitas

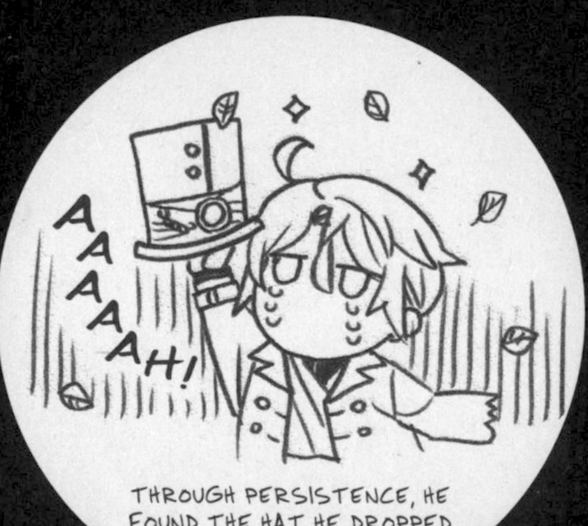
AAAAAAH!

THROUGH PERSISTENCE, HE FOUND THE HAT HE DROPPED WAY BACK IN VOL. 5!!

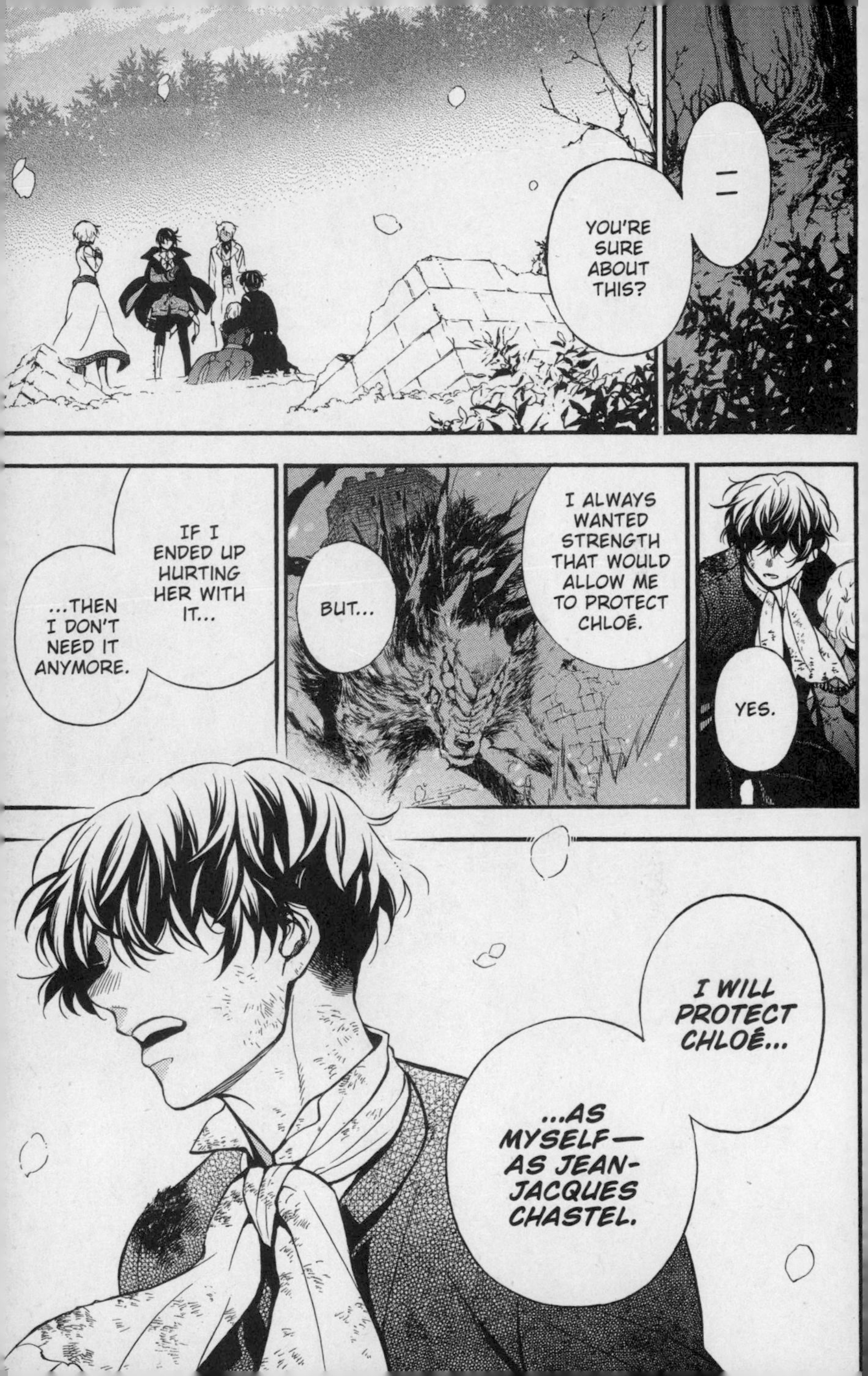
YOU'RE SURE ABOUT THIS?
YES.
I ALWAYS WANTED STRENGTH THAT WOULD ALLOW ME TO PROTECT CHLOÉ.
BUT...
IF I ENDED UP HURTING HER WITH IT...
...THEN I DON'T NEED IT ANYMORE.
I WILL PROTECT CHLOÉ...
...AS MYSELF—AS JEAN-JACQUES CHASTEL.

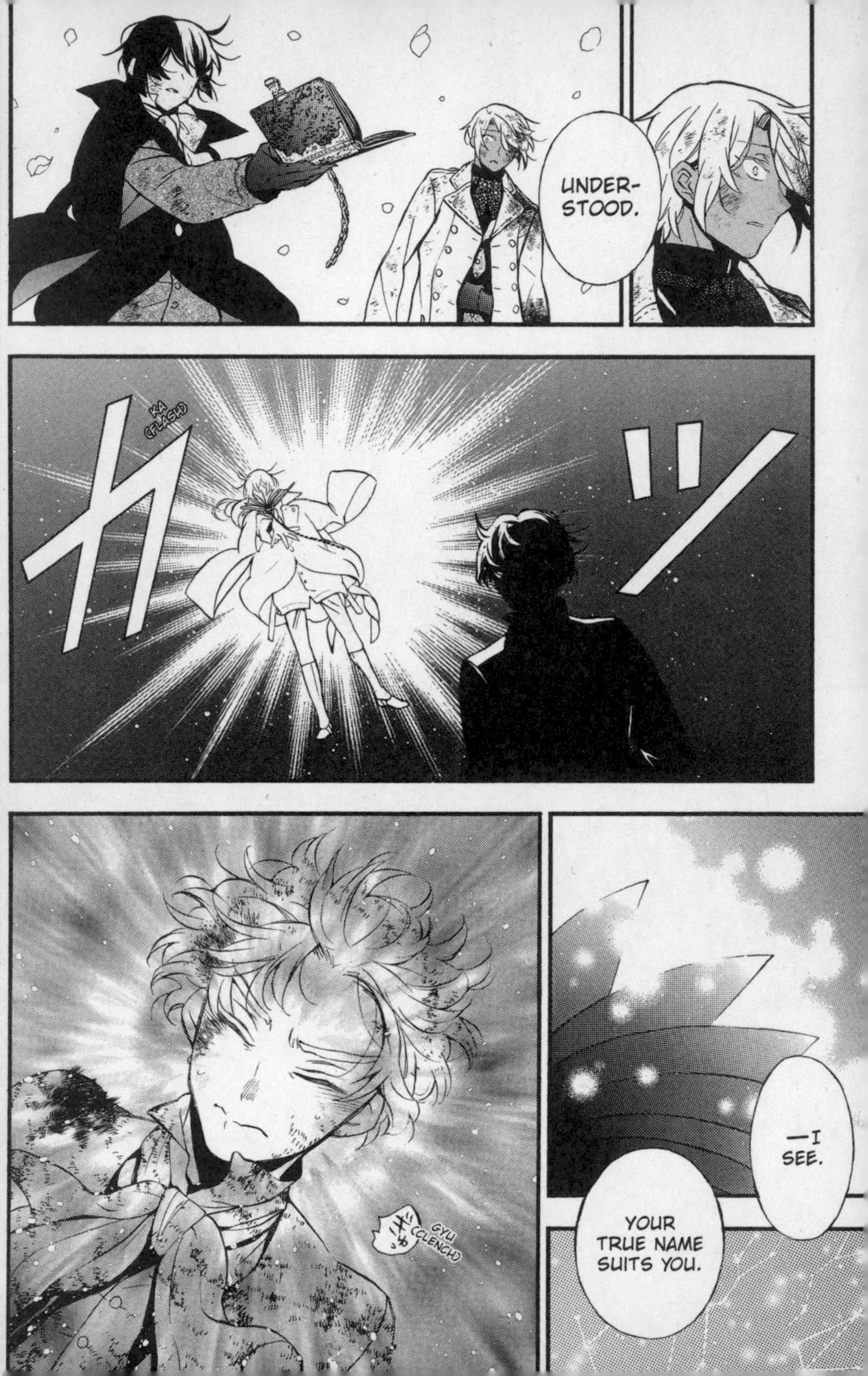
UNDER-
STOOD.
KA (FLASH)
—I SEE.
YOUR TRUE NAME SUITS YOU.
GYU (CLENCH)

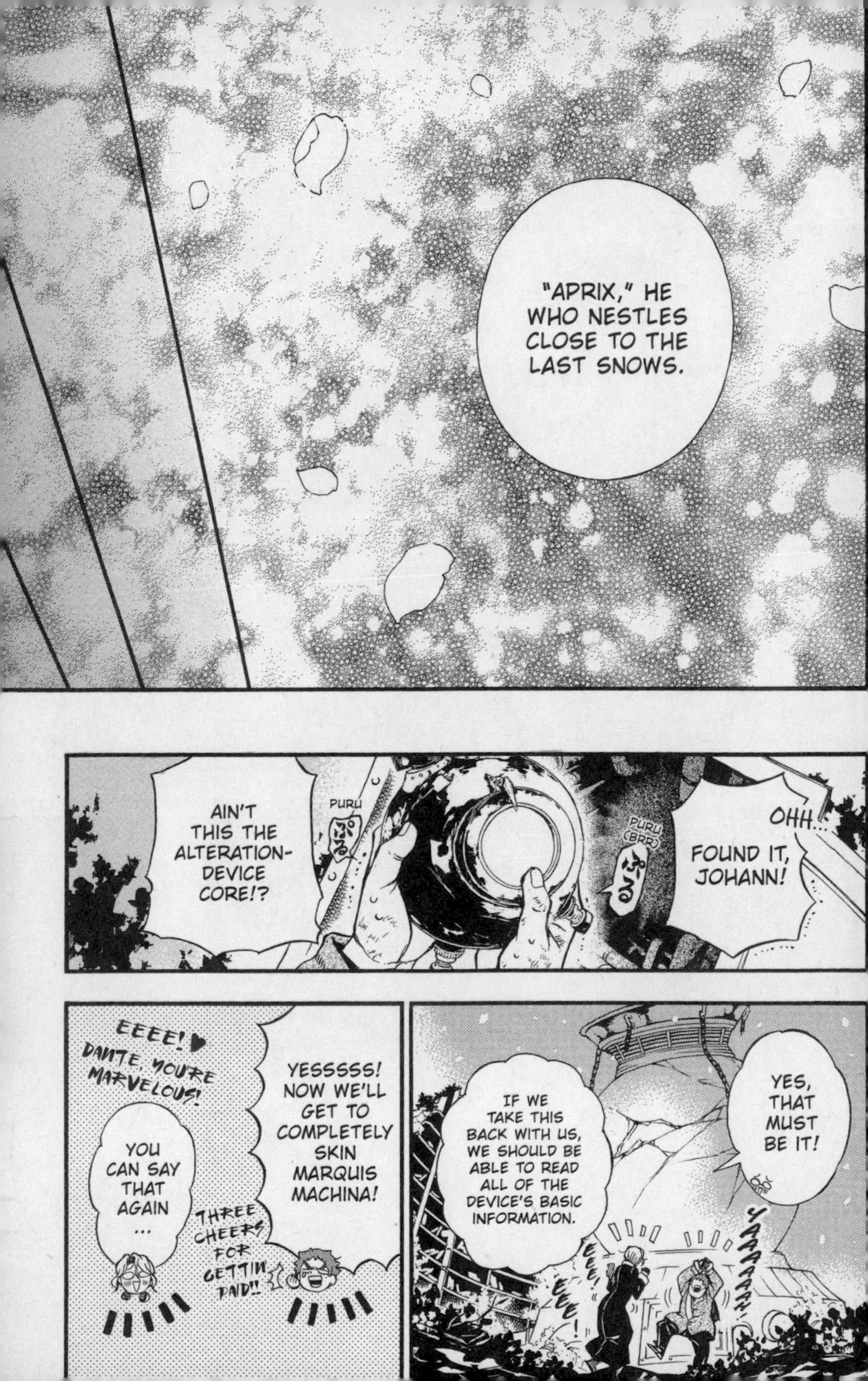
"APRIX," HE WHO NESTLES CLOSE TO THE LAST SNOWS.
OHH... FOUND IT, JOHANN!
PURU (BRR)
ぷる
PURU
ぷる
AIN'T THIS THE ALTERATION-DEVICE CORE!?
YES, THAT MUST BE IT!
YAAAAAAN!
IF WE TAKE THIS BACK WITH US, WE SHOULD BE ABLE TO READ ALL OF THE DEVICE'S BASIC INFORMATION.
EEE! EEE!
YESSSSS! NOW WE'LL GET TO COMPLETELY SKIN MARQUIS MACHINA!
THREE CHEERS FOR GETTIN' PAID!!
EEEE!♥ DANTE, YOU'RE MARVELOUS!
YOU CAN SAY THAT AGAIN ...

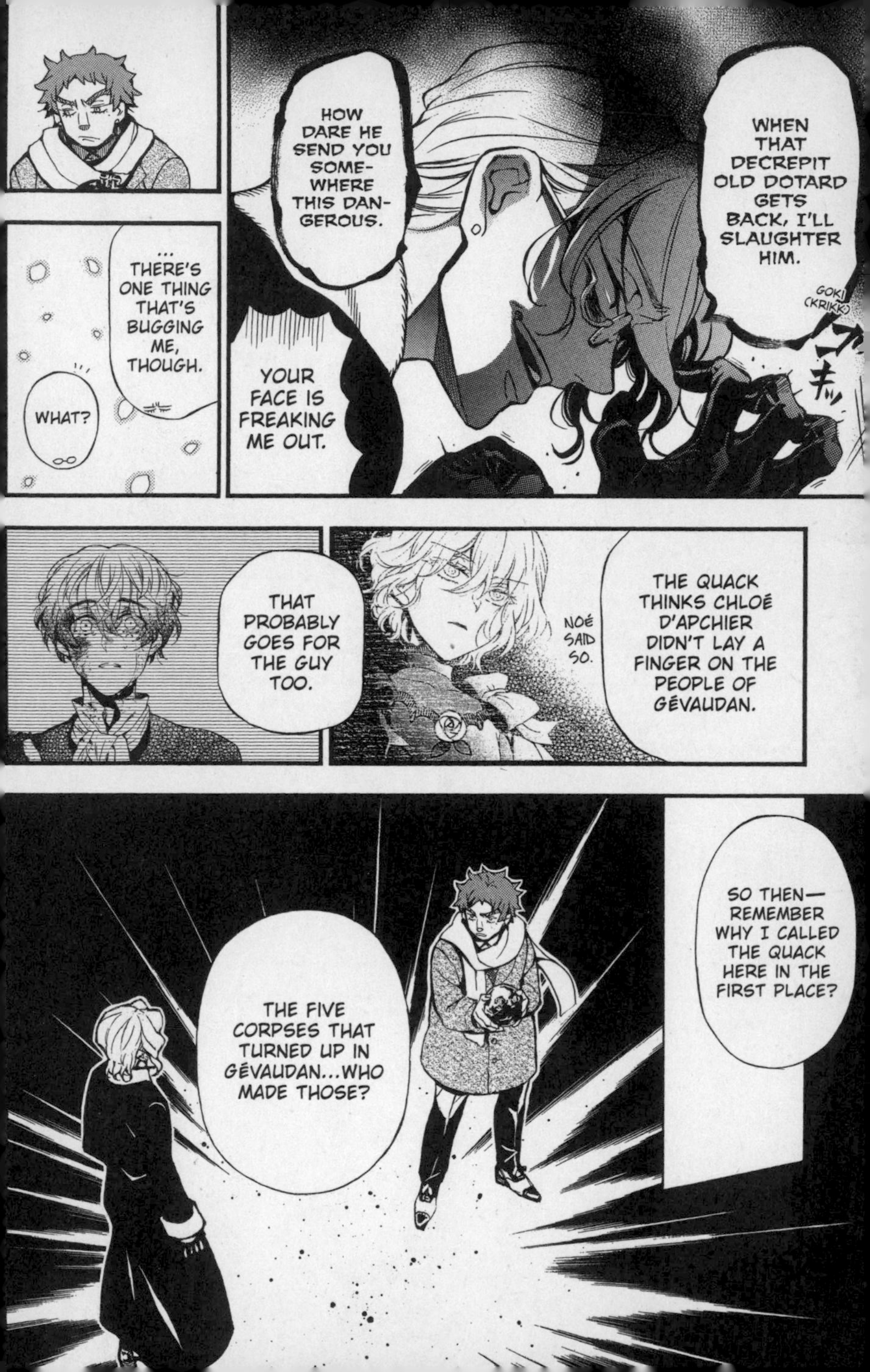
WHEN THAT DECREPIT OLD DOTARD GETS BACK, I'LL SLAUGHTER HIM.
HOW DARE HE SEND YOU SOME-WHERE THIS DAN-GEROUS.
GOKI (KRIKK)
YOUR FACE IS FREAKING ME OUT.
... THERE'S ONE THING THAT'S BUGGING ME, THOUGH.
WHAT?
THE QUACK THINKS CHLOÉ D'APCHIER DIDN'T LAY A FINGER ON THE PEOPLE OF GÉVAUDAN.
NOÉ SAID SO.
THAT PROBABLY GOES FOR THE GUY TOO.
SO THEN—REMEMBER WHY I CALLED THE QUACK HERE IN THE FIRST PLACE?
THE FIVE CORPSES THAT TURNED UP IN GÉVAUDAN...WHO MADE THOSE?

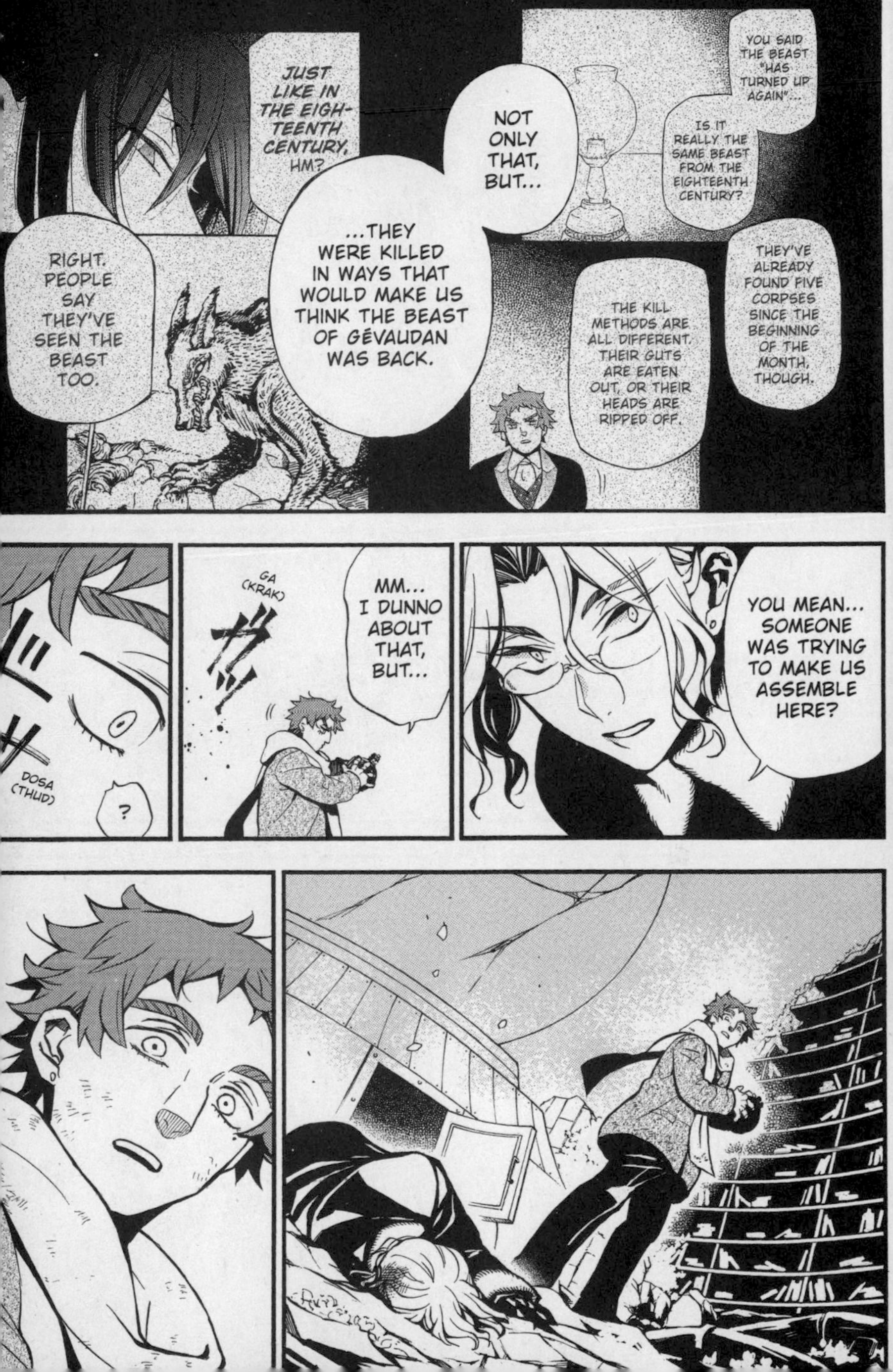
YOU SAID THE BEAST "HAS TURNED UP AGAIN"...
IS IT REALLY THE SAME BEAST FROM THE EIGHTEENTH CENTURY?
THEY'VE ALREADY FOUND FIVE CORPSES SINCE THE BEGINNING OF THE MONTH, THOUGH.
THE KILL METHODS ARE ALL DIFFERENT. THEIR GUTS ARE EATEN OUT, OR THEIR HEADS ARE RIPPED OFF.
NOT ONLY THAT, BUT...
...THEY WERE KILLED IN WAYS THAT WOULD MAKE US THINK THE BEAST OF GÉVAUDAN WAS BACK.
JUST LIKE IN THE EIGHTEENTH CENTURY, HM?
RIGHT. PEOPLE SAY THEY'VE SEEN THE BEAST TOO.
YOU MEAN... SOMEONE WAS TRYING TO MAKE US ASSEMBLE HERE?
MM... I DUNNO ABOUT THAT, BUT...
GA (KRAK)
DOSA (THUD)
?

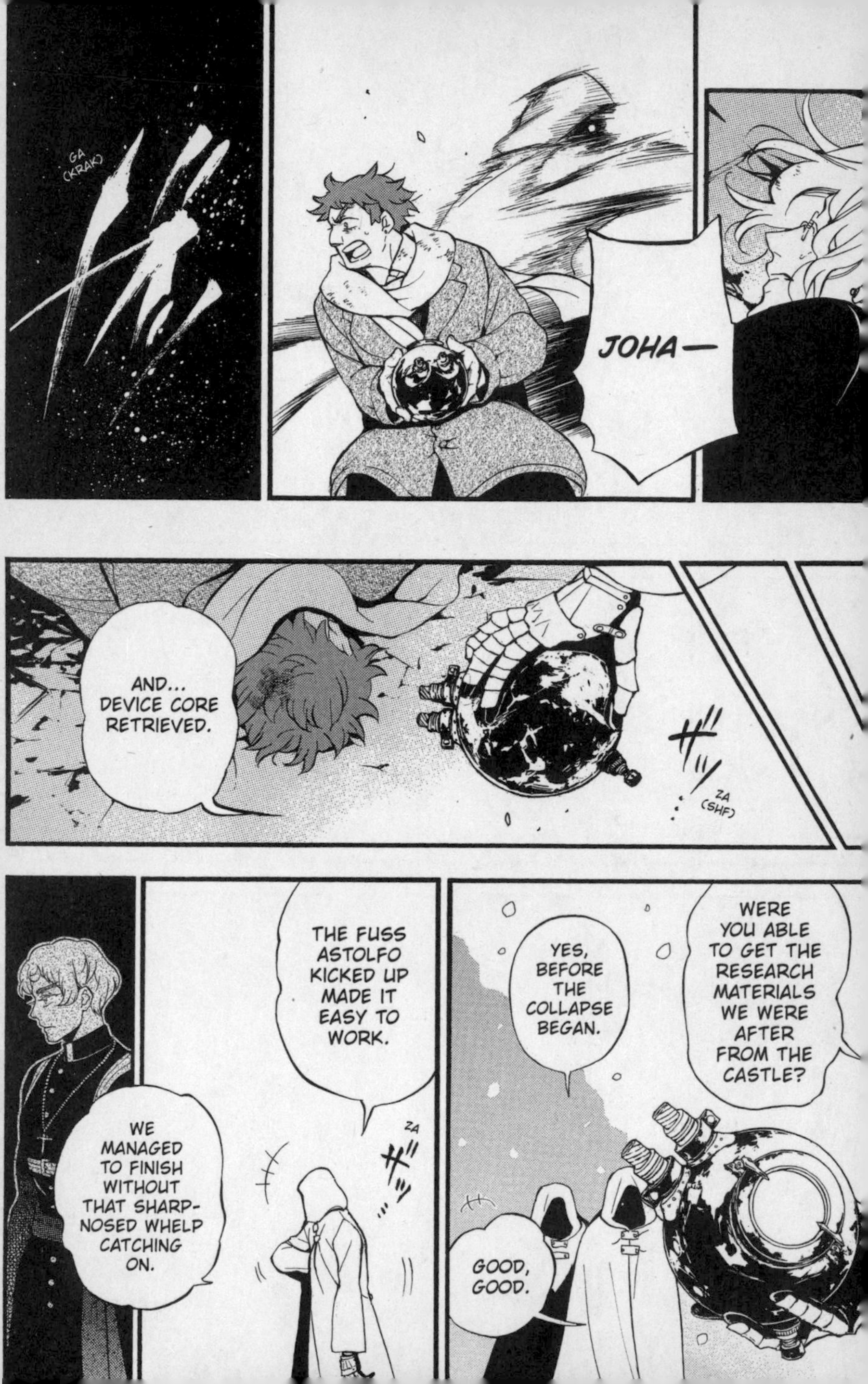
JOHA—
GA (KRAK)
ZA (SHF)
AND... DEVICE CORE RETRIEVED.
WERE YOU ABLE TO GET THE RESEARCH MATERIALS WE WERE AFTER FROM THE CASTLE?
YES, BEFORE THE COLLAPSE BEGAN.
GOOD, GOOD.
THE FUSS ASTOLFO KICKED UP MADE IT EASY TO WORK.
ZA
WE MANAGED TO FINISH WITHOUT THAT SHARP-NOSED WHELP CATCHING ON.

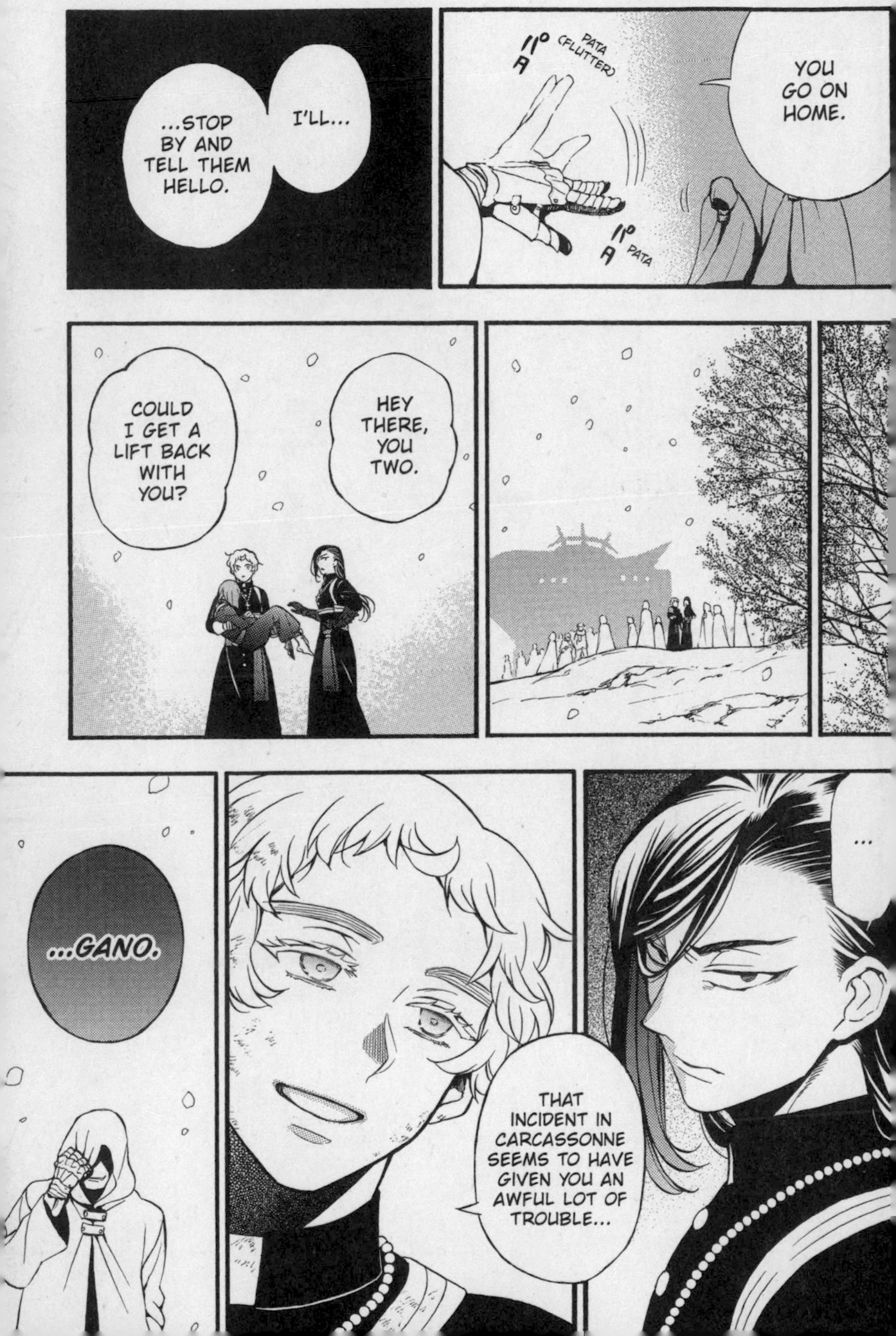
YOU GO ON HOME.
パタ
PATA (FLUTTER)
パタ
PATA
I'LL...
...STOP BY AND TELL THEM HELLO.
HEY THERE, YOU TWO.
COULD I GET A LIFT BACK WITH YOU?
...
THAT INCIDENT IN CARCASSONNE SEEMS TO HAVE GIVEN YOU AN AWFUL LOT OF TROUBLE...
...GANO.

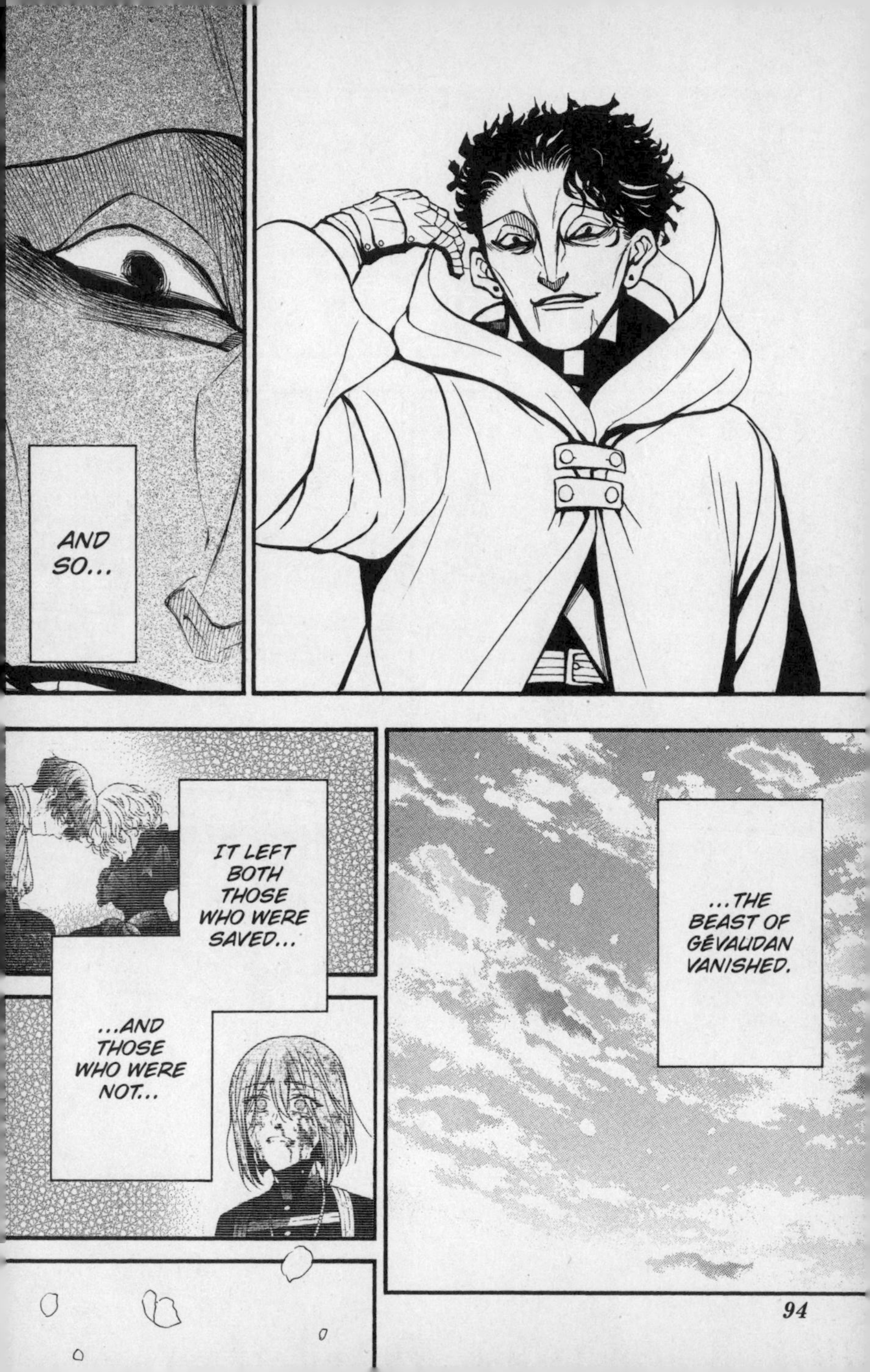
AND SO...
...THE BEAST OF GÉVAUDAN VANISHED.
IT LEFT BOTH THOSE WHO WERE SAVED...
...AND THOSE WHO WERE NOT...

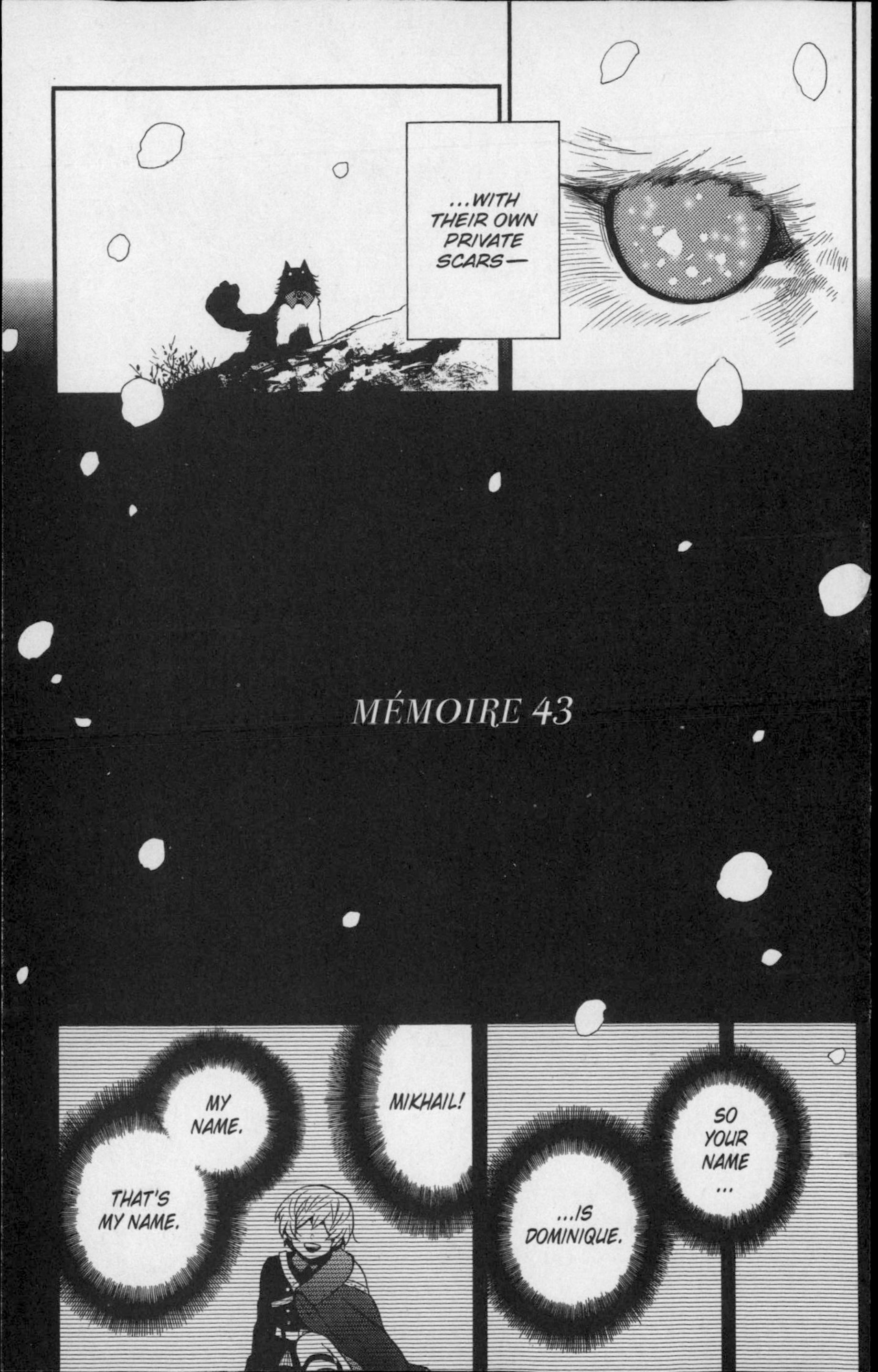
...WITH THEIR OWN PRIVATE SCARS—
MÉMOIRE 43
SO YOUR NAME ...
...IS DOMINIQUE.
MIKHAIL!
MY NAME.
THAT'S MY NAME.

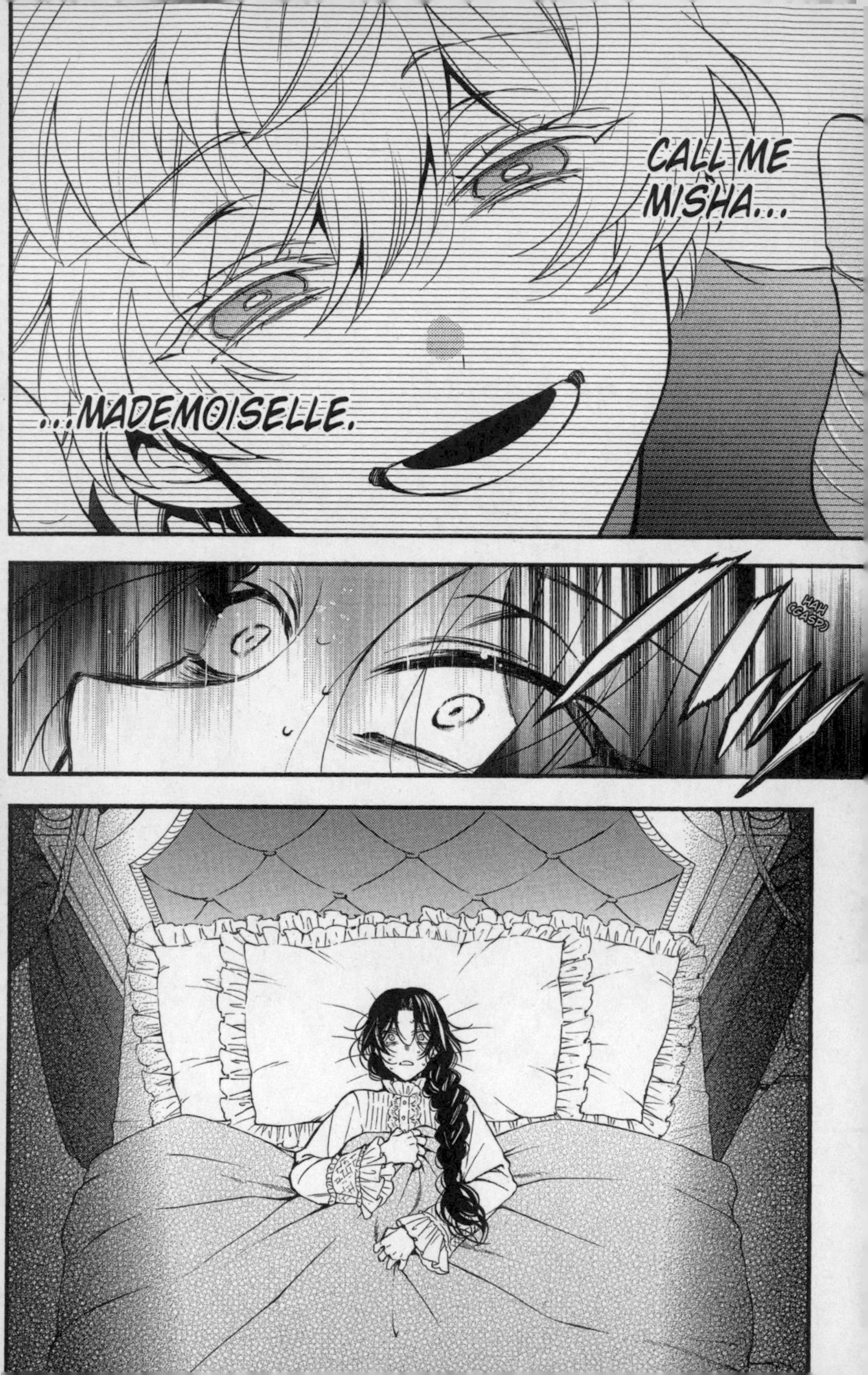
CALL ME MISHA...
...MADEMOISELLE.
HAH (GASP)

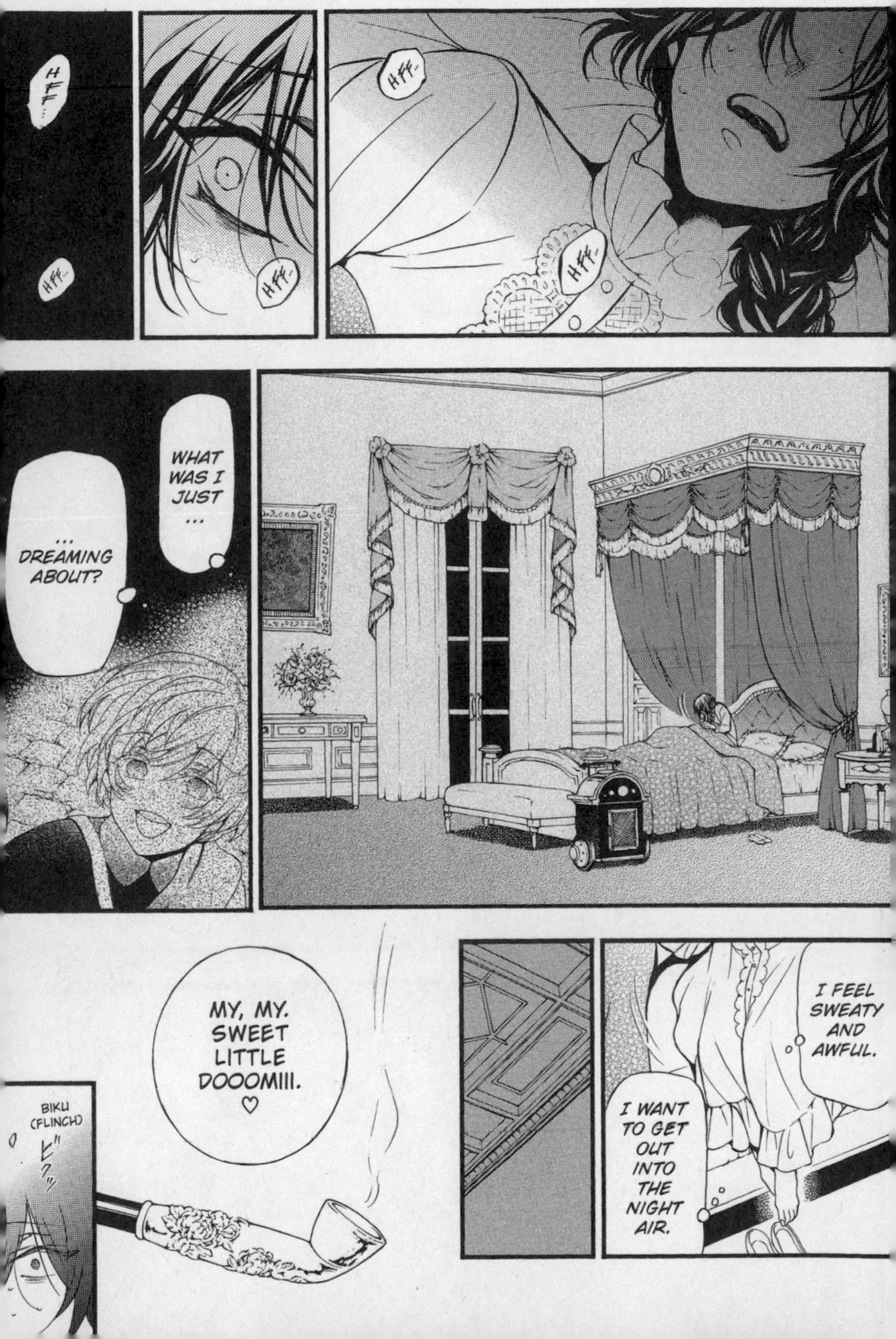
HFF...
HFF...
HFF...
HFF...
HFF...
WHAT WAS I JUST...
...DREAMING ABOUT?
I FEEL SWEATY AND AWFUL.
I WANT TO GET OUT INTO THE NIGHT AIR.
MY, MY. SWEET LITTLE DOOOMIII. ♡
BIKU (FLINCH)
ビクッ

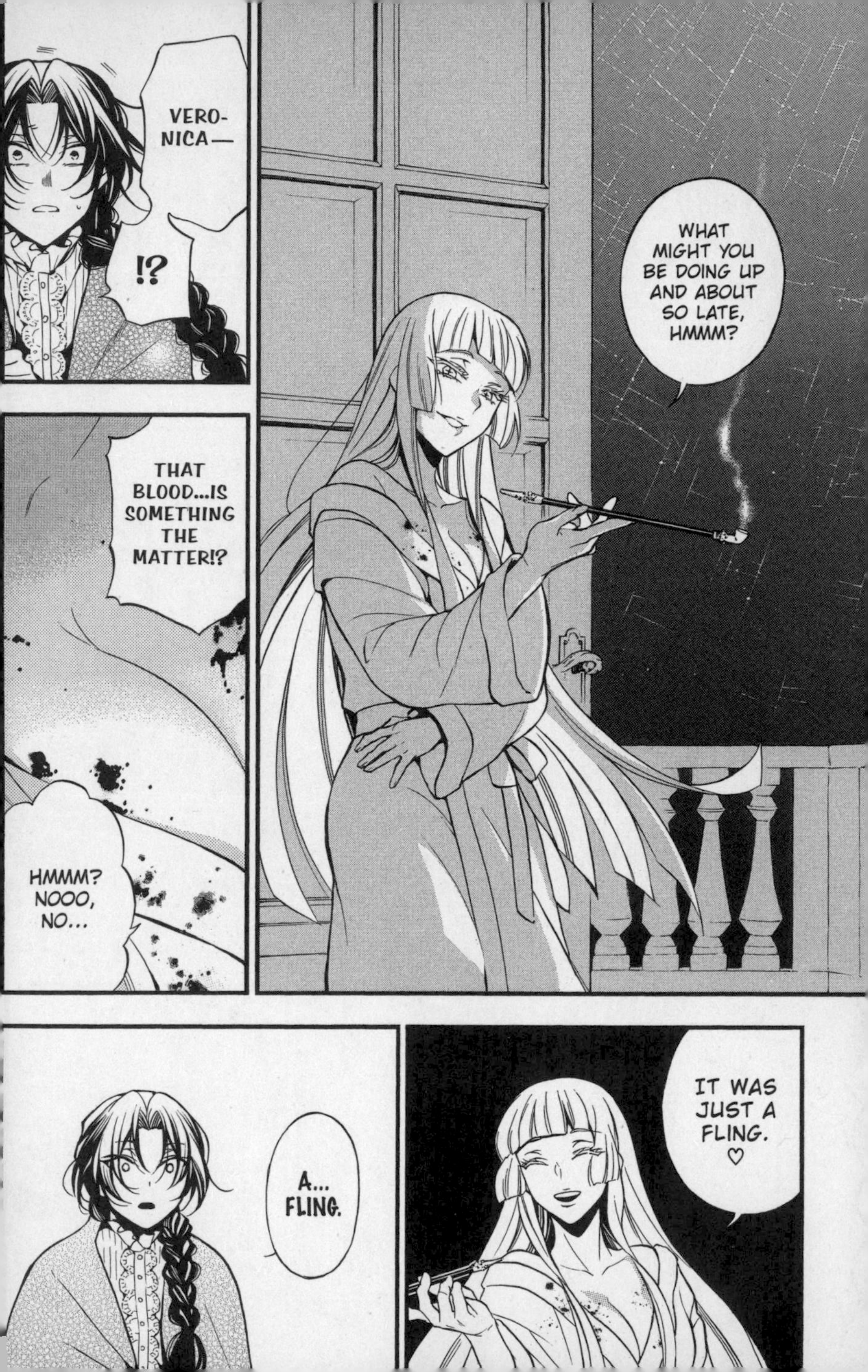
WHAT MIGHT YOU BE DOING UP AND ABOUT SO LATE, HMMM?
VERO-NICA—
!?
THAT BLOOD...IS SOMETHING THE MATTER!?
HMMM? NOOO, NO...
IT WAS JUST A FLING. ♡
A... FLING.

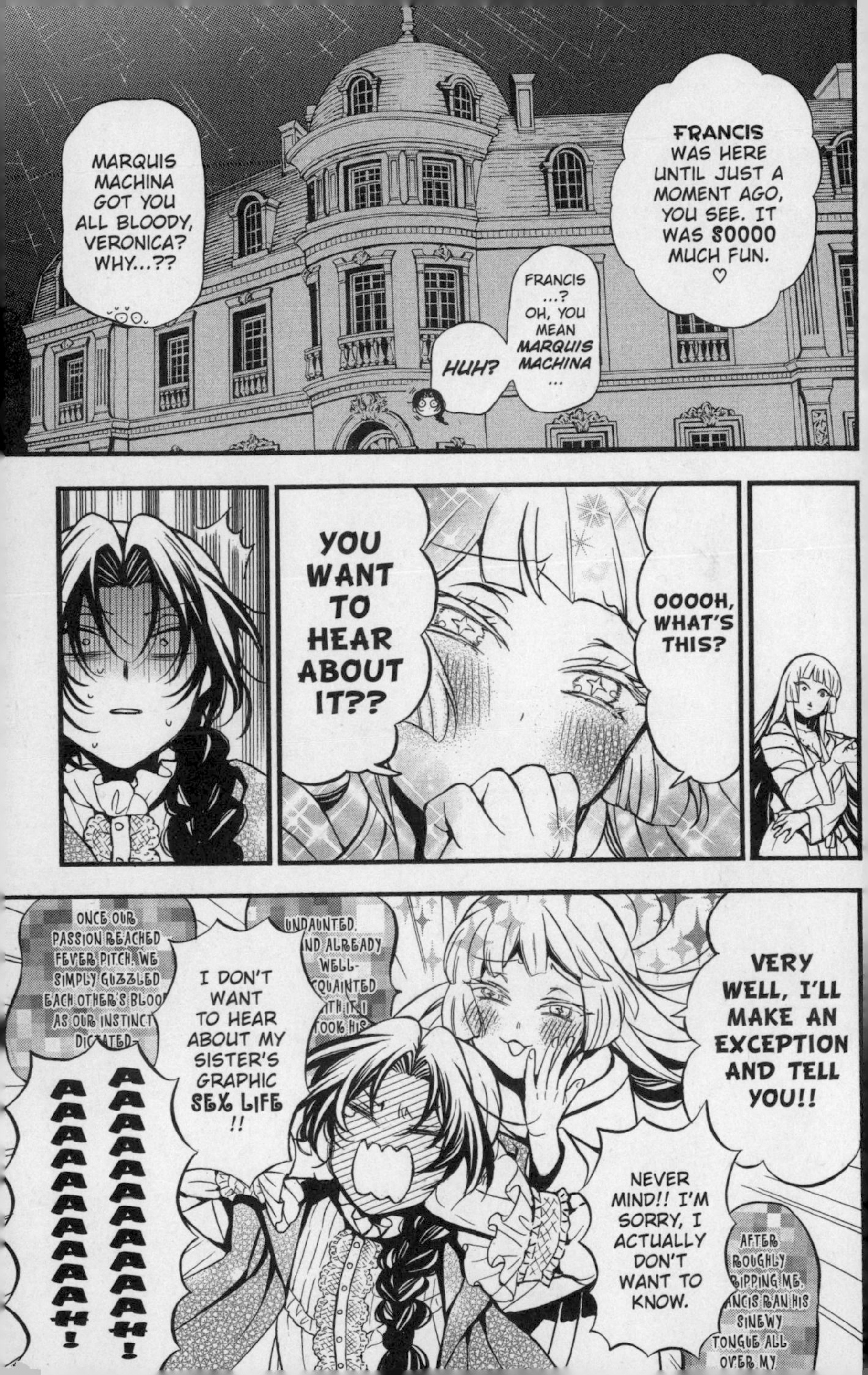
FRANCIS WAS HERE UNTIL JUST A MOMENT AGO, YOU SEE. IT WAS SOOOO MUCH FUN. ♡
FRANCIS ...? OH, YOU MEAN MARQUIS MACHINA ...
HUH?
MARQUIS MACHINA GOT YOU ALL BLOODY, VERONICA? WHY...??
OOOOH, WHAT'S THIS?
YOU WANT TO HEAR ABOUT IT??
VERY WELL, I'LL MAKE AN EXCEPTION AND TELL YOU!!
AFTER ROUGHLY RIPPING ME, ANCIS RAN HIS SINEWY TONGUE ALL OVER MY
NEVER MIND!! I'M SORRY, I ACTUALLY DON'T WANT TO KNOW.
UNDAUNTED, ND ALREADY WELL-CQUAINTED ITH IT, I TOOK HIS
I DON'T WANT TO HEAR ABOUT MY SISTER'S GRAPHIC SEX LIFE!!
ONCE OUR PASSION REACHED FEVER PITCH, WE SIMPLY GUZZLED EACH OTHER'S BLOO AS OUR INSTINCT DICTATED—
AAAAAAAAAAAAAH!
AAAAAAAAAAAAAAH!

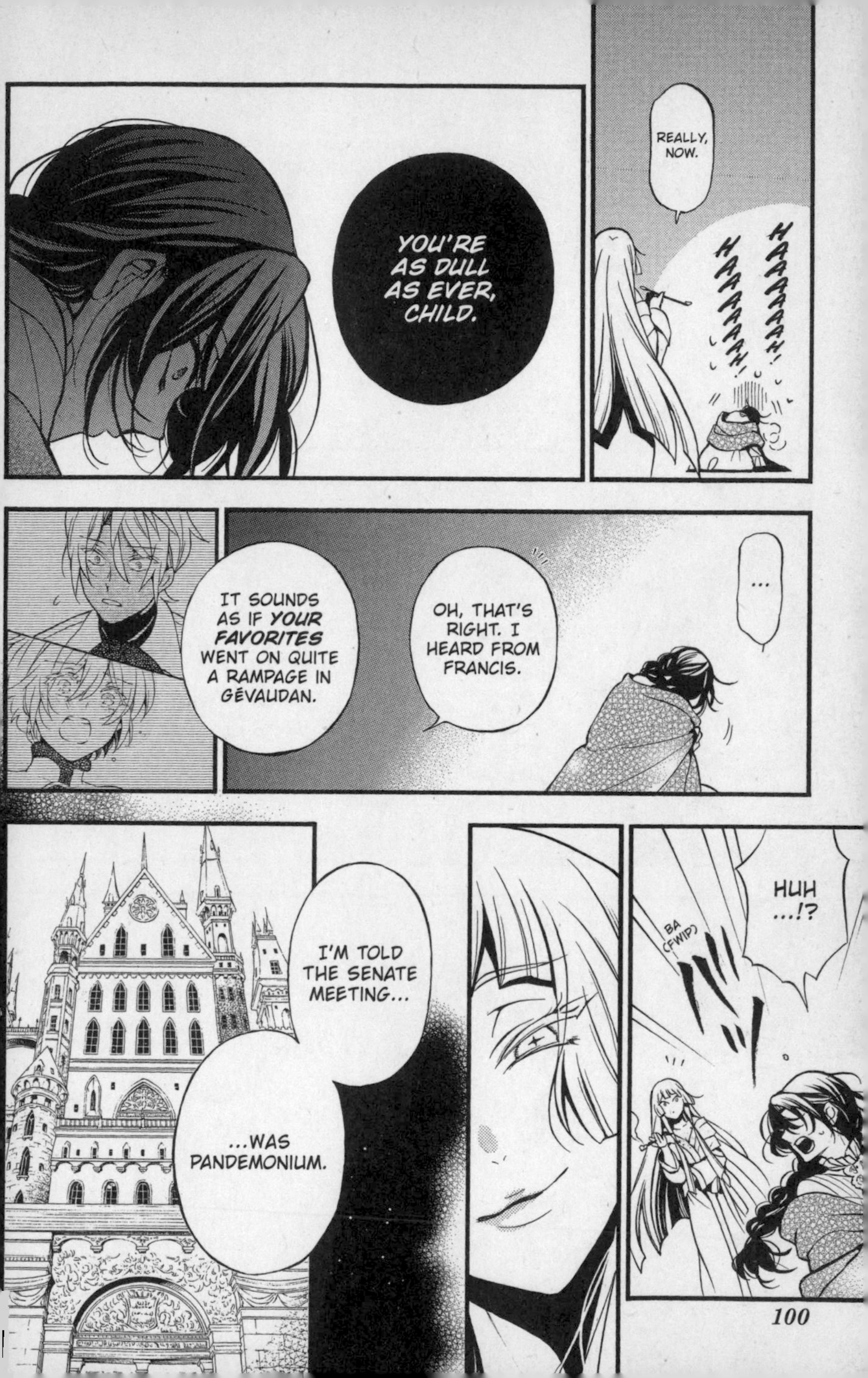
REALLY, NOW.
HAAAAAAH!
HAAAAAAH!
YOU'RE AS DULL AS EVER, CHILD.
...
OH, THAT'S RIGHT. I HEARD FROM FRANCIS.
IT SOUNDS AS IF *YOUR FAVORITES* WENT ON QUITE A RAMPAGE IN GÉVAUDAN.
HUH ...!?
BA (FWIP)
I'M TOLD THE SENATE MEETING...
...WAS PANDEMONIUM.

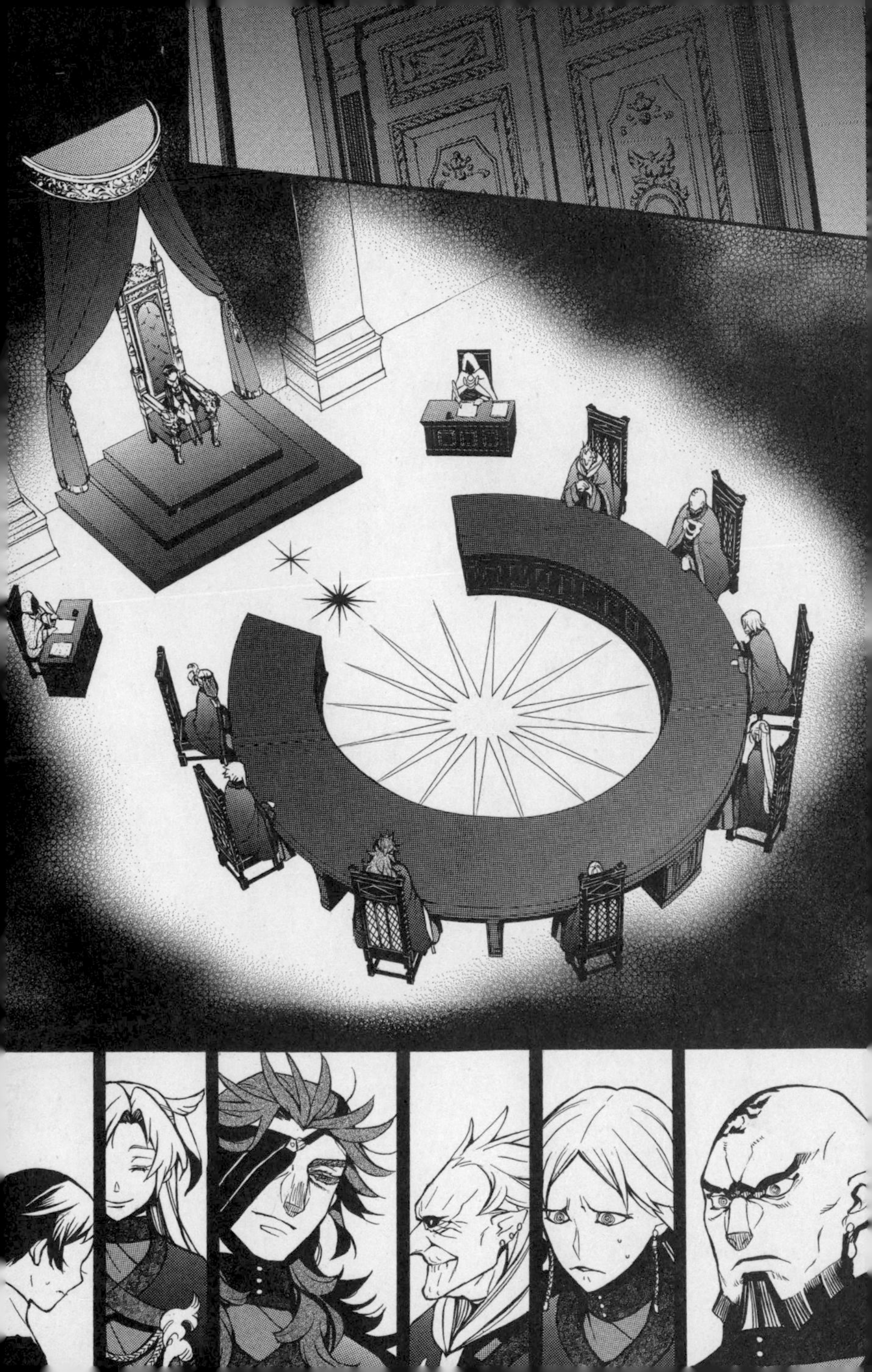

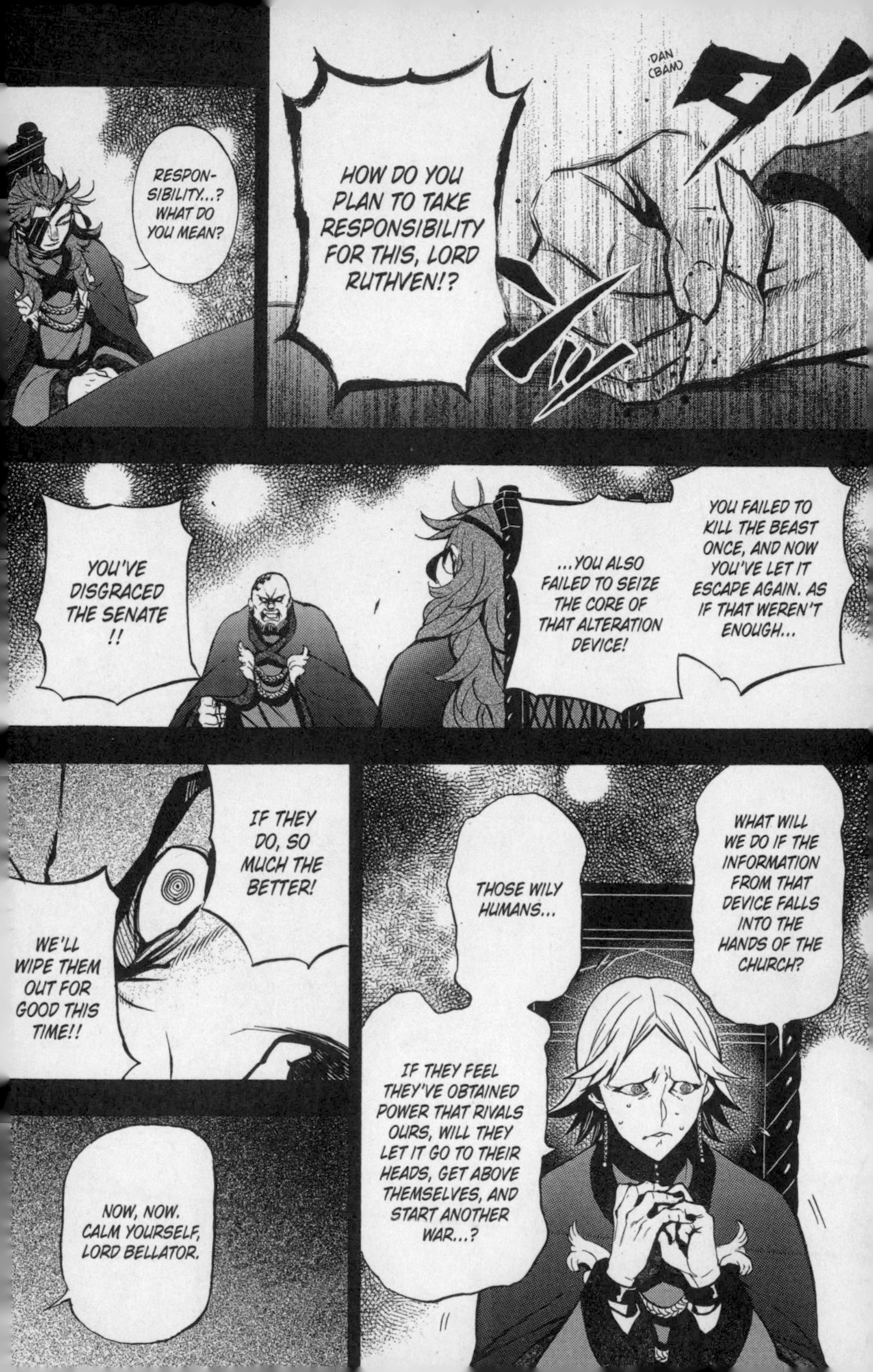
DAN (BAM)
HOW DO YOU PLAN TO TAKE RESPONSIBILITY FOR THIS, LORD RUTHVEN!?
RESPON-SIBILITY...? WHAT DO YOU MEAN?
YOU FAILED TO KILL THE BEAST ONCE, AND NOW YOU'VE LET IT ESCAPE AGAIN. AS IF THAT WEREN'T ENOUGH...
...YOU ALSO FAILED TO SEIZE THE CORE OF THAT ALTERATION DEVICE!
YOU'VE DISGRACED THE SENATE !!
WHAT WILL WE DO IF THE INFORMATION FROM THAT DEVICE FALLS INTO THE HANDS OF THE CHURCH?
THOSE WILY HUMANS...
IF THEY FEEL THEY'VE OBTAINED POWER THAT RIVALS OURS, WILL THEY LET IT GO TO THEIR HEADS, GET ABOVE THEMSELVES, AND START ANOTHER WAR...?
IF THEY DO, SO MUCH THE BETTER!
WE'LL WIPE THEM OUT FOR GOOD THIS TIME!!
NOW, NOW. CALM YOURSELF, LORD BELLATOR.

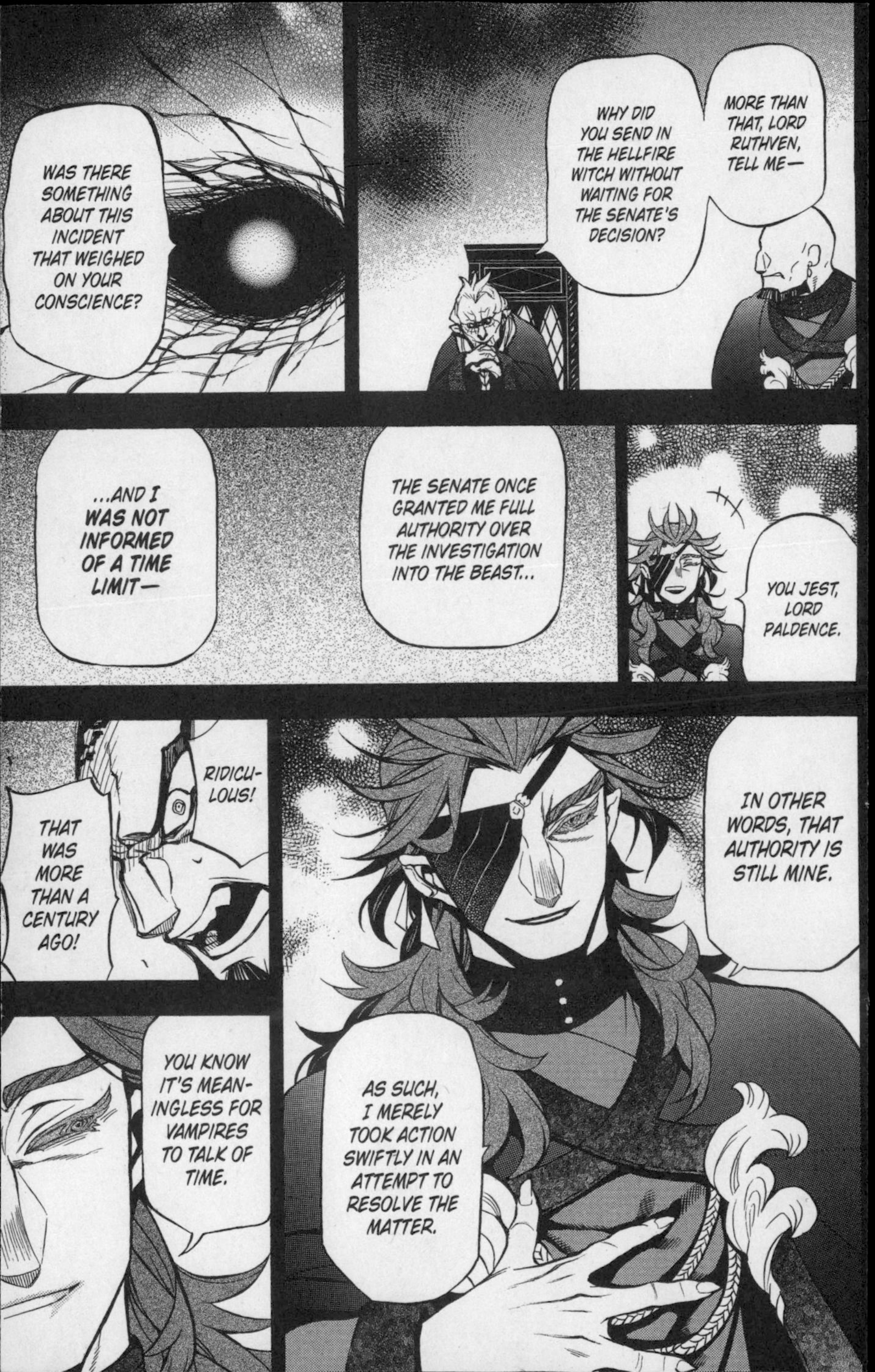
MORE THAN THAT, LORD RUTHVEN, TELL ME—
WHY DID YOU SEND IN THE HELLFIRE WITCH WITHOUT WAITING FOR THE SENATE'S DECISION?
WAS THERE SOMETHING ABOUT THIS INCIDENT THAT WEIGHED ON YOUR CONSCIENCE?
YOU JEST, LORD PALDENCE.
THE SENATE ONCE GRANTED ME FULL AUTHORITY OVER THE INVESTIGATION INTO THE BEAST...
...AND I WAS NOT INFORMED OF A TIME LIMIT—
IN OTHER WORDS, THAT AUTHORITY IS STILL MINE.
AS SUCH, I MERELY TOOK ACTION SWIFTLY IN AN ATTEMPT TO RESOLVE THE MATTER.
RIDICU-LOUS!
THAT WAS MORE THAN A CENTURY AGO!
YOU KNOW IT'S MEAN-INGLESS FOR VAMPIRES TO TALK OF TIME.

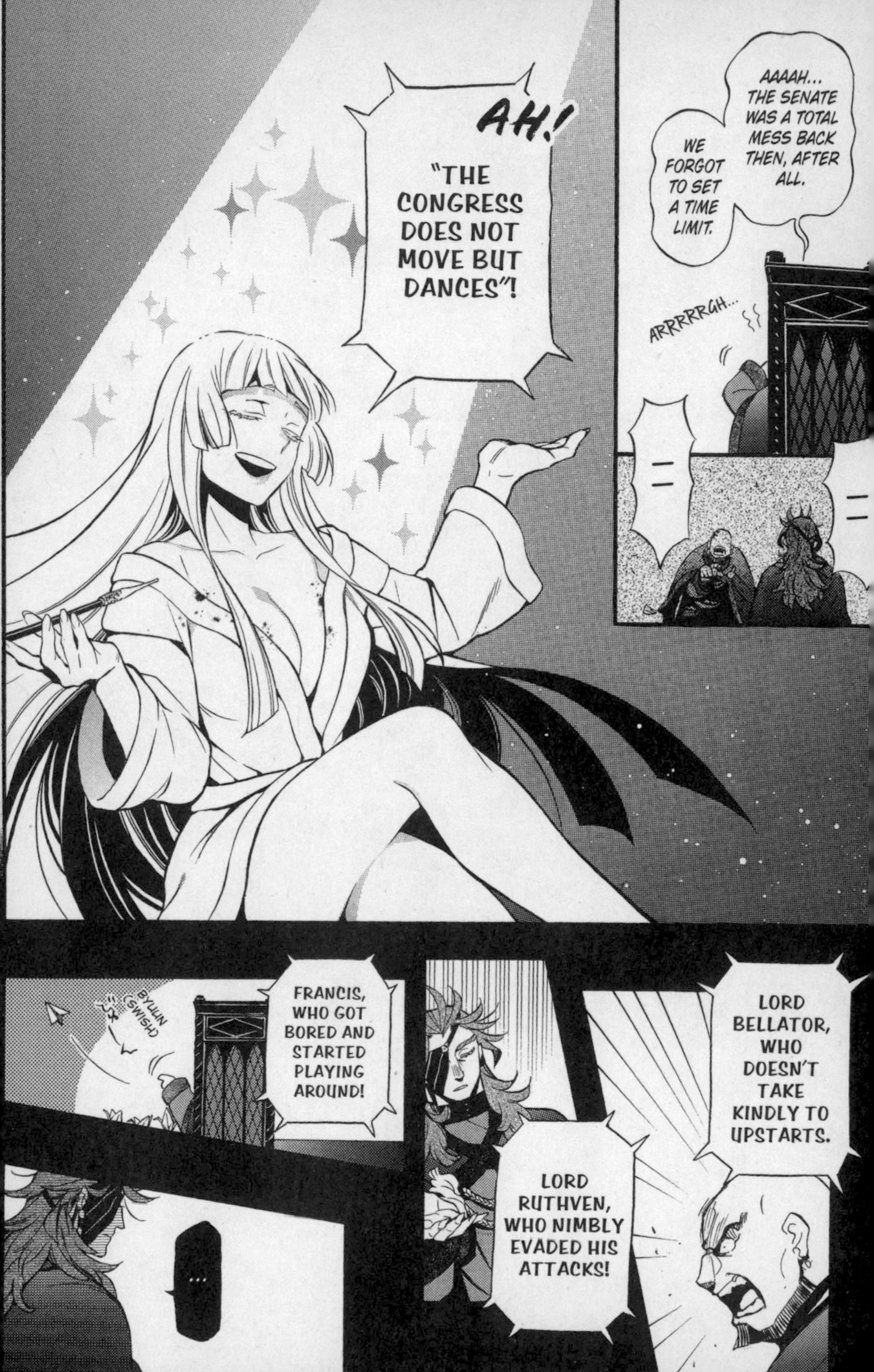
AAAAH... THE SENATE WAS A TOTAL MESS BACK THEN, AFTER ALL.
WE FORGOT TO SET A TIME LIMIT.
ARRRRRGH...
AH!
"THE CONGRESS DOES NOT MOVE BUT DANCES"!
LORD BELLATOR, WHO DOESN'T TAKE KINDLY TO UPSTARTS.
LORD RUTHVEN, WHO NIMBLY EVADED HIS ATTACKS!
FRANCIS, WHO GOT BORED AND STARTED PLAYING AROUND!
BYUUN (SWISH)
...

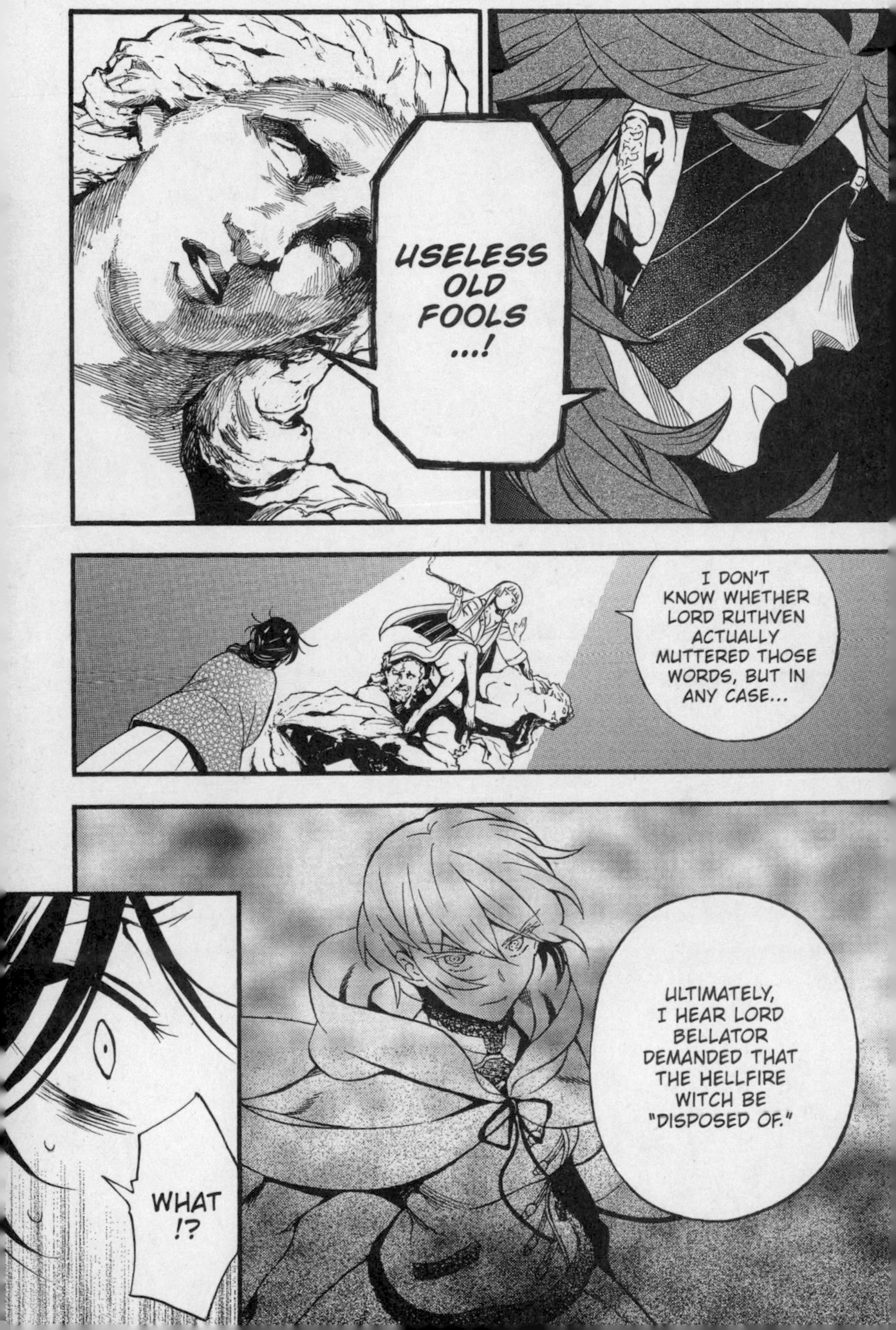
USELESS OLD FOOLS ...!
I DON'T KNOW WHETHER LORD RUTHVEN ACTUALLY MUTTERED THOSE WORDS, BUT IN ANY CASE...
ULTIMATELY, I HEAR LORD BELLATOR DEMANDED THAT THE HELLFIRE WITCH BE "DISPOSED OF."
WHAT !?

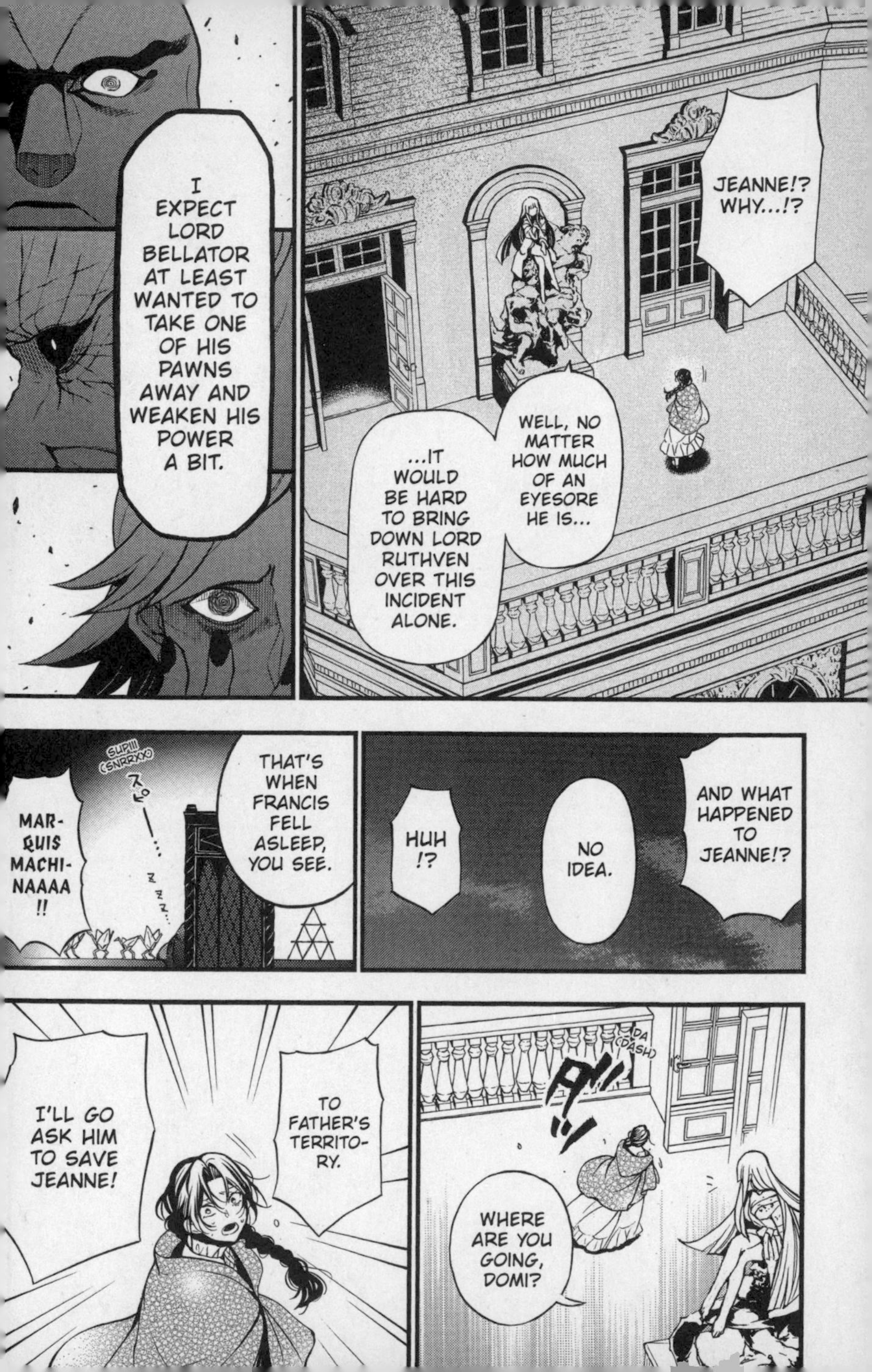
JEANNE!? WHY...!?
WELL, NO MATTER HOW MUCH OF AN EYESORE HE IS...
...IT WOULD BE HARD TO BRING DOWN LORD RUTHVEN OVER THIS INCIDENT ALONE.
I EXPECT LORD BELLATOR AT LEAST WANTED TO TAKE ONE OF HIS PAWNS AWAY AND WEAKEN HIS POWER A BIT.
AND WHAT HAPPENED TO JEANNE!?
NO IDEA.
HUH!?
THAT'S WHEN FRANCIS FELL ASLEEP, YOU SEE.
SUPIII (SNRRXX)
MARQUIS MACHINAAAA!!
Z Z Z...
DA (DASH)
WHERE ARE YOU GOING, DOMI?
TO FATHER'S TERRITORY.
I'LL GO ASK HIM TO SAVE JEANNE!

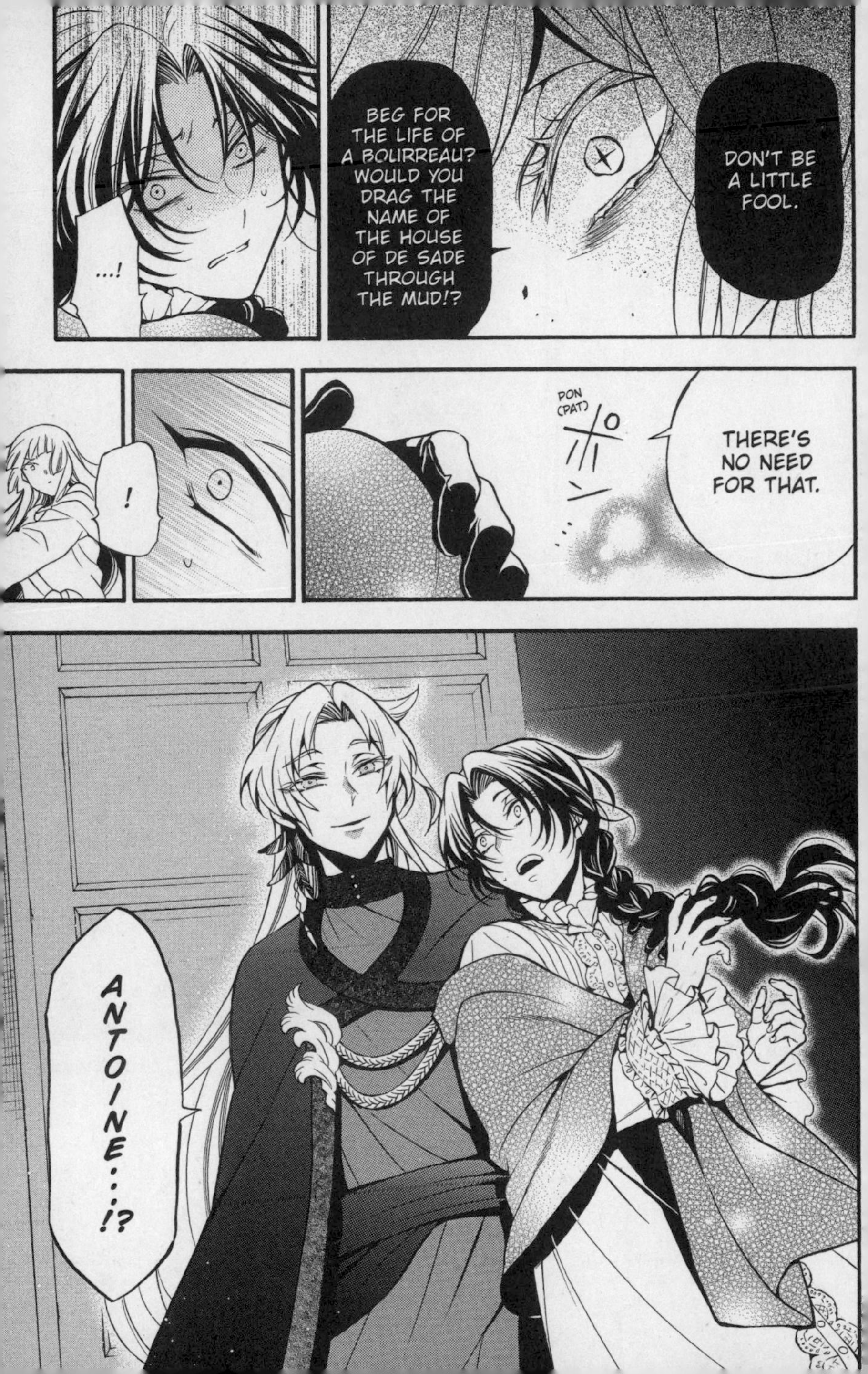
DON'T BE A LITTLE FOOL.
BEG FOR THE LIFE OF A BOURREAU? WOULD YOU DRAG THE NAME OF THE HOUSE OF DE SADE THROUGH THE MUD!?
...!
THERE'S NO NEED FOR THAT.
PON (PAT)
!
ANTOINE...!?

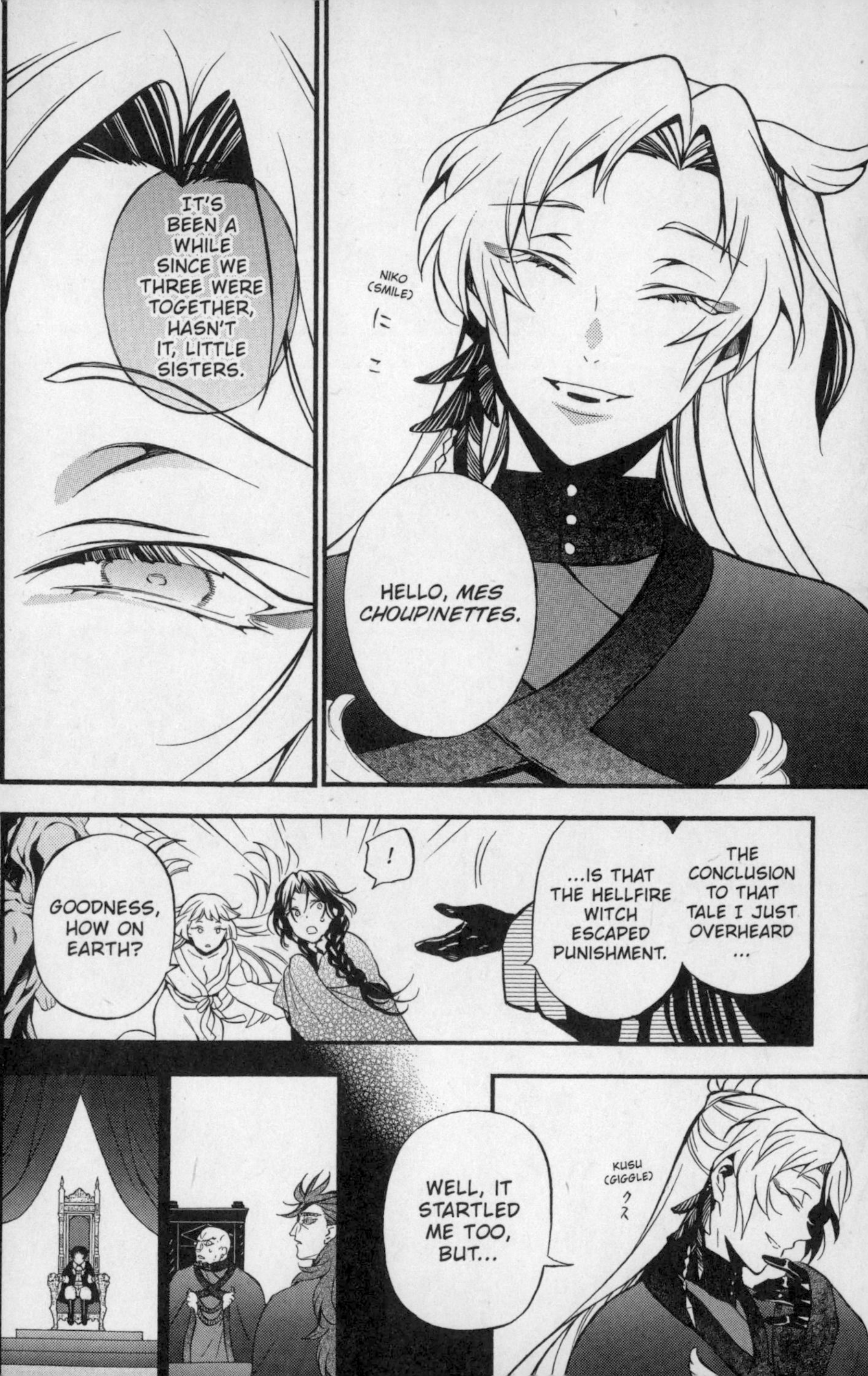
NIKO (SMILE)
にこ
HELLO, *MES CHOUPINETTES.*
IT'S BEEN A WHILE SINCE WE THREE WERE TOGETHER, HASN'T IT, LITTLE SISTERS.
THE CONCLUSION TO THAT TALE I JUST OVERHEARD ...
...IS THAT THE HELLFIRE WITCH ESCAPED PUNISHMENT.
!
GOODNESS, HOW ON EARTH?
KUSU (GIGGLE)
クス
WELL, IT STARTLED ME TOO, BUT...

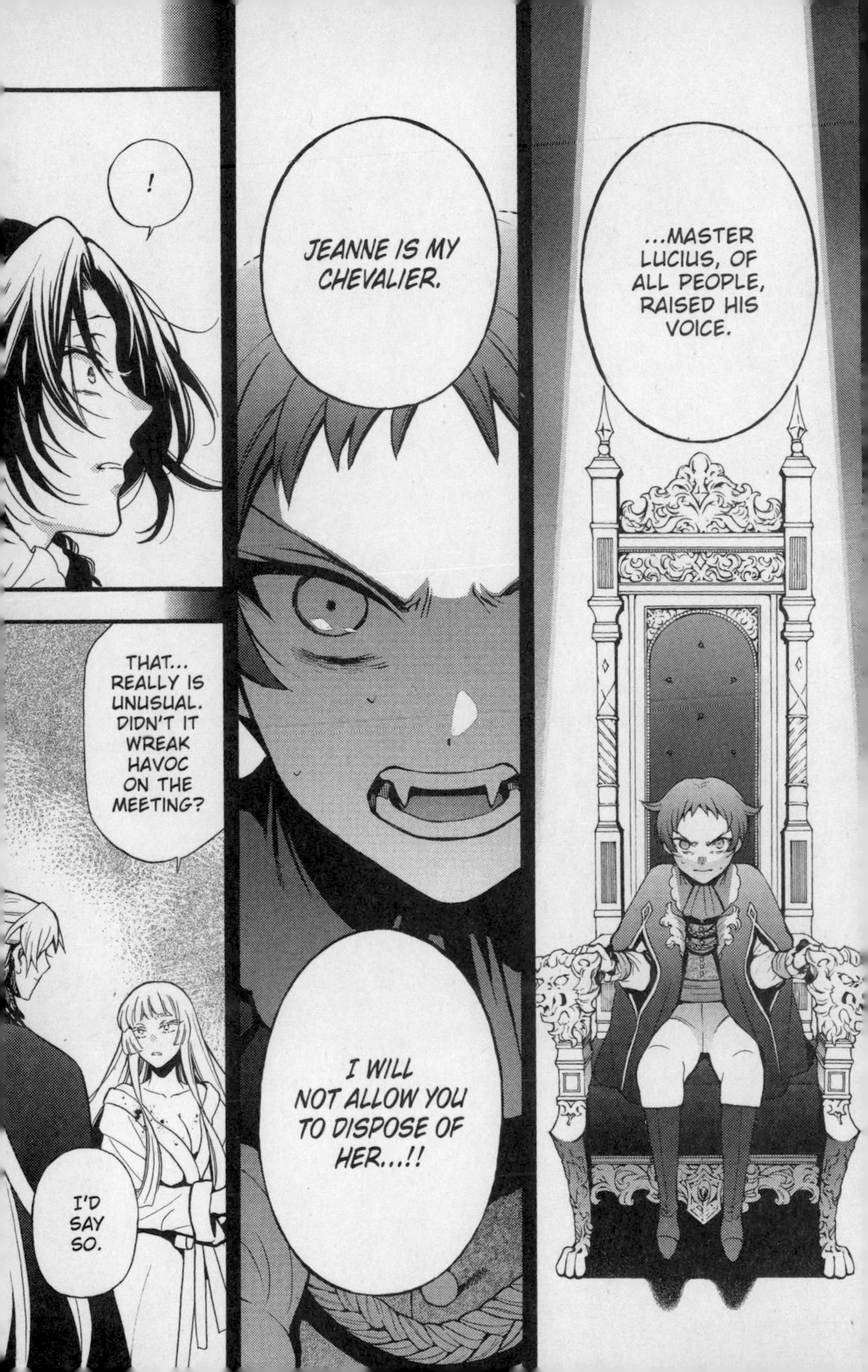
...MASTER LUCIUS, OF ALL PEOPLE, RAISED HIS VOICE.
JEANNE IS MY CHEVALIER.
I WILL NOT ALLOW YOU TO DISPOSE OF HER...!!
!
THAT... REALLY IS UNUSUAL. DIDN'T IT WREAK HAVOC ON THE MEETING?
I'D SAY SO.

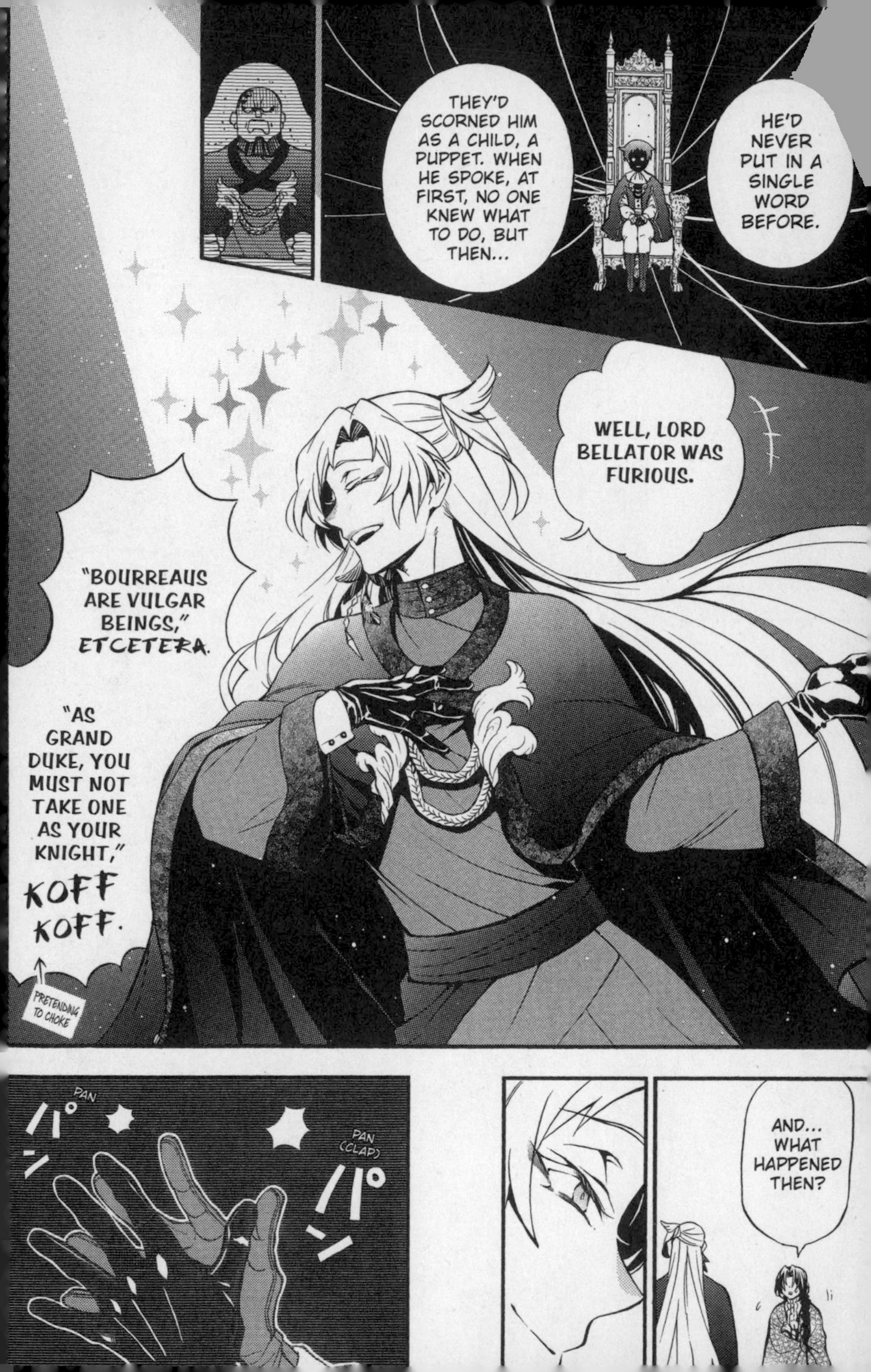
HE'D NEVER PUT IN A SINGLE WORD BEFORE.
THEY'D SCORNED HIM AS A CHILD, A PUPPET. WHEN HE SPOKE, AT FIRST, NO ONE KNEW WHAT TO DO, BUT THEN...
WELL, LORD BELLATOR WAS FURIOUS.
"BOURREAUS ARE VULGAR BEINGS," ETCETERA.
"AS GRAND DUKE, YOU MUST NOT TAKE ONE AS YOUR KNIGHT," KOFF KOFF.
PRETENDING TO CHOKE
AND... WHAT HAPPENED THEN?
PAN
PAN (CLAP)

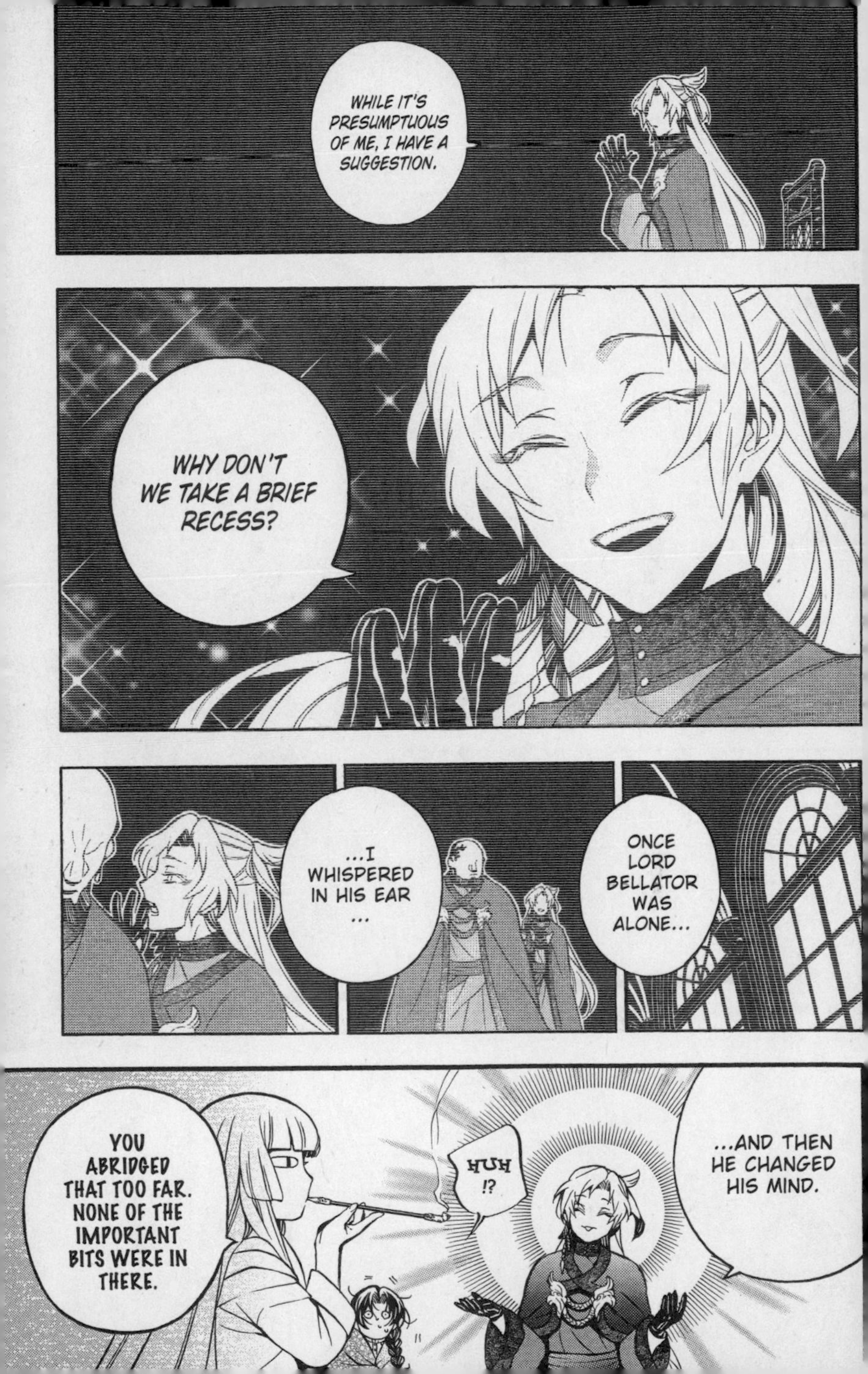
WHILE IT'S PRESUMPTUOUS OF ME, I HAVE A SUGGESTION.
WHY DON'T WE TAKE A BRIEF RECESS?
ONCE LORD BELLATOR WAS ALONE...
...I WHISPERED IN HIS EAR ...
...AND THEN HE CHANGED HIS MIND.
HUH!?
YOU ABRIDGED THAT TOO FAR. NONE OF THE IMPORTANT BITS WERE IN THERE.

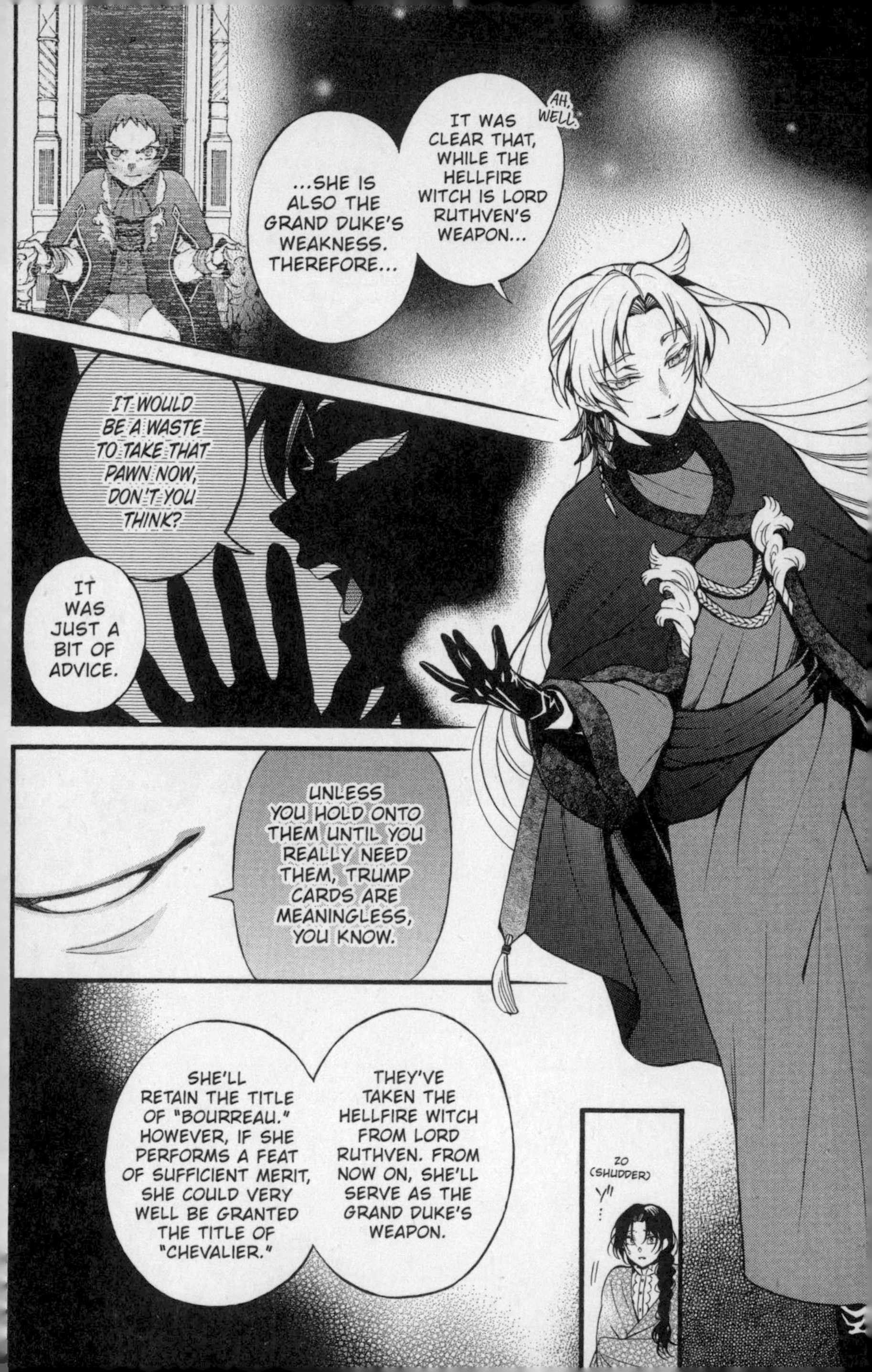
AH, WELL.
IT WAS CLEAR THAT, WHILE THE HELLFIRE WITCH IS LORD RUTHVEN'S WEAPON...
...SHE IS ALSO THE GRAND DUKE'S WEAKNESS. THEREFORE...
IT WOULD BE A WASTE TO TAKE THAT PAWN NOW, DON'T YOU THINK?
IT WAS JUST A BIT OF ADVICE.
UNLESS YOU HOLD ONTO THEM UNTIL YOU REALLY NEED THEM, TRUMP CARDS ARE MEANINGLESS, YOU KNOW.
THEY'VE TAKEN THE HELLFIRE WITCH FROM LORD RUTHVEN. FROM NOW ON, SHE'LL SERVE AS THE GRAND DUKE'S WEAPON.
SHE'LL RETAIN THE TITLE OF "BOURREAU." HOWEVER, IF SHE PERFORMS A FEAT OF SUFFICIENT MERIT, SHE COULD VERY WELL BE GRANTED THE TITLE OF "CHEVALIER."
ZO (SHUDDER)

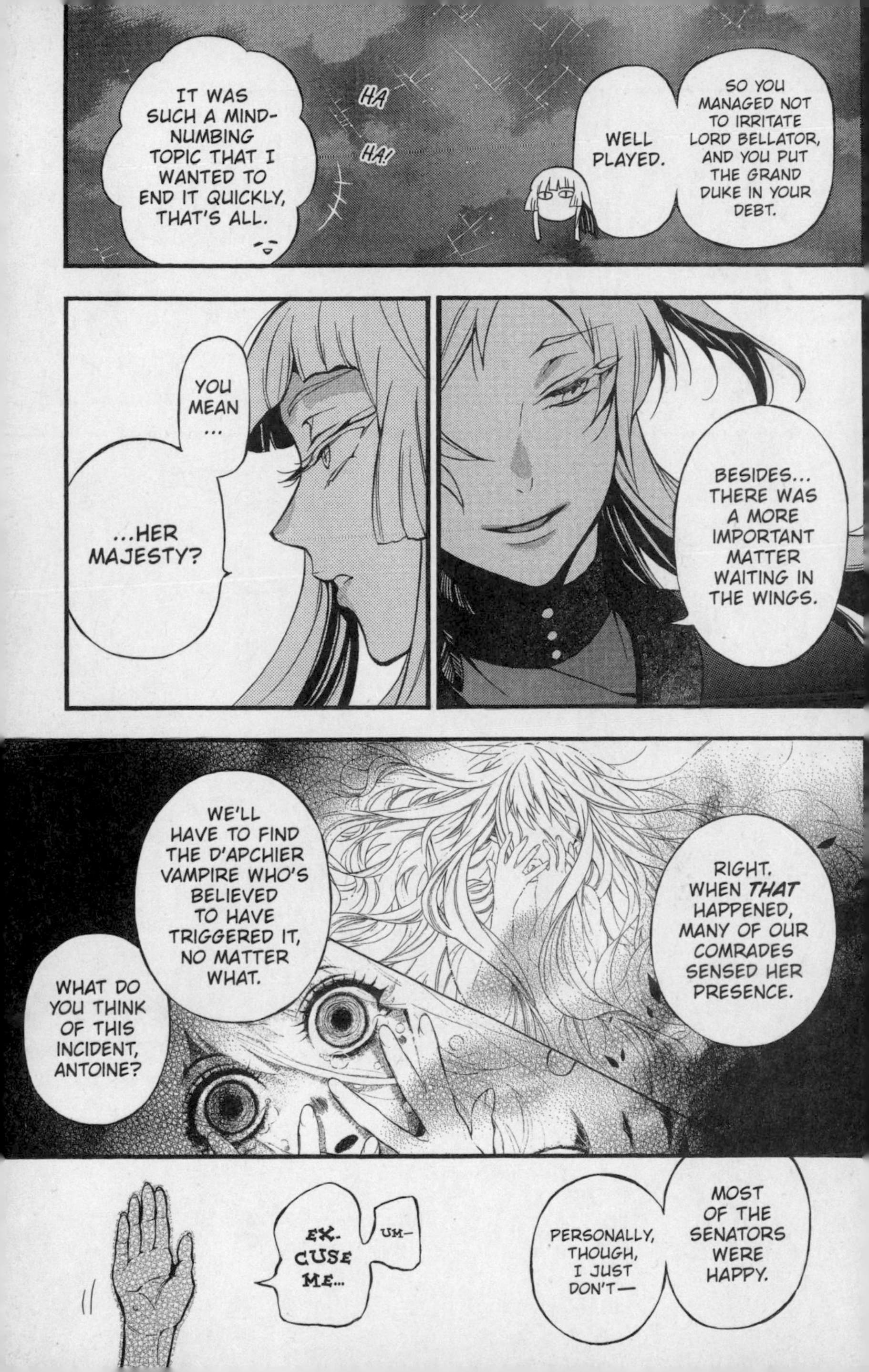
SO YOU MANAGED NOT TO IRRITATE LORD BELLATOR, AND YOU PUT THE GRAND DUKE IN YOUR DEBT.
WELL PLAYED.
HA HA!
IT WAS SUCH A MIND-NUMBING TOPIC THAT I WANTED TO END IT QUICKLY, THAT'S ALL.
BESIDES... THERE WAS A MORE IMPORTANT MATTER WAITING IN THE WINGS.
YOU MEAN ...
...HER MAJESTY?
RIGHT. WHEN *THAT* HAPPENED, MANY OF OUR COMRADES SENSED HER PRESENCE.
WE'LL HAVE TO FIND THE D'APCHIER VAMPIRE WHO'S BELIEVED TO HAVE TRIGGERED IT, NO MATTER WHAT.
WHAT DO YOU THINK OF THIS INCIDENT, ANTOINE?
MOST OF THE SENATORS WERE HAPPY.
PERSONALLY, THOUGH, I JUST DON'T—
UM—
EX-CUSE ME...

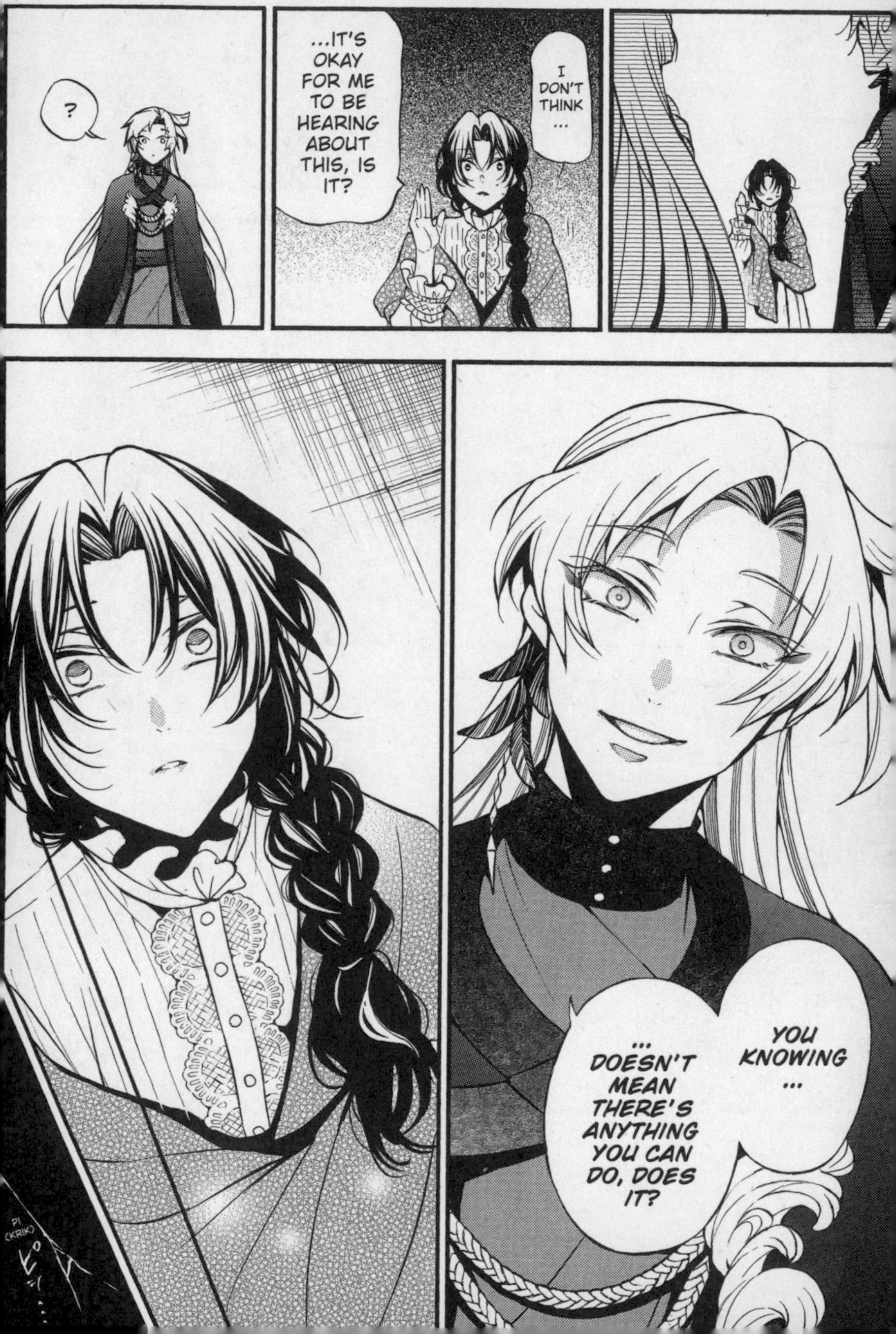
I DON'T THINK ...
...IT'S OKAY FOR ME TO BE HEARING ABOUT THIS, IS IT?
?
YOU KNOWING ...
... DOESN'T MEAN THERE'S ANYTHING YOU CAN DO, DOES IT?
PI (KRIK)

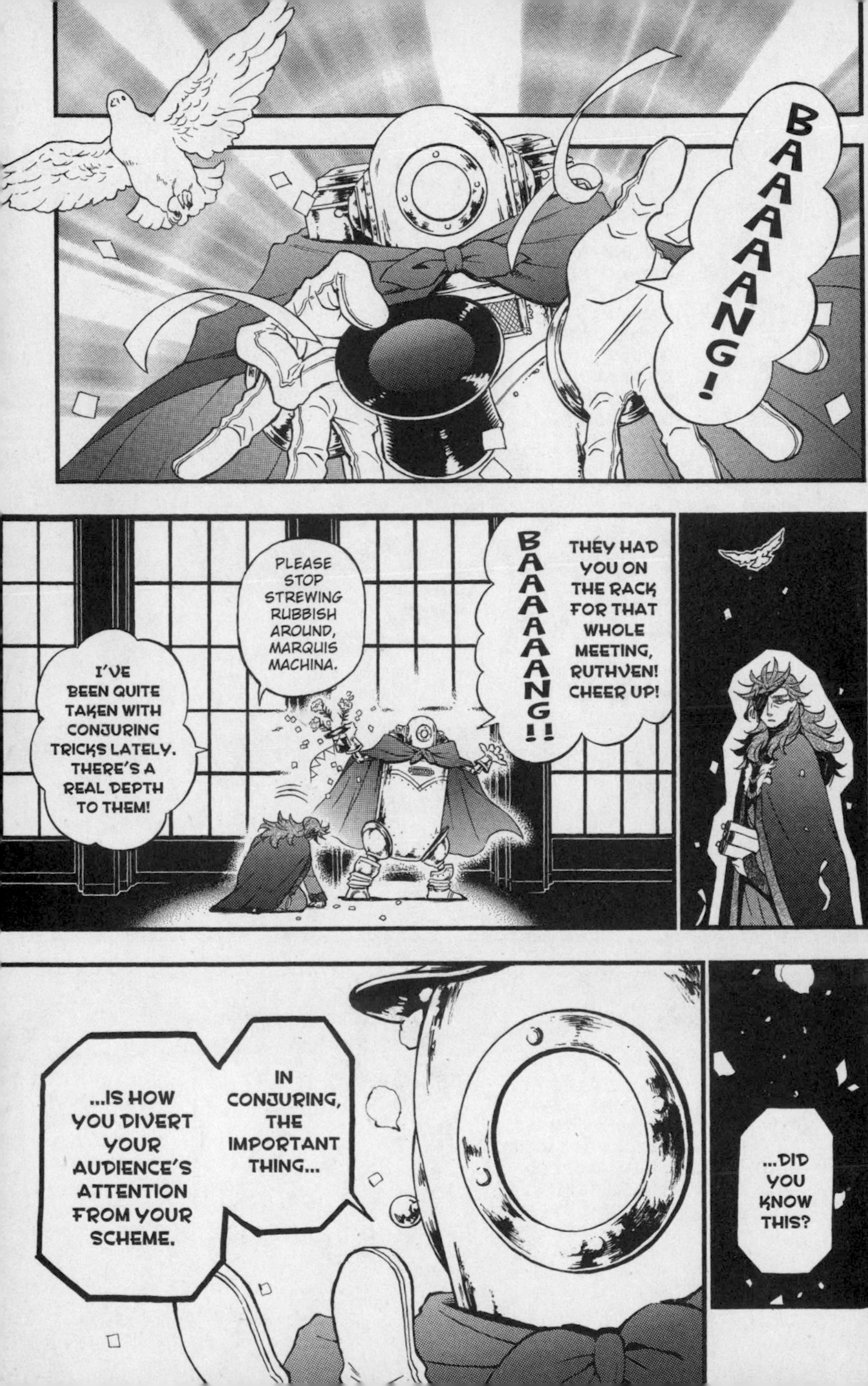

BAAAAANG!
BAAAAAANG!! THEY HAD YOU ON THE RACK FOR THAT WHOLE MEETING, RUTHVEN! CHEER UP!
PLEASE STOP STREWING RUBBISH AROUND, MARQUIS MACHINA.
I'VE BEEN QUITE TAKEN WITH CONJURING TRICKS LATELY. THERE'S A REAL DEPTH TO THEM!
...DID YOU KNOW THIS?
IN CONJURING, THE IMPORTANT THING...
...IS HOW YOU DIVERT YOUR AUDIENCE'S ATTENTION FROM YOUR SCHEME.

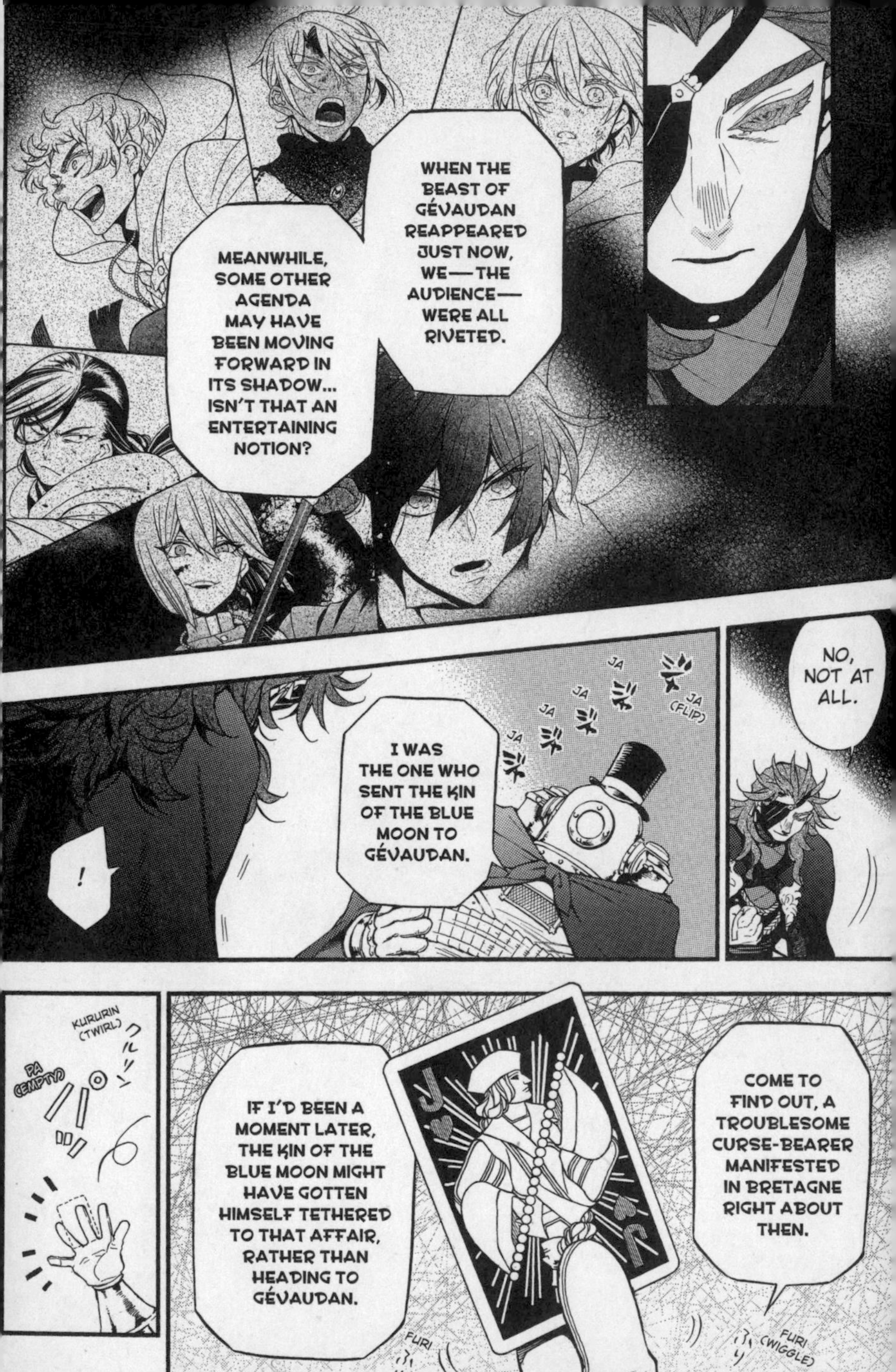
WHEN THE BEAST OF GÉVAUDAN REAPPEARED JUST NOW, WE—THE AUDIENCE—WERE ALL RIVETED.
MEANWHILE, SOME OTHER AGENDA MAY HAVE BEEN MOVING FORWARD IN ITS SHADOW... ISN'T THAT AN ENTERTAINING NOTION?
NO, NOT AT ALL.
JA (FLIP)
JA
JA
JA
JA
I WAS THE ONE WHO SENT THE KIN OF THE BLUE MOON TO GÉVAUDAN.
!
COME TO FIND OUT, A TROUBLESOME CURSE-BEARER MANIFESTED IN BRETAGNE RIGHT ABOUT THEN.
FURI (WIGGLE)
IF I'D BEEN A MOMENT LATER, THE KIN OF THE BLUE MOON MIGHT HAVE GOTTEN HIMSELF TETHERED TO THAT AFFAIR, RATHER THAN HEADING TO GÉVAUDAN.
FURI
KURURIN (TWIRL)
PA (EMPTY)

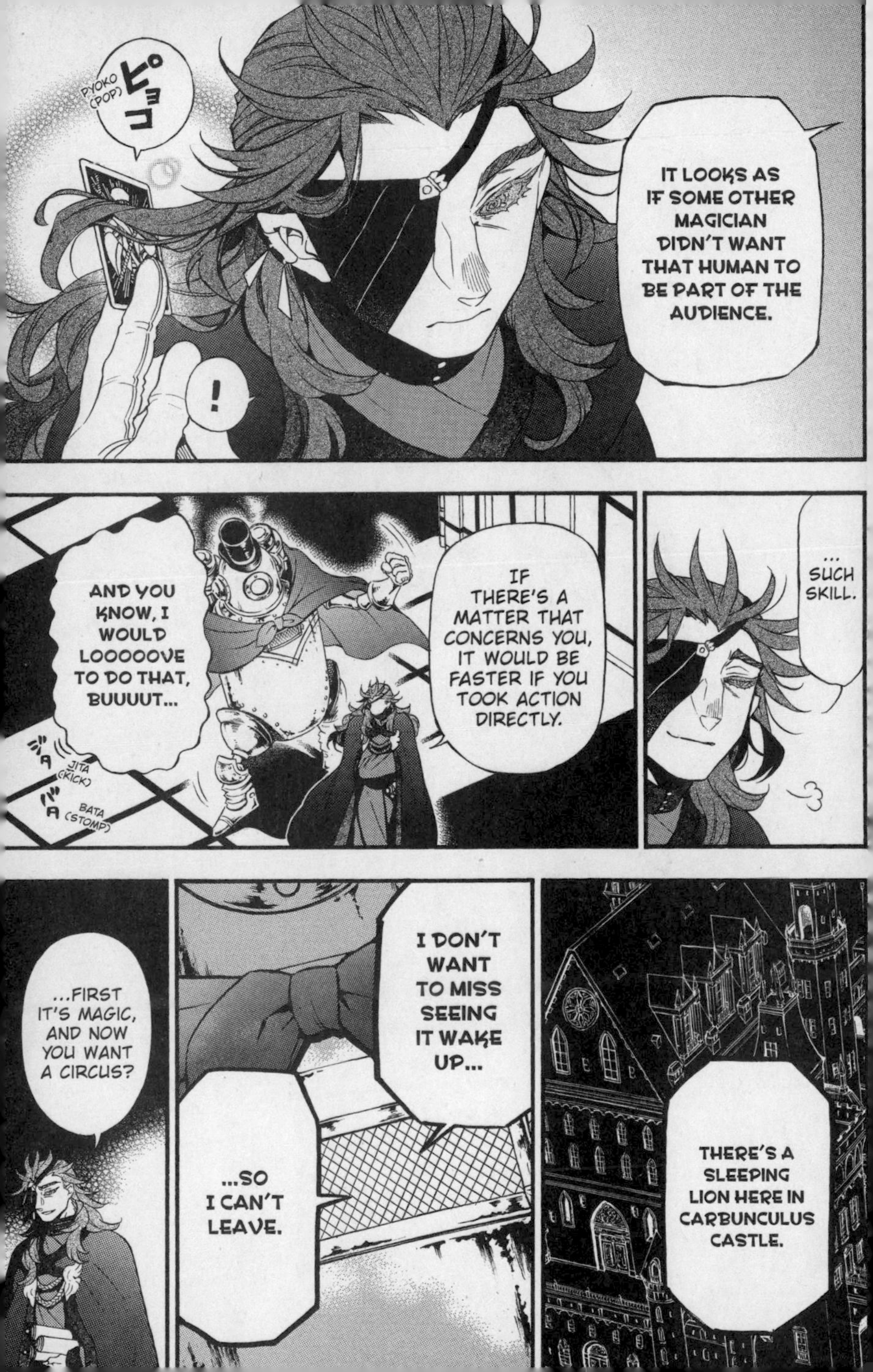
IT LOOKS AS IF SOME OTHER MAGICIAN DIDN'T WANT THAT HUMAN TO BE PART OF THE AUDIENCE.
ピョコ
PYOKO (POP)
!
...SUCH SKILL.
IF THERE'S A MATTER THAT CONCERNS YOU, IT WOULD BE FASTER IF YOU TOOK ACTION DIRECTLY.
AND YOU KNOW, I WOULD LOOOOOVE TO DO THAT, BUUUUT...
ジタ
JITA (KICK)
バタ
BATA (STOMP)
THERE'S A SLEEPING LION HERE IN CARBUNCULUS CASTLE.
I DON'T WANT TO MISS SEEING IT WAKE UP...
...SO I CAN'T LEAVE.
...FIRST IT'S MAGIC, AND NOW YOU WANT A CIRCUS?

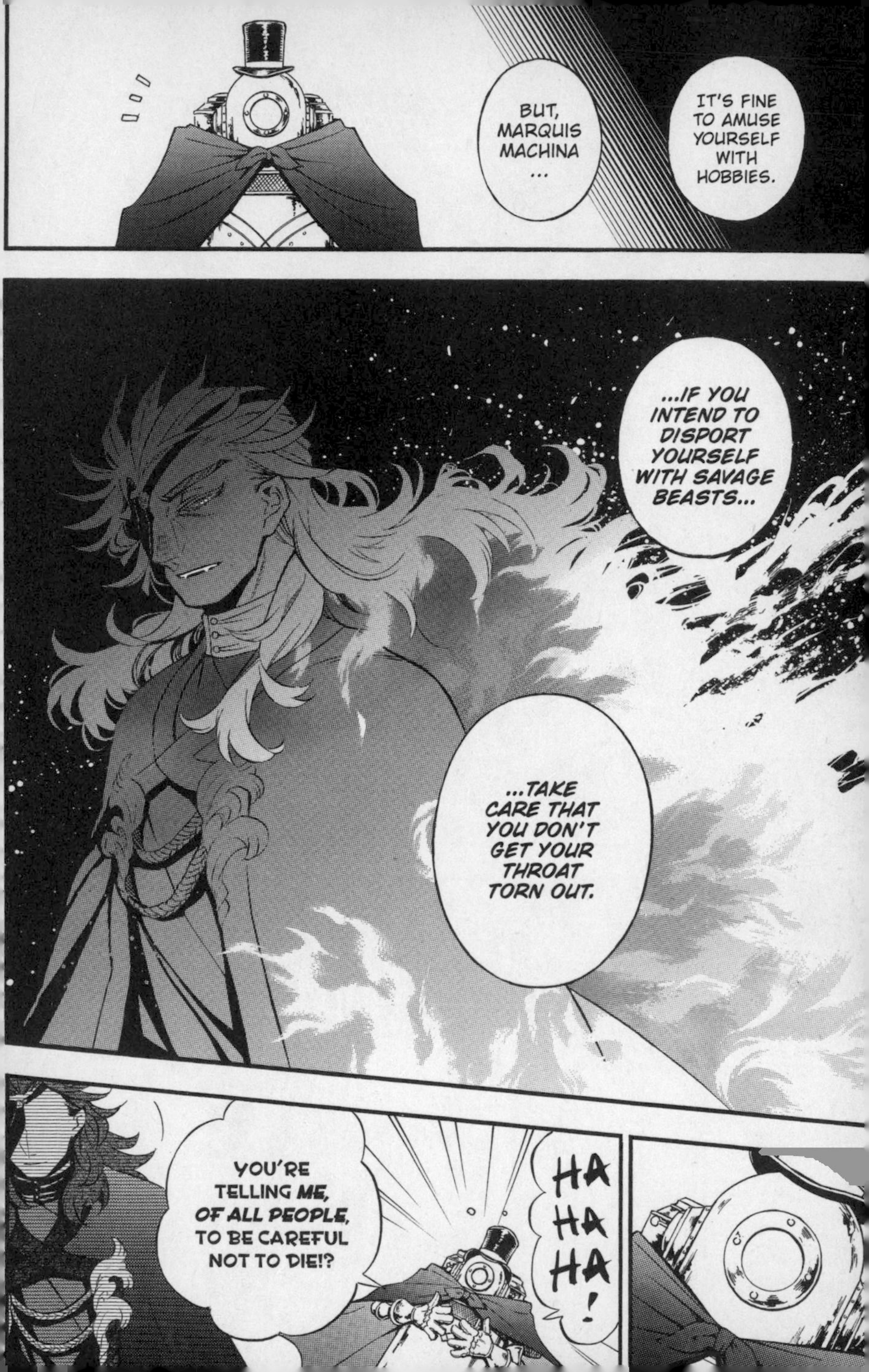
IT'S FINE TO AMUSE YOURSELF WITH HOBBIES.
BUT, MARQUIS MACHINA ...
...IF YOU INTEND TO DISPORT YOURSELF WITH SAVAGE BEASTS...
...TAKE CARE THAT YOU DON'T GET YOUR THROAT TORN OUT.
HA HA HA!
YOU'RE TELLING *ME*, *OF ALL PEOPLE*, TO BE CAREFUL NOT TO DIE!?

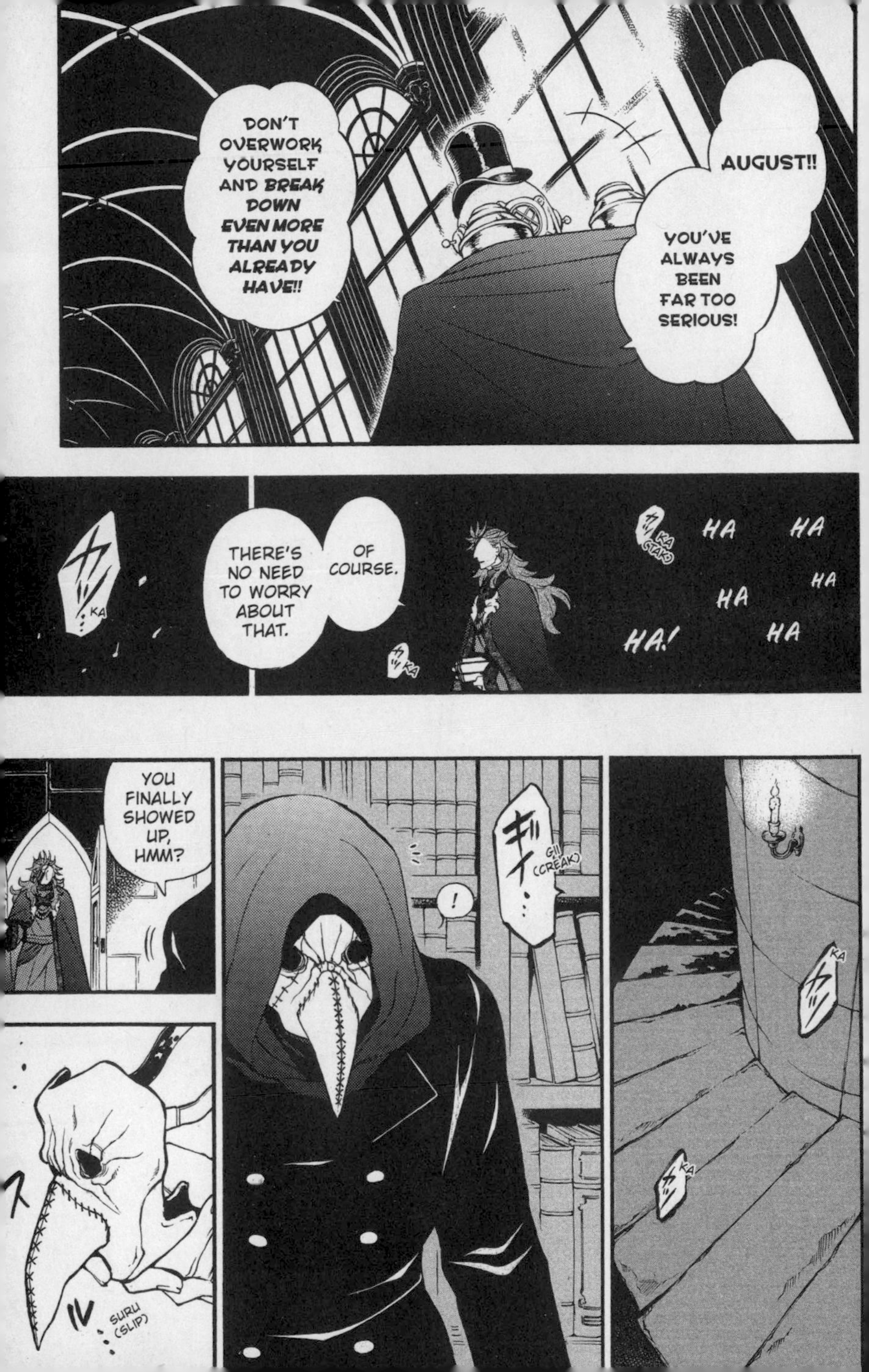
AUGUST!!
YOU'VE ALWAYS BEEN FAR TOO SERIOUS!
DON'T OVERWORK YOURSELF AND BREAK DOWN EVEN MORE THAN YOU ALREADY HAVE!!
KA (STAK)
HA HA HA HA HA HA!
OF COURSE.
THERE'S NO NEED TO WORRY ABOUT THAT.
KA
KA
KA
KA
GII (CREAK)
!
YOU FINALLY SHOWED UP, HMM?
SURU (SLIP)

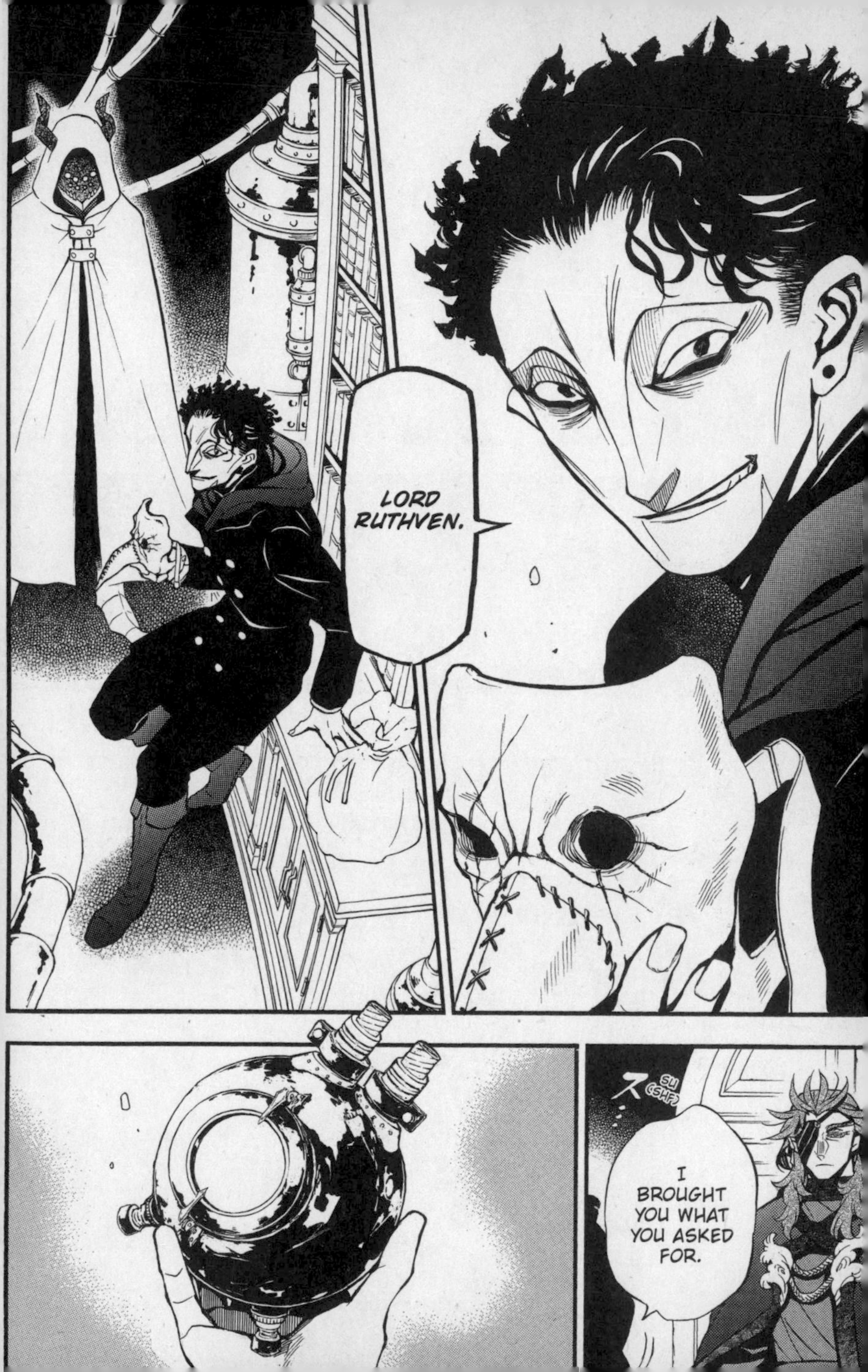
LORD RUTHVEN.
ス
SU (SHF)
I BROUGHT YOU WHAT YOU ASKED FOR.

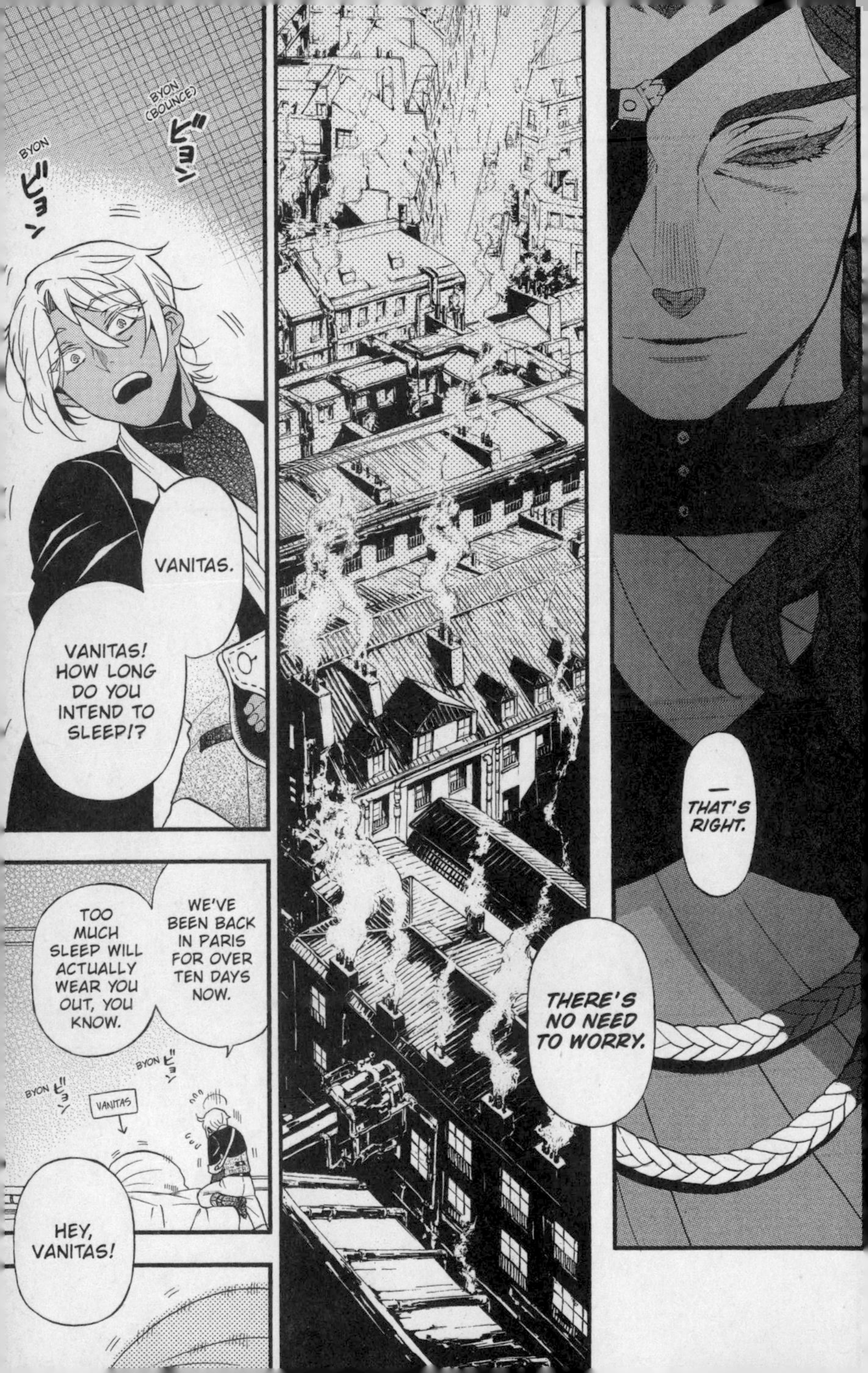
—THAT'S RIGHT.
THERE'S NO NEED TO WORRY.
BYON (BOUNCE)
ビョン
BYON
ビョン
VANITAS.
VANITAS! HOW LONG DO YOU INTEND TO SLEEP!?
WE'VE BEEN BACK IN PARIS FOR OVER TEN DAYS NOW.
TOO MUCH SLEEP WILL ACTUALLY WEAR YOU OUT, YOU KNOW.
BYON ビョン
BYON ビョン
VANITAS
HEY, VANITAS!

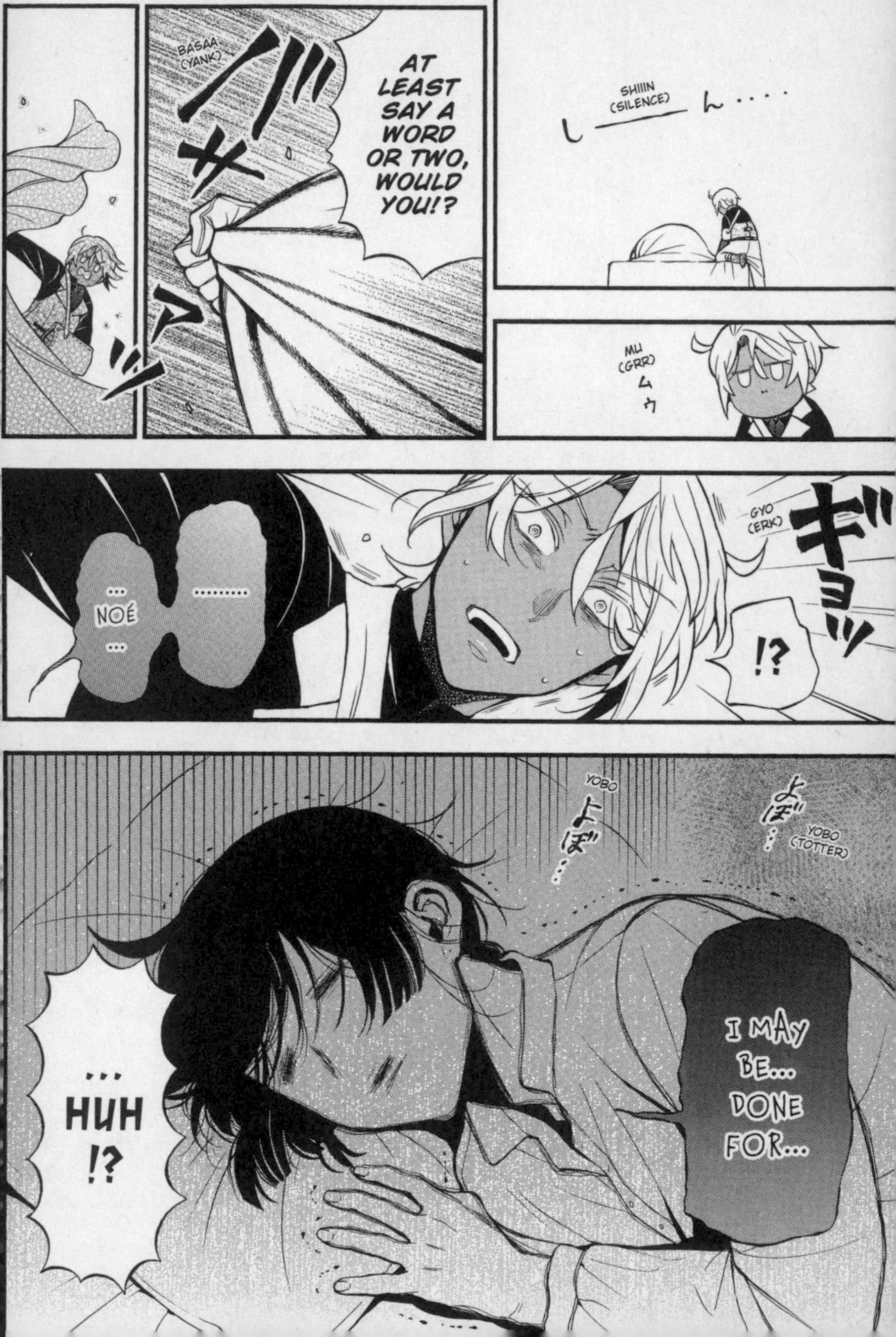
SHIIIN (SILENCE)
し――ん・・・・
MU (GRR)
ムウ
AT LEAST SAY A WORD OR TWO, WOULD YOU!?
BASAA (YANK)
バサァッ
GYO (ERK)
ギョッ
!?
....
... NOÉ ...
YOBO (TOTTER)
よぼ・・・
YOBO
よぼ・・・
I MAY BE... DONE FOR...
...HUH!?

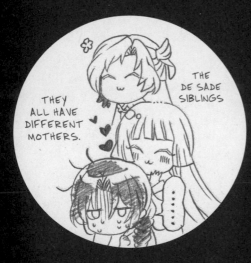

THE DE SADE SIBLINGS
THEY ALL HAVE DIFFERENT MOTHERS.
....

※ THE "MONSIEUR ANTOINE" WHO WAS MENTIONED IN PASSING IN VOLUME 5 IS NOT VERONICA AND DOMI'S OLDER BROTHER.

Les Mémoires de Vanitas

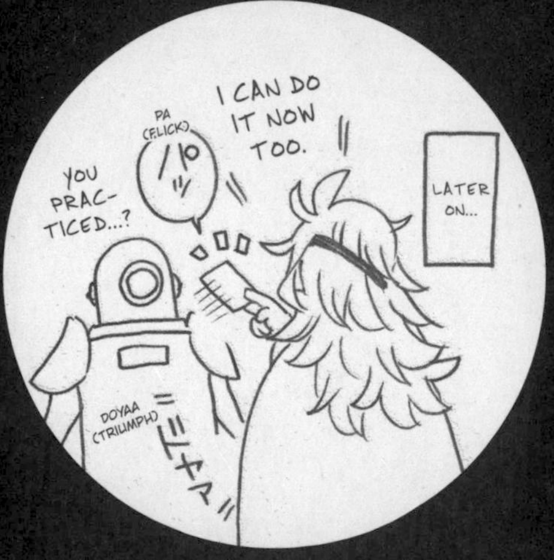
LATER ON...
I CAN DO IT NOW TOO.
PA (FLICK)
YOU PRAC-TICED...?
DOYAA (TRIUMPH)

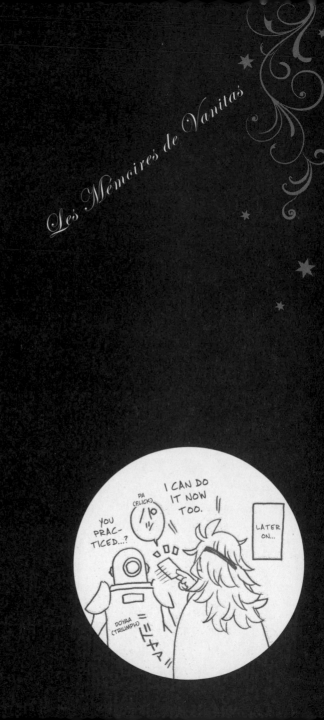

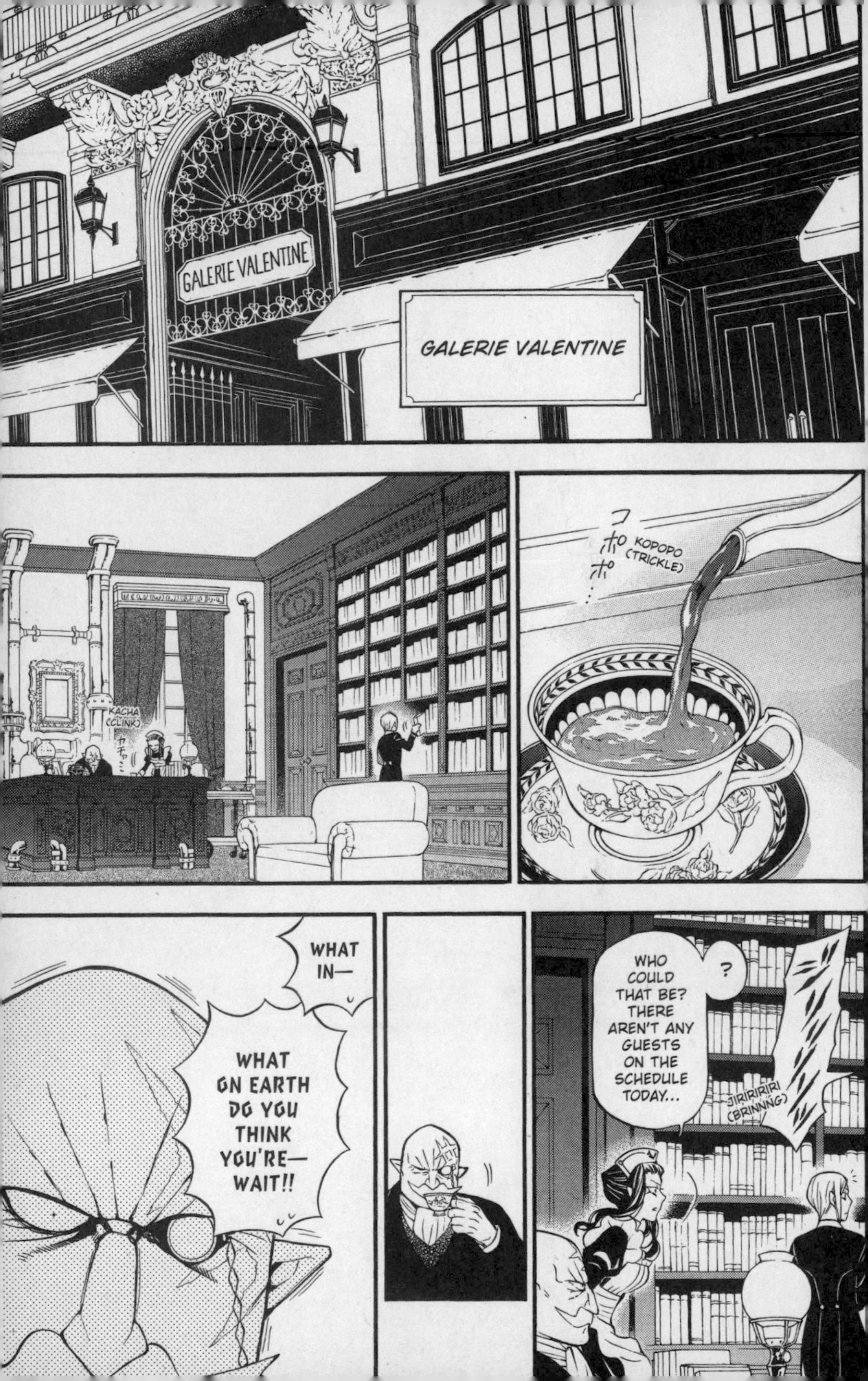
GALERIE VALENTINE
GALERIE VALENTINE
KOPOPO (TRICKLE)
KACHA (CLINK)
?
WHO COULD THAT BE? THERE AREN'T ANY GUESTS ON THE SCHEDULE TODAY...
JIRIRIRIRI (BRINNNG)
WHAT IN—
WHAT ON EARTH DO YOU THINK YOU'RE— WAIT!!

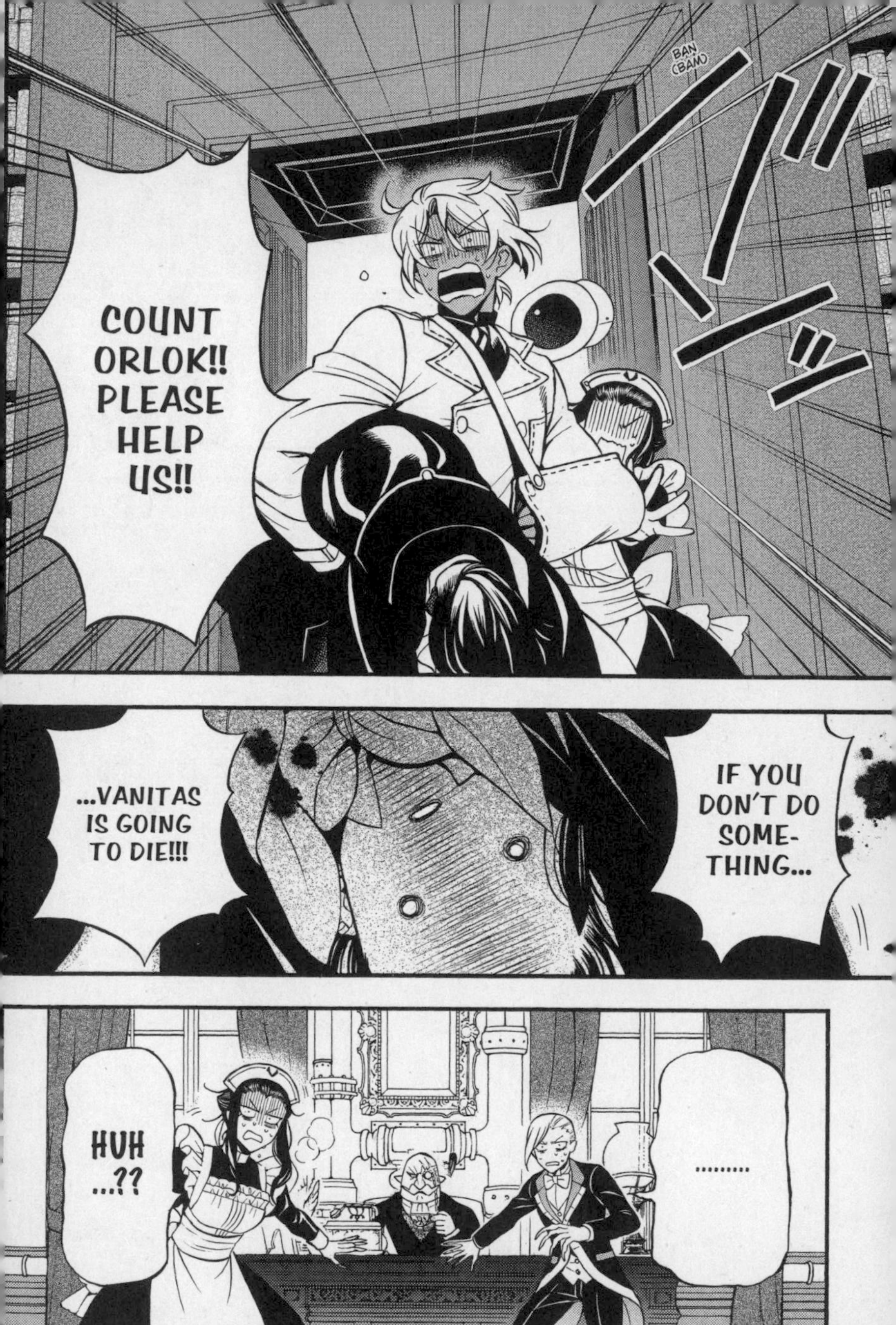
BAN (BAM)
COUNT ORLOK!! PLEASE HELP US!!
IF YOU DON'T DO SOME-THING...
...VANITAS IS GOING TO DIE!!!
....
HUH ...??

MÉMOIRE 44

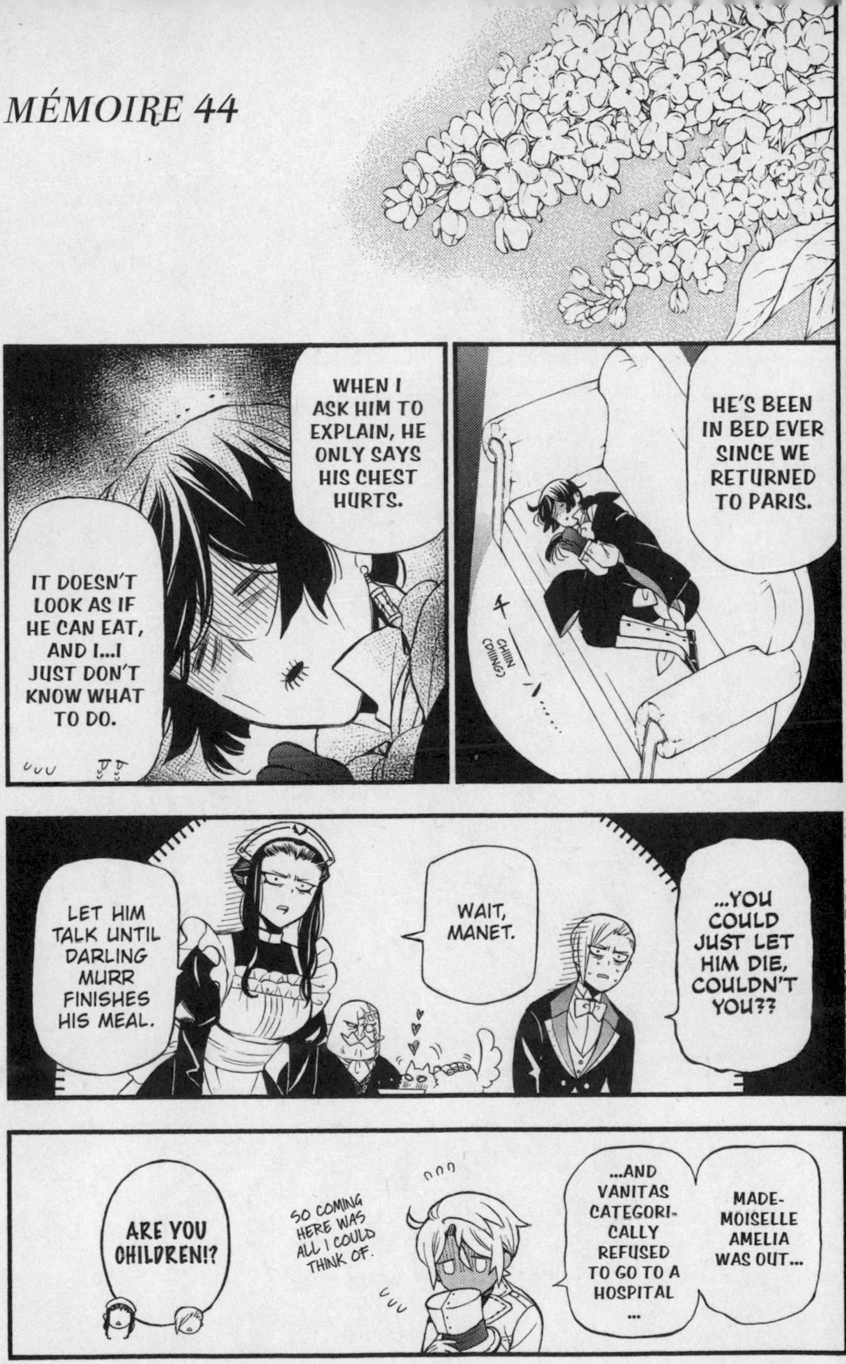
HE'S BEEN IN BED EVER SINCE WE RETURNED TO PARIS.
CHIIN (CHING)
WHEN I ASK HIM TO EXPLAIN, HE ONLY SAYS HIS CHEST HURTS.
IT DOESN'T LOOK AS IF HE CAN EAT, AND I...I JUST DON'T KNOW WHAT TO DO.
...YOU COULD JUST LET HIM DIE, COULDN'T YOU??
WAIT, MANET.
LET HIM TALK UNTIL DARLING MURR FINISHES HIS MEAL.
MADE-MOISELLE AMELIA WAS OUT...
...AND VANITAS CATEGORI-CALLY REFUSED TO GO TO A HOSPITAL ...
SO COMING HERE WAS ALL I COULD THINK OF.
ARE YOU CHILDREN!?

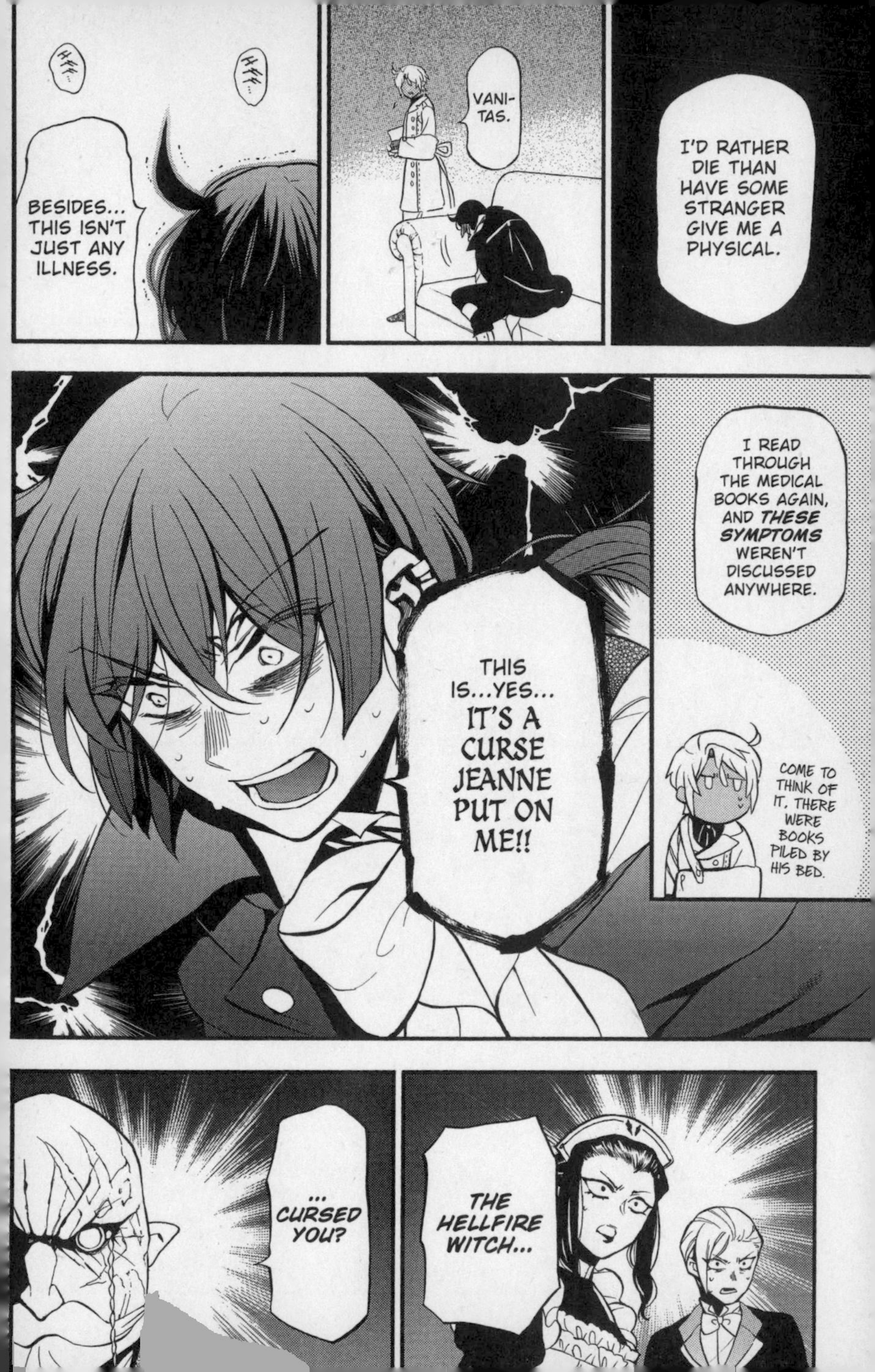
I'D RATHER DIE THAN HAVE SOME STRANGER GIVE ME A PHYSICAL.
VANITAS.
BESIDES... THIS ISN'T JUST ANY ILLNESS.
I READ THROUGH THE MEDICAL BOOKS AGAIN, AND *THESE SYMPTOMS* WEREN'T DISCUSSED ANYWHERE.
COME TO THINK OF IT, THERE WERE BOOKS PILED BY HIS BED.
THIS IS...YES... **IT'S A CURSE JEANNE PUT ON ME!!**
THE HELLFIRE WITCH...
...CURSED YOU?

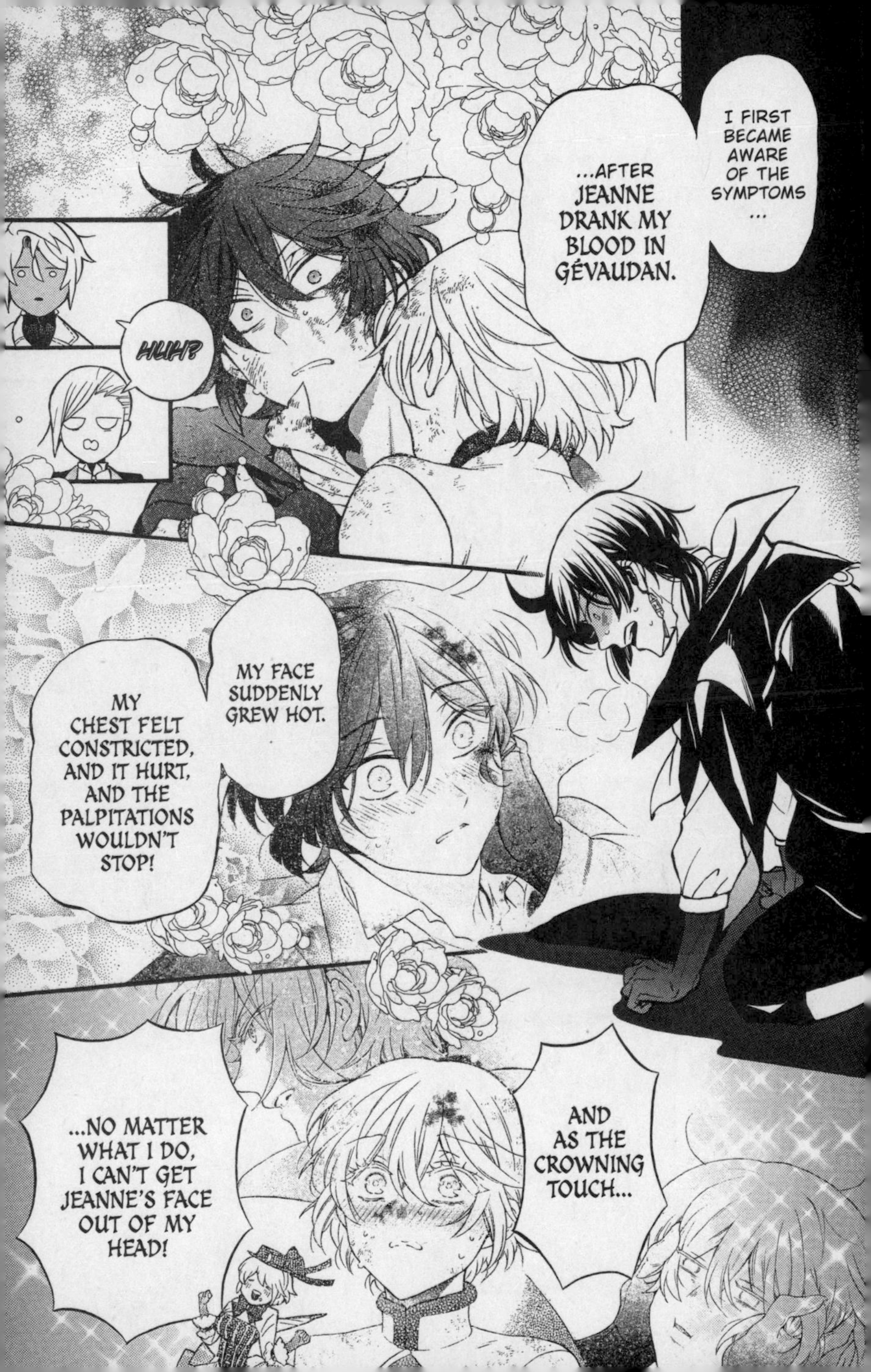
I FIRST BECAME AWARE OF THE SYMPTOMS ...
...AFTER JEANNE DRANK MY BLOOD IN GÉVAUDAN.
HUH?
MY FACE SUDDENLY GREW HOT.
MY CHEST FELT CONSTRICTED, AND IT HURT, AND THE PALPITATIONS WOULDN'T STOP!
AND AS THE CROWNING TOUCH...
...NO MATTER WHAT I DO, I CAN'T GET JEANNE'S FACE OUT OF MY HEAD!

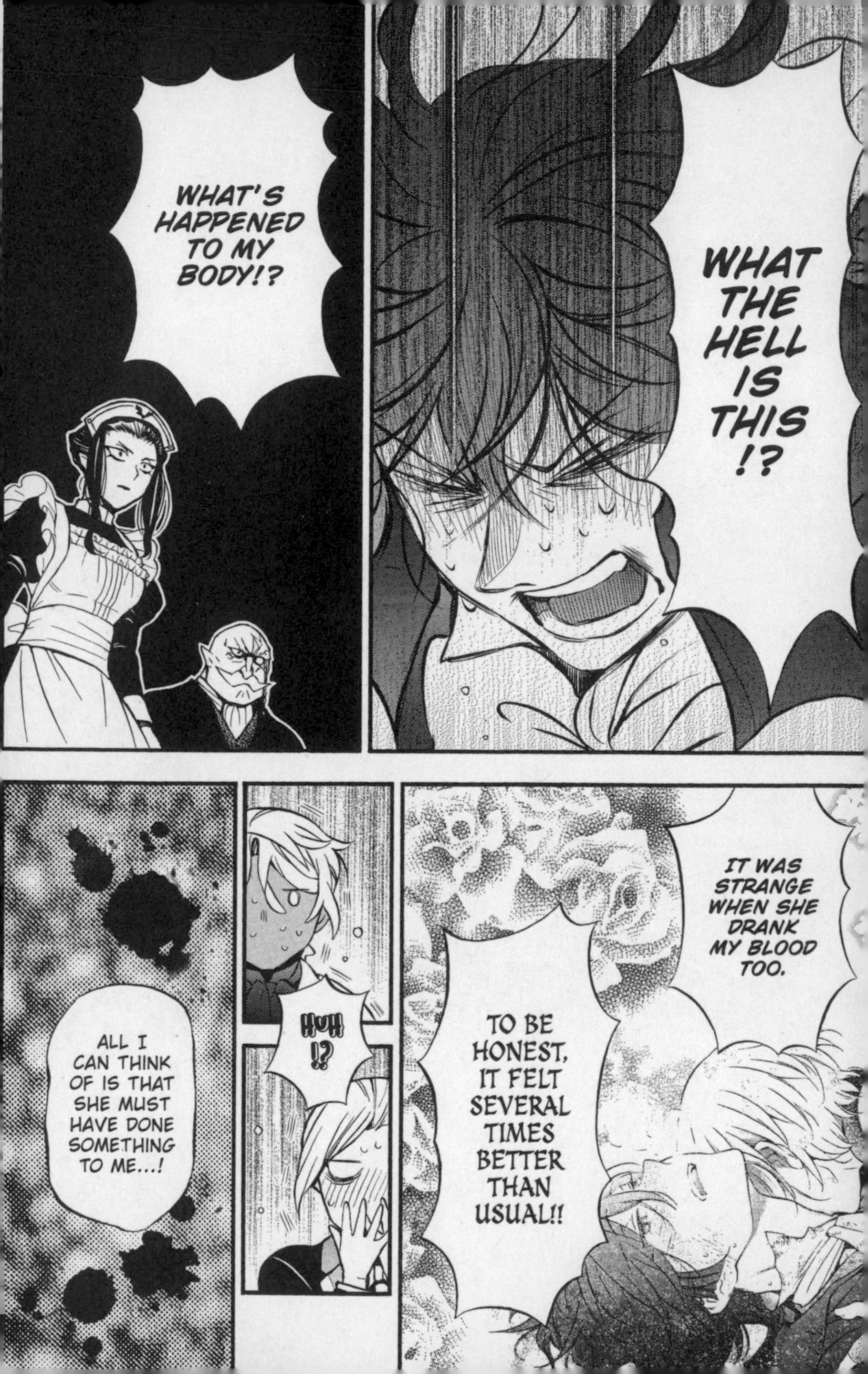
WHAT THE HELL IS THIS!?
WHAT'S HAPPENED TO MY BODY!?
IT WAS STRANGE WHEN SHE DRANK MY BLOOD TOO.
TO BE HONEST, IT FELT SEVERAL TIMES BETTER THAN USUAL!!
HUH!?
ALL I CAN THINK OF IS THAT SHE MUST HAVE DONE SOMETHING TO ME...!

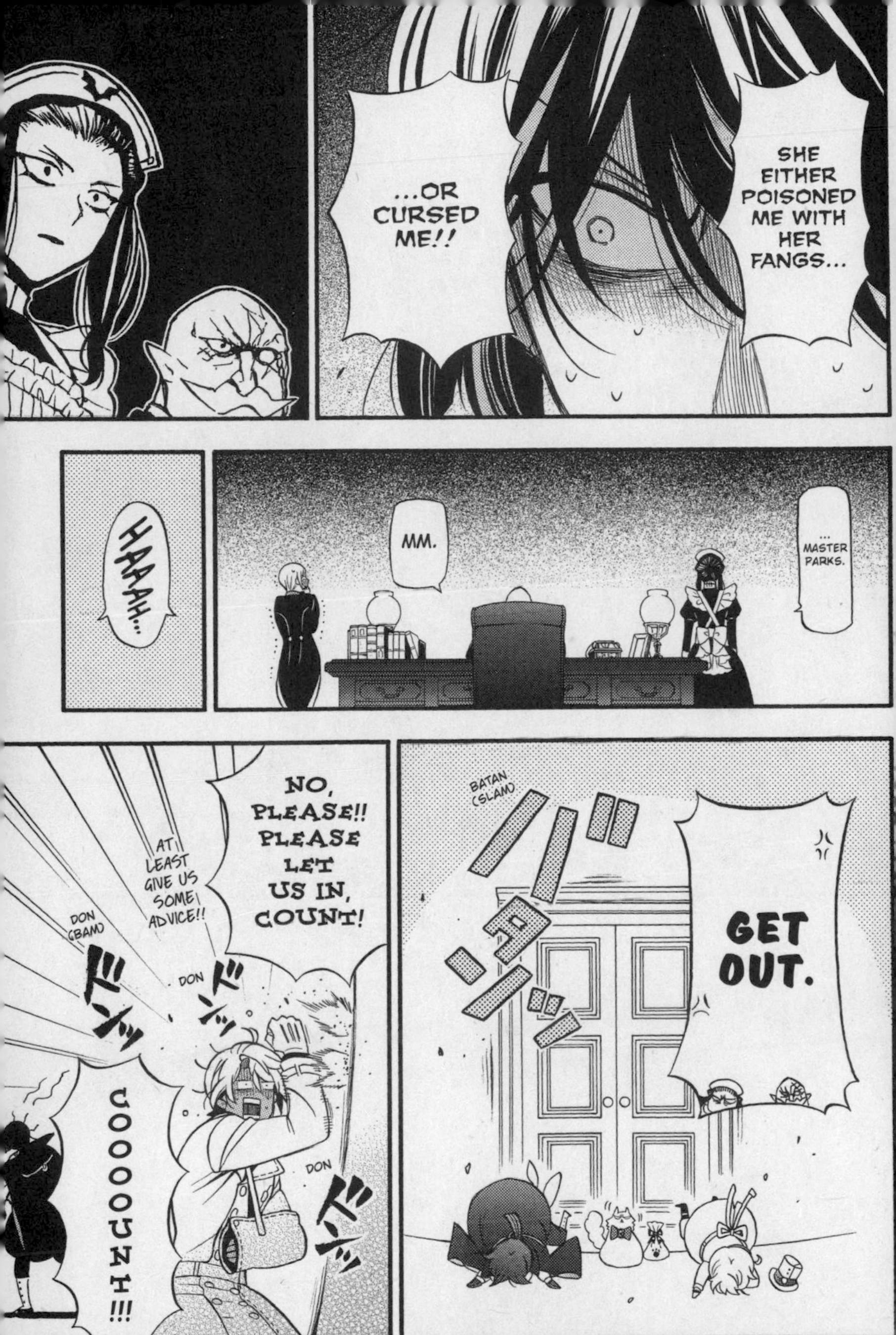
SHE EITHER POISONED ME WITH HER FANGS...
...OR CURSED ME!!
... MASTER PARKS.
MM.
HAAAAH...
BATAN (SLAM)
GET OUT.
NO, PLEASE!! PLEASE LET US IN, COUNT!
AT LEAST GIVE US SOME ADVICE!!
DON (BAM)
DON
DON
UOOOOOUNH!!!

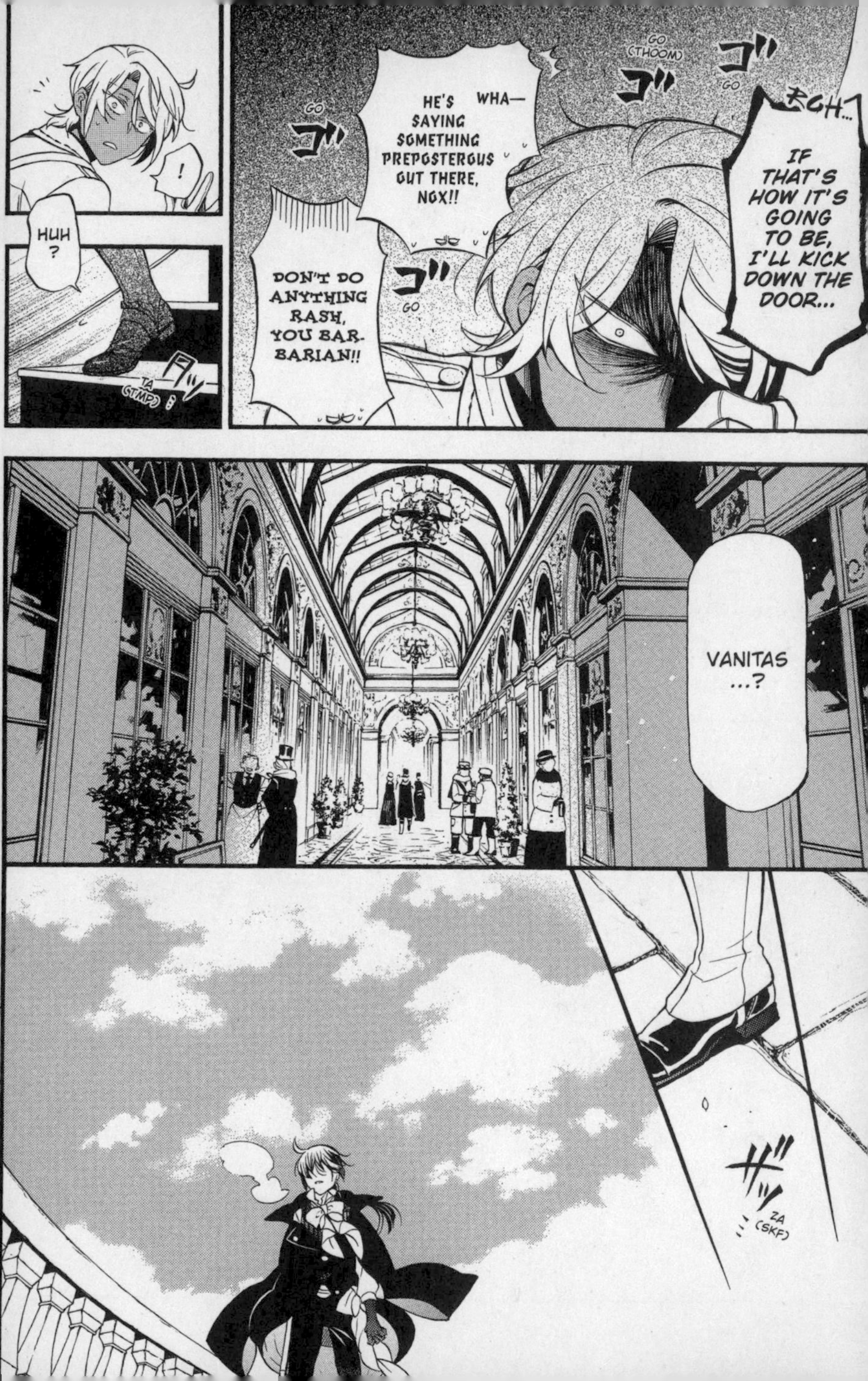
GO (THOOM)
GO
RGH...
IF THAT'S HOW IT'S GOING TO BE, I'LL KICK DOWN THE DOOR...
WHA—
HE'S SAYING SOMETHING PREPOSTEROUS OUT THERE, NOX!!
GO
DON'T DO ANYTHING RASH, YOU BAR-BARIAN!!
GO
!
HUH ?
TA (TMP)
VANITAS ...?
ZA (SKF)

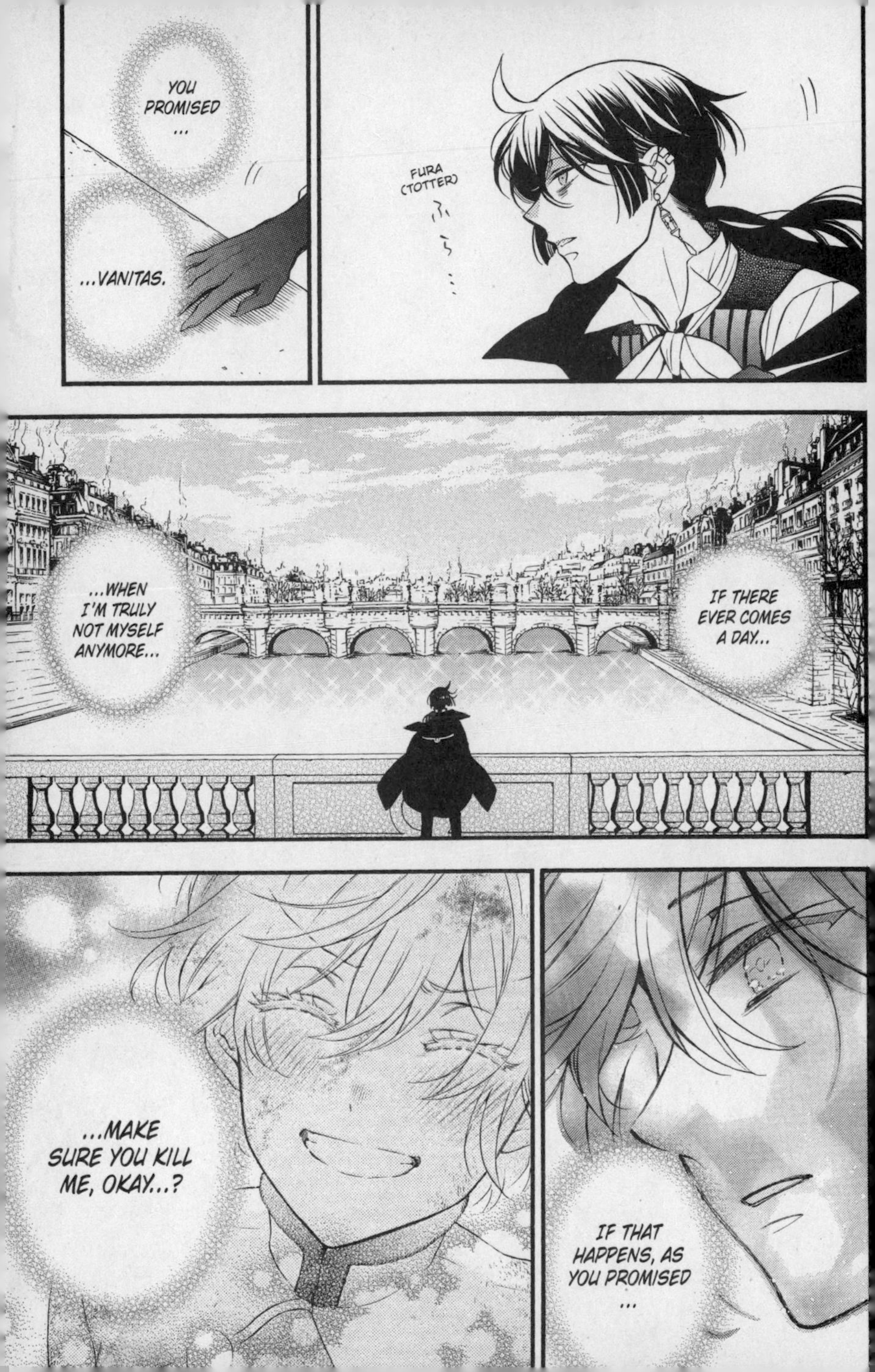
FURA (TOTTER)
ふら…
YOU PROMISED …
…VANITAS.
IF THERE EVER COMES A DAY…
…WHEN I'M TRULY NOT MYSELF ANYMORE…
IF THAT HAPPENS, AS YOU PROMISED …
…MAKE SURE YOU KILL ME, OKAY…?

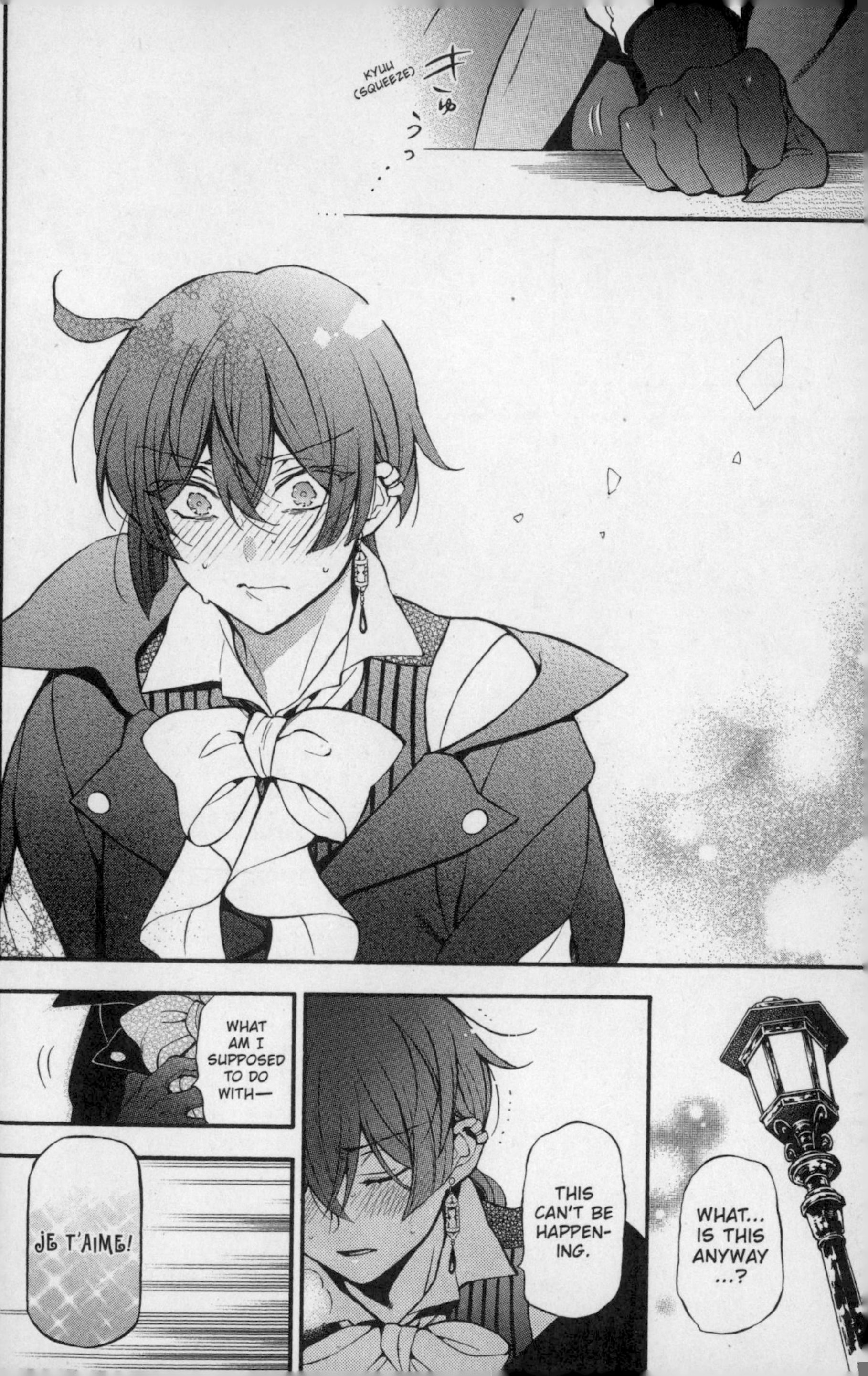
KYUU (SQUEEZE)
WHAT... IS THIS ANYWAY ...?
THIS CAN'T BE HAPPEN- ING.
WHAT AM I SUPPOSED TO DO WITH—
JE T'AIME!

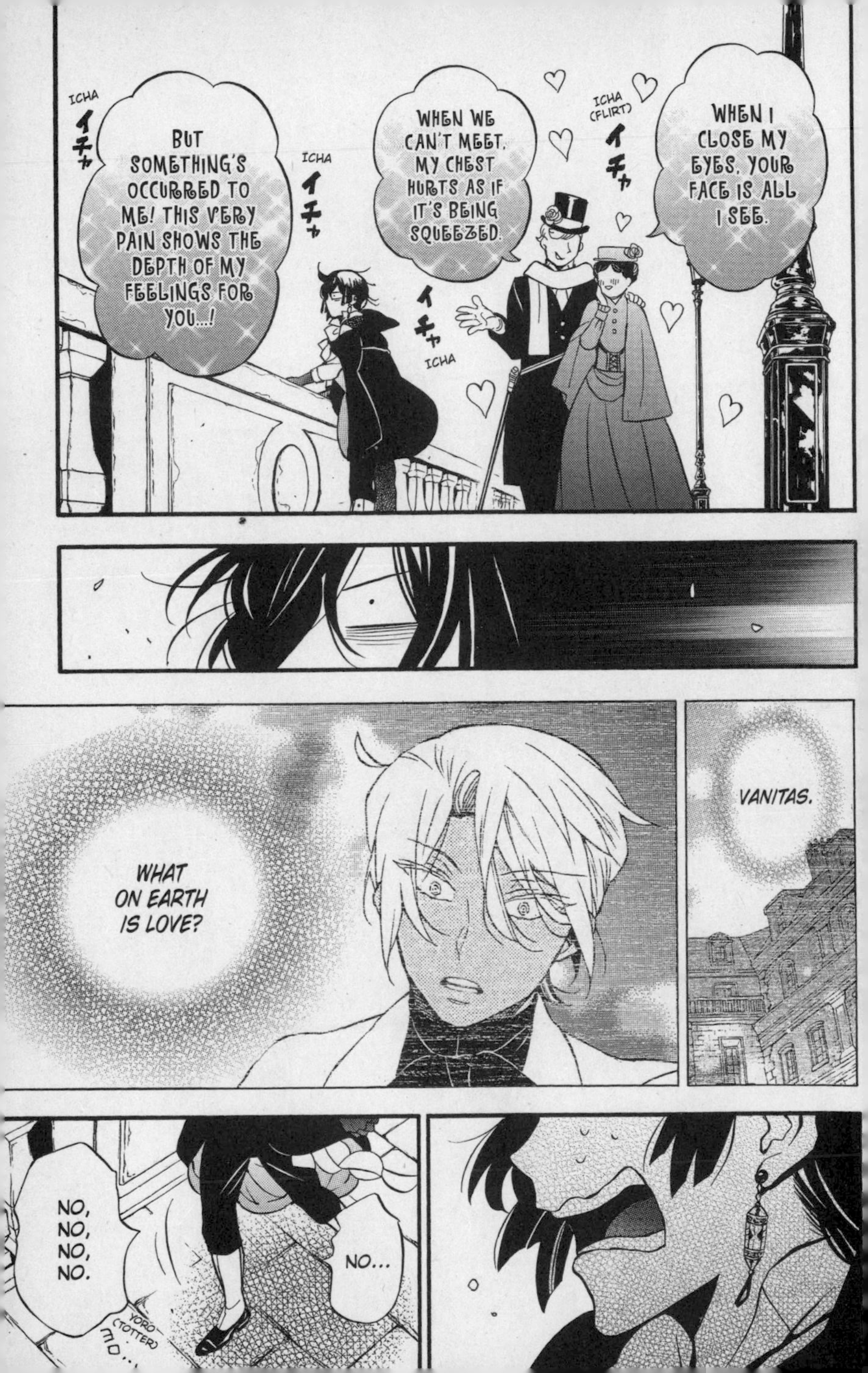
WHEN I CLOSE MY EYES, YOUR FACE IS ALL I SEE.
ICHA (FLIRT) イチャ
WHEN WE CAN'T MEET, MY CHEST HURTS AS IF IT'S BEING SQUEEZED.
イチャ ICHA
ICHA イチャ
ICHA イチャ
BUT SOMETHING'S OCCURRED TO ME! THIS VERY PAIN SHOWS THE DEPTH OF MY FEELINGS FOR YOU...!
VANITAS.
WHAT ON EARTH IS LOVE?
NO...
NO, NO, NO, NO.
YORO (TOTTER) ヨロ...

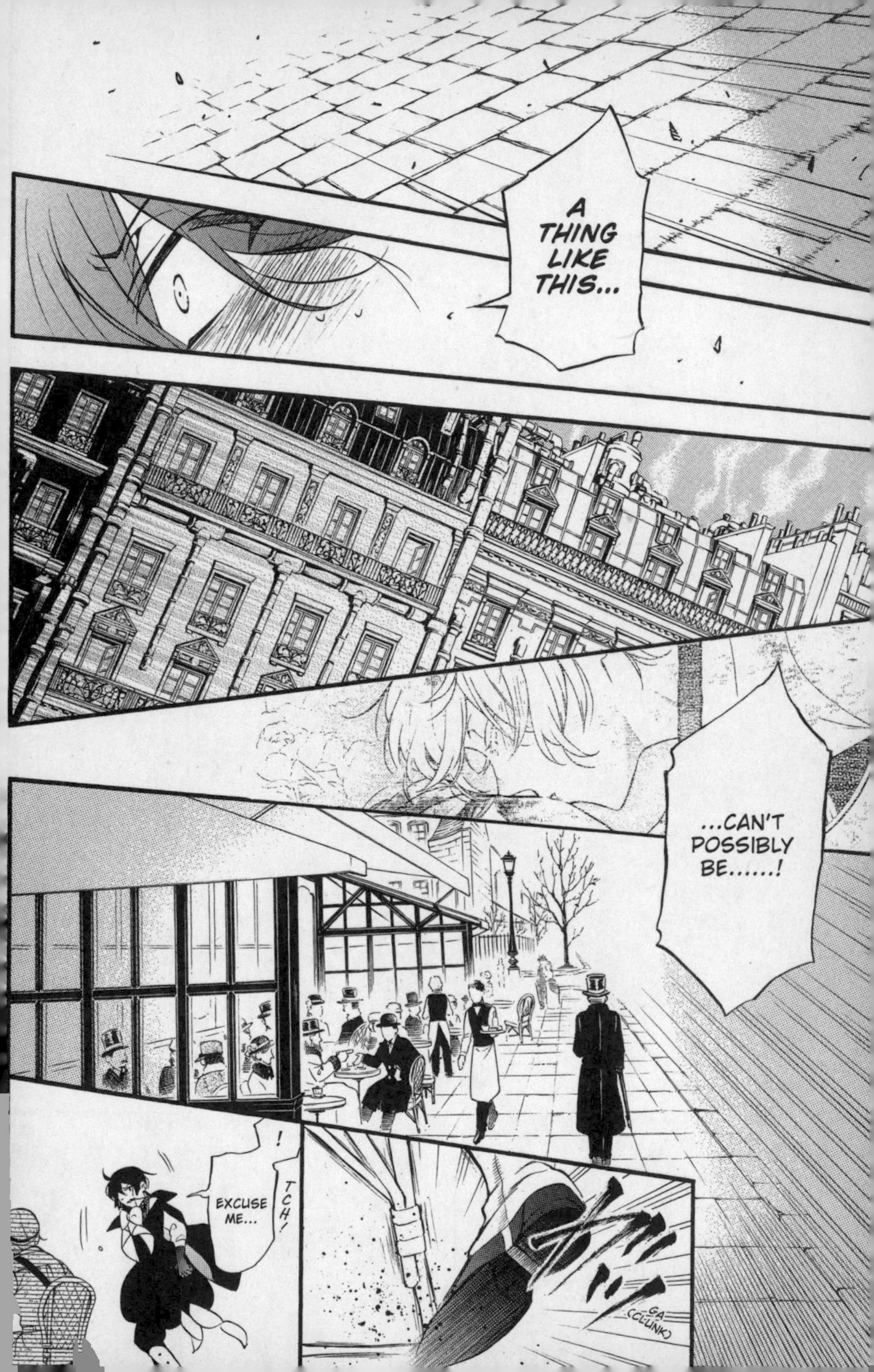
A THING LIKE THIS...
...CAN'T POSSIBLY BE......!
GA (CLUNK)
!
TCH!
EXCUSE ME...

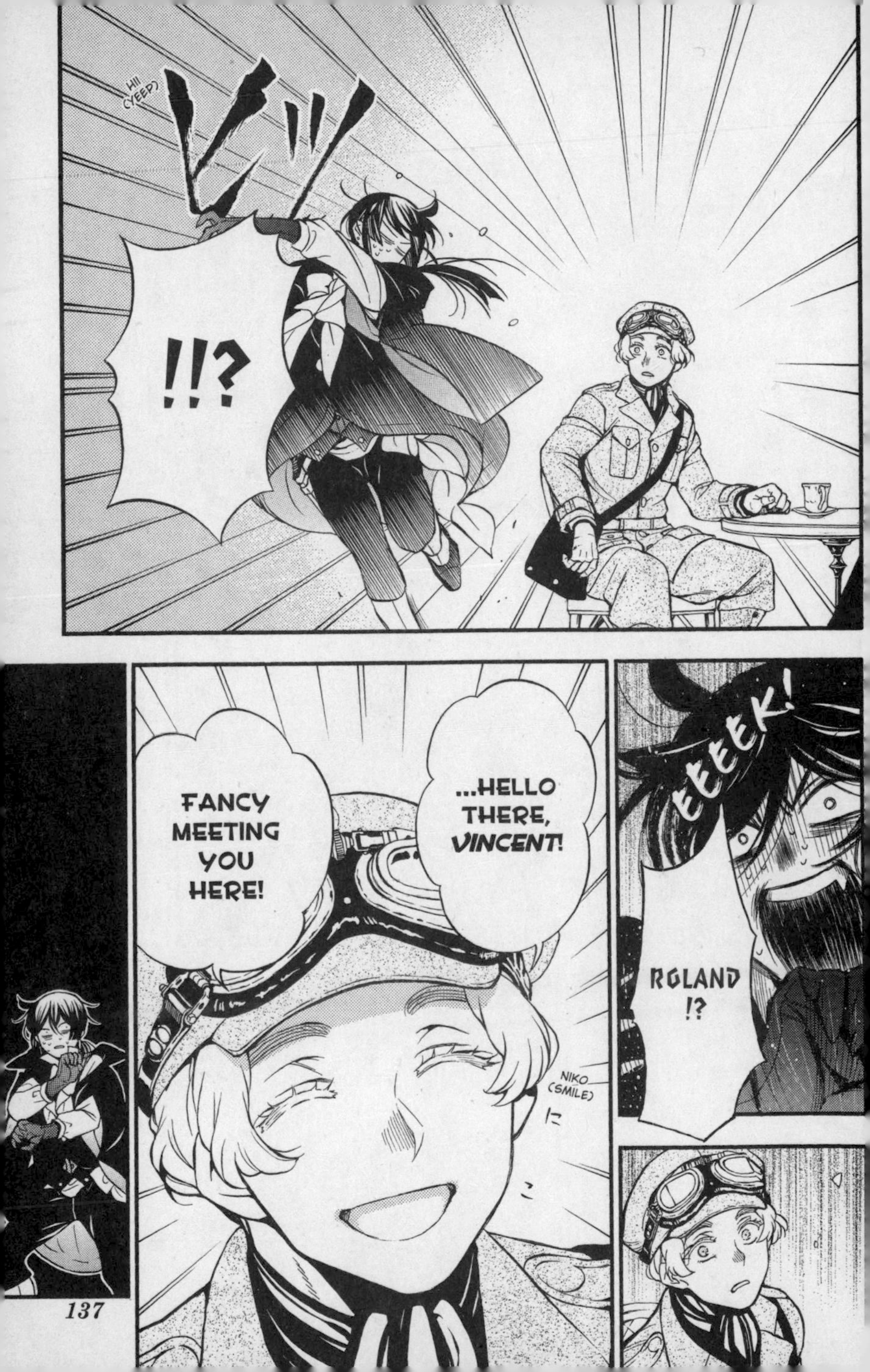
HII (YEEP)
!!?
EEEEK!
ROLAND !?
...HELLO THERE, VINCENT!
FANCY MEETING YOU HERE!
NIKO (SMILE)

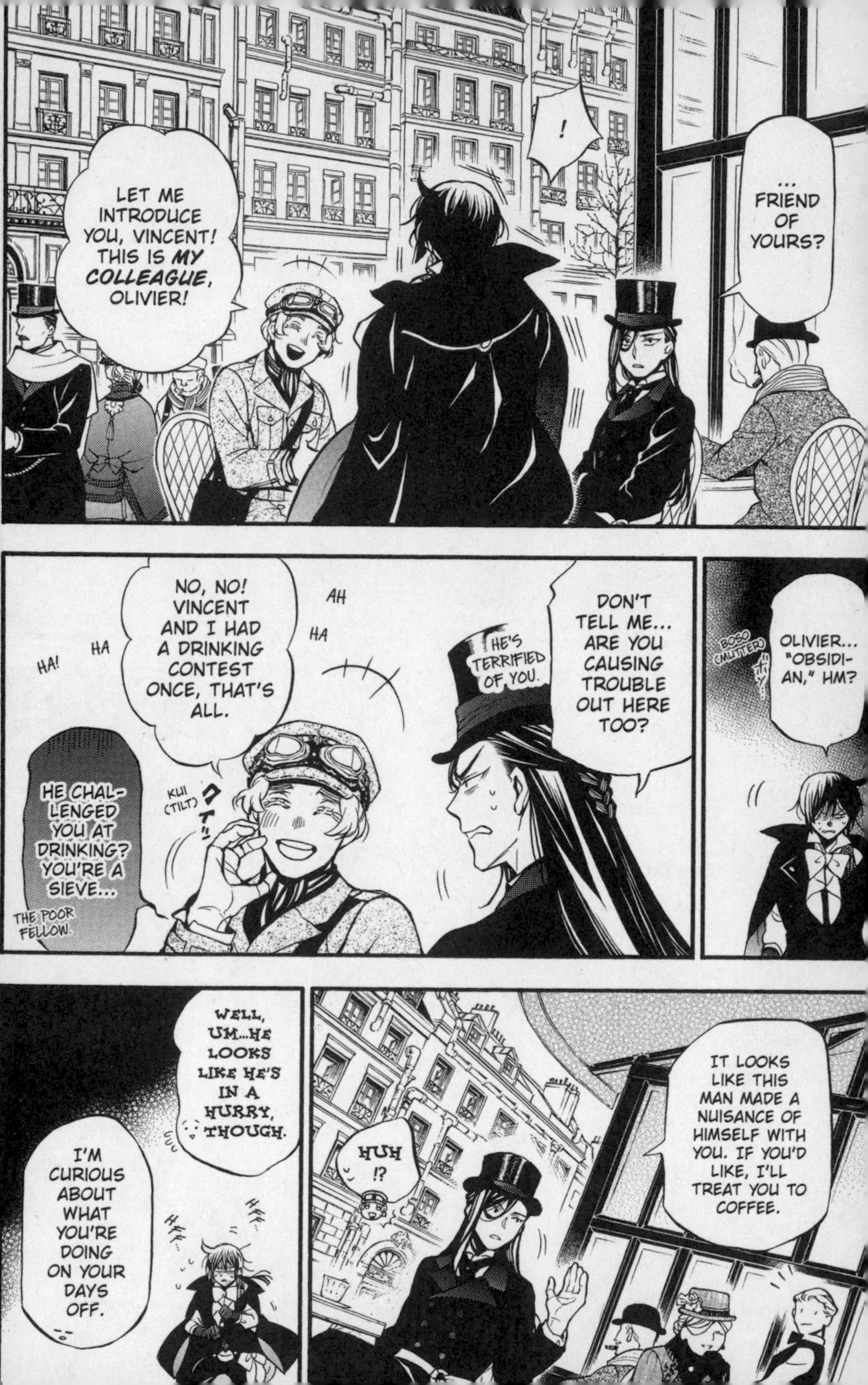
... FRIEND OF YOURS?
!
LET ME INTRODUCE YOU, VINCENT! THIS IS *MY COLLEAGUE*, OLIVIER!
BOSO (MUTTER)
OLIVIER... "OBSIDIAN," HM?
DON'T TELL ME... ARE YOU CAUSING TROUBLE OUT HERE TOO?
HE'S TERRIFIED OF YOU.
AH HA
HA HA!
NO, NO! VINCENT AND I HAD A DRINKING CONTEST ONCE, THAT'S ALL.
KUI (TILT)
HE CHAL-LENGED YOU AT DRINKING? YOU'RE A SIEVE...
THE POOR FELLOW.
IT LOOKS LIKE THIS MAN MADE A NUISANCE OF HIMSELF WITH YOU. IF YOU'D LIKE, I'LL TREAT YOU TO COFFEE.
HUH !?
WELL, UM...HE LOOKS LIKE HE'S IN A HURRY, THOUGH.
I'M CURIOUS ABOUT WHAT YOU'RE DOING ON YOUR DAYS OFF.

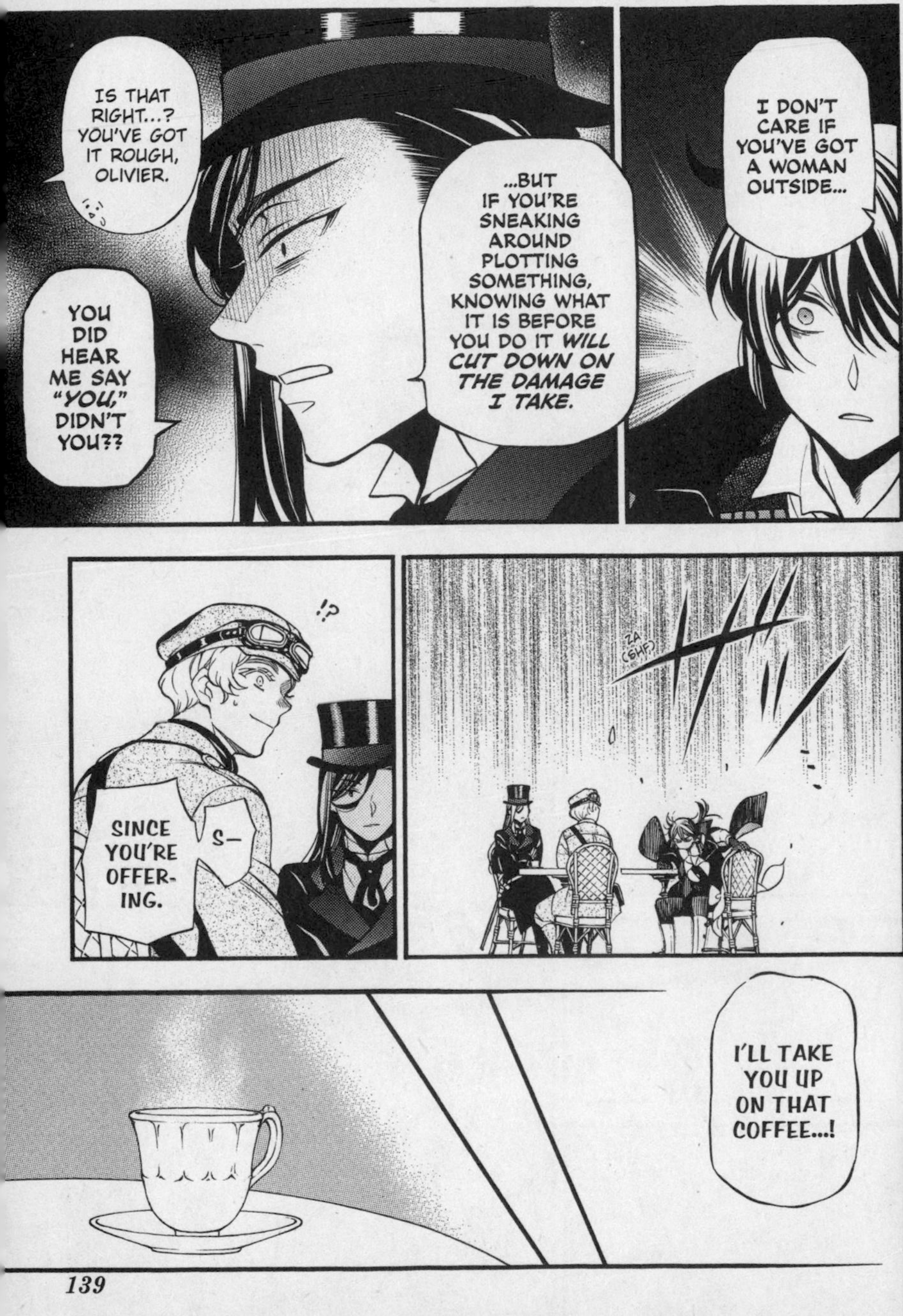
I DON'T CARE IF YOU'VE GOT A WOMAN OUTSIDE...
...BUT IF YOU'RE SNEAKING AROUND PLOTTING SOMETHING, KNOWING WHAT IT IS BEFORE YOU DO IT *WILL CUT DOWN ON THE DAMAGE I TAKE.*
IS THAT RIGHT...? YOU'VE GOT IT ROUGH, OLIVIER.
YOU DID HEAR ME SAY "*YOU*," DIDN'T YOU??
ZA (SHF)
!?
S—
SINCE YOU'RE OFFER-ING.
I'LL TAKE YOU UP ON THAT COFFEE...!

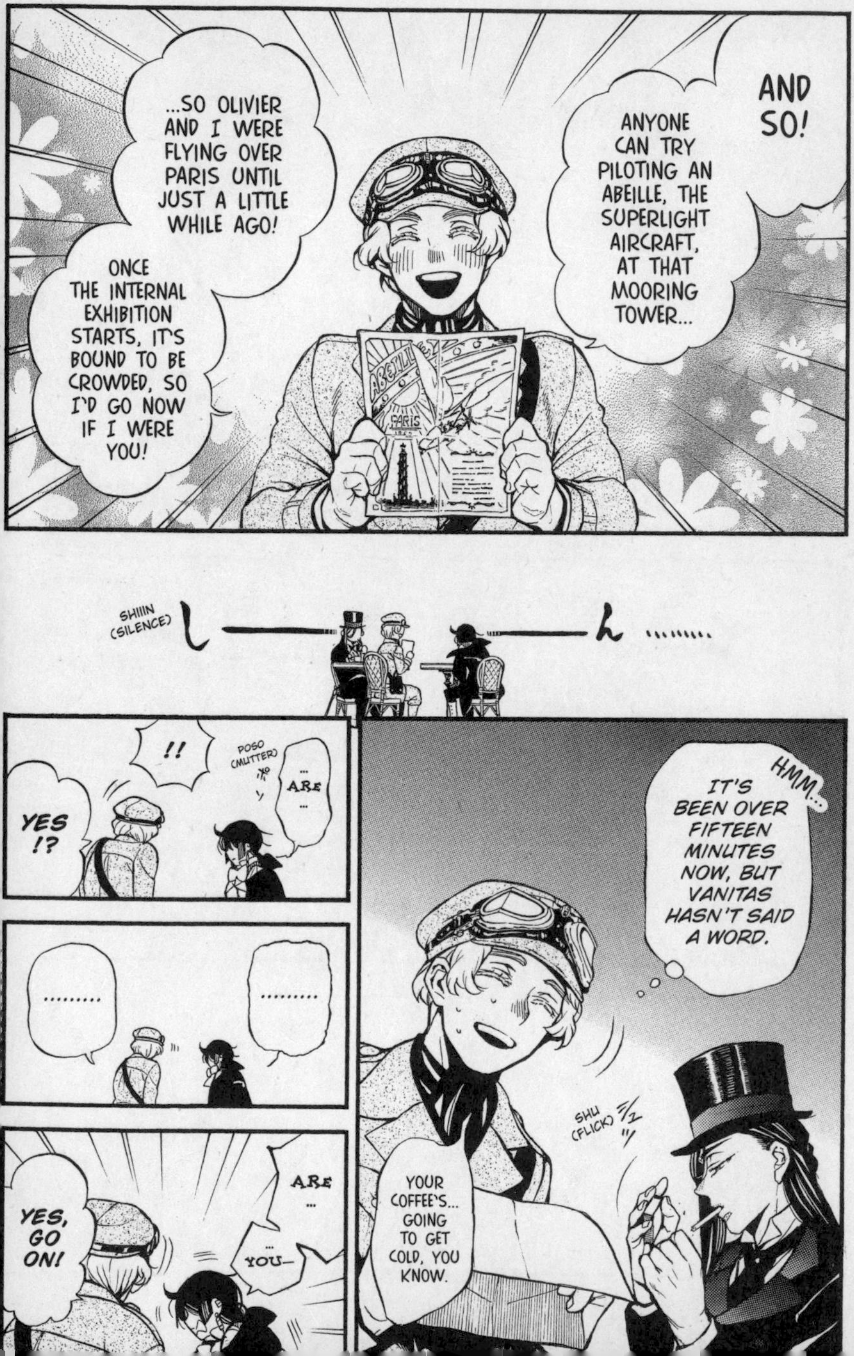
AND SO!
ANYONE CAN TRY PILOTING AN ABEILLE, THE SUPERLIGHT AIRCRAFT, AT THAT MOORING TOWER...
...SO OLIVIER AND I WERE FLYING OVER PARIS UNTIL JUST A LITTLE WHILE AGO!
ONCE THE INTERNAL EXHIBITION STARTS, IT'S BOUND TO BE CROWDED, SO I'D GO NOW IF I WERE YOU!
ABEILLE
PARIS
SHIIIN (SILENCE)
し――ん……
HMM...
IT'S BEEN OVER FIFTEEN MINUTES NOW, BUT VANITAS HASN'T SAID A WORD.
SHU (FLICK)
YOUR COFFEE'S... GOING TO GET COLD, YOU KNOW.
POSO (MUTTER)
...ARE...
!!
YES!?
....
....
ARE...
...YOU—
YES, GO ON!

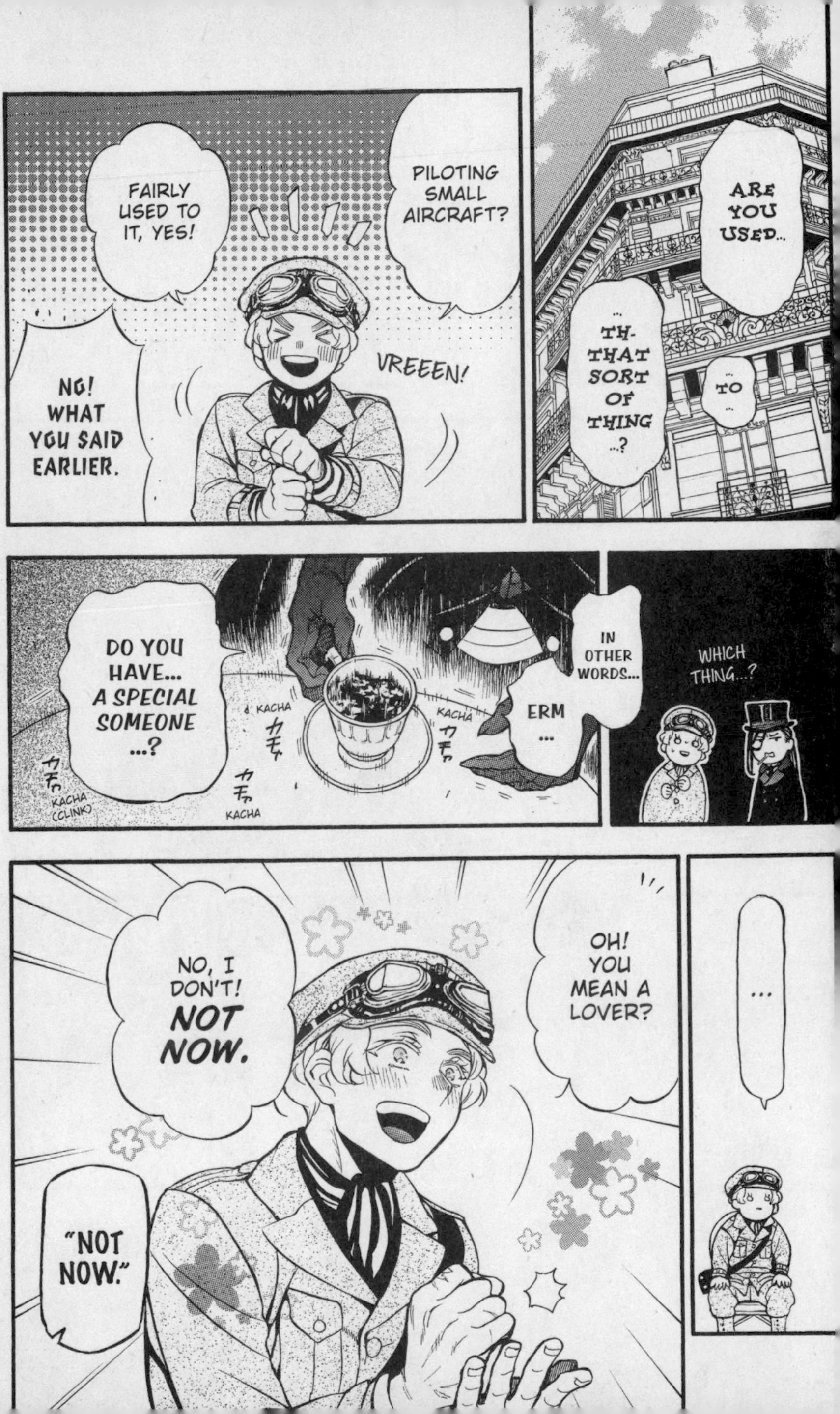
ARE YOU USED...
...TO...
...TH-THAT SORT OF THING...?
PILOTING SMALL AIRCRAFT?
VREEEN!
FAIRLY USED TO IT, YES!
NO! WHAT YOU SAID EARLIER.
WHICH THING...?
IN OTHER WORDS...
ERM...
KACHA
カチャ
KACHA
カチャ
DO YOU HAVE... A SPECIAL SOMEONE ...?
カチャ
KACHA
カチャ
KACHA (CLINK)
...
OH! YOU MEAN A LOVER?
NO, I DON'T! NOT NOW.
"NOT NOW."

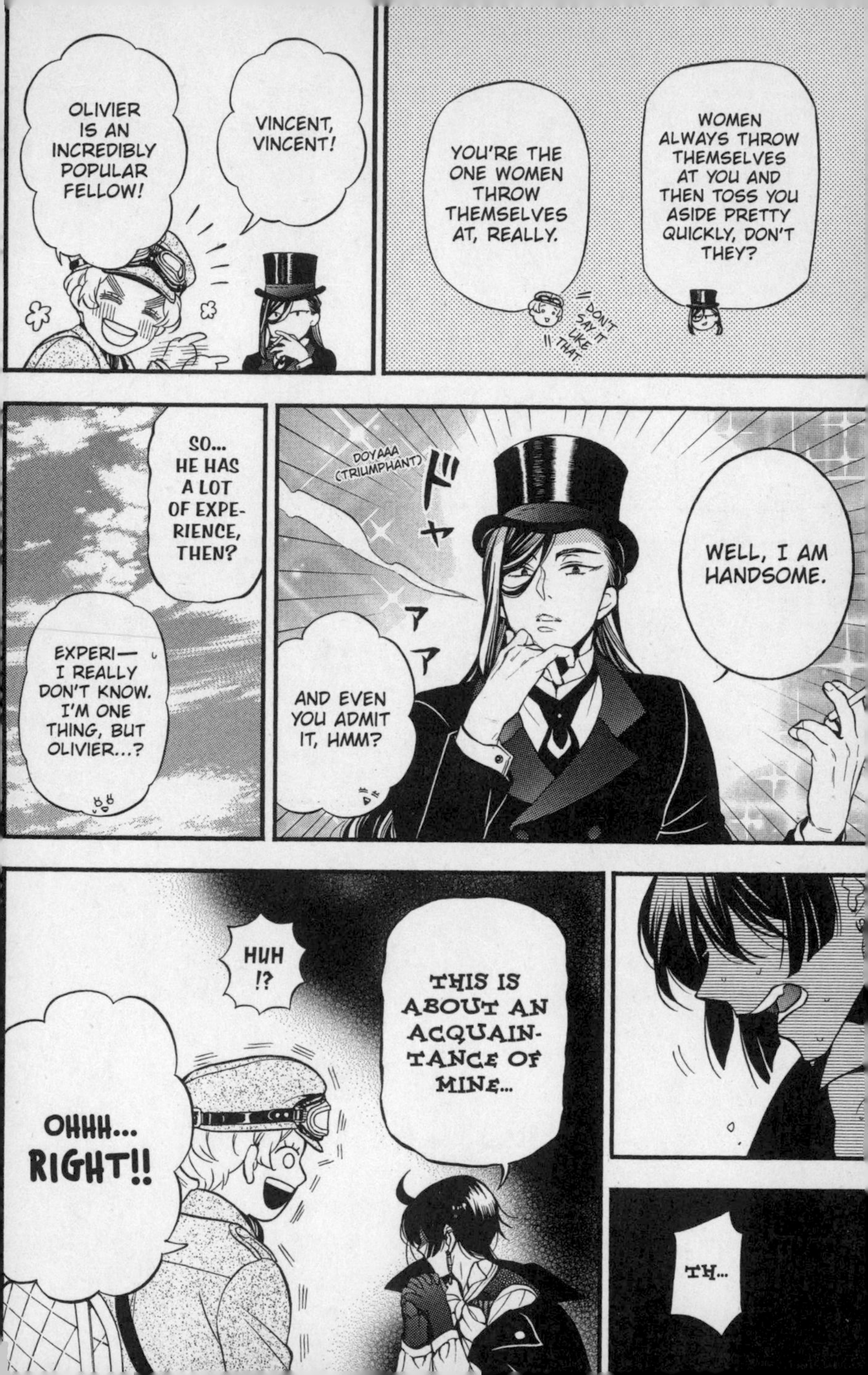
WOMEN ALWAYS THROW THEMSELVES AT YOU AND THEN TOSS YOU ASIDE PRETTY QUICKLY, DON'T THEY?
YOU'RE THE ONE WOMEN THROW THEMSELVES AT, REALLY.
DON'T SAY IT LIKE THAT
VINCENT, VINCENT!
OLIVIER IS AN INCREDIBLY POPULAR FELLOW!
WELL, I AM HANDSOME.
DOYAAA (TRIUMPHANT)
AND EVEN YOU ADMIT IT, HMM?
SO... HE HAS A LOT OF EXPE-RIENCE, THEN?
EXPERI— I REALLY DON'T KNOW. I'M ONE THING, BUT OLIVIER...?
TH...
THIS IS ABOUT AN ACQUAIN-TANCE OF MINE...
HUH !?
OHHH... RIGHT!!

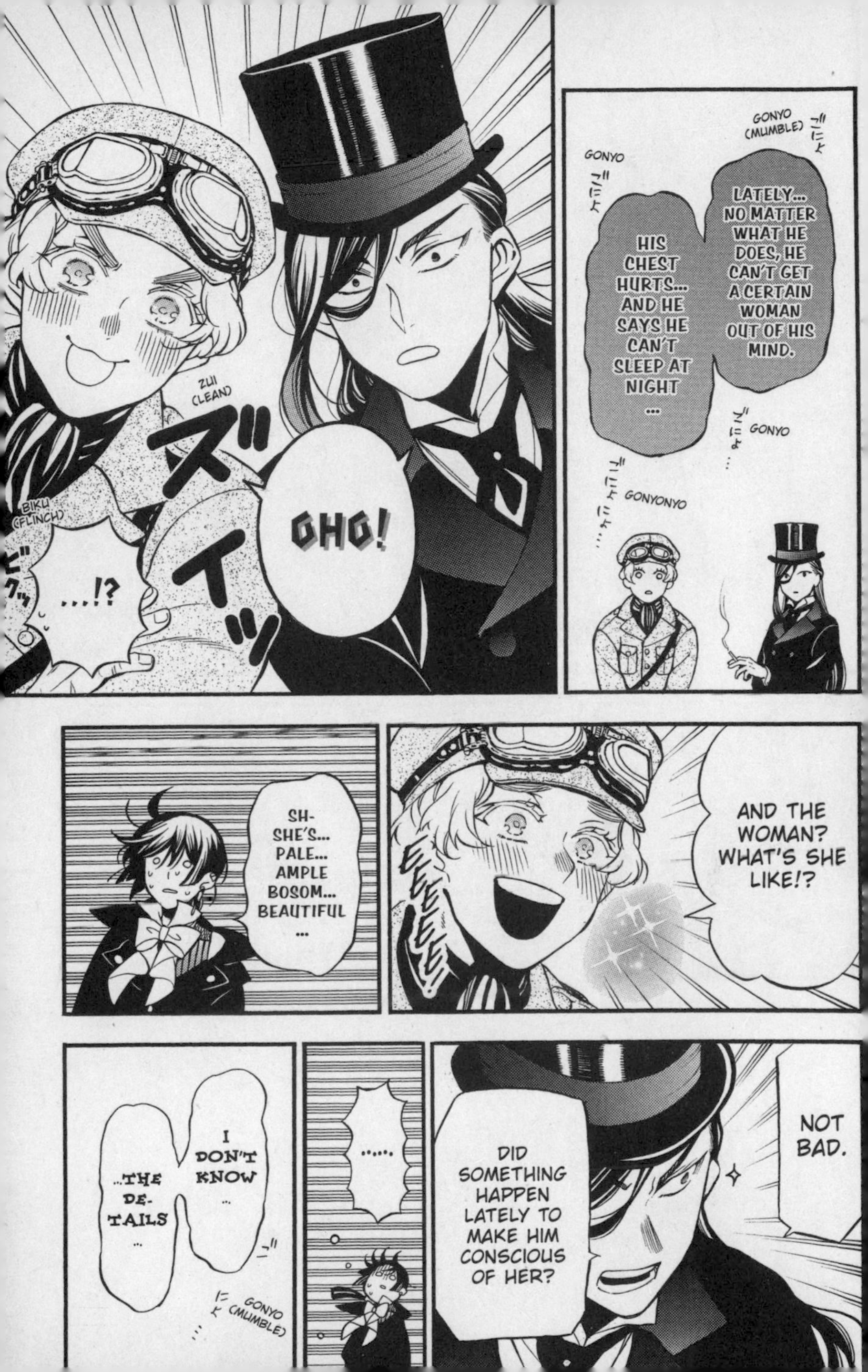
GONYO (MUMBLE)
LATELY... NO MATTER WHAT HE DOES, HE CAN'T GET A CERTAIN WOMAN OUT OF HIS MIND.
GONYO
HIS CHEST HURTS... AND HE SAYS HE CAN'T SLEEP AT NIGHT ...
GONYO
GONYONYO
ZUI (LEAN)
GHG!
BIKU (FLINCH)
...!?
AND THE WOMAN? WHAT'S SHE LIKE!?
SH-SHE'S... PALE... AMPLE BOSOM... BEAUTIFUL ...
NOT BAD.
DID SOMETHING HAPPEN LATELY TO MAKE HIM CONSCIOUS OF HER?
......
I DON'T KNOW ...
...THE DETAILS ...
GONYO (MUMBLE)

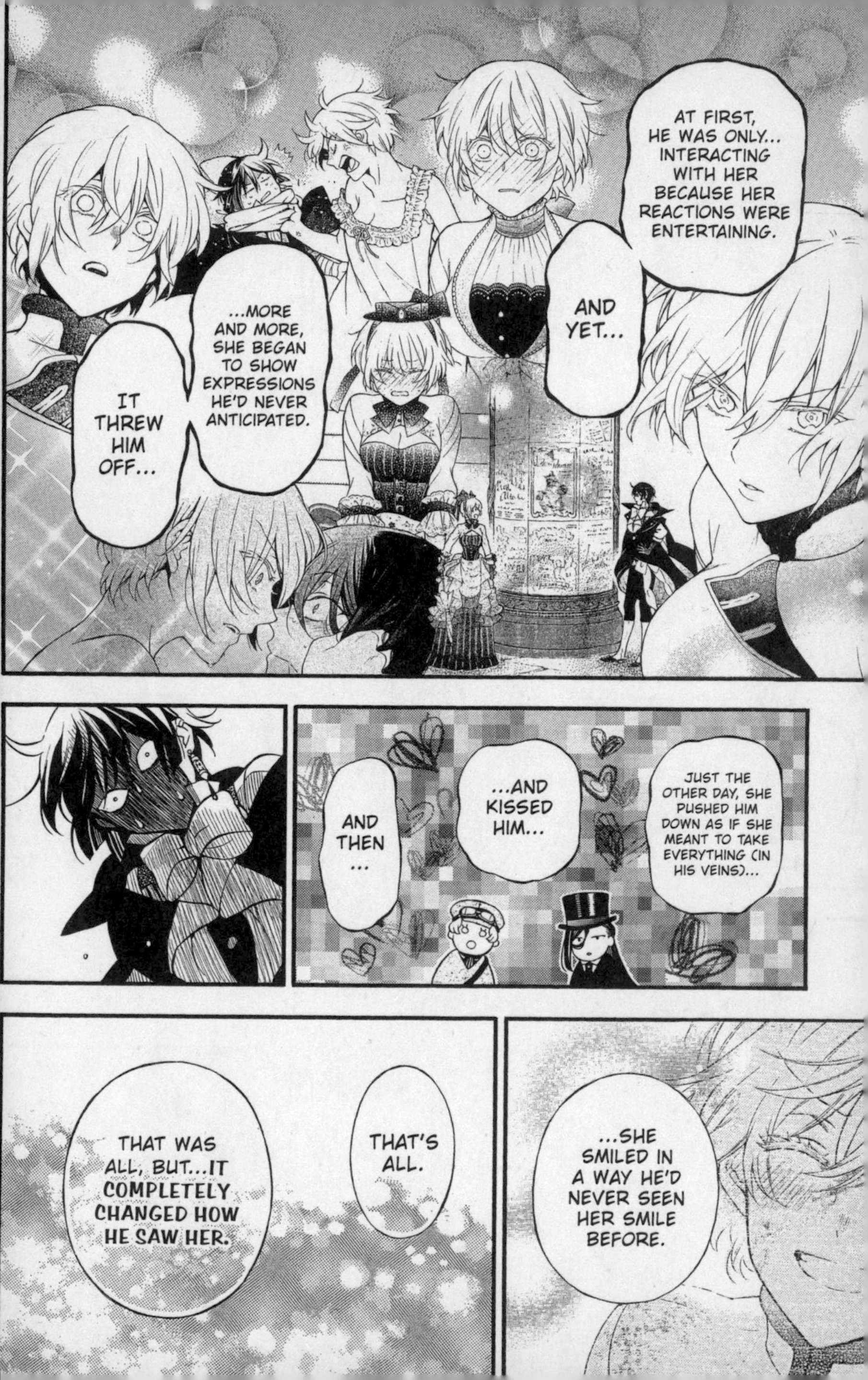
AT FIRST, HE WAS ONLY... INTERACTING WITH HER BECAUSE HER REACTIONS WERE ENTERTAINING.
AND YET...
...MORE AND MORE, SHE BEGAN TO SHOW EXPRESSIONS HE'D NEVER ANTICIPATED.
IT THREW HIM OFF...
JUST THE OTHER DAY, SHE PUSHED HIM DOWN AS IF SHE MEANT TO TAKE EVERYTHING (IN HIS VEINS)...
...AND KISSED HIM...
AND THEN ...
...SHE SMILED IN A WAY HE'D NEVER SEEN HER SMILE BEFORE.
THAT'S ALL.
THAT WAS ALL, BUT...IT COMPLETELY CHANGED HOW HE SAW HER.

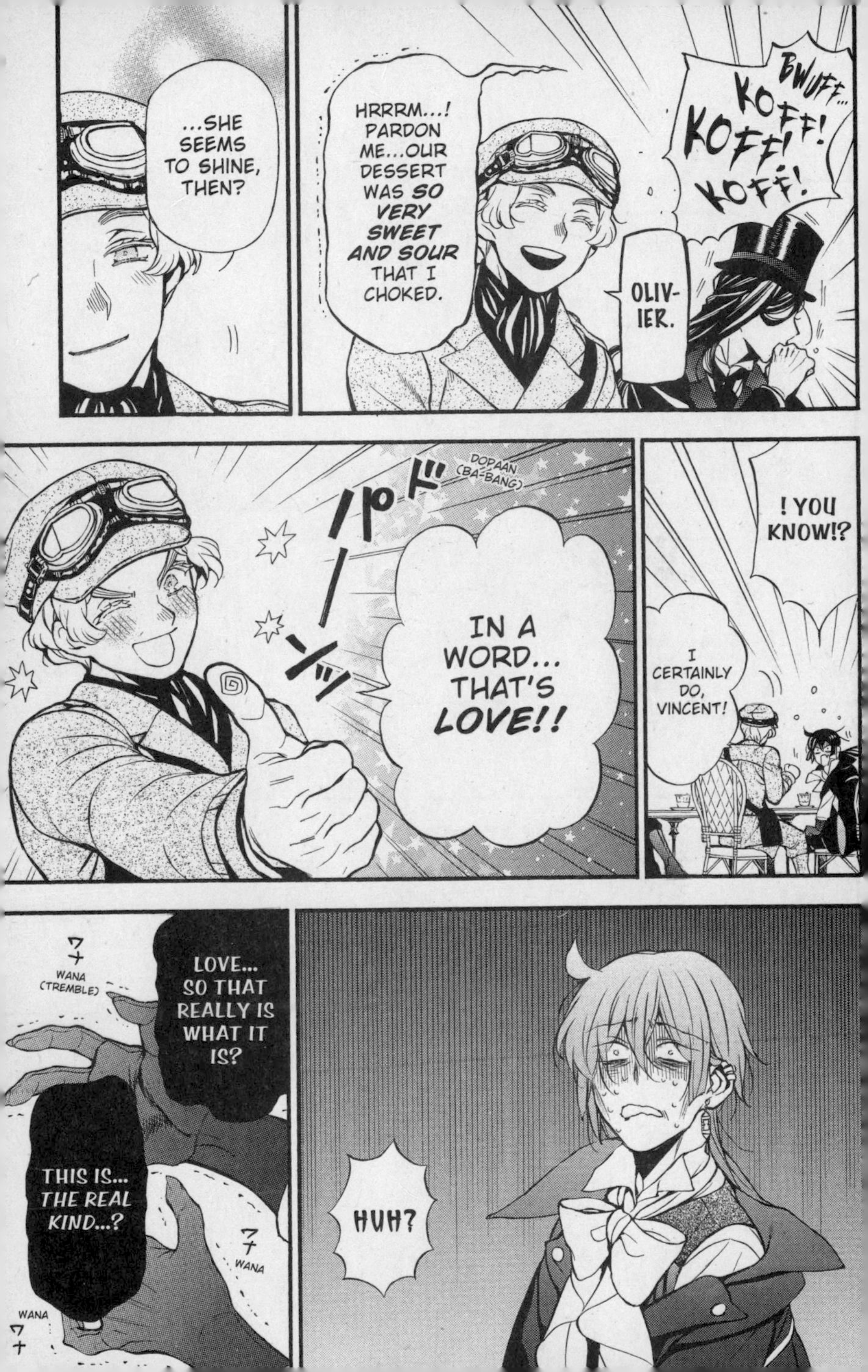
BWUFF...
KOFF! KOFF! KOFF!
OLIV-IER.
HRRRM...! PARDON ME...OUR DESSERT WAS SO VERY SWEET AND SOUR THAT I CHOKED.
...SHE SEEMS TO SHINE, THEN?
! YOU KNOW!?
I CERTAINLY DO, VINCENT!
パドーンッ
DOPAAN (BA-BANG)
IN A WORD... THAT'S LOVE!!
HUH?
ワナ
WANA (TREMBLE)
LOVE... SO THAT REALLY IS WHAT IT IS?
THIS IS... THE REAL KIND...?
ワナ
WANA
WANA
ワナ

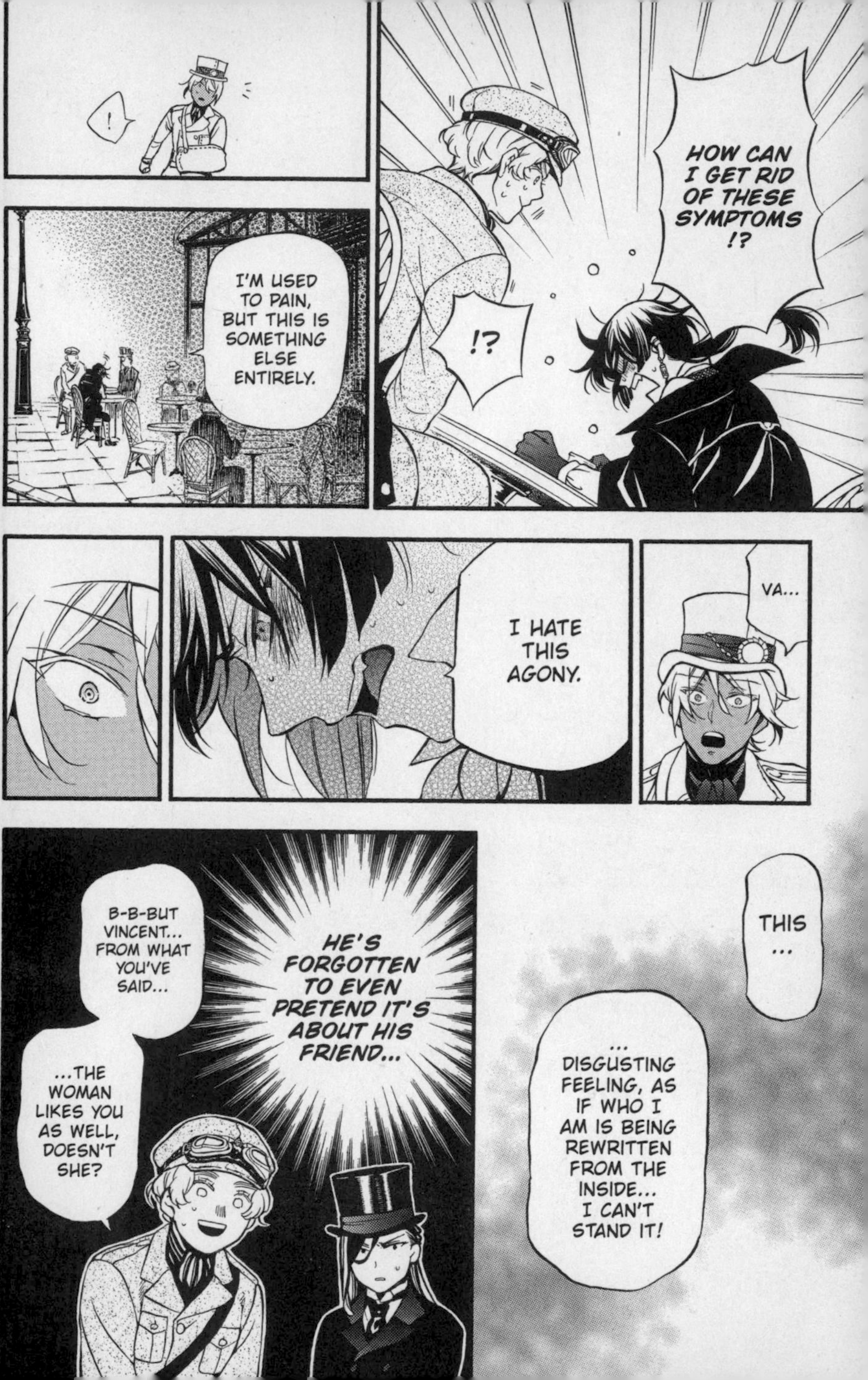
HOW CAN I GET RID OF THESE SYMPTOMS !?
!?
!
I'M USED TO PAIN, BUT THIS IS SOMETHING ELSE ENTIRELY.
VA...
I HATE THIS AGONY.
THIS ...
... DISGUSTING FEELING, AS IF WHO I AM IS BEING REWRITTEN FROM THE INSIDE... I CAN'T STAND IT!
HE'S FORGOTTEN TO EVEN PRETEND IT'S ABOUT HIS FRIEND...
B-B-BUT VINCENT... FROM WHAT YOU'VE SAID...
...THE WOMAN LIKES YOU AS WELL, DOESN'T SHE?

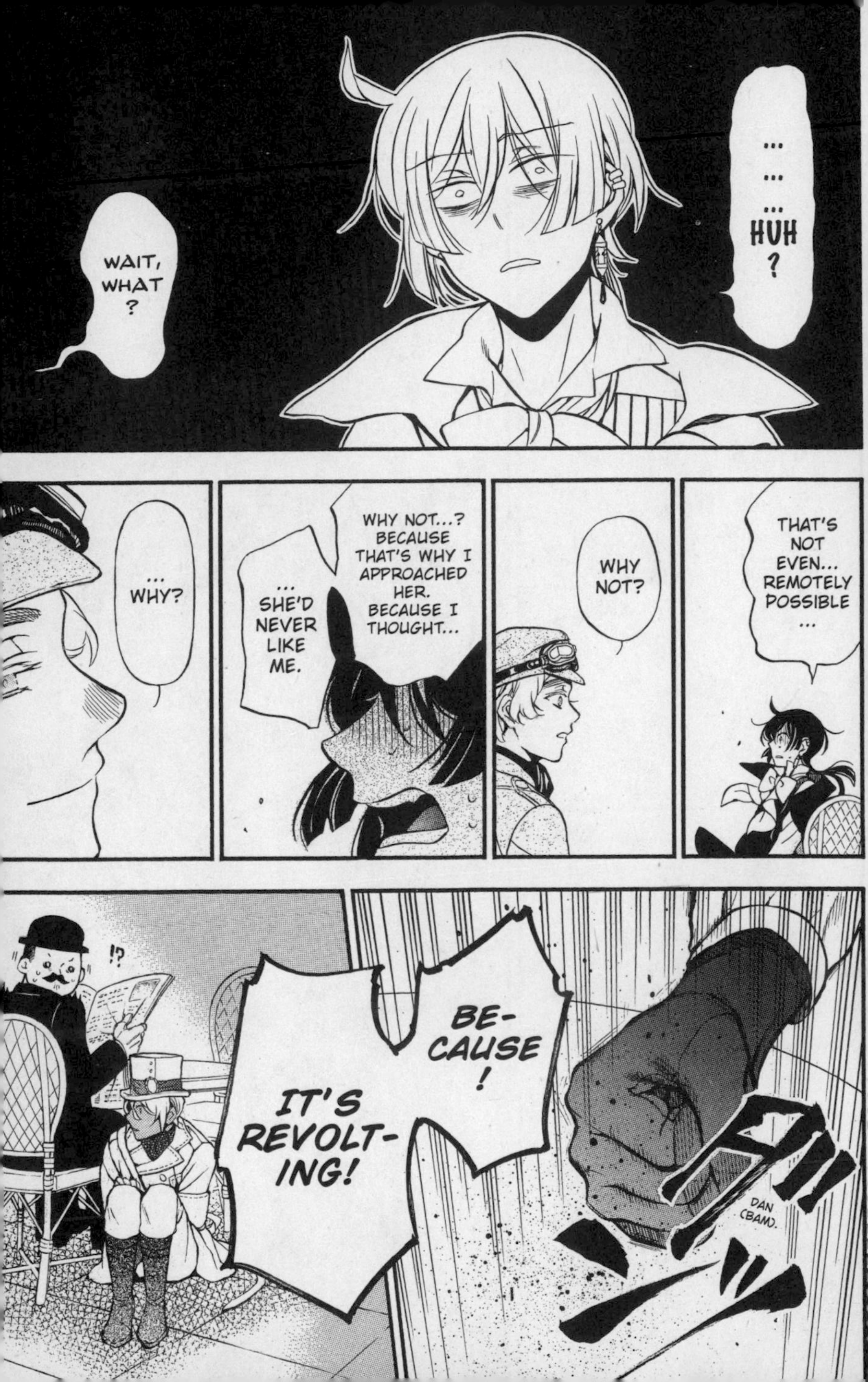
... ... HUH?
WAIT, WHAT?
THAT'S NOT EVEN... REMOTELY POSSIBLE ...
WHY NOT?
WHY NOT...? BECAUSE THAT'S WHY I APPROACHED HER. BECAUSE I THOUGHT...
... SHE'D NEVER LIKE ME.
... WHY?
BE-CAUSE! IT'S REVOLT-ING!
DAN (BAM).
!?

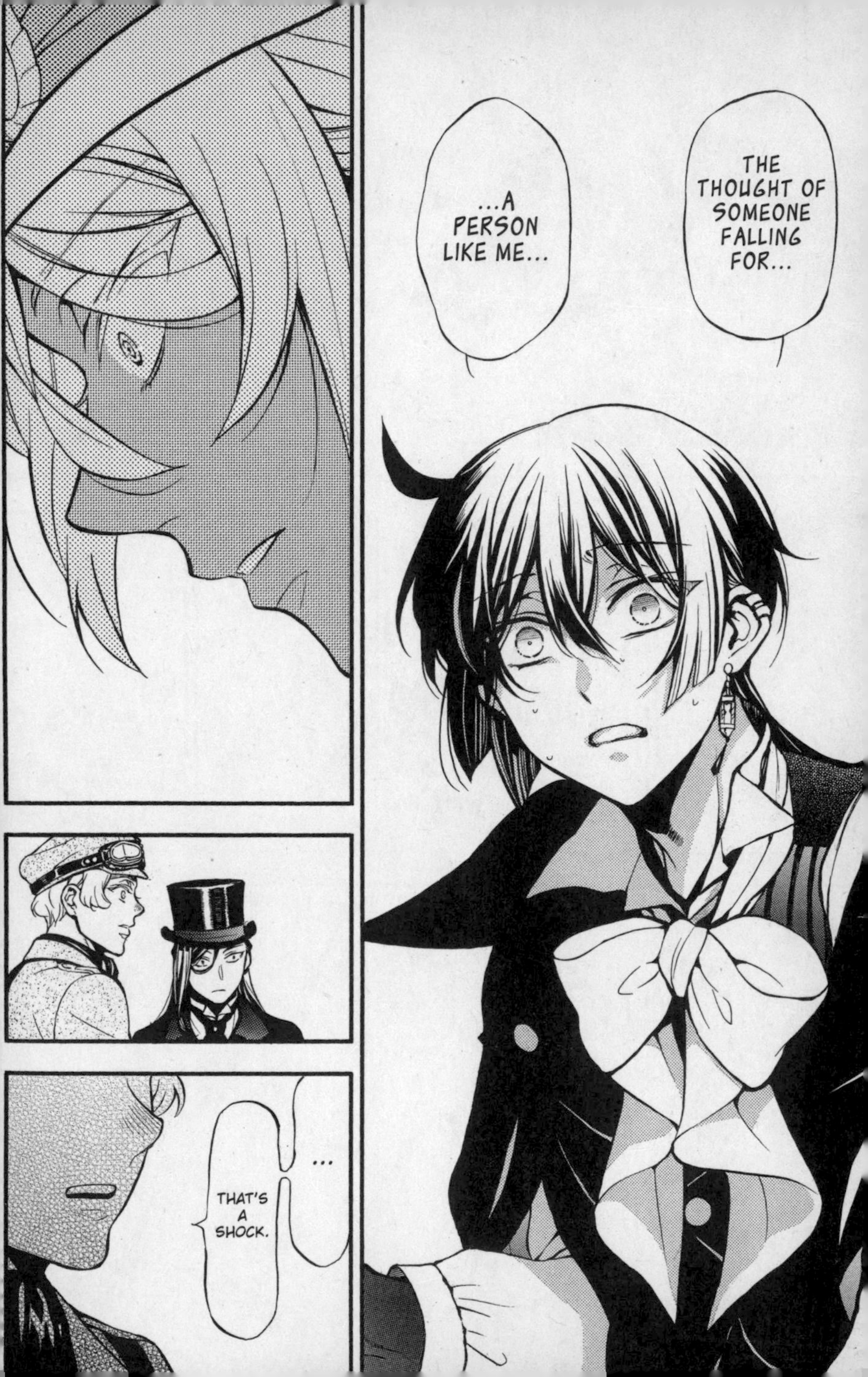

THE THOUGHT OF SOMEONE FALLING FOR...
...A PERSON LIKE ME...
...
THAT'S A SHOCK.

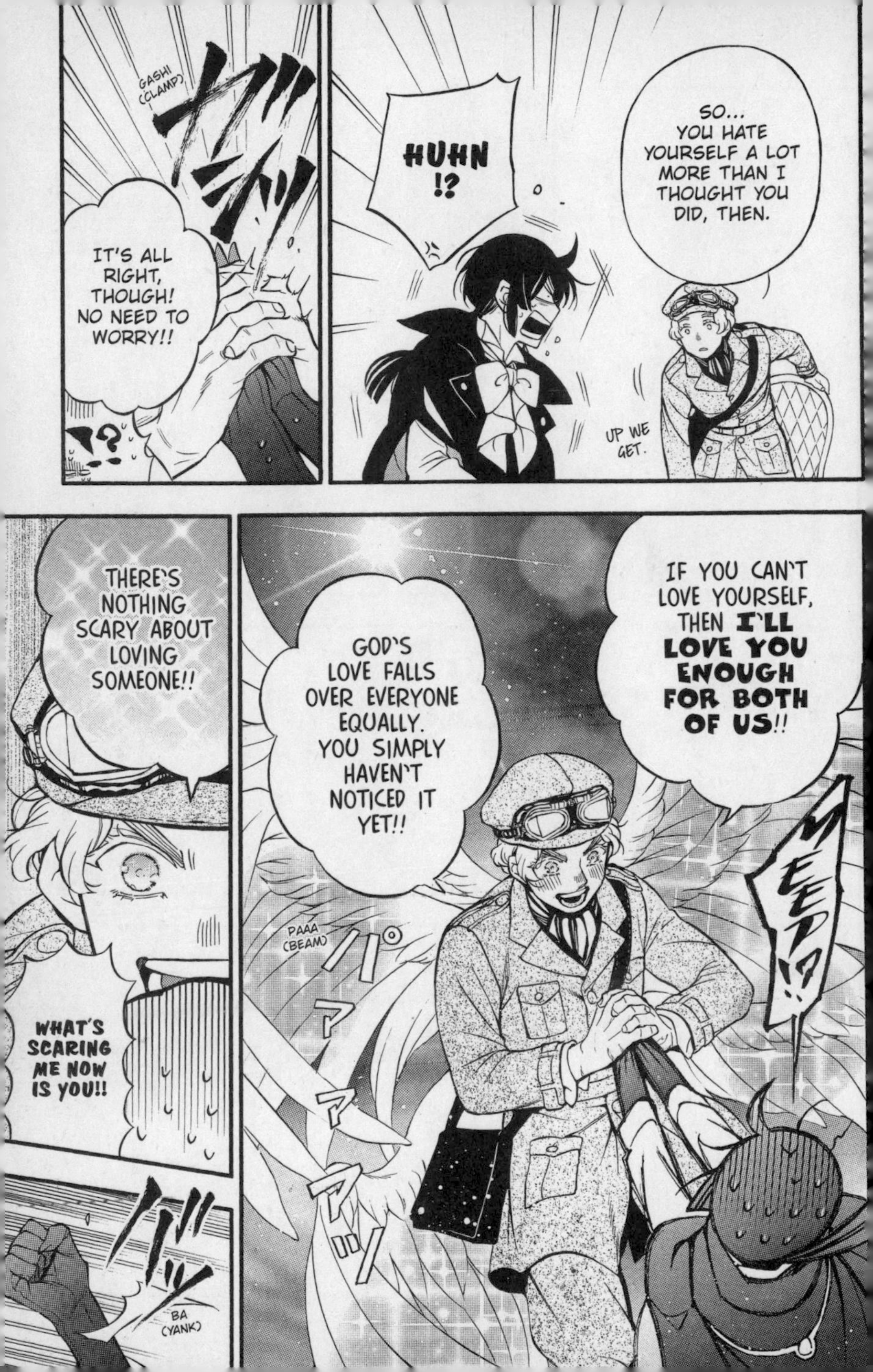
SO... YOU HATE YOURSELF A LOT MORE THAN I THOUGHT YOU DID, THEN.
UP WE GET.
HUHN !?
GASHI (CLAMP)
IT'S ALL RIGHT, THOUGH! NO NEED TO WORRY!!
IF YOU CAN'T LOVE YOURSELF, THEN I'LL LOVE YOU ENOUGH FOR BOTH OF US!!
GOD'S LOVE FALLS OVER EVERYONE EQUALLY. YOU SIMPLY HAVEN'T NOTICED IT YET!!
PAAA (BEAM)
THERE'S NOTHING SCARY ABOUT LOVING SOMEONE!!
WHAT'S SCARING ME NOW IS YOU!!
BA (YANK)

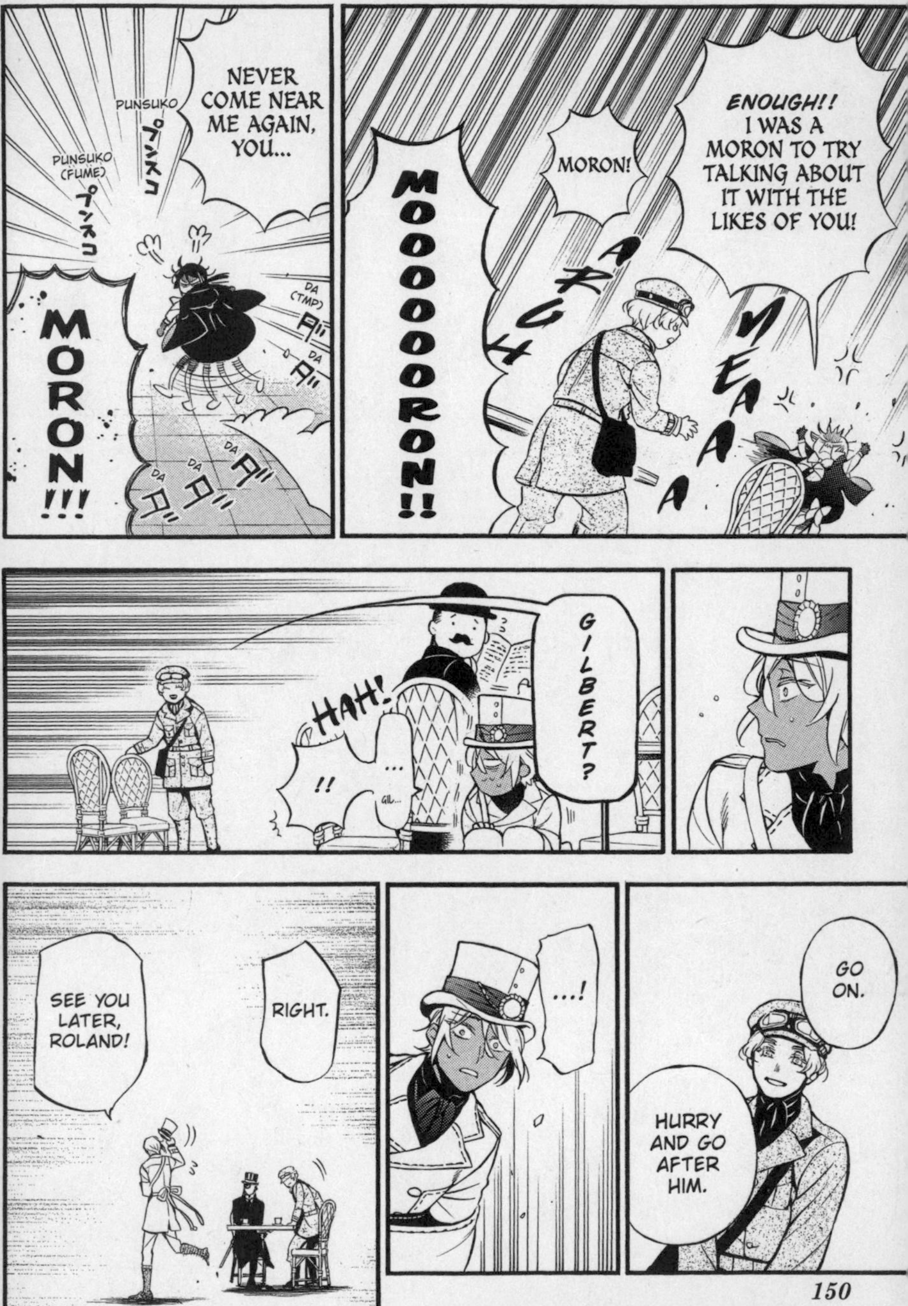
ENOUGH!! I WAS A MORON TO TRY TALKING ABOUT IT WITH THE LIKES OF YOU!
MORON!
MOOOOOOORON!!
ARGH
MEAAA
NEVER COME NEAR ME AGAIN, YOU...
PUNSUKO
PUNSUKO (FUME)
MORON!!!
DA (TMP)
DA
DA
DA
DA
GILBERT?
HAH!
...
!!
GIL...
GO ON.
HURRY AND GO AFTER HIM.
...!
RIGHT.
SEE YOU LATER, ROLAND!

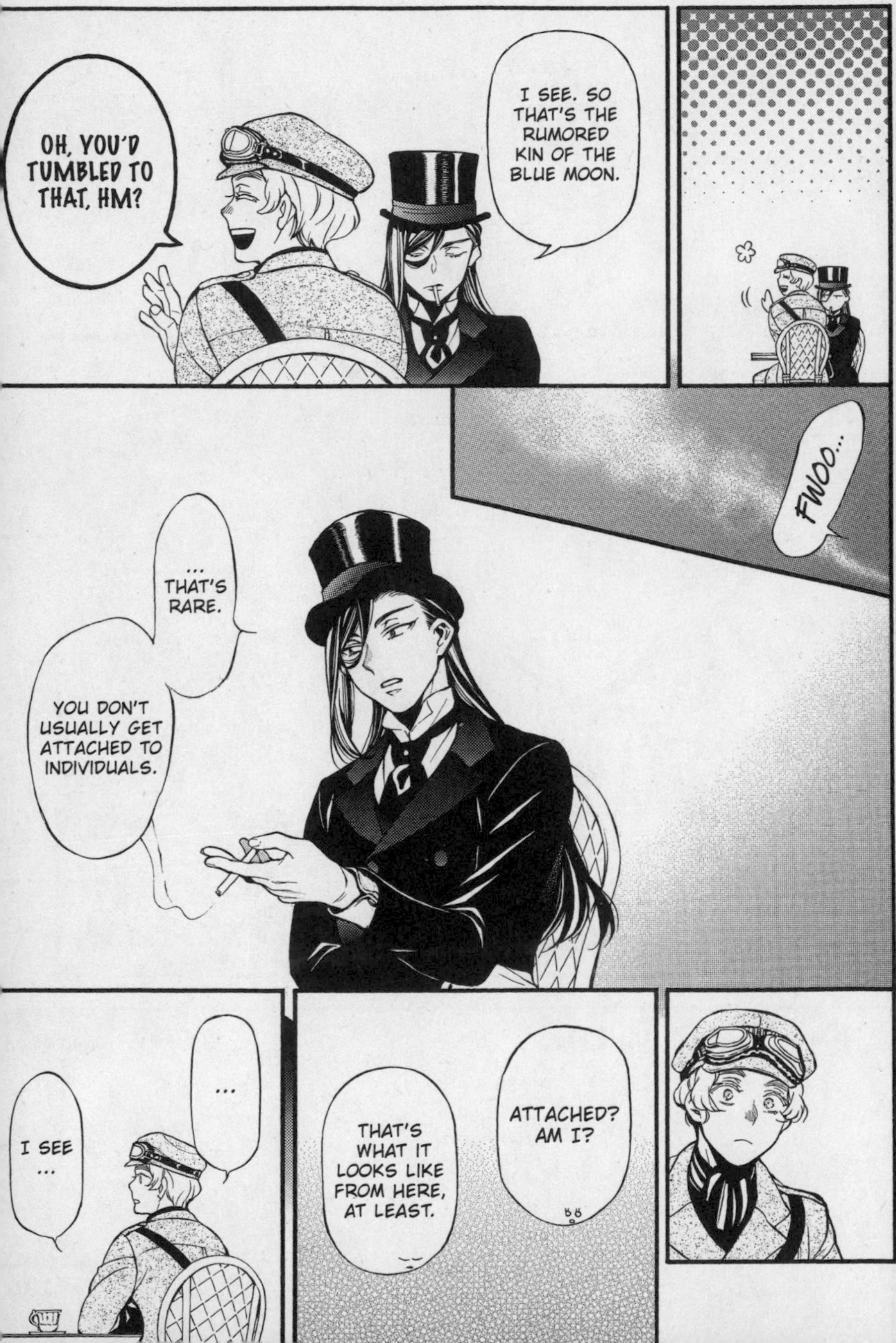
I SEE. SO THAT'S THE RUMORED KIN OF THE BLUE MOON.
OH, YOU'D TUMBLED TO THAT, HM?
FWOO...
... THAT'S RARE.
YOU DON'T USUALLY GET ATTACHED TO INDIVIDUALS.
ATTACHED? AM I?
THAT'S WHAT IT LOOKS LIKE FROM HERE, AT LEAST.
...
I SEE ...

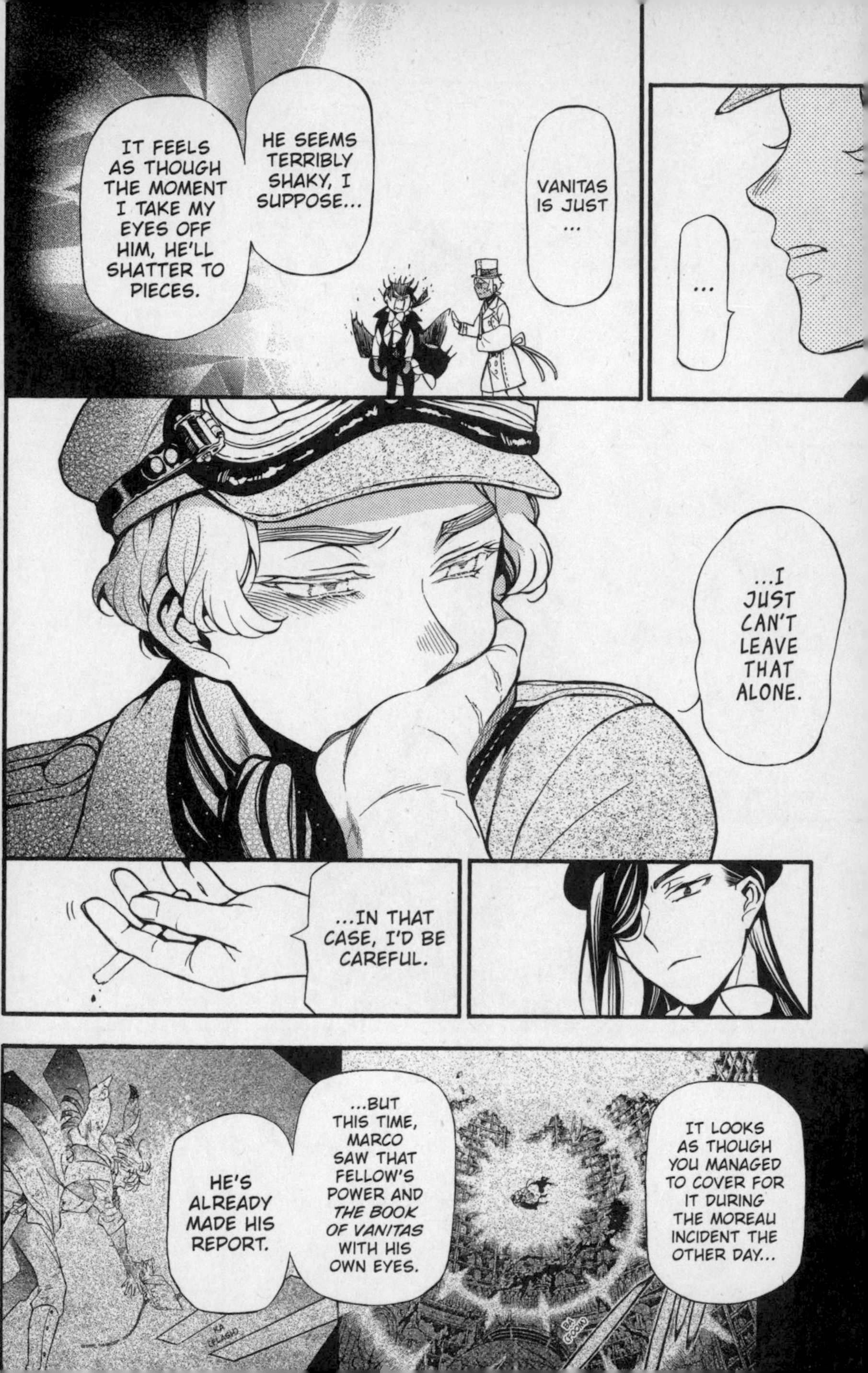
...
VANITAS IS JUST ...
HE SEEMS TERRIBLY SHAKY, I SUPPOSE...
IT FEELS AS THOUGH THE MOMENT I TAKE MY EYES OFF HIM, HE'LL SHATTER TO PIECES.
...I JUST CAN'T LEAVE THAT ALONE.
...IN THAT CASE, I'D BE CAREFUL.
IT LOOKS AS THOUGH YOU MANAGED TO COVER FOR IT DURING THE MOREAU INCIDENT THE OTHER DAY...
BA GOOM
...BUT THIS TIME, MARCO SAW THAT FELLOW'S POWER AND *THE BOOK OF VANITAS* WITH HIS OWN EYES.
HE'S ALREADY MADE HIS REPORT.
KA (FLASH)

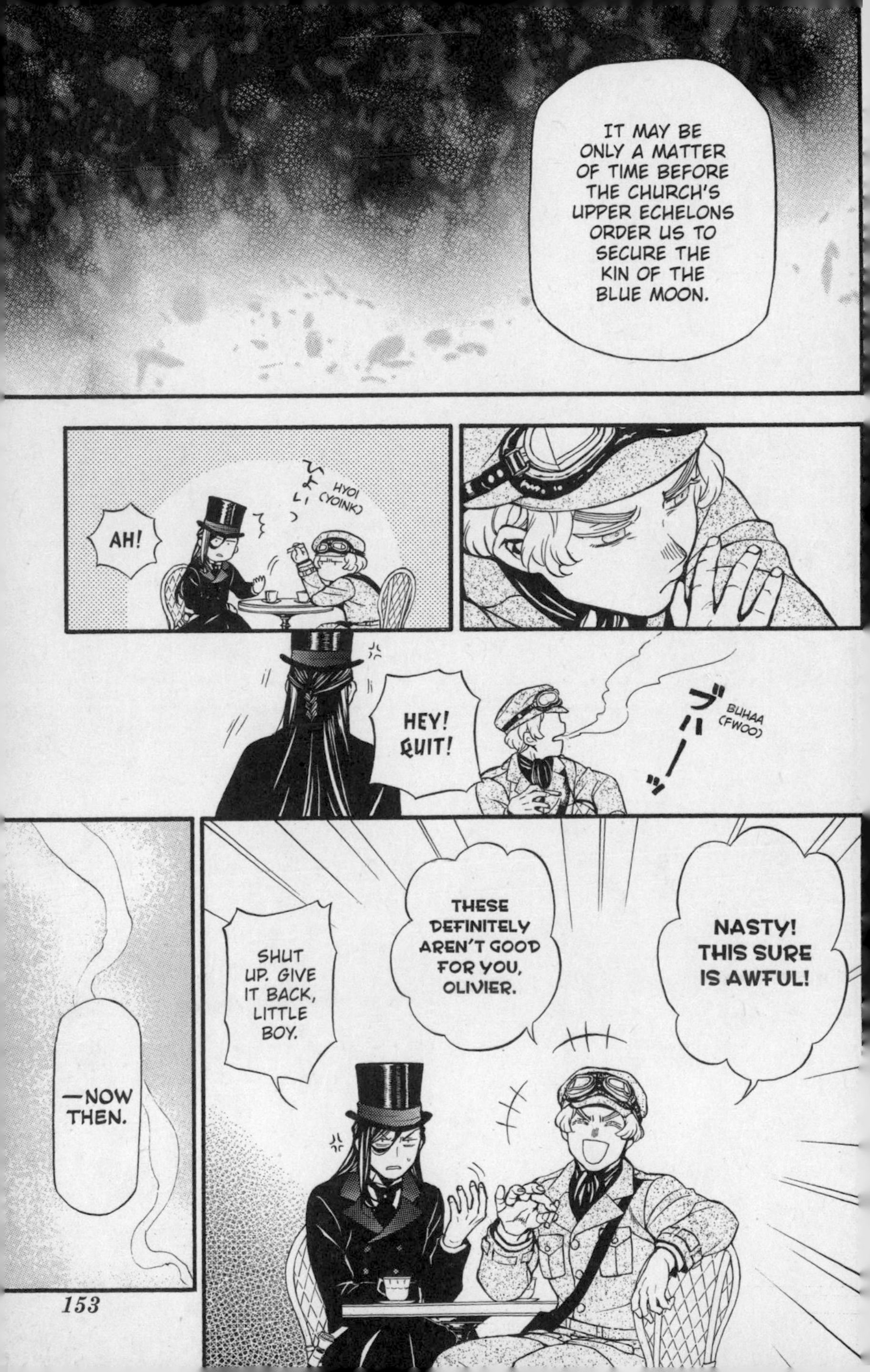
IT MAY BE ONLY A MATTER OF TIME BEFORE THE CHURCH'S UPPER ECHELONS ORDER US TO SECURE THE KIN OF THE BLUE MOON.
HYOI (YOINK)
AH!
BUHAA (FWOO)
HEY! QUIT!
NASTY! THIS SURE IS AWFUL!
THESE DEFINITELY AREN'T GOOD FOR YOU, OLIVIER.
SHUT UP. GIVE IT BACK, LITTLE BOY.
—NOW THEN.

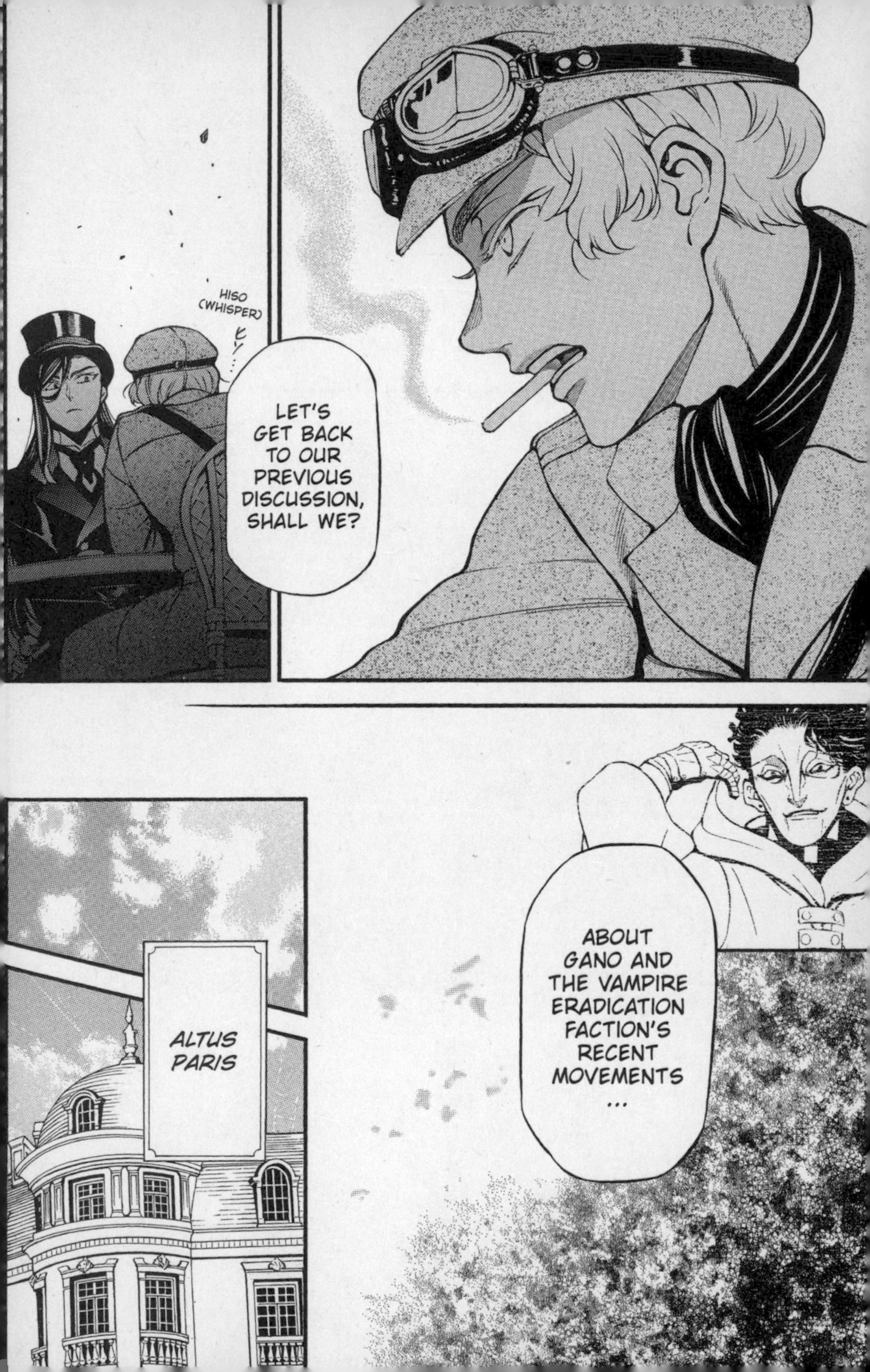
LET'S GET BACK TO OUR PREVIOUS DISCUSSION, SHALL WE?
HISO (WHISPER)
ヒソ…
ABOUT GANO AND THE VAMPIRE ERADICATION FACTION'S RECENT MOVEMENTS…
ALTUS PARIS

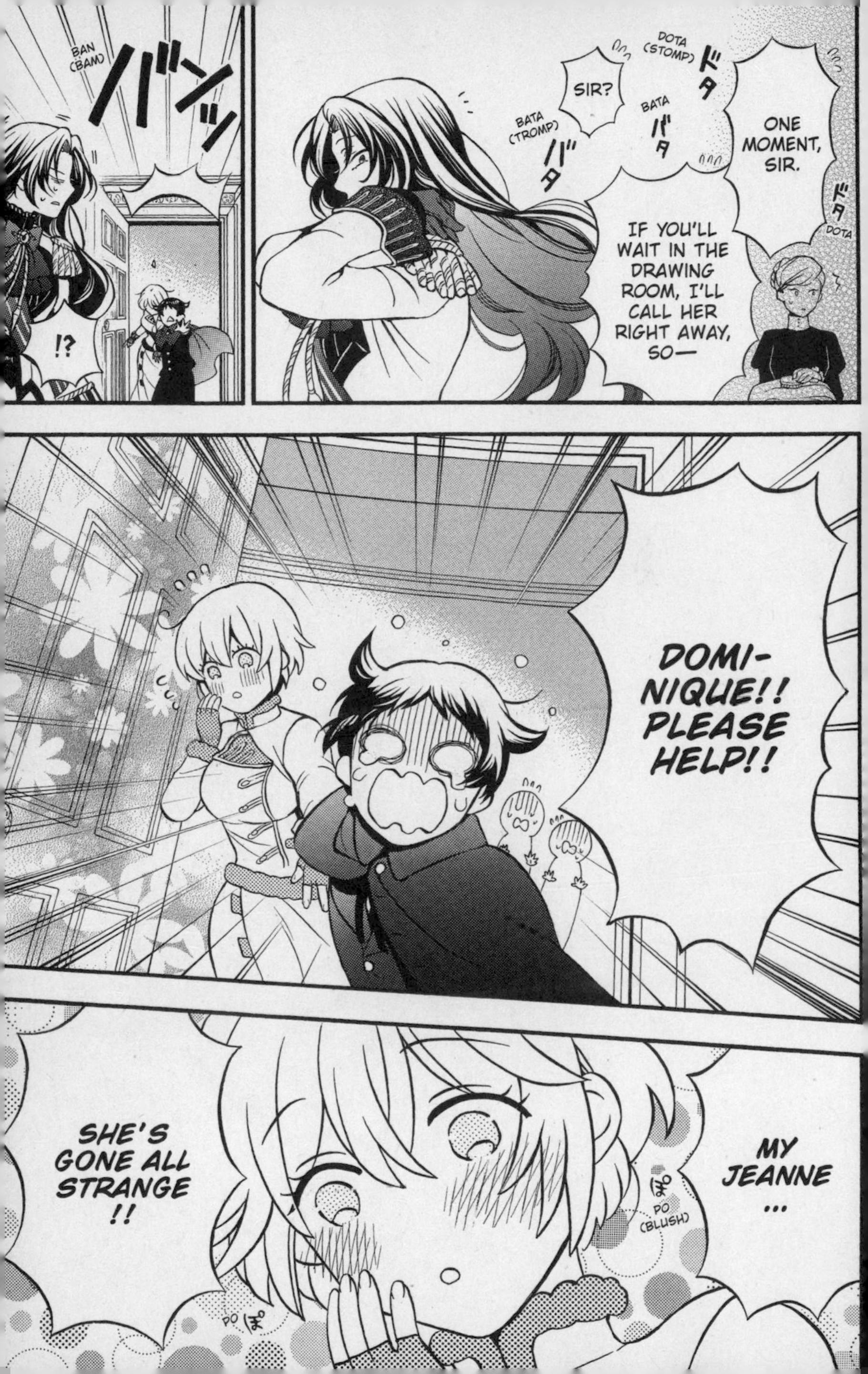
ドタ DOTA
ONE MOMENT, SIR.
IF YOU'LL WAIT IN THE DRAWING ROOM, I'LL CALL HER RIGHT AWAY, SO—
ドタ DOTA (STOMP)
バタ BATA
SIR?
バタ BATA (TROMP)
バンッ BAN (BAM)
!?
DOMI-NIQUE!! PLEASE HELP!!
MY JEANNE...
ぽ PO (BLUSH)
ぽ PO
SHE'S GONE ALL STRANGE!!

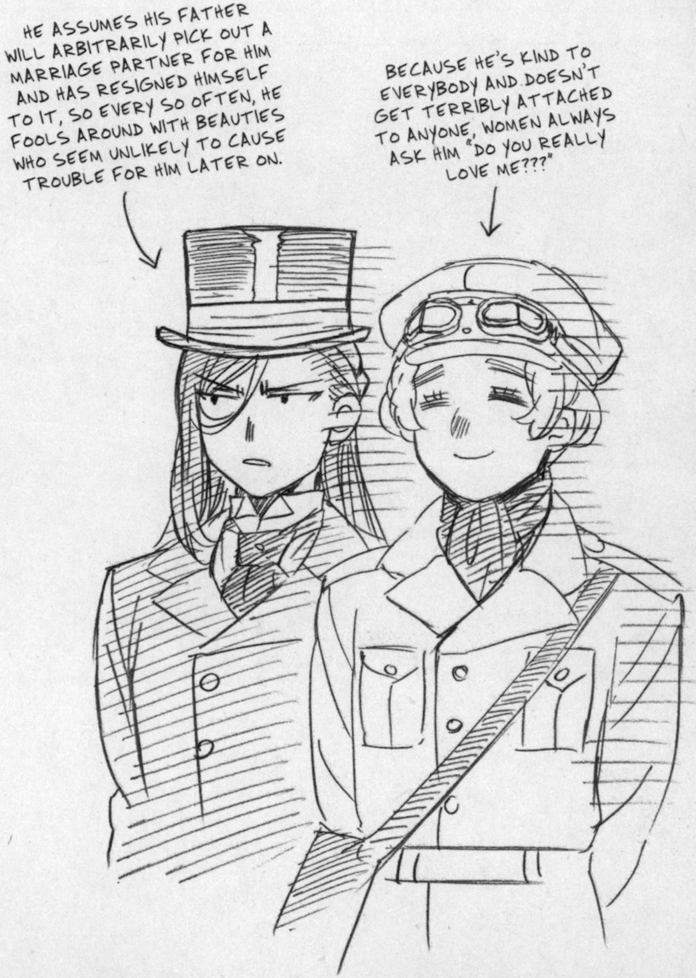
BECAUSE HE'S KIND TO EVERYBODY AND DOESN'T GET TERRIBLY ATTACHED TO ANYONE, WOMEN ALWAYS ASK HIM "DO YOU REALLY LOVE ME???"
HE ASSUMES HIS FATHER WILL ARBITRARILY PICK OUT A MARRIAGE PARTNER FOR HIM AND HAS RESIGNED HIMSELF TO IT, SO EVERY SO OFTEN, HE FOOLS AROUND WITH BEAUTIES WHO SEEM UNLIKELY TO CAUSE TROUBLE FOR HIM LATER ON.

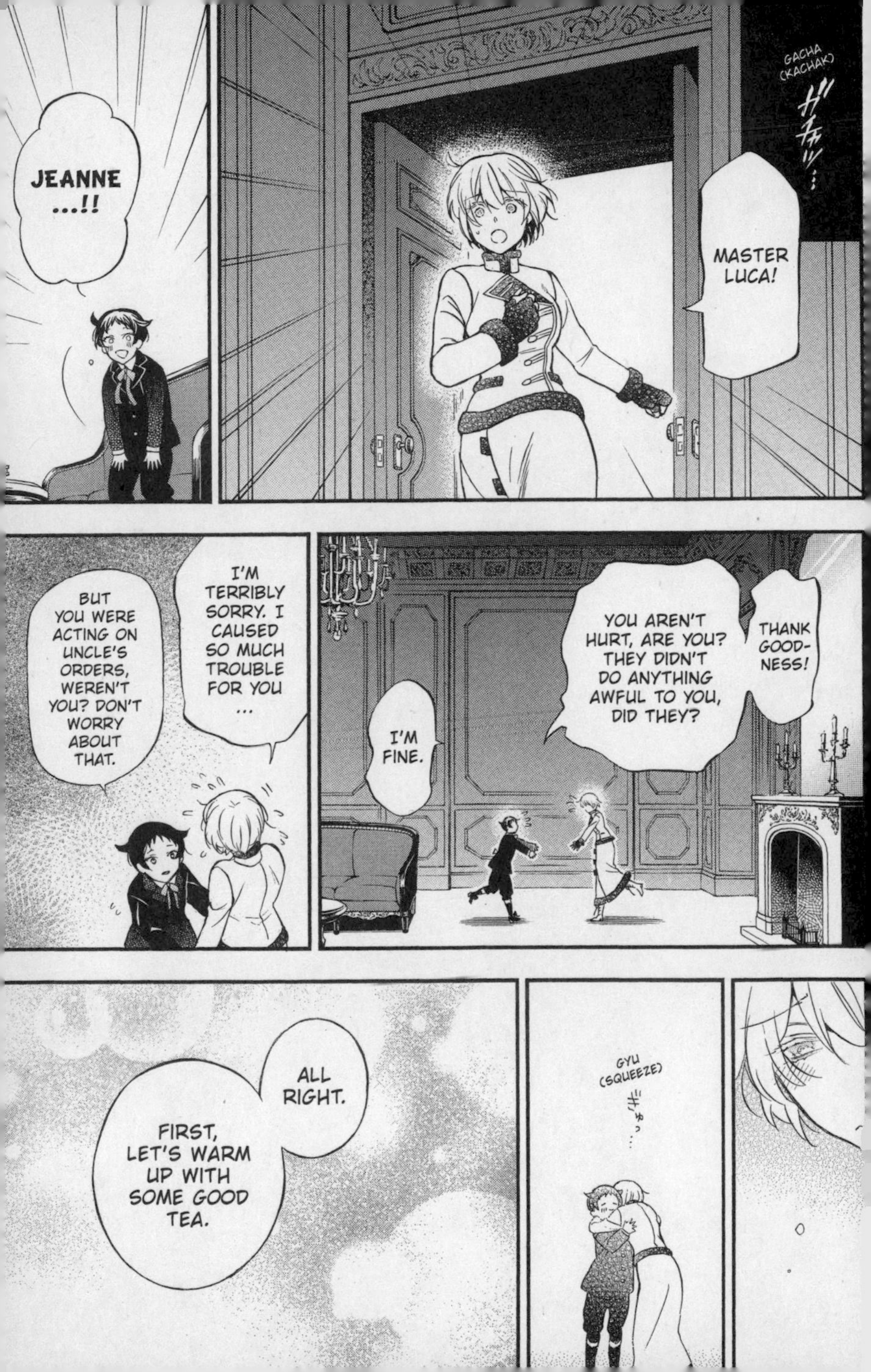
GACHA (KACHAK)
ガチャッ…
MASTER LUCA!
JEANNE ...!!
THANK GOOD-NESS!
YOU AREN'T HURT, ARE YOU? THEY DIDN'T DO ANYTHING AWFUL TO YOU, DID THEY?
I'M FINE.
I'M TERRIBLY SORRY. I CAUSED SO MUCH TROUBLE FOR YOU ...
BUT YOU WERE ACTING ON UNCLE'S ORDERS, WEREN'T YOU? DON'T WORRY ABOUT THAT.
GYU (SQUEEZE)
ぎゅっ…
ALL RIGHT.
FIRST, LET'S WARM UP WITH SOME GOOD TEA.

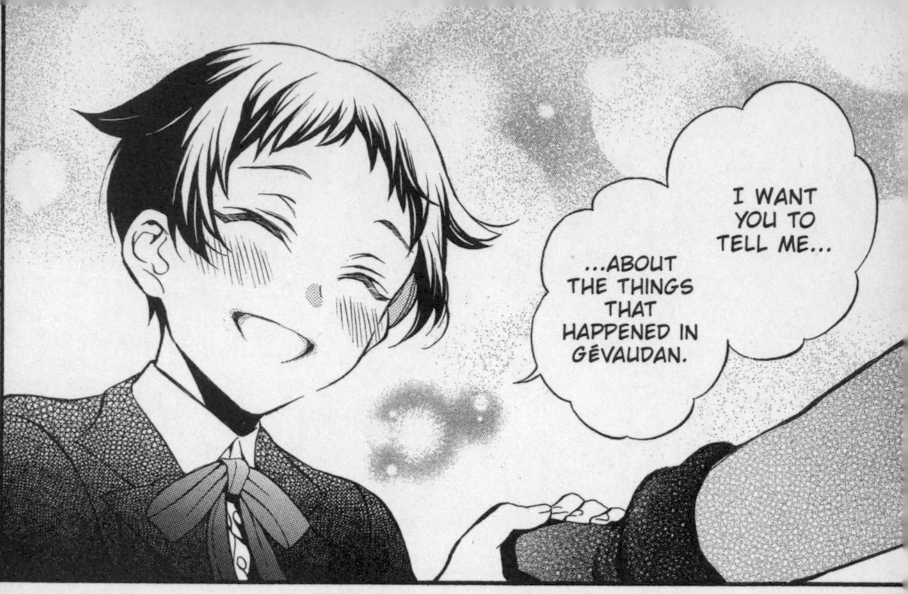
I WANT YOU TO TELL ME...
...ABOUT THE THINGS THAT HAPPENED IN GÉVAUDAN.

MÉMOIRE 45

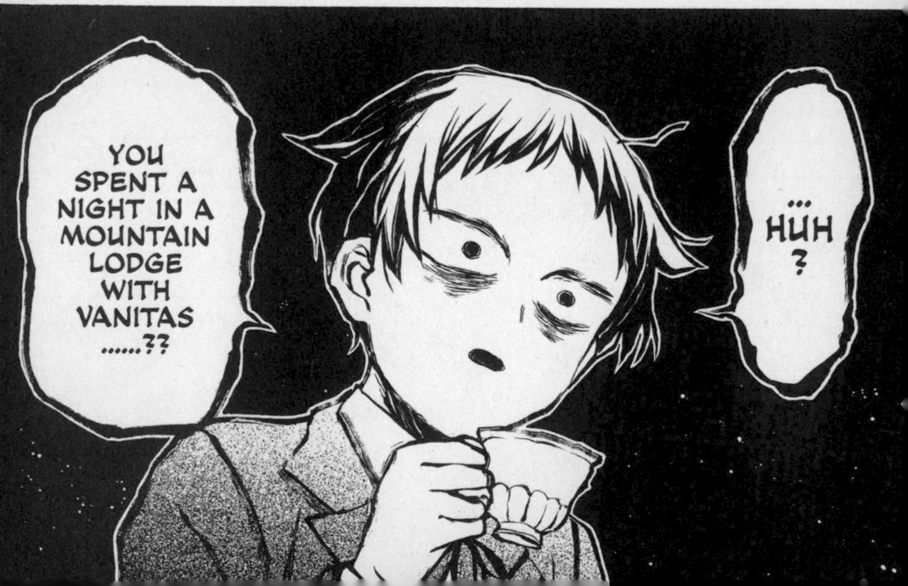
...HUH?
YOU SPENT A NIGHT IN A MOUNTAIN LODGE WITH VANITAS ......??

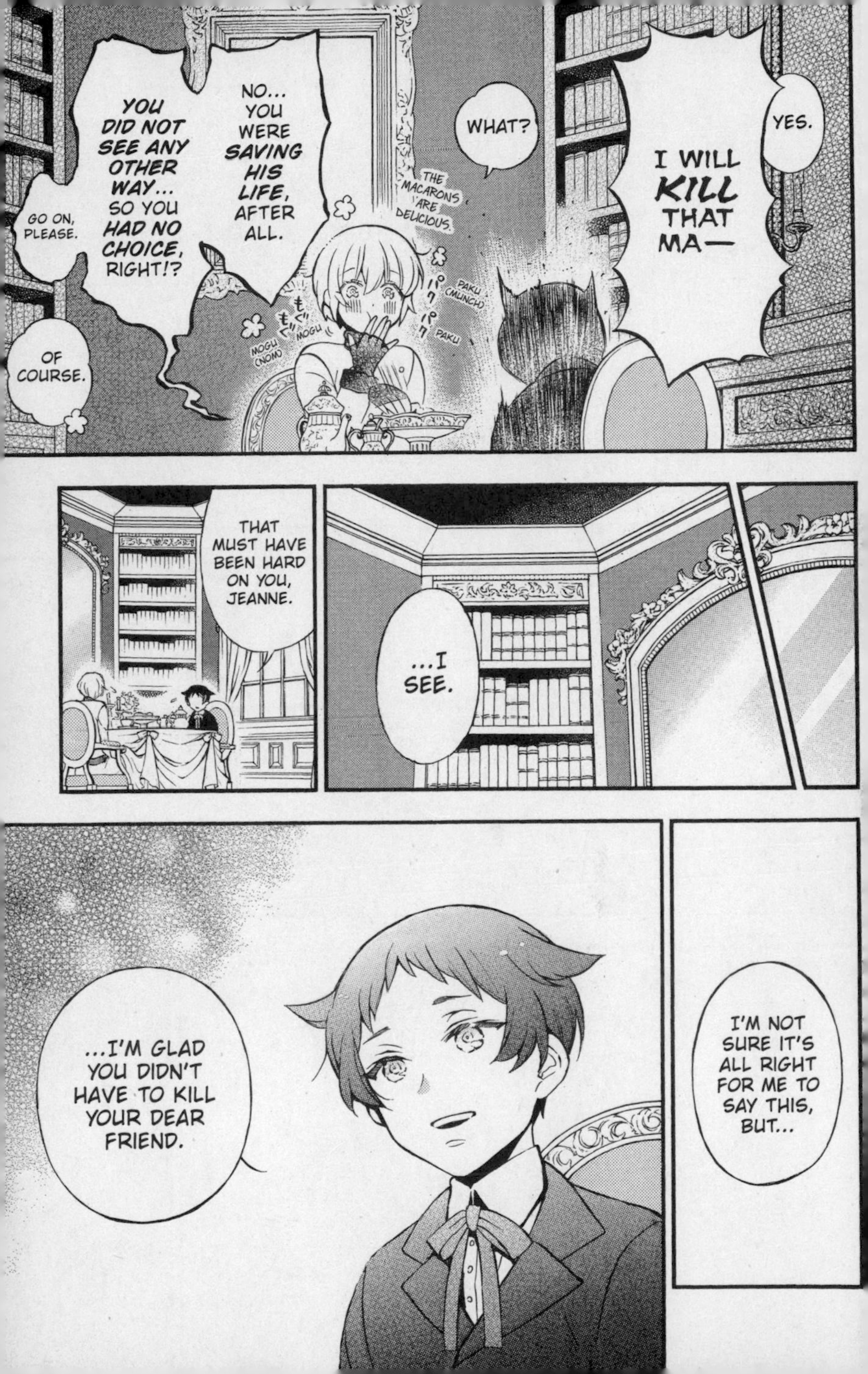
YES.
I WILL KILL THAT MA—
WHAT?
THE MACARONS ARE DELICIOUS.
パクパク
PAKU (MUNCH) PAKU
もぐもぐ
MOGU (NOM) MOGU
NO... YOU WERE SAVING HIS LIFE, AFTER ALL.
YOU DID NOT SEE ANY OTHER WAY... SO YOU HAD NO CHOICE, RIGHT!?
GO ON, PLEASE.
OF COURSE.
...I SEE.
THAT MUST HAVE BEEN HARD ON YOU, JEANNE.
I'M NOT SURE IT'S ALL RIGHT FOR ME TO SAY THIS, BUT...
...I'M GLAD YOU DIDN'T HAVE TO KILL YOUR DEAR FRIEND.

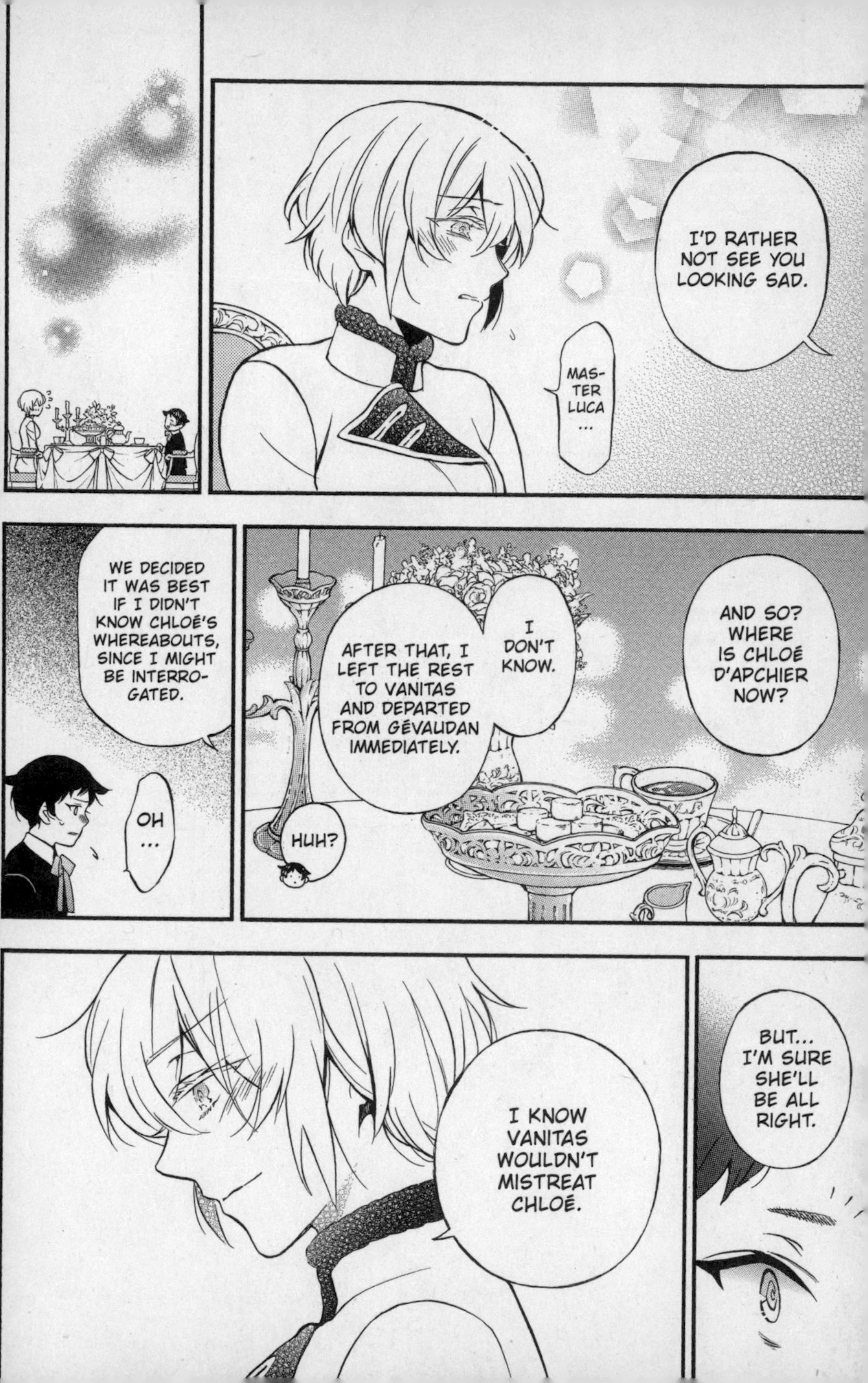
I'D RATHER NOT SEE YOU LOOKING SAD.
MAS-TER LUCA ...
AND SO? WHERE IS CHLOÉ D'APCHIER NOW?
I DON'T KNOW.
AFTER THAT, I LEFT THE REST TO VANITAS AND DEPARTED FROM GÉVAUDAN IMMEDIATELY.
HUH?
WE DECIDED IT WAS BEST IF I DIDN'T KNOW CHLOÉ'S WHEREABOUTS, SINCE I MIGHT BE INTERRO-GATED.
OH ...
BUT... I'M SURE SHE'LL BE ALL RIGHT.
I KNOW VANITAS WOULDN'T MISTREAT CHLOÉ.

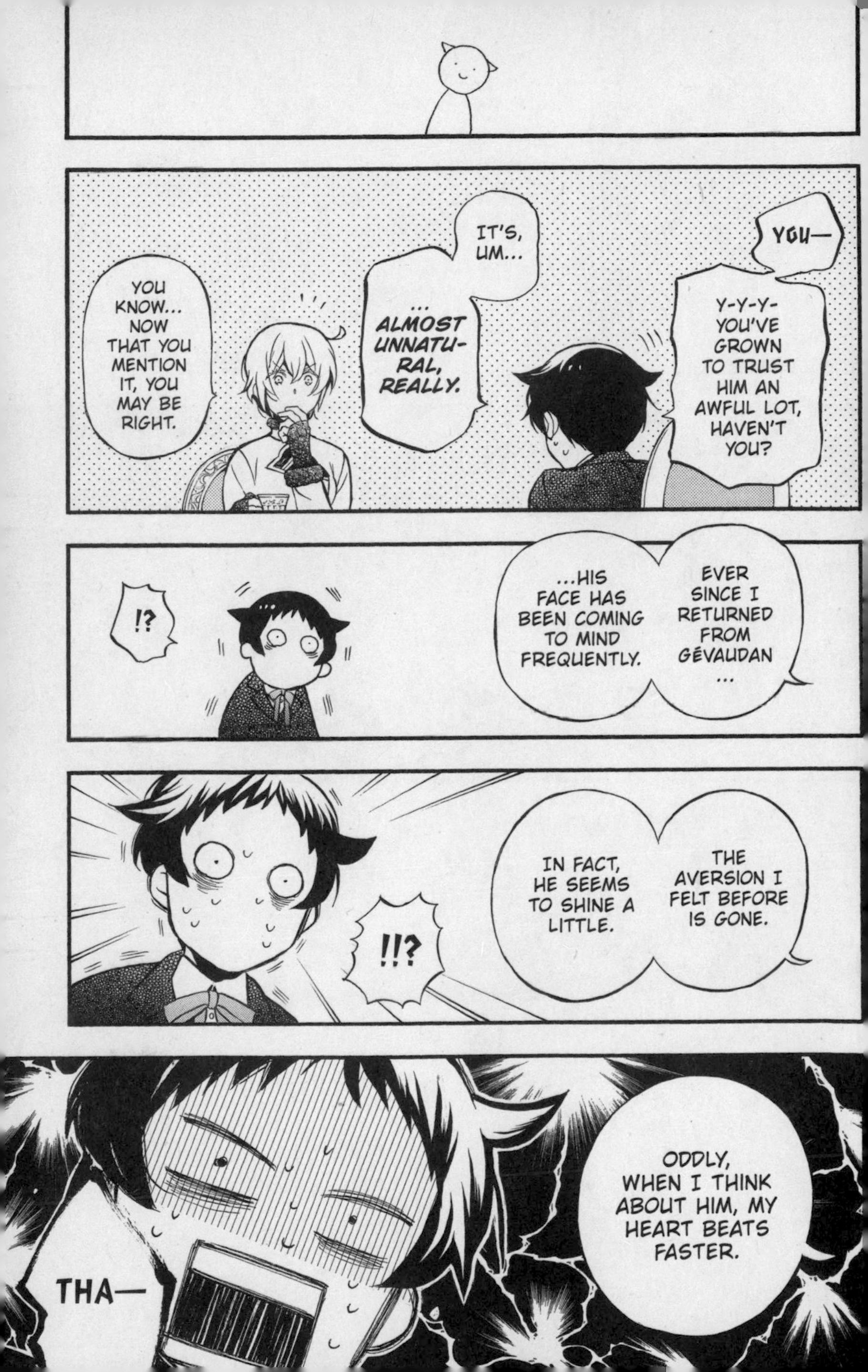
YOU—
Y-Y-Y-YOU'VE GROWN TO TRUST HIM AN AWFUL LOT, HAVEN'T YOU?
IT'S, UM...
...ALMOST UNNATURAL, REALLY.
YOU KNOW... NOW THAT YOU MENTION IT, YOU MAY BE RIGHT.
EVER SINCE I RETURNED FROM GÉVAUDAN ...
...HIS FACE HAS BEEN COMING TO MIND FREQUENTLY.
!?
THE AVERSION I FELT BEFORE IS GONE.
IN FACT, HE SEEMS TO SHINE A LITTLE.
!!?
ODDLY, WHEN I THINK ABOUT HIM, MY HEART BEATS FASTER.
THA—

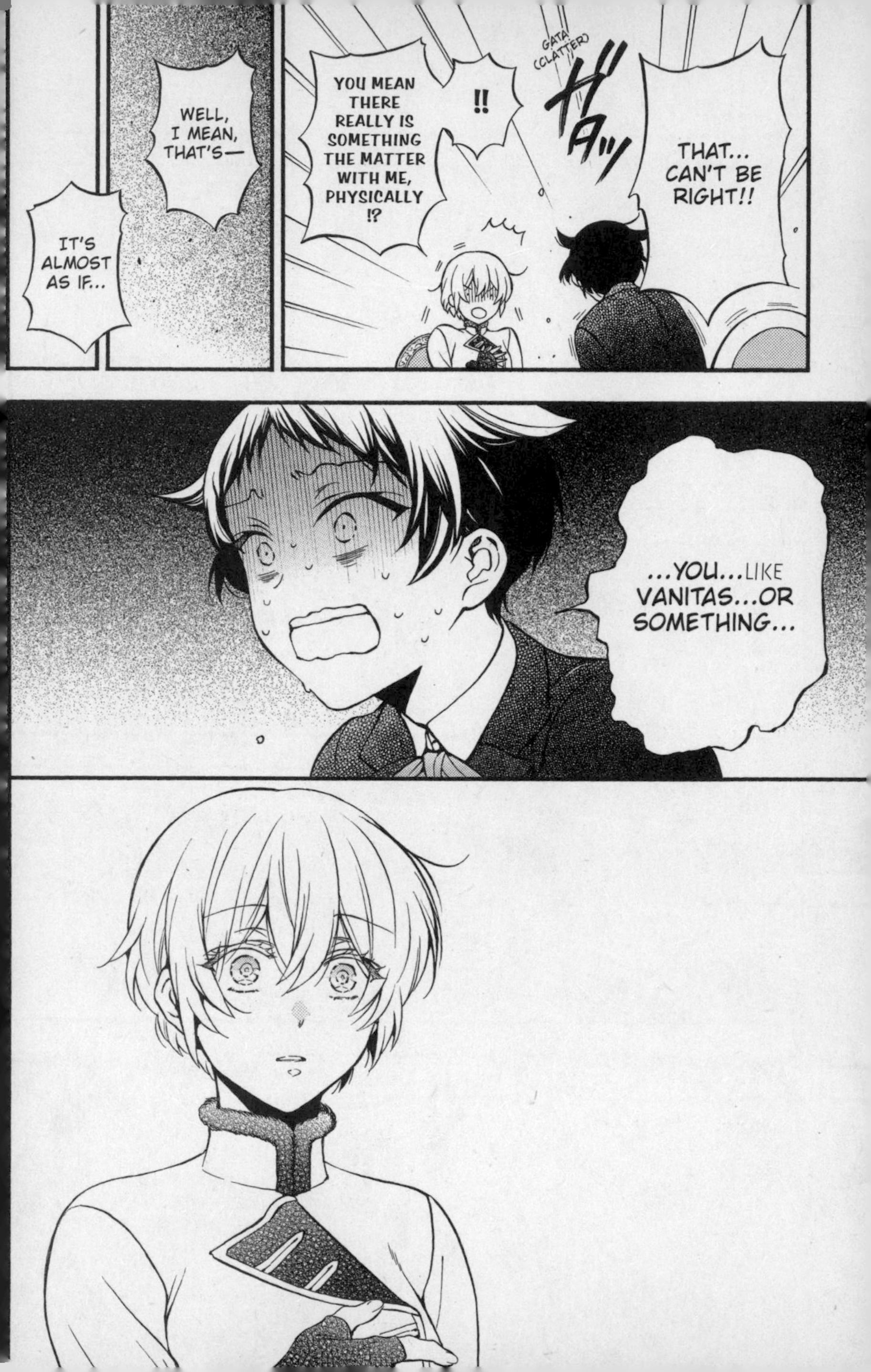
THAT... CAN'T BE RIGHT!!
GATA (CLATTER)
ガタッ
YOU MEAN THERE REALLY IS SOMETHING THE MATTER WITH ME, PHYSICALLY!?
!!
WELL, I MEAN, THAT'S—
IT'S ALMOST AS IF...
...YOU...LIKE VANITAS...OR SOMETHING...

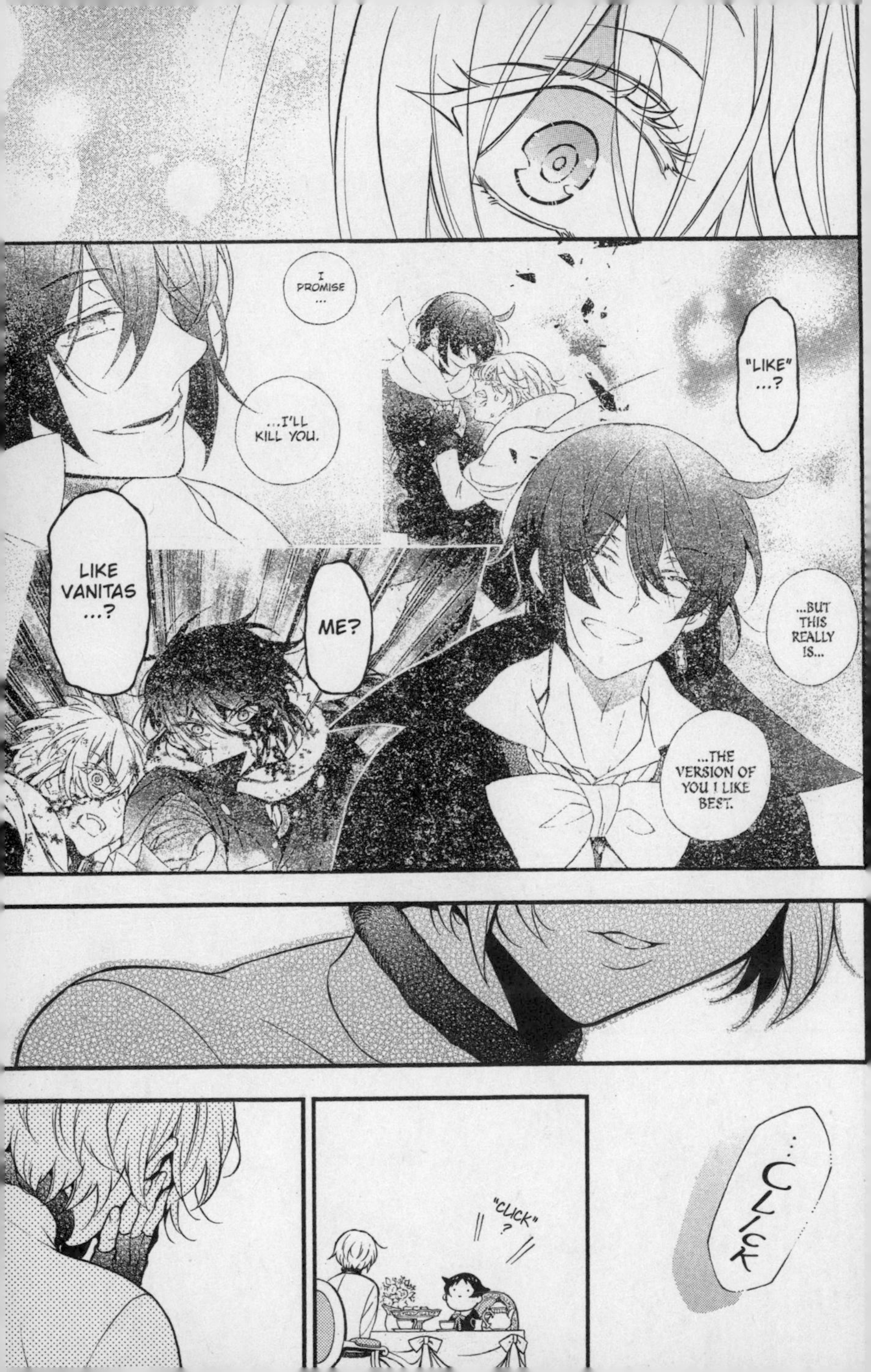
"LIKE" ...?
I PROMISE ...
...I'LL KILL YOU.
...BUT THIS REALLY IS...
...THE VERSION OF YOU I LIKE BEST.
ME?
LIKE VANITAS ...?
...CLICK
"CLICK" ?

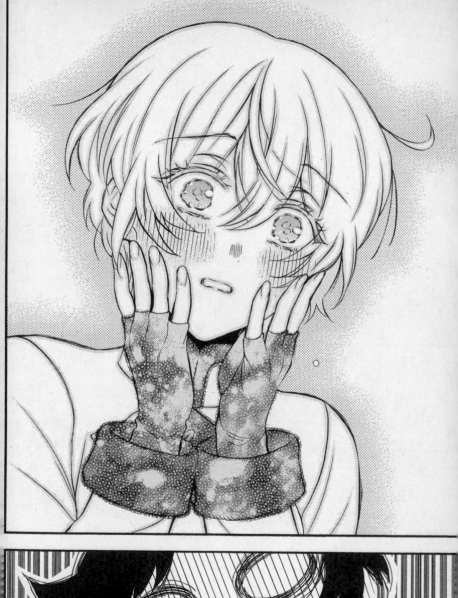
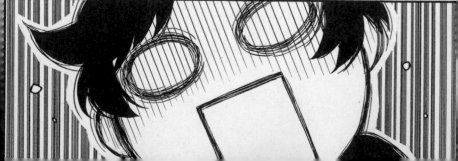

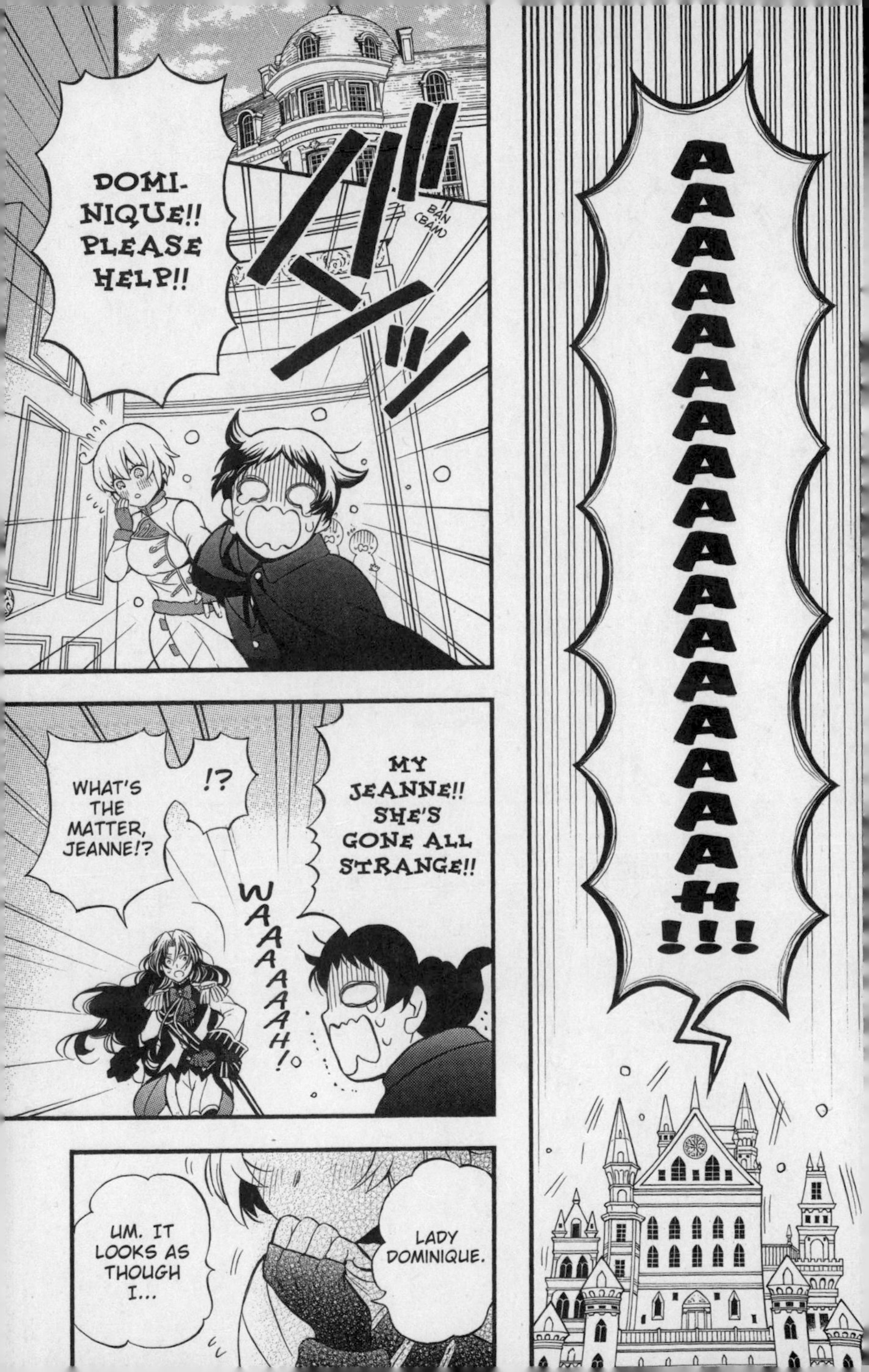
AAAAAAAAAAAAAAAAAH!!!
BAN (BAM)
DOMI-NIQUE!! PLEASE HELP!!
MY JEANNE!! SHE'S GONE ALL STRANGE!!
WAAAAAAH!
!?
WHAT'S THE MATTER, JEANNE!?
LADY DOMINIQUE.
UM. IT LOOKS AS THOUGH I...

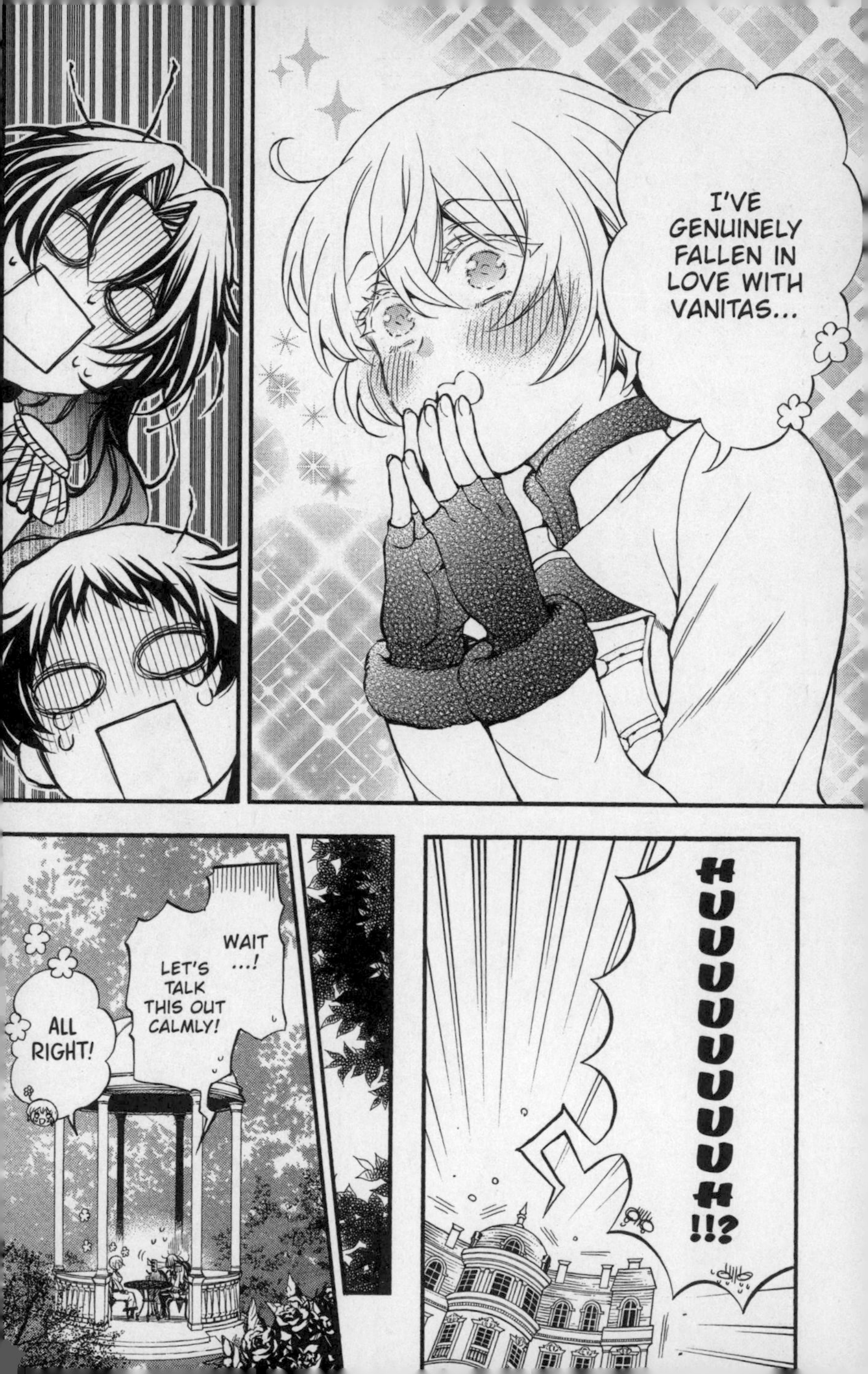
I'VE GENUINELY FALLEN IN LOVE WITH VANITAS...
HUUUUUUUUH!!?
WAIT...!
LET'S TALK THIS OUT CALMLY!
ALL RIGHT!

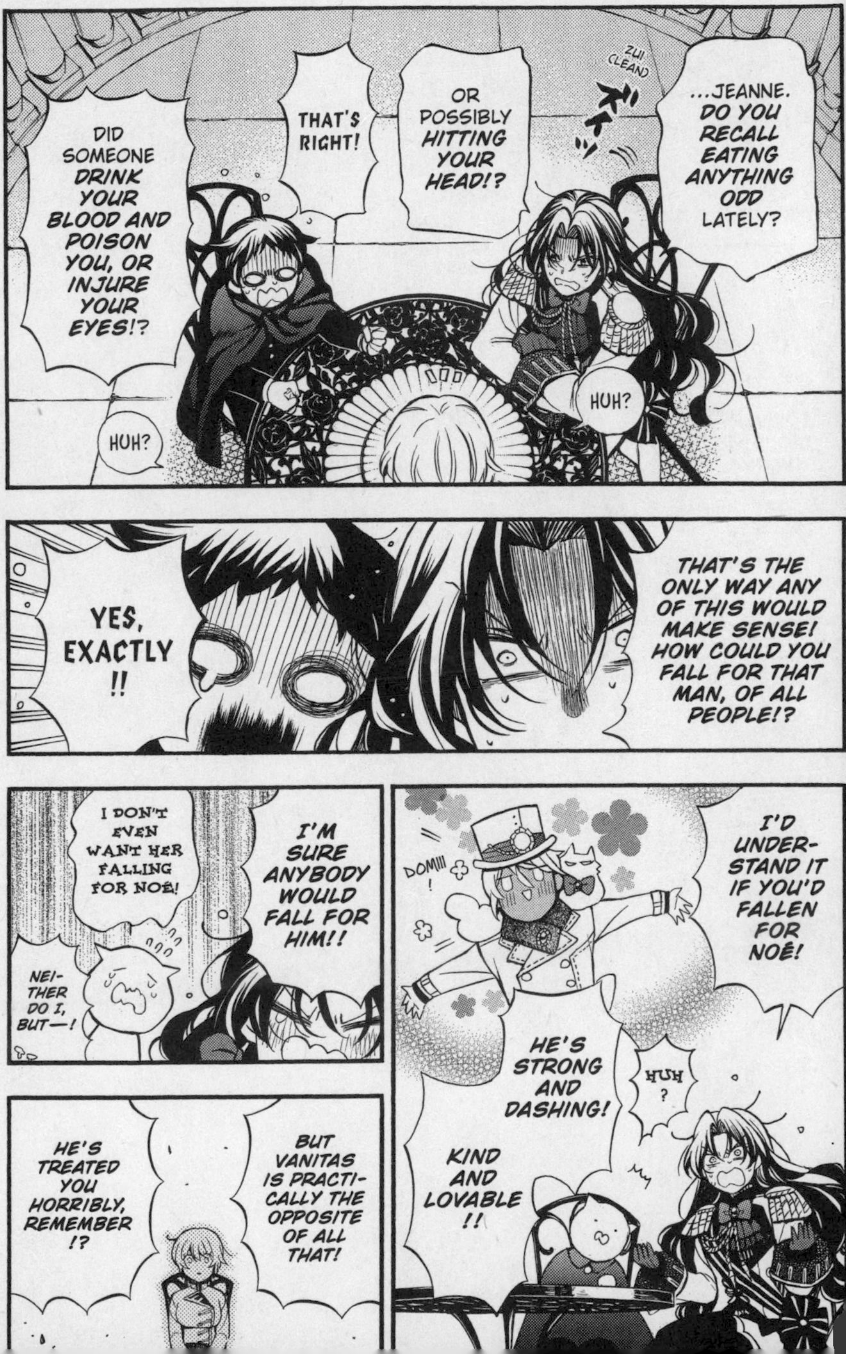
...JEANNE. DO YOU RECALL EATING ANYTHING ODD LATELY?
ZUI (LEAN)
OR POSSIBLY HITTING YOUR HEAD!?
THAT'S RIGHT!
DID SOMEONE DRINK YOUR BLOOD AND POISON YOU, OR INJURE YOUR EYES!?
HUH?
HUH?
THAT'S THE ONLY WAY ANY OF THIS WOULD MAKE SENSE! HOW COULD YOU FALL FOR THAT MAN, OF ALL PEOPLE!?
YES, EXACTLY !!
I'D UNDER-STAND IT IF YOU'D FALLEN FOR NOÉ!
DOM!!!
HUH?
HE'S STRONG AND DASHING!
KIND AND LOVABLE!!
I'M SURE ANYBODY WOULD FALL FOR HIM!!
I DON'T EVEN WANT HER FALLING FOR NOÉ!
NEI-THER DO I, BUT—!
BUT VANITAS IS PRACTI-CALLY THE OPPOSITE OF ALL THAT!
HE'S TREATED YOU HORRIBLY, REMEMBER!?

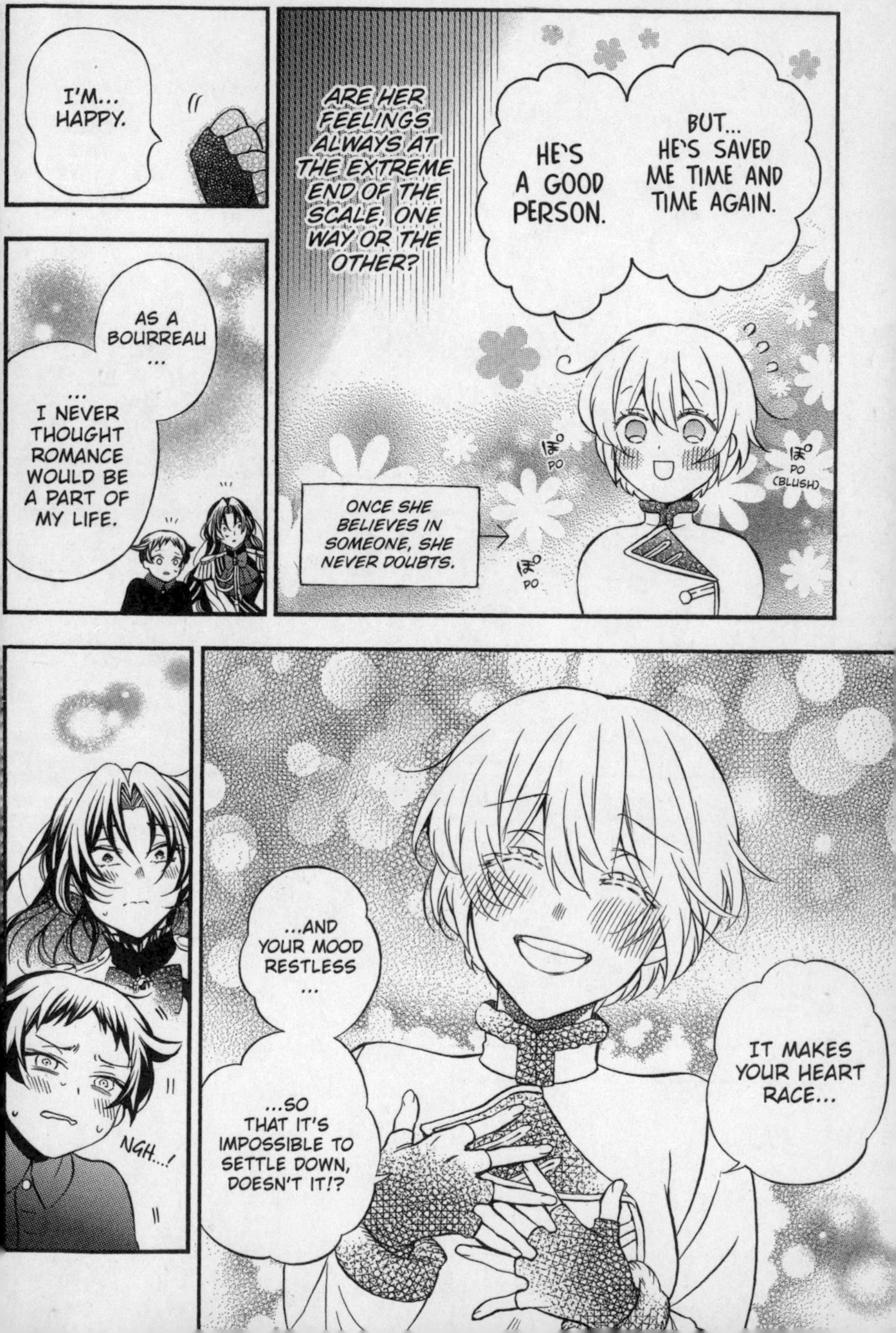
BUT... HE'S SAVED ME TIME AND TIME AGAIN.
HE'S A GOOD PERSON.
ARE HER FEELINGS ALWAYS AT THE EXTREME END OF THE SCALE, ONE WAY OR THE OTHER?
ぽ PO (BLUSH)
ぽ PO
ぽ PO
ONCE SHE BELIEVES IN SOMEONE, SHE NEVER DOUBTS.
I'M... HAPPY.
AS A BOURREAU...
...I NEVER THOUGHT ROMANCE WOULD BE A PART OF MY LIFE.
IT MAKES YOUR HEART RACE...
...AND YOUR MOOD RESTLESS...
...SO THAT IT'S IMPOSSIBLE TO SETTLE DOWN, DOESN'T IT!?
NGH...!

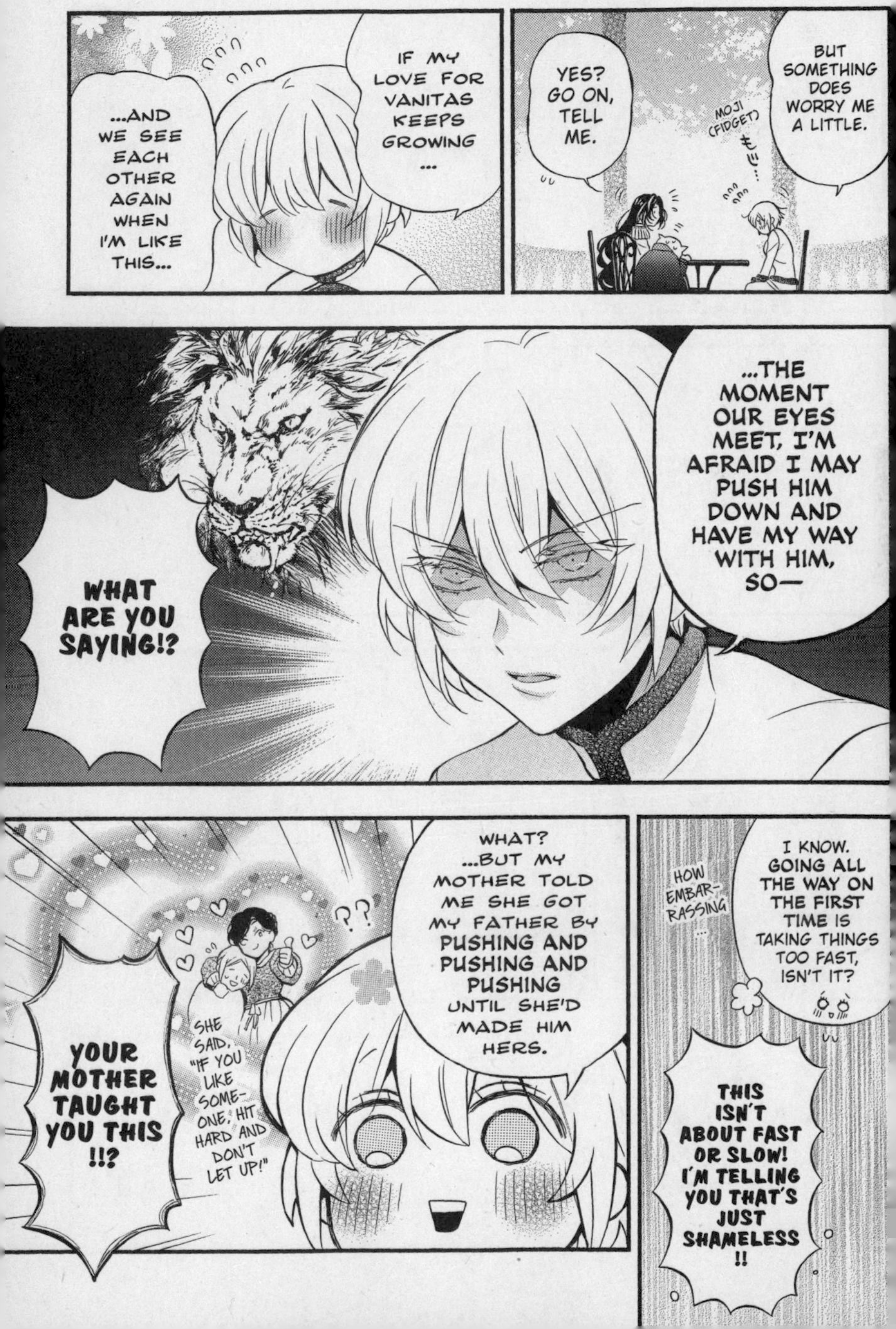
BUT SOMETHING DOES WORRY ME A LITTLE.
MOJI (FIDGET)
もじ…
YES? GO ON, TELL ME.
IF MY LOVE FOR VANITAS KEEPS GROWING...
...AND WE SEE EACH OTHER AGAIN WHEN I'M LIKE THIS...
...THE MOMENT OUR EYES MEET, I'M AFRAID I MAY PUSH HIM DOWN AND HAVE MY WAY WITH HIM, SO—
WHAT ARE YOU SAYING!?
I KNOW. GOING ALL THE WAY ON THE FIRST TIME IS TAKING THINGS TOO FAST, ISN'T IT?
HOW EMBAR-RASSING...
THIS ISN'T ABOUT FAST OR SLOW! I'M TELLING YOU THAT'S JUST SHAMELESS!!
WHAT? ...BUT MY MOTHER TOLD ME SHE GOT MY FATHER BY PUSHING AND PUSHING AND PUSHING UNTIL SHE'D MADE HIM HERS.
SHE SAID, "IF YOU LIKE SOME-ONE, HIT HARD AND DON'T LET UP!"
YOUR MOTHER TAUGHT YOU THIS!!?

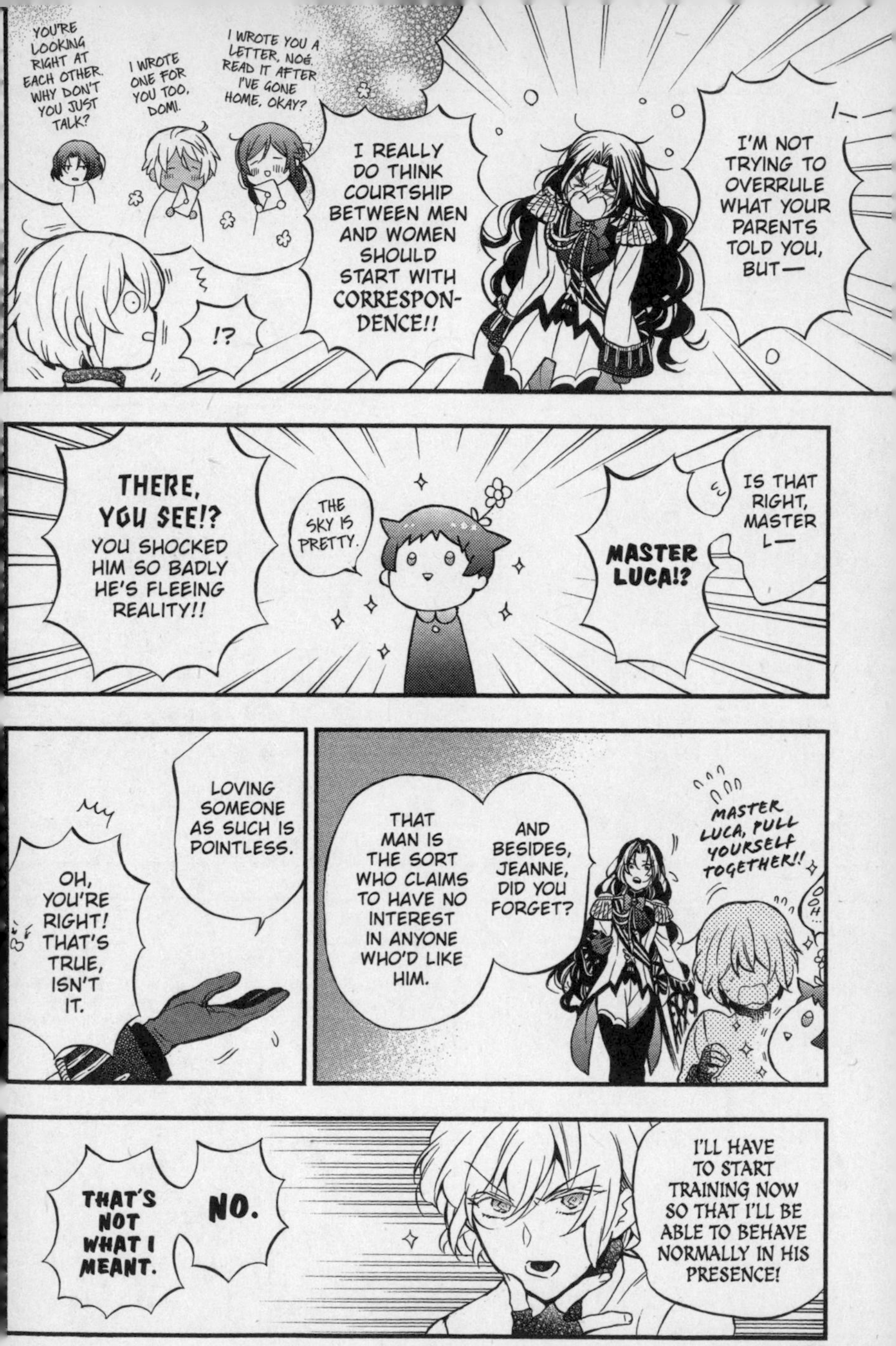
I—
I'M NOT TRYING TO OVERRULE WHAT YOUR PARENTS TOLD YOU, BUT—
I REALLY DO THINK COURTSHIP BETWEEN MEN AND WOMEN SHOULD START WITH CORRESPONDENCE!!
I WROTE YOU A LETTER, NOÉ. READ IT AFTER I'VE GONE HOME, OKAY?
I WROTE ONE FOR YOU TOO, DOMI.
YOU'RE LOOKING RIGHT AT EACH OTHER. WHY DON'T YOU JUST TALK?
!?
IS THAT RIGHT, MASTER L—
MASTER LUCA!?
THE SKY IS PRETTY.
THERE, YOU SEE!? YOU SHOCKED HIM SO BADLY HE'S FLEEING REALITY!!
MASTER LUCA, PULL YOURSELF TOGETHER!!
AND BESIDES, JEANNE, DID YOU FORGET?
THAT MAN IS THE SORT WHO CLAIMS TO HAVE NO INTEREST IN ANYONE WHO'D LIKE HIM.
LOVING SOMEONE AS SUCH IS POINTLESS.
OH, YOU'RE RIGHT! THAT'S TRUE, ISN'T IT.
I'LL HAVE TO START TRAINING NOW SO THAT I'LL BE ABLE TO BEHAVE NORMALLY IN HIS PRESENCE!
NO.
THAT'S NOT WHAT I MEANT.

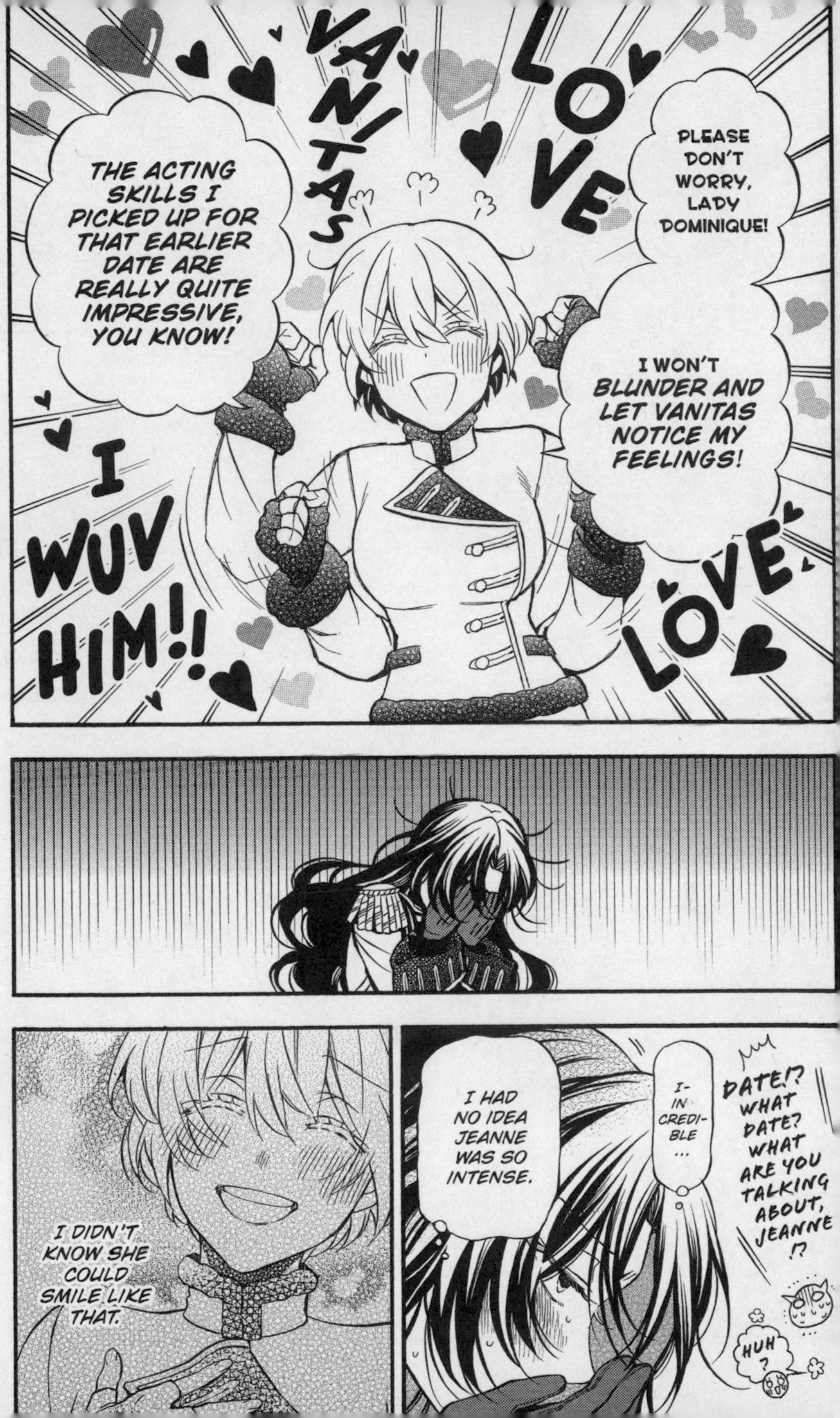
LOVE
PLEASE DON'T WORRY, LADY DOMINIQUE!
VANITAS
THE ACTING SKILLS I PICKED UP FOR THAT EARLIER DATE ARE REALLY QUITE IMPRESSIVE, YOU KNOW!
I WON'T BLUNDER AND LET VANITAS NOTICE MY FEELINGS!
LOVE
I WUV HIM!!
DATE!? WHAT DATE? WHAT ARE YOU TALKING ABOUT, JEANNE!?
I-INCREDIBLE...
I HAD NO IDEA JEANNE WAS SO INTENSE.
HUH?
I DIDN'T KNOW SHE COULD SMILE LIKE THAT.

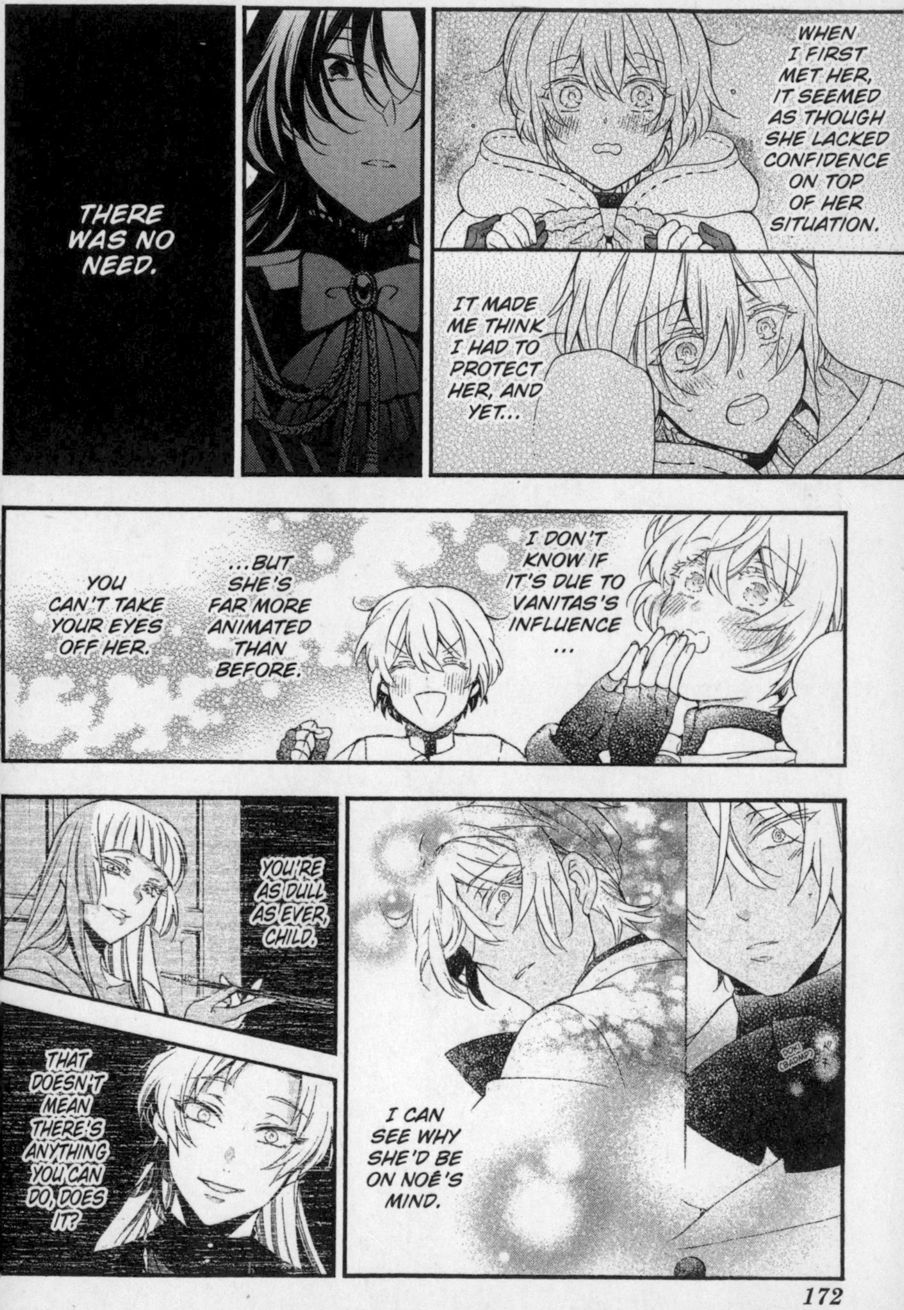
WHEN I FIRST MET HER, IT SEEMED AS THOUGH SHE LACKED CONFIDENCE ON TOP OF HER SITUATION.
IT MADE ME THINK I HAD TO PROTECT HER, AND YET...
THERE WAS NO NEED.
I DON'T KNOW IF IT'S DUE TO VANITAS'S INFLUENCE ...
...BUT SHE'S FAR MORE ANIMATED THAN BEFORE.
YOU CAN'T TAKE YOUR EYES OFF HER.
DOKI (BADMP)
I CAN SEE WHY SHE'D BE ON NOÊ'S MIND.
YOU'RE AS DULL AS EVER, CHILD.
THAT DOESN'T MEAN THERE'S ANYTHING YOU CAN DO, DOES IT?

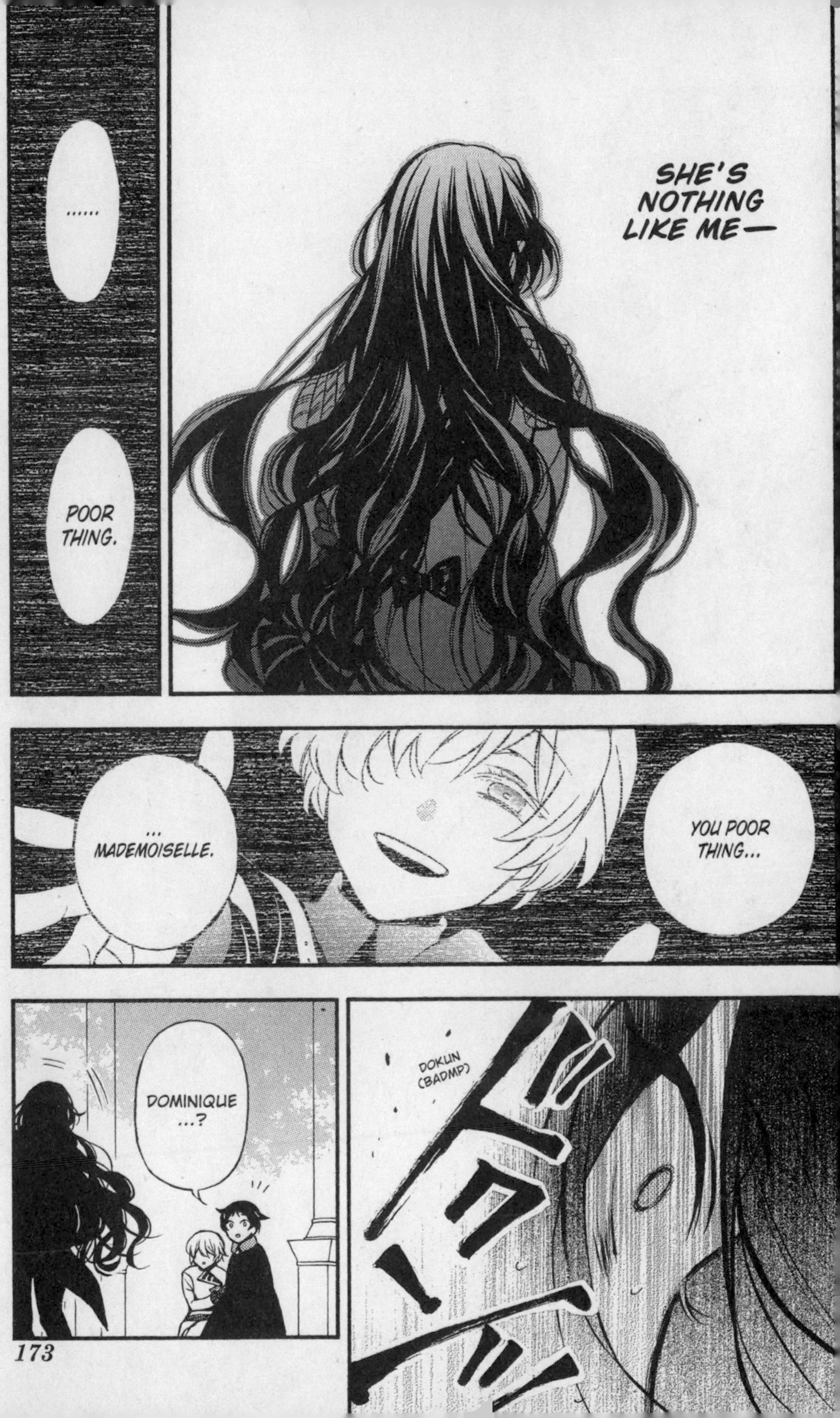
SHE'S NOTHING LIKE ME—
......
POOR THING.
YOU POOR THING...
... MADEMOISELLE.
DOKUN (BADMP)
DOMINIQUE ...?

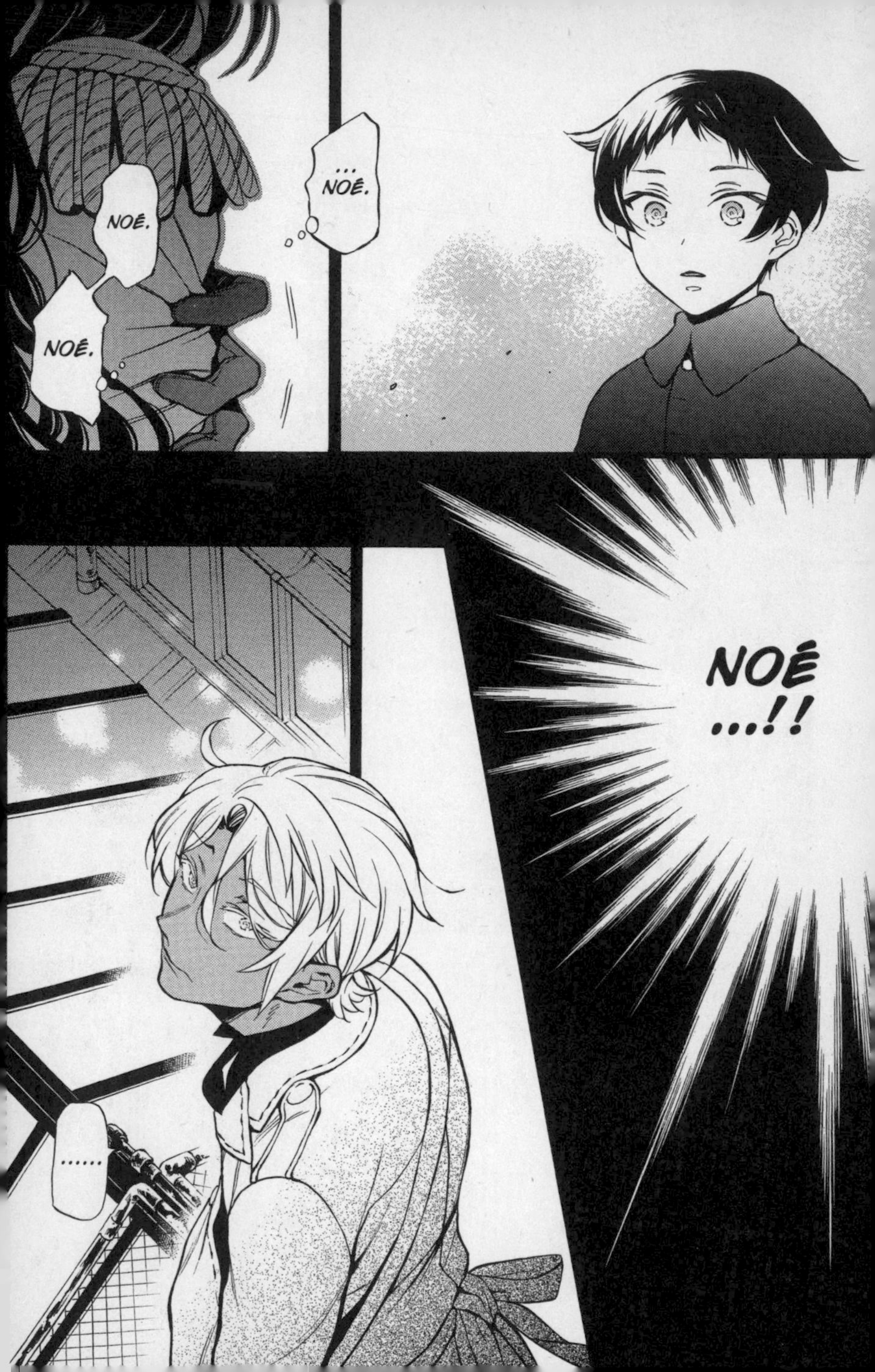
... NOÉ.
NOÉ.
NOÉ.
NOÉ ...!!
......

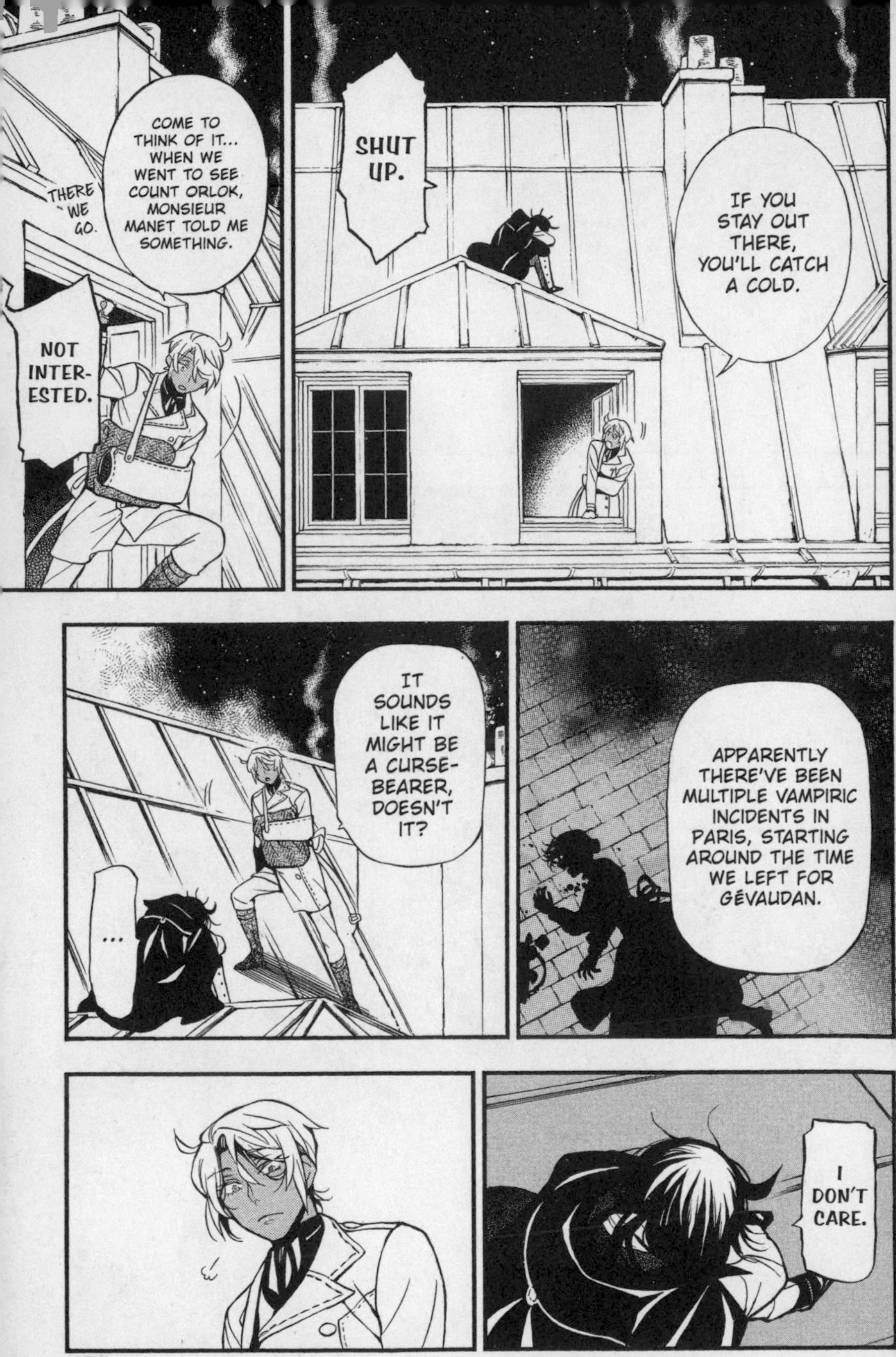
IF YOU STAY OUT THERE, YOU'LL CATCH A COLD.
SHUT UP.
COME TO THINK OF IT... WHEN WE WENT TO SEE COUNT ORLOK, MONSIEUR MANET TOLD ME SOMETHING.
THERE WE GO.
NOT INTER-ESTED.
APPARENTLY THERE'VE BEEN MULTIPLE VAMPIRIC INCIDENTS IN PARIS, STARTING AROUND THE TIME WE LEFT FOR GÉVAUDAN.
IT SOUNDS LIKE IT MIGHT BE A CURSE-BEARER, DOESN'T IT?
...
I DON'T CARE.

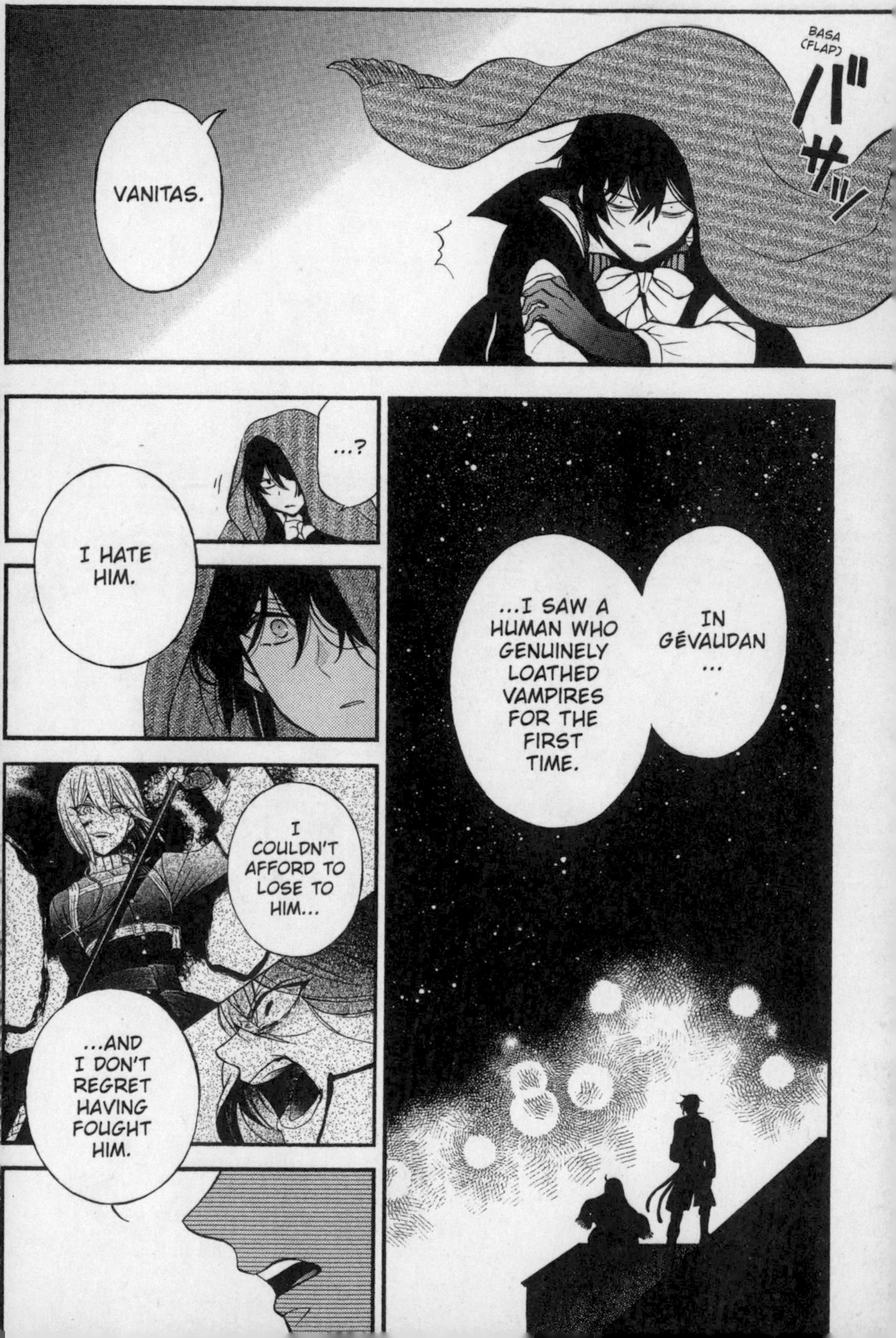
BASA (FLAP)
バサッ
VANITAS.
IN GÉVAUDAN ...
...I SAW A HUMAN WHO GENUINELY LOATHED VAMPIRES FOR THE FIRST TIME.
...?
I HATE HIM.
I COULDN'T AFFORD TO LOSE TO HIM...
...AND I DON'T REGRET HAVING FOUGHT HIM.

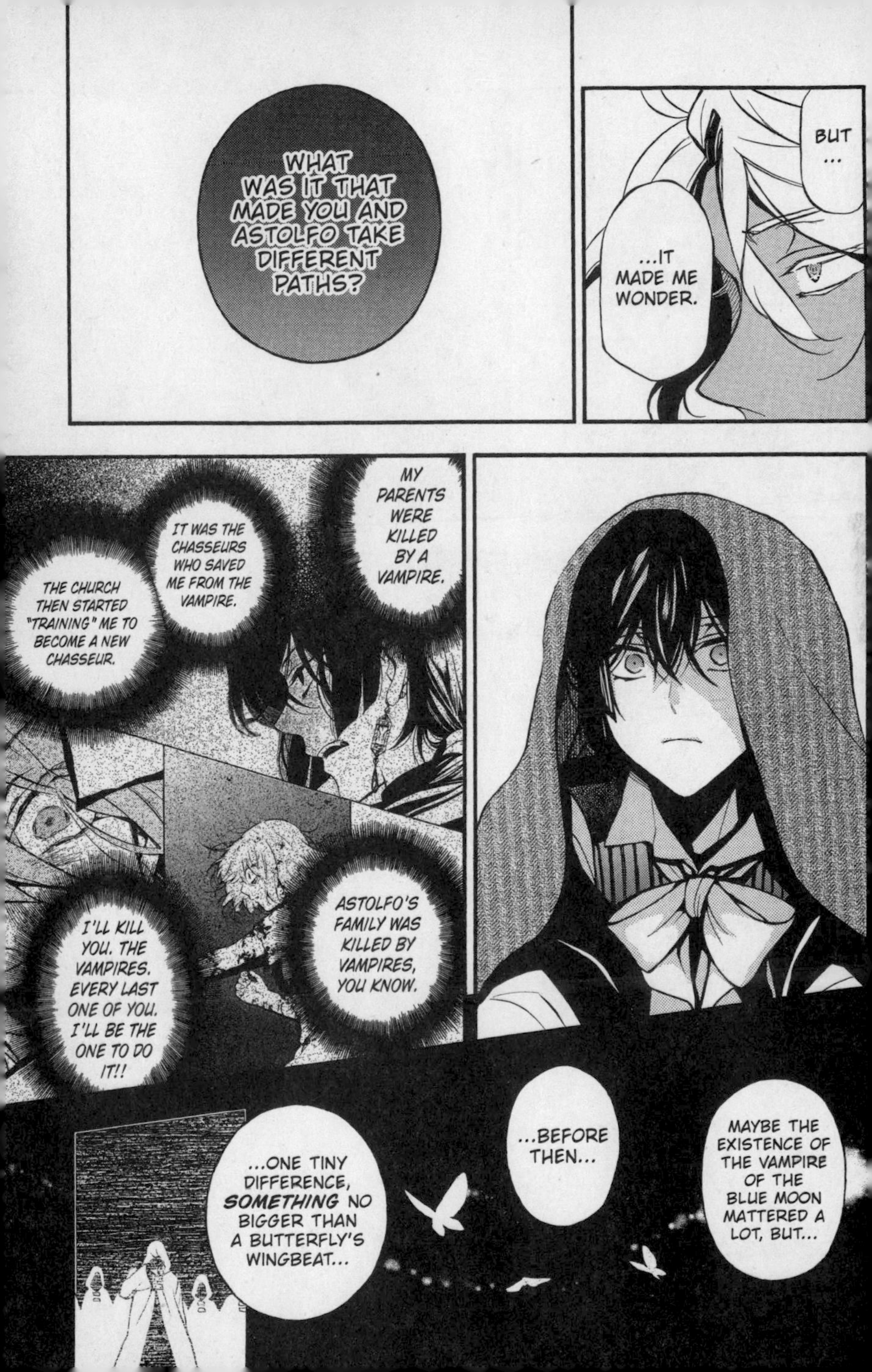
BUT...
...IT MADE ME WONDER.
WHAT WAS IT THAT MADE YOU AND ASTOLFO TAKE DIFFERENT PATHS?
MY PARENTS WERE KILLED BY A VAMPIRE.
IT WAS THE CHASSEURS WHO SAVED ME FROM THE VAMPIRE.
THE CHURCH THEN STARTED "TRAINING" ME TO BECOME A NEW CHASSEUR.
ASTOLFO'S FAMILY WAS KILLED BY VAMPIRES, YOU KNOW.
I'LL KILL YOU. THE VAMPIRES. EVERY LAST ONE OF YOU. I'LL BE THE ONE TO DO IT!!
MAYBE THE EXISTENCE OF THE VAMPIRE OF THE BLUE MOON MATTERED A LOT, BUT...
...BEFORE THEN...
...ONE TINY DIFFERENCE, SOMETHING NO BIGGER THAN A BUTTERFLY'S WINGBEAT...

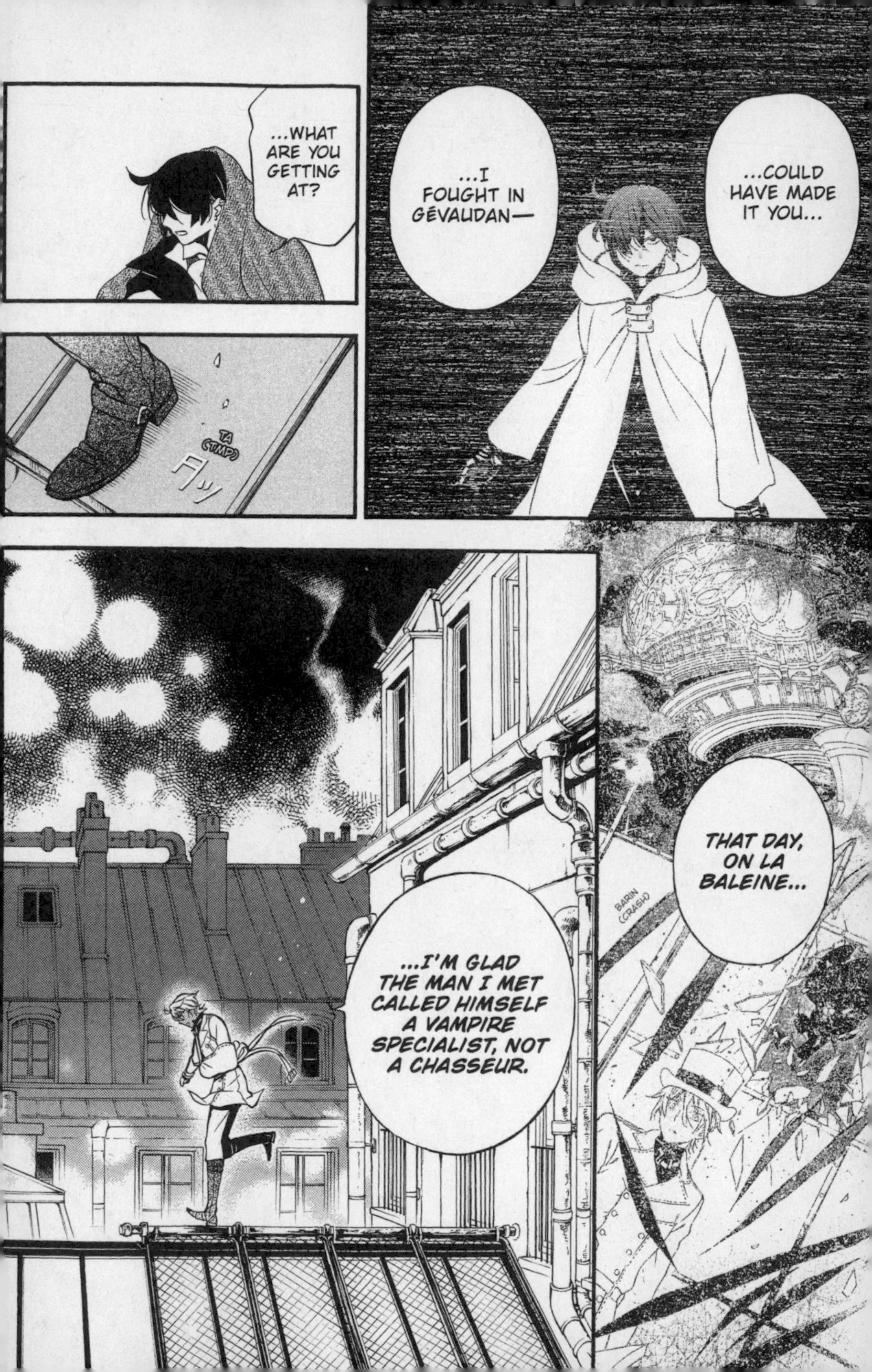
...COULD HAVE MADE IT YOU...
...I FOUGHT IN GÉVAUDAN—
...WHAT ARE YOU GETTING AT?
TA (TMP)
タッ
THAT DAY, ON LA BALEINE...
BARIN (CRASH)
...I'M GLAD THE MAN I MET CALLED HIMSELF A VAMPIRE SPECIALIST, NOT A CHASSEUR.

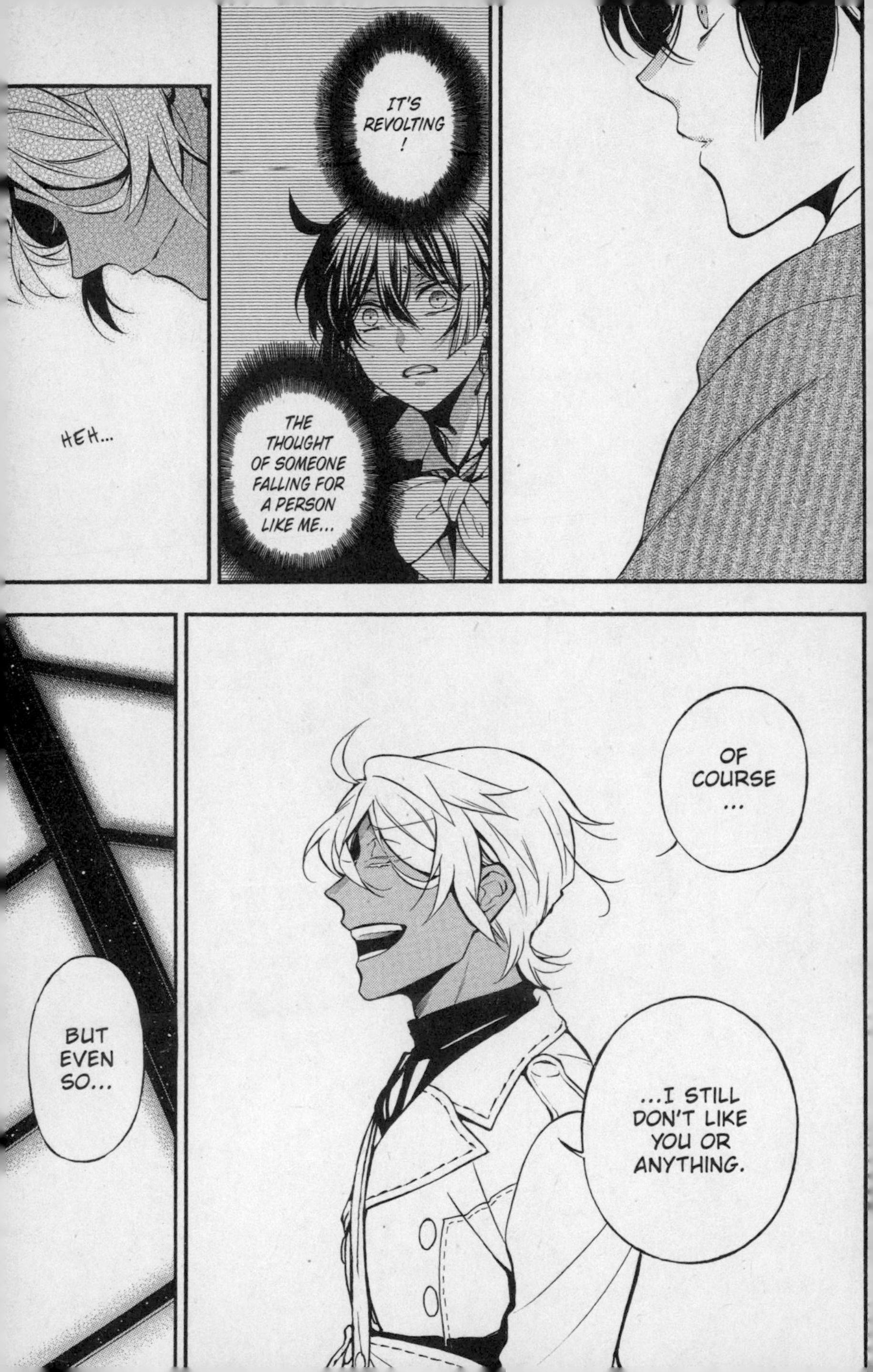
IT'S REVOLTING!
THE THOUGHT OF SOMEONE FALLING FOR A PERSON LIKE ME...
HEH...
OF COURSE...
...I STILL DON'T LIKE YOU OR ANYTHING.
BUT EVEN SO...

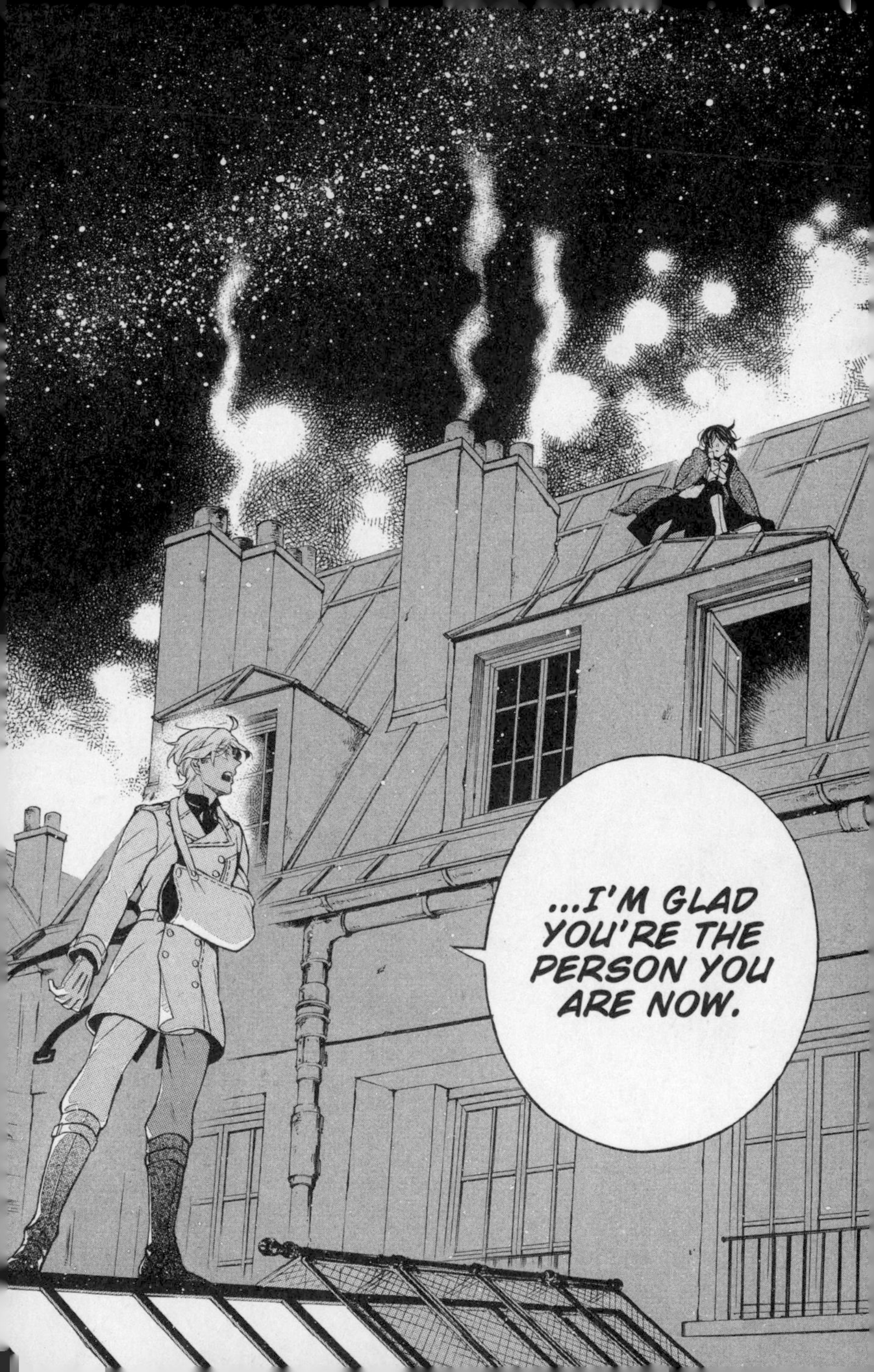
...I'M GLAD YOU'RE THE PERSON YOU ARE NOW.

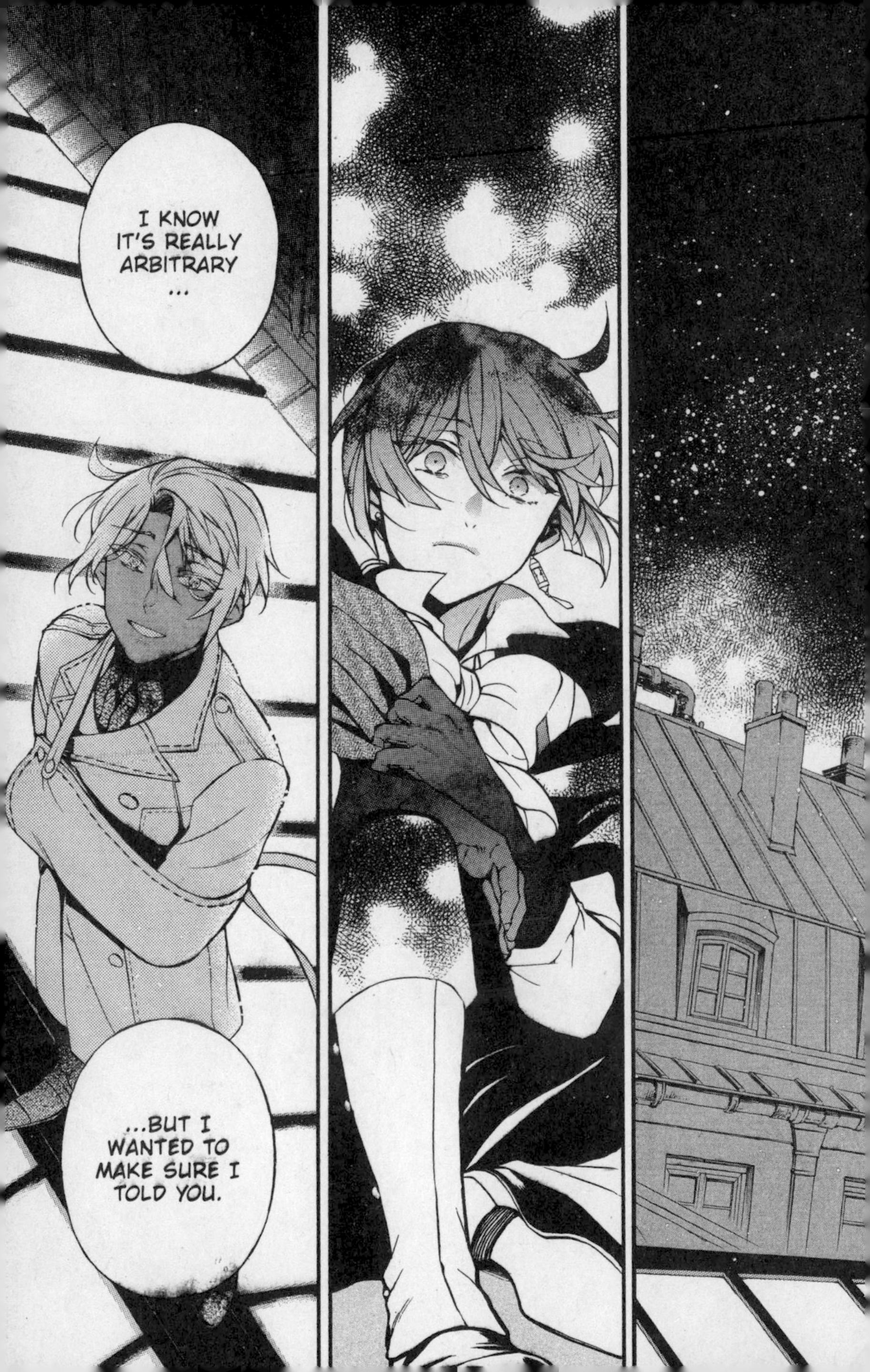
I KNOW IT'S REALLY ARBITRARY ...
...BUT I WANTED TO MAKE SURE I TOLD YOU.

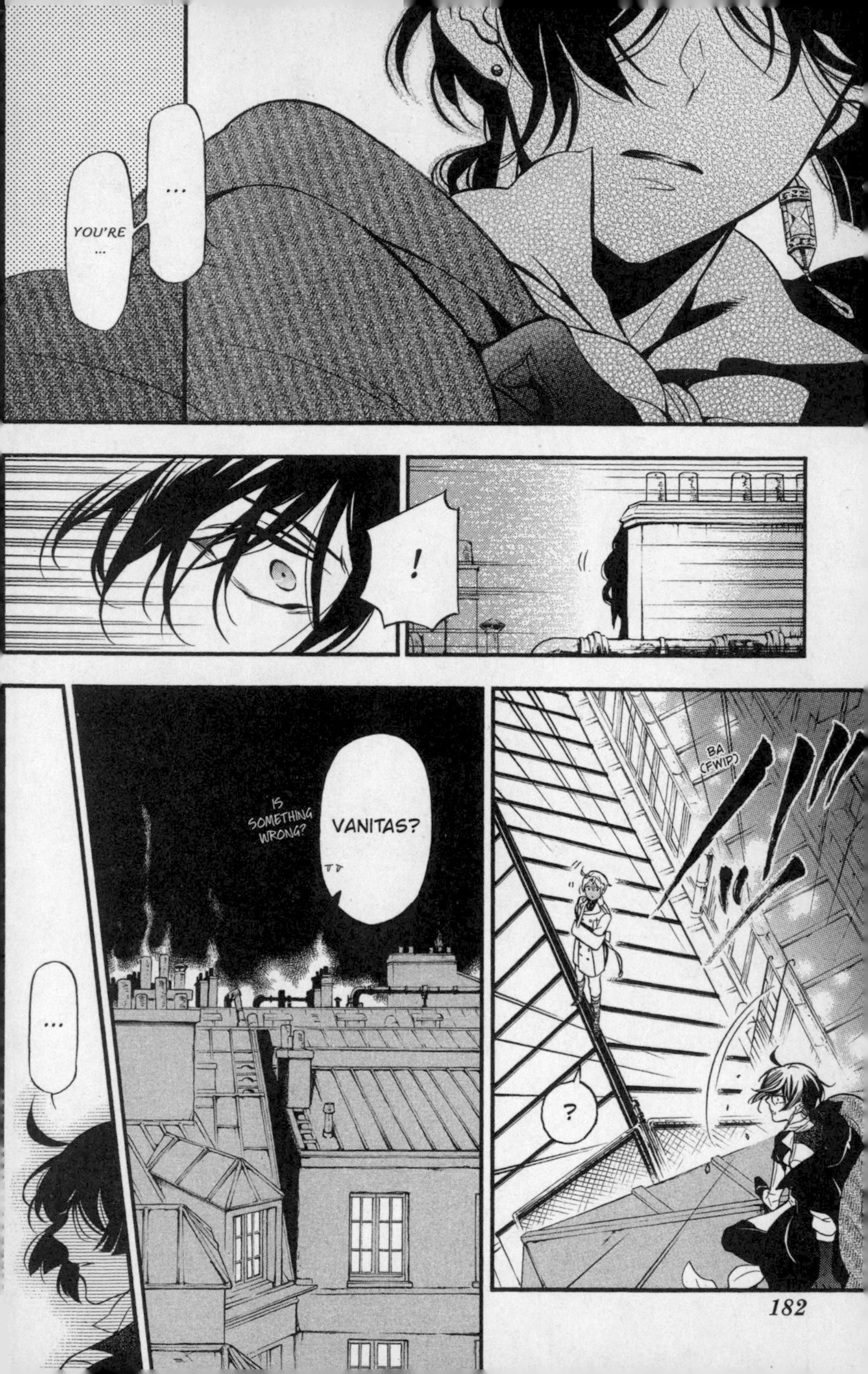
...
YOU'RE ...
!
BA (FWIP)
?
VANITAS?
IS SOMETHING WRONG?
...

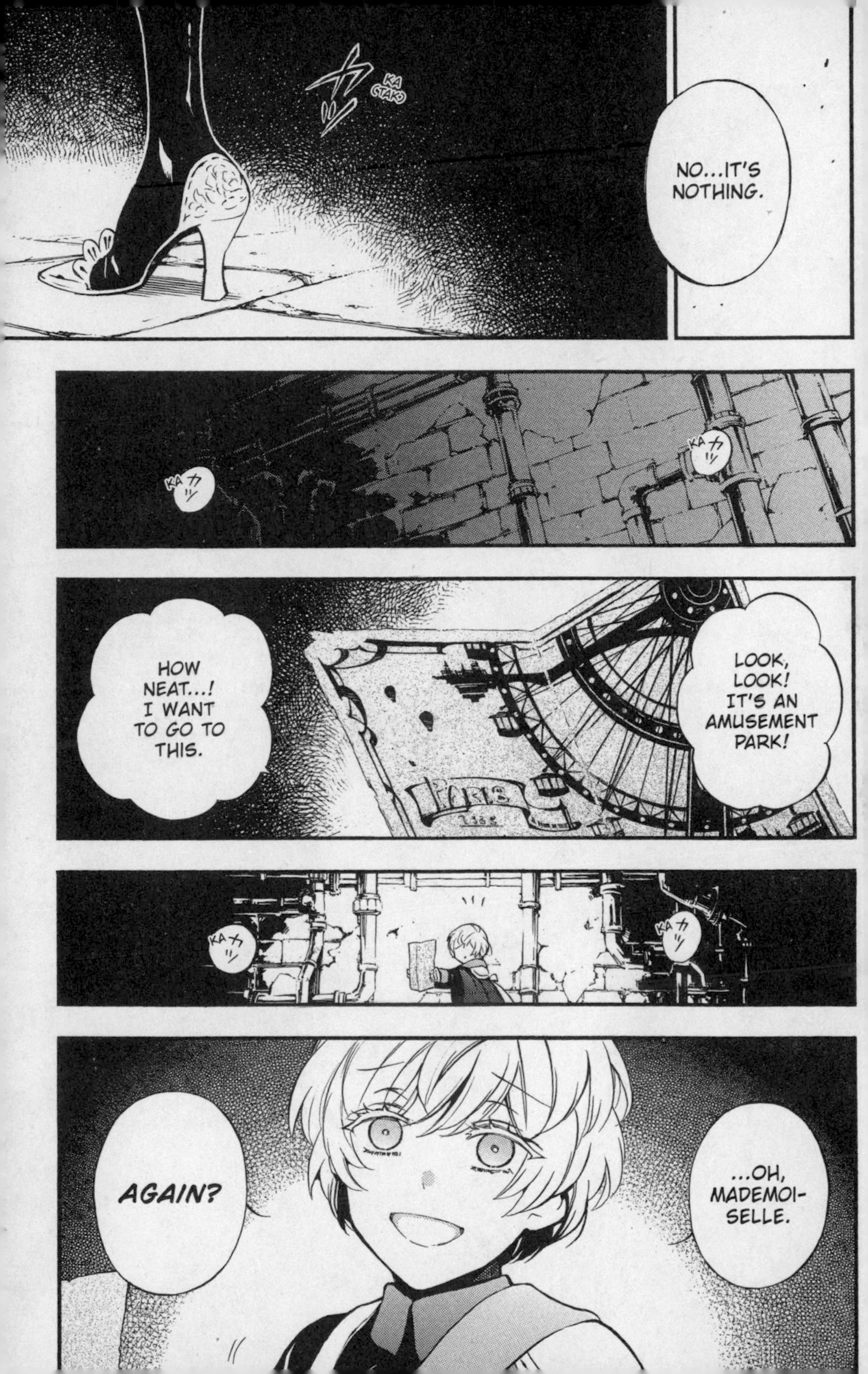
NO...IT'S NOTHING.
KA (TAK)
KA
KA
LOOK, LOOK! IT'S AN AMUSEMENT PARK!
HOW NEAT...! I WANT TO GO TO THIS.
KA
KA
...OH, MADEMOI-SELLE.
AGAIN?

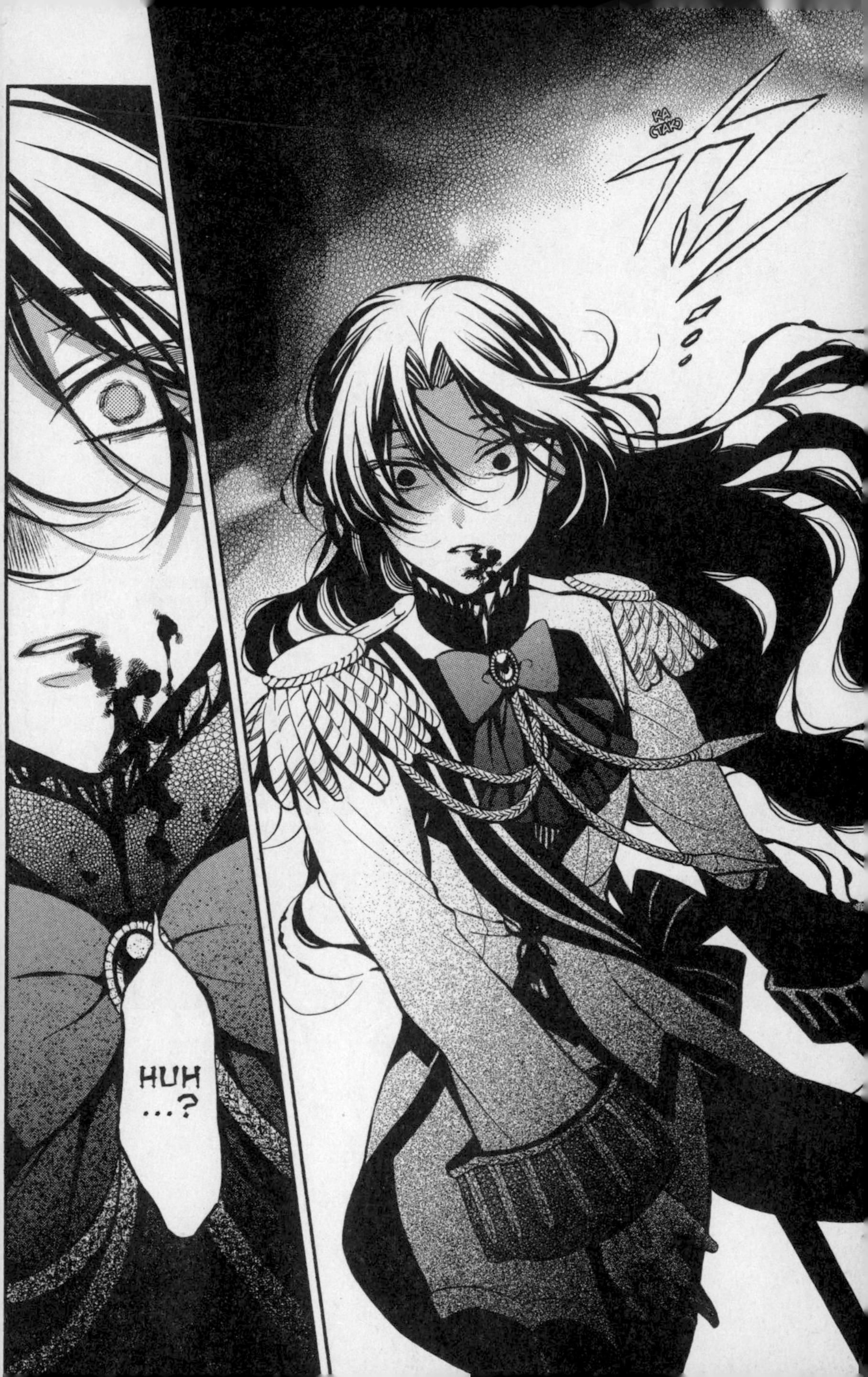
KA (TAK)
HUH ...?

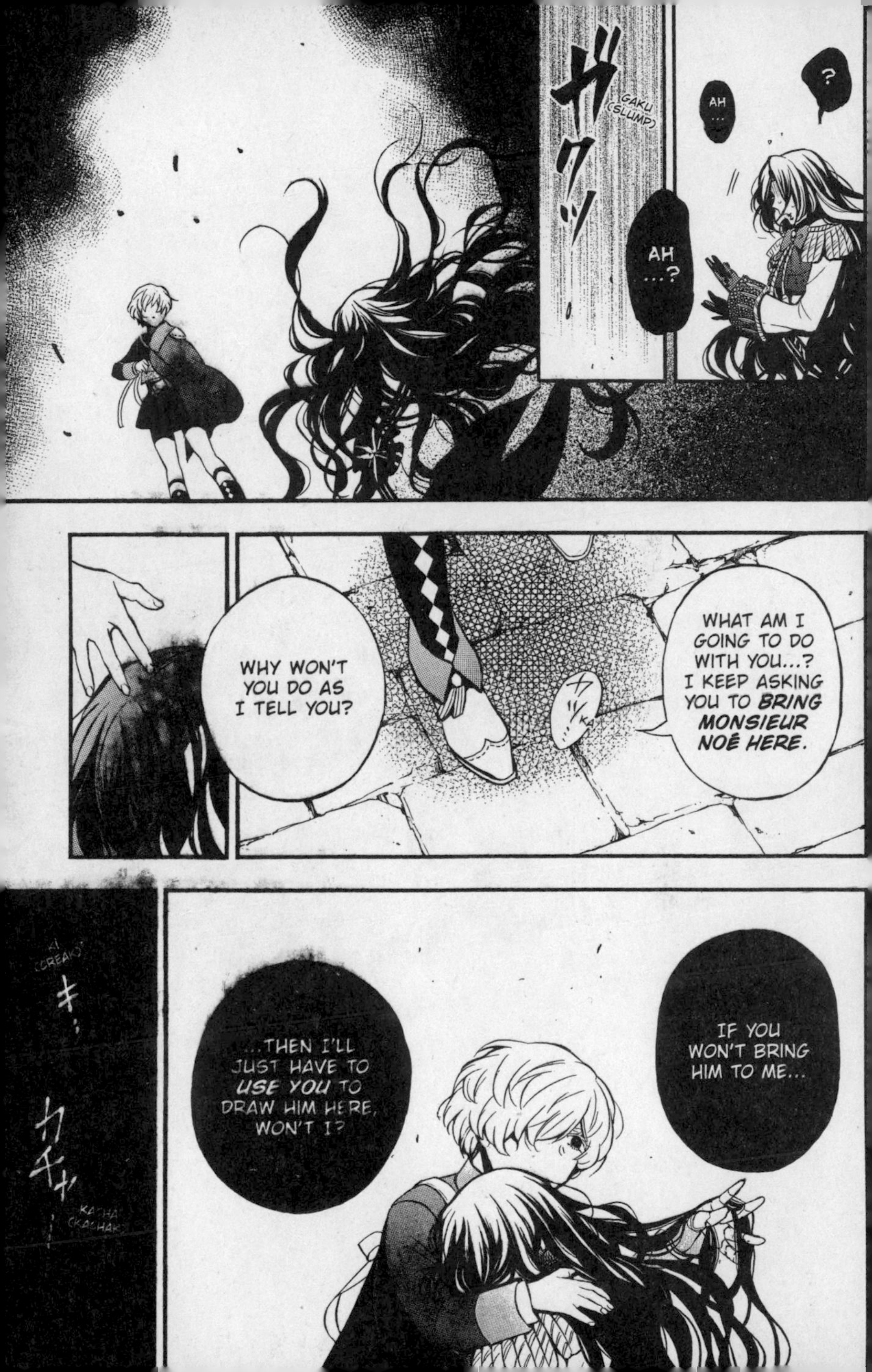
?
AH ...
GAKU (SLUMP)
AH ...?
WHAT AM I GOING TO DO WITH YOU...? I KEEP ASKING YOU TO **BRING MONSIEUR NOÊ HERE**.
WHY WON'T YOU DO AS I TELL YOU?
IF YOU WON'T BRING HIM TO ME...
...THEN I'LL JUST HAVE TO ***USE YOU*** TO DRAW HIM HERE, WON'T I?
KI (CREAK)
KACHA (KACHAK)

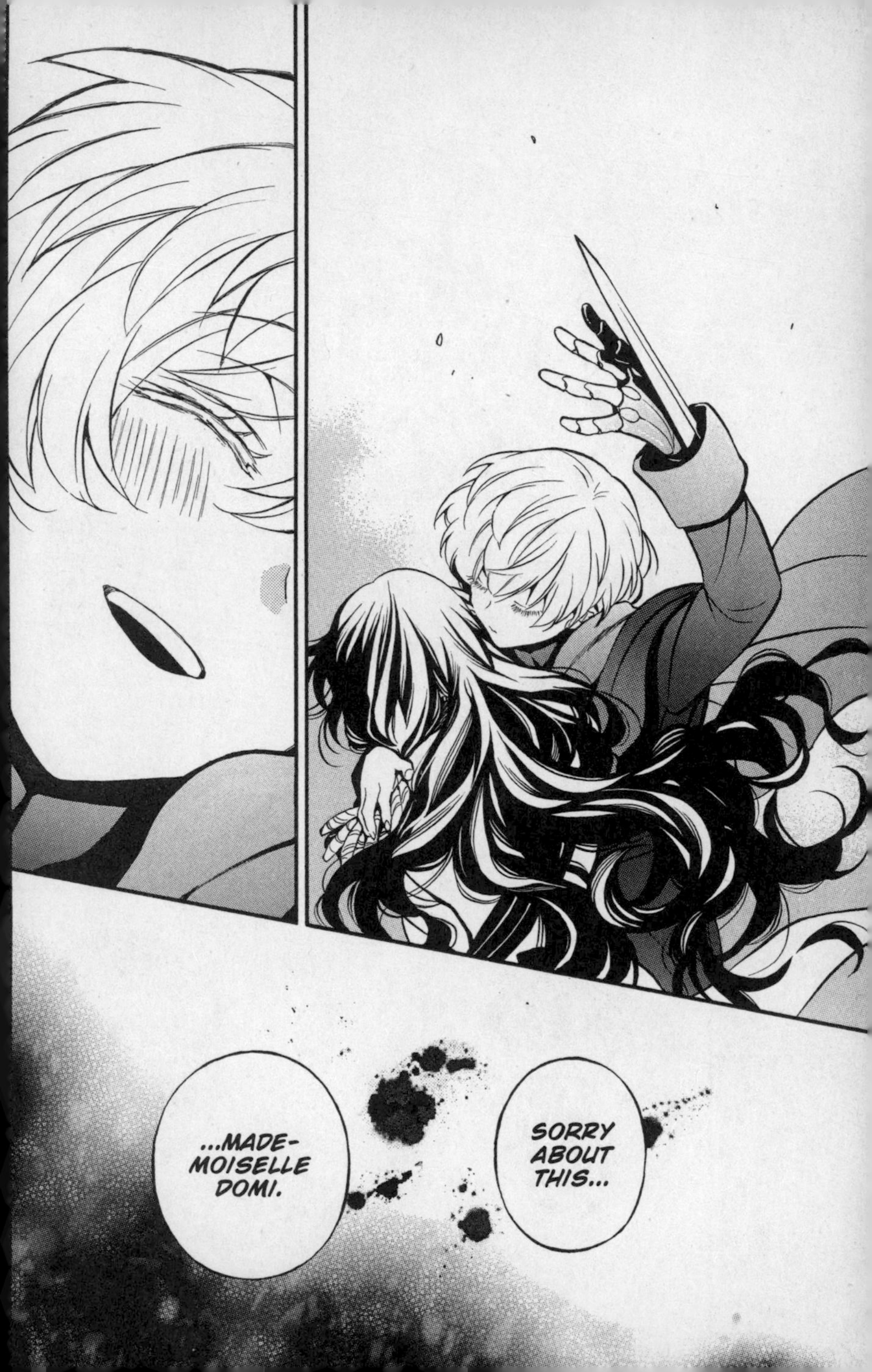
SORRY ABOUT THIS...
...MADE-MOISELLE DOMI.

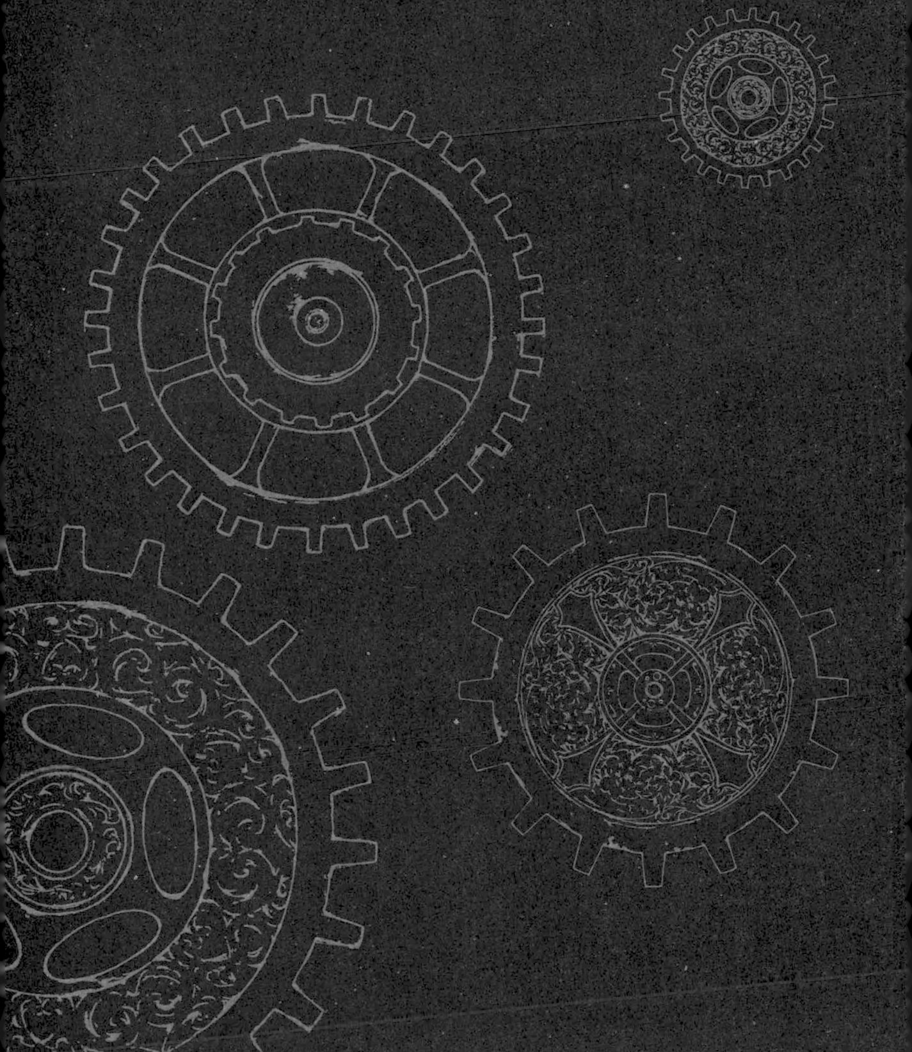

Mémoire 45
Mal d'Amour THE INCURABLE ILLNESS (PART 2)

Les Mémoires de Vanitas

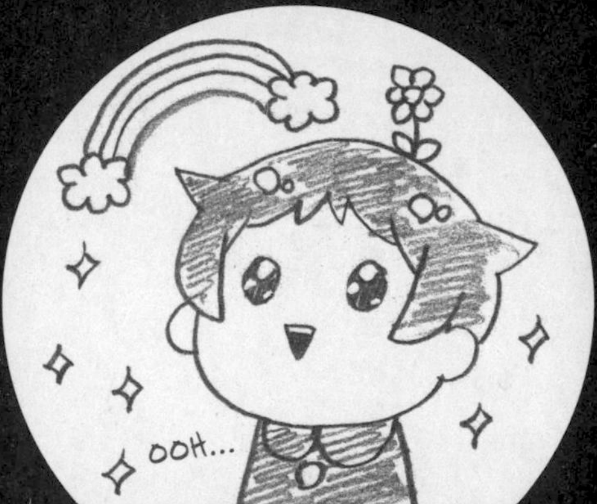
OOH...

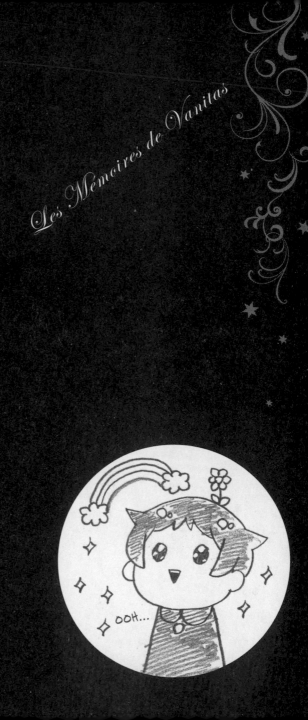

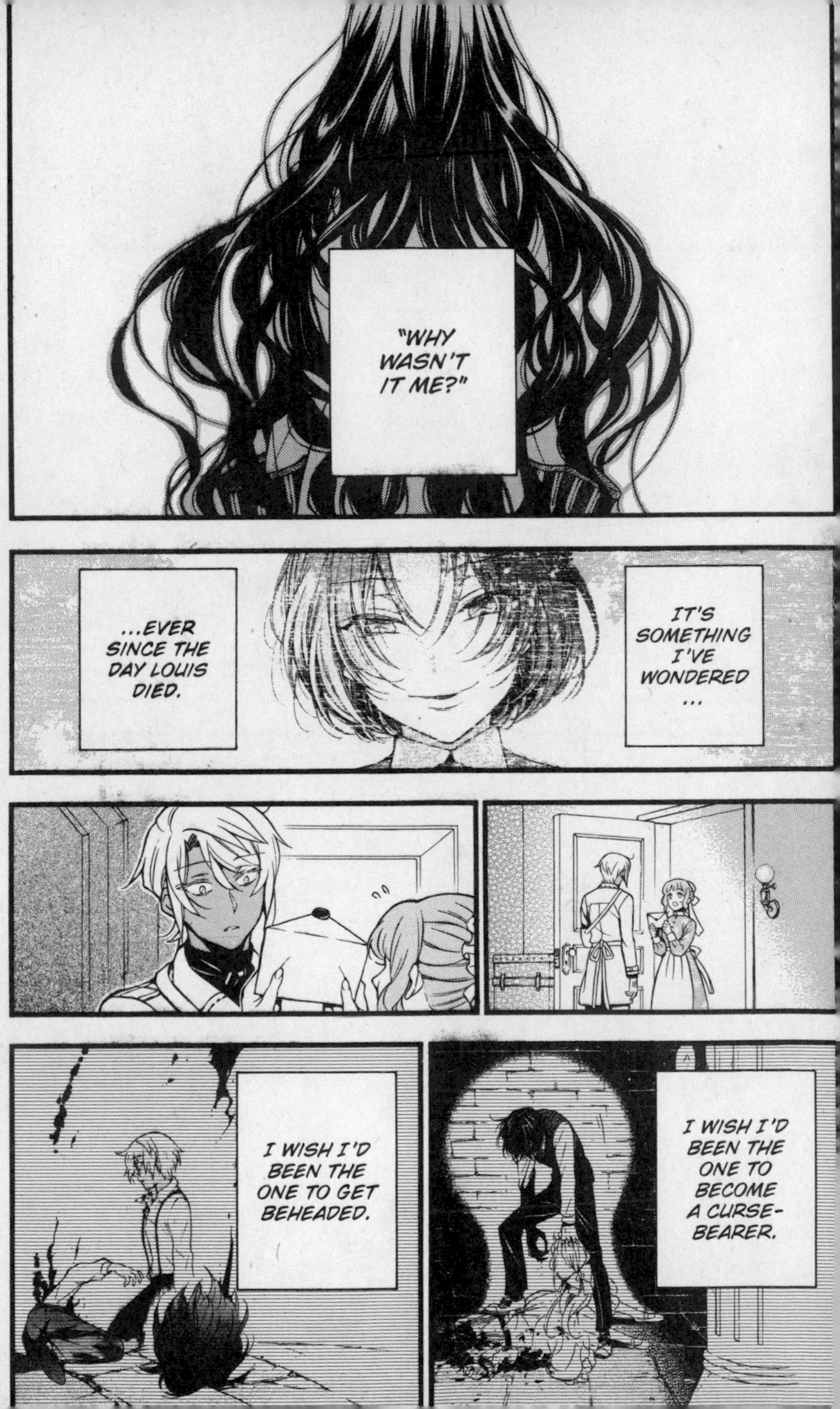
"WHY WASN'T IT ME?"
IT'S SOMETHING I'VE WONDERED ...
...EVER SINCE THE DAY LOUIS DIED.
I WISH I'D BEEN THE ONE TO BECOME A CURSE-BEARER.
I WISH I'D BEEN THE ONE TO GET BEHEADED.

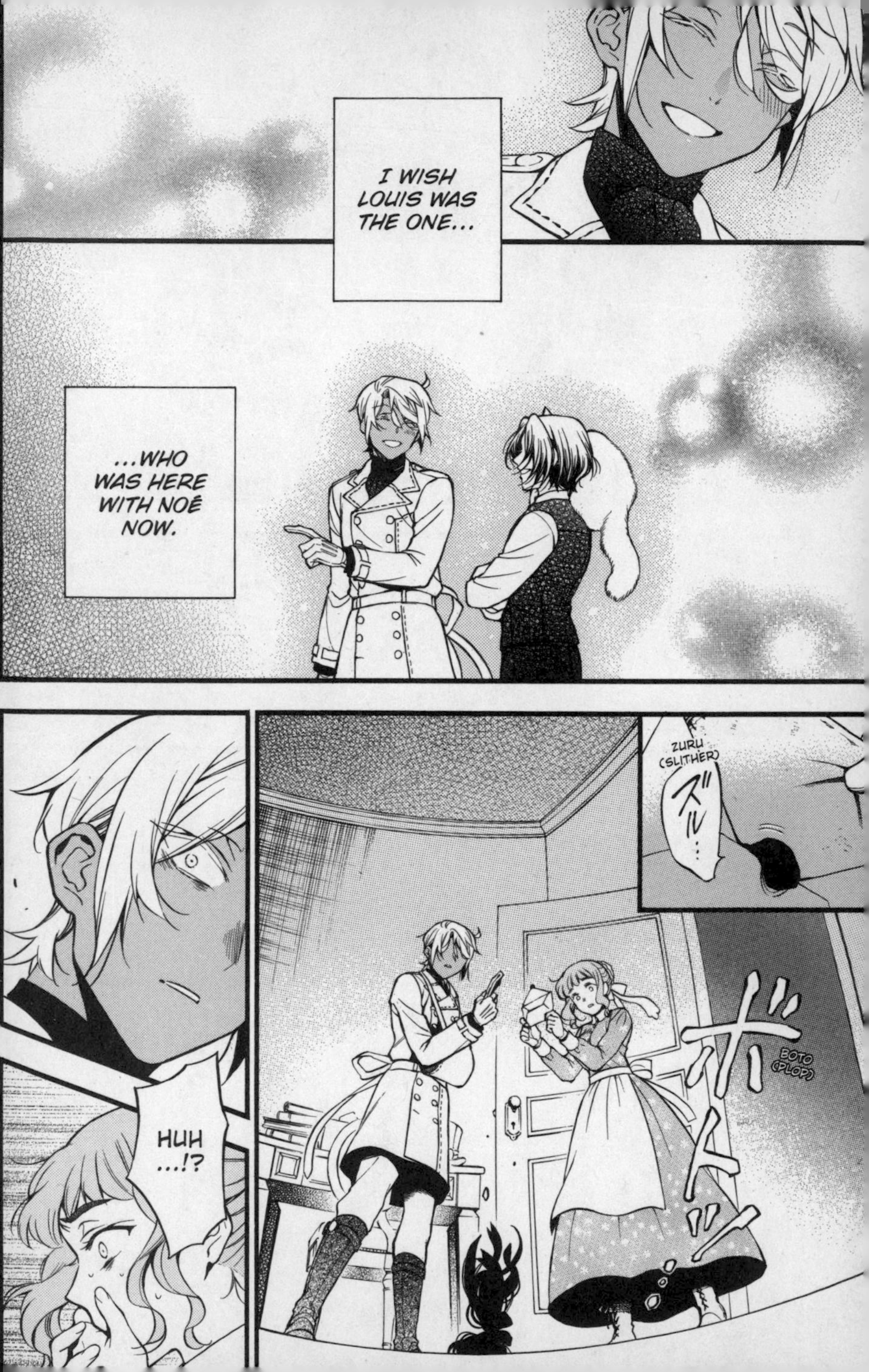
I WISH LOUIS WAS THE ONE...
...WHO WAS HERE WITH NOÉ NOW.
ZURU (SLITHER)
ズル…
BOTO (PLOP)
HUH ...!?

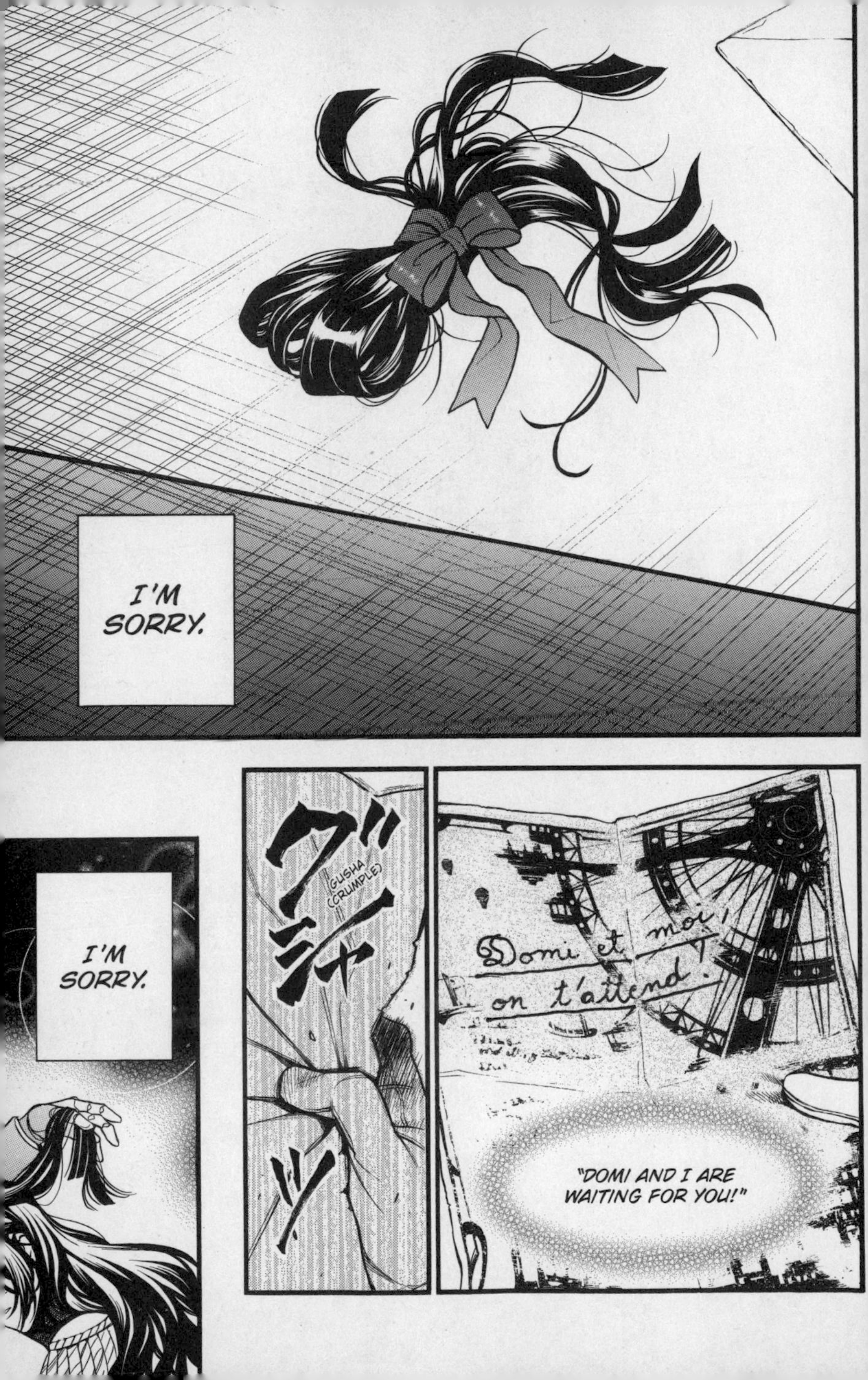
I'M SORRY.
Domi et moi, on t'attend!
"DOMI AND I ARE WAITING FOR YOU!"
GUSHA (CRUMPLE)
I'M SORRY.

MÉMOIRE 46

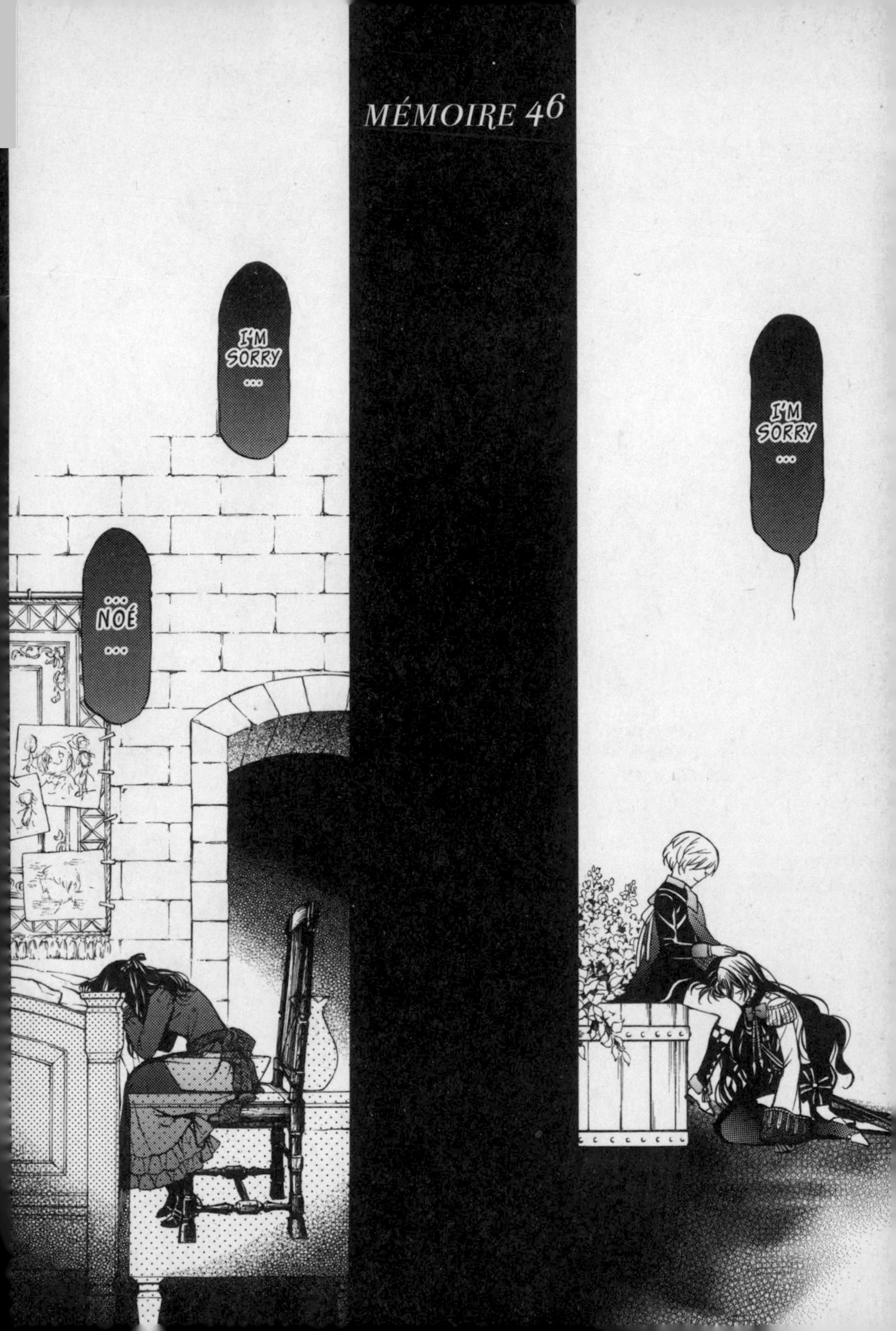
I'M SORRY ...
I'M SORRY ...
... NOÉ ...

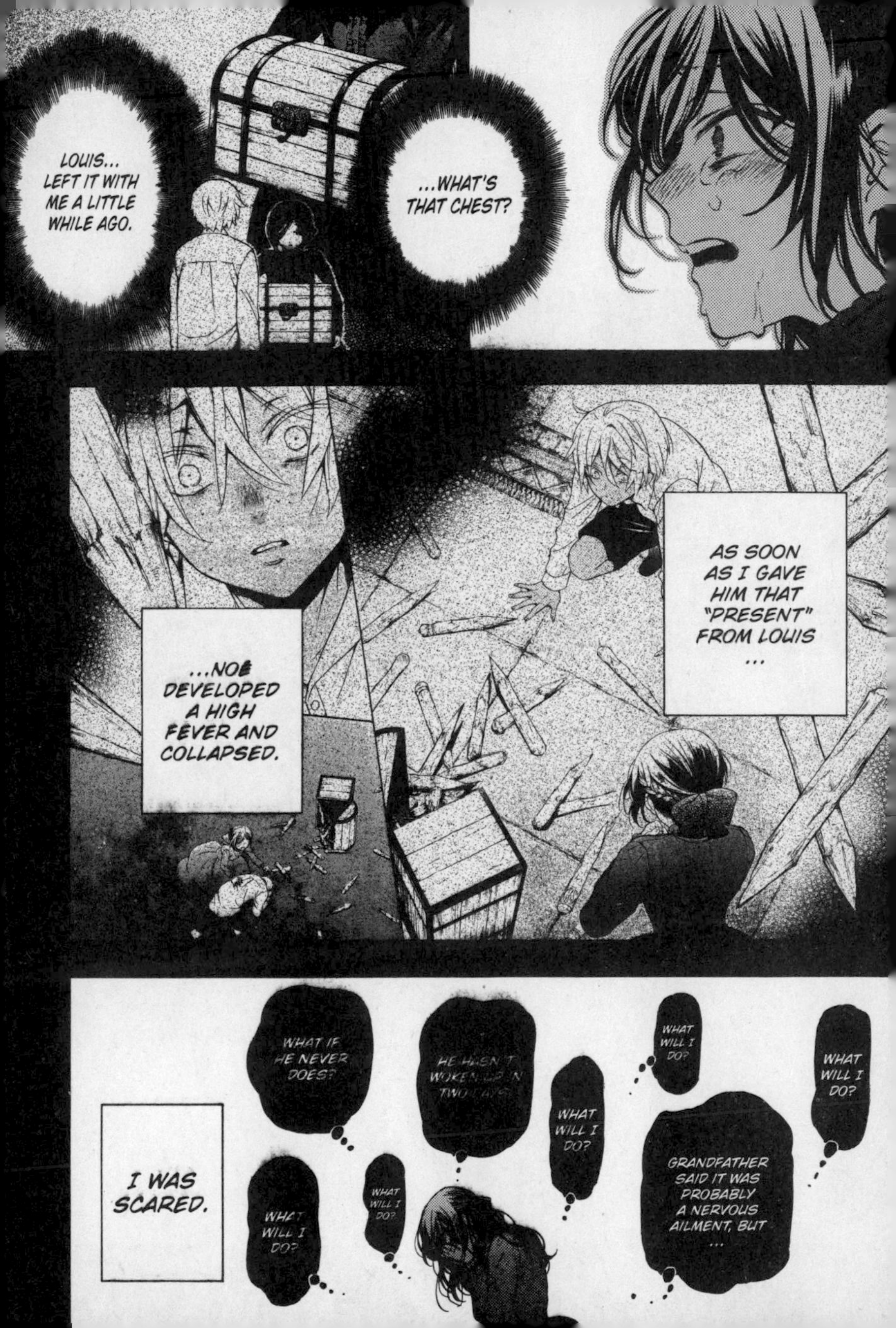
...WHAT'S THAT CHEST?
LOUIS... LEFT IT WITH ME A LITTLE WHILE AGO.
AS SOON AS I GAVE HIM THAT "PRESENT" FROM LOUIS ...
...NOÉ DEVELOPED A HIGH FEVER AND COLLAPSED.
WHAT WILL I DO?
WHAT WILL I DO?
GRANDFATHER SAID IT WAS PROBABLY A NERVOUS AILMENT, BUT ...
WHAT WILL I DO?
HE HASN'T WOKEN UP IN TWO DAYS.
WHAT IF HE NEVER DOES?
WHAT WILL I DO?
WHAT WILL I DO?
I WAS SCARED.

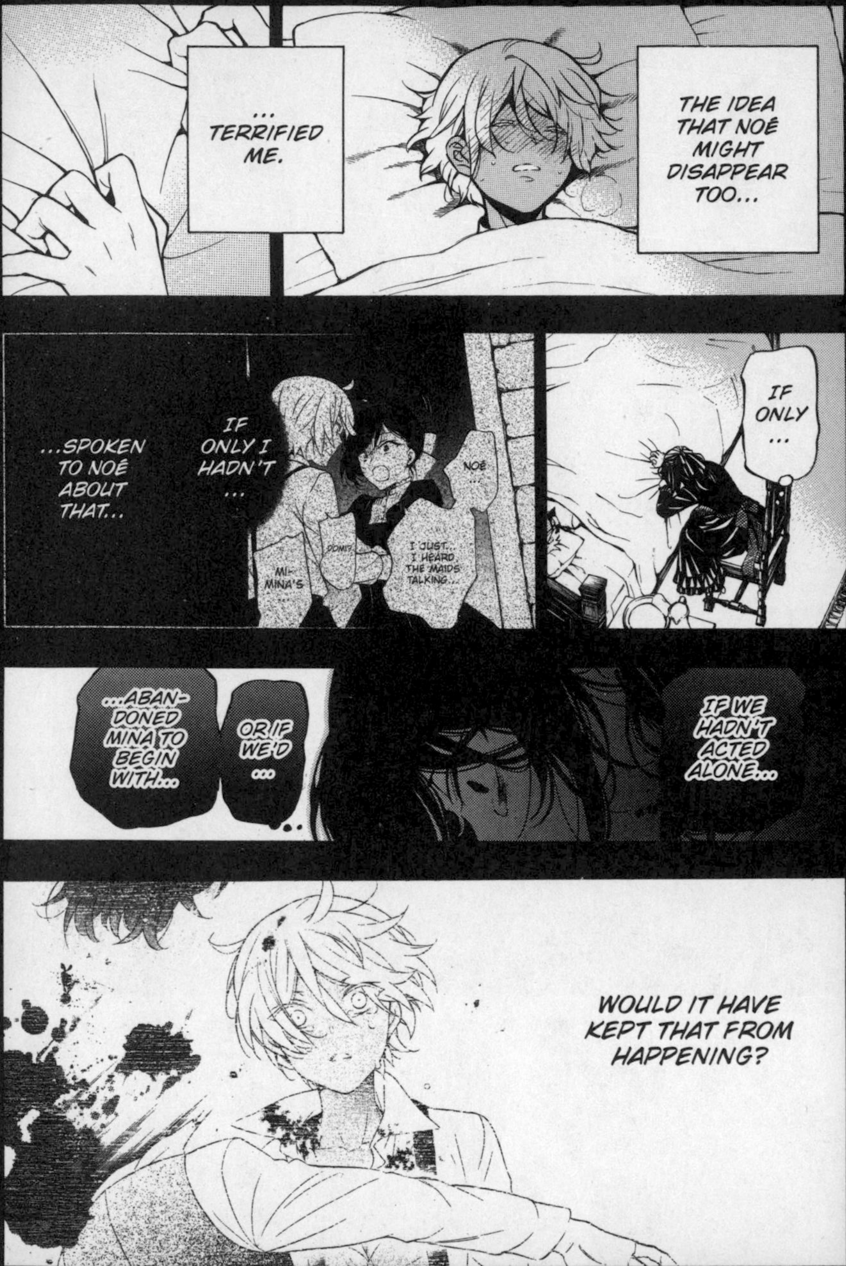
THE IDEA THAT NOÉ MIGHT DISAPPEAR TOO...
... TERRIFIED ME.
IF ONLY ...
IF ONLY I HADN'T ...
...SPOKEN TO NOÉ ABOUT THAT...
NOÉ ...
I JUST... I HEARD THE MAIDS TALKING...
DOMI?
MI-MINA'S ...
IF WE HADN'T ACTED ALONE...
OR IF WE'D ...
...ABAN-DONED MINA TO BEGIN WITH...
WOULD IT HAVE KEPT THAT FROM HAPPENING?

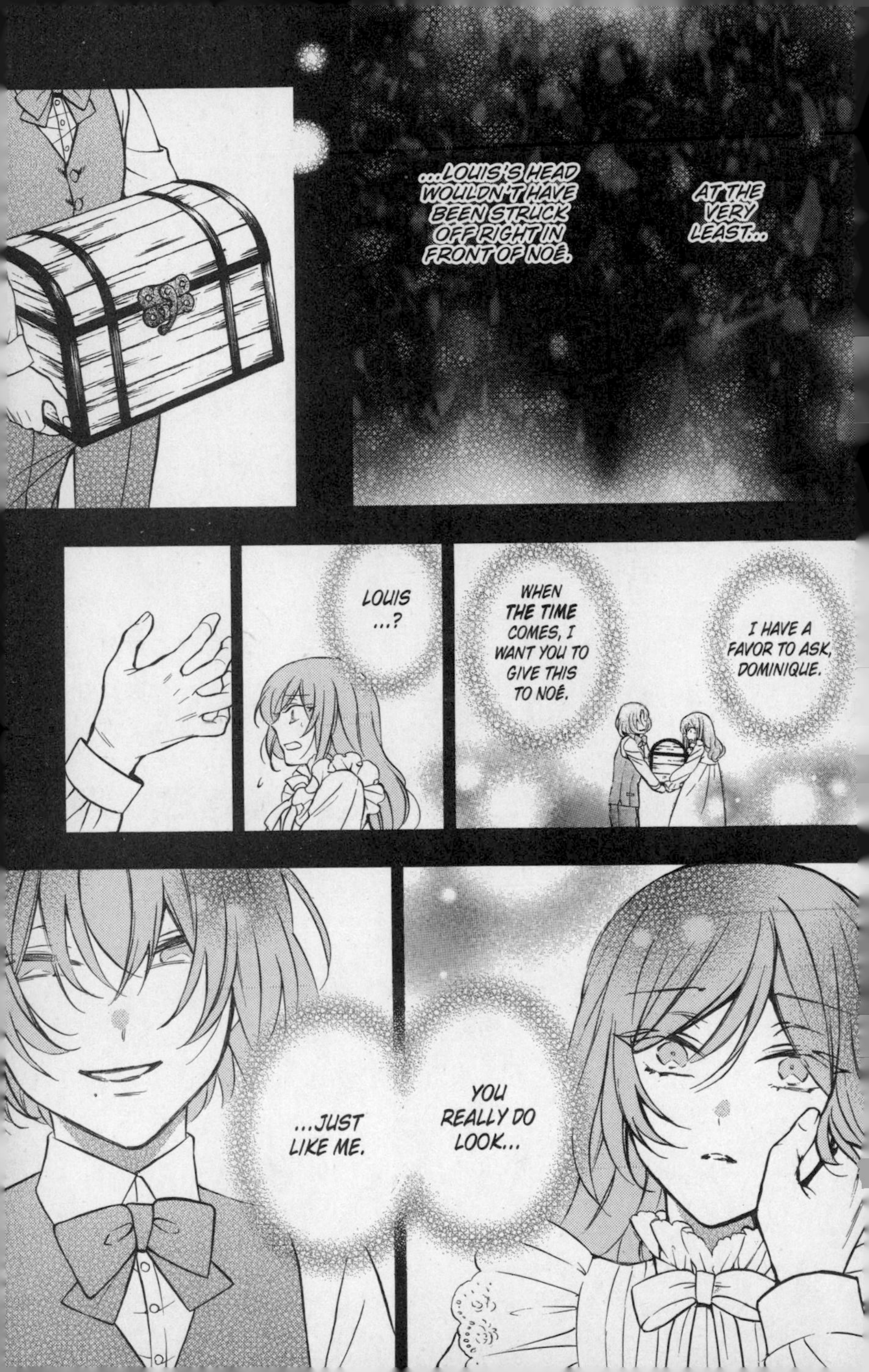
AT THE VERY LEAST...
...LOUIS'S HEAD WOULDN'T HAVE BEEN STRUCK OFF RIGHT IN FRONT OF NOÉ.
I HAVE A FAVOR TO ASK, DOMINIQUE.
WHEN THE TIME COMES, I WANT YOU TO GIVE THIS TO NOÉ.
LOUIS ...?
YOU REALLY DO LOOK...
...JUST LIKE ME.

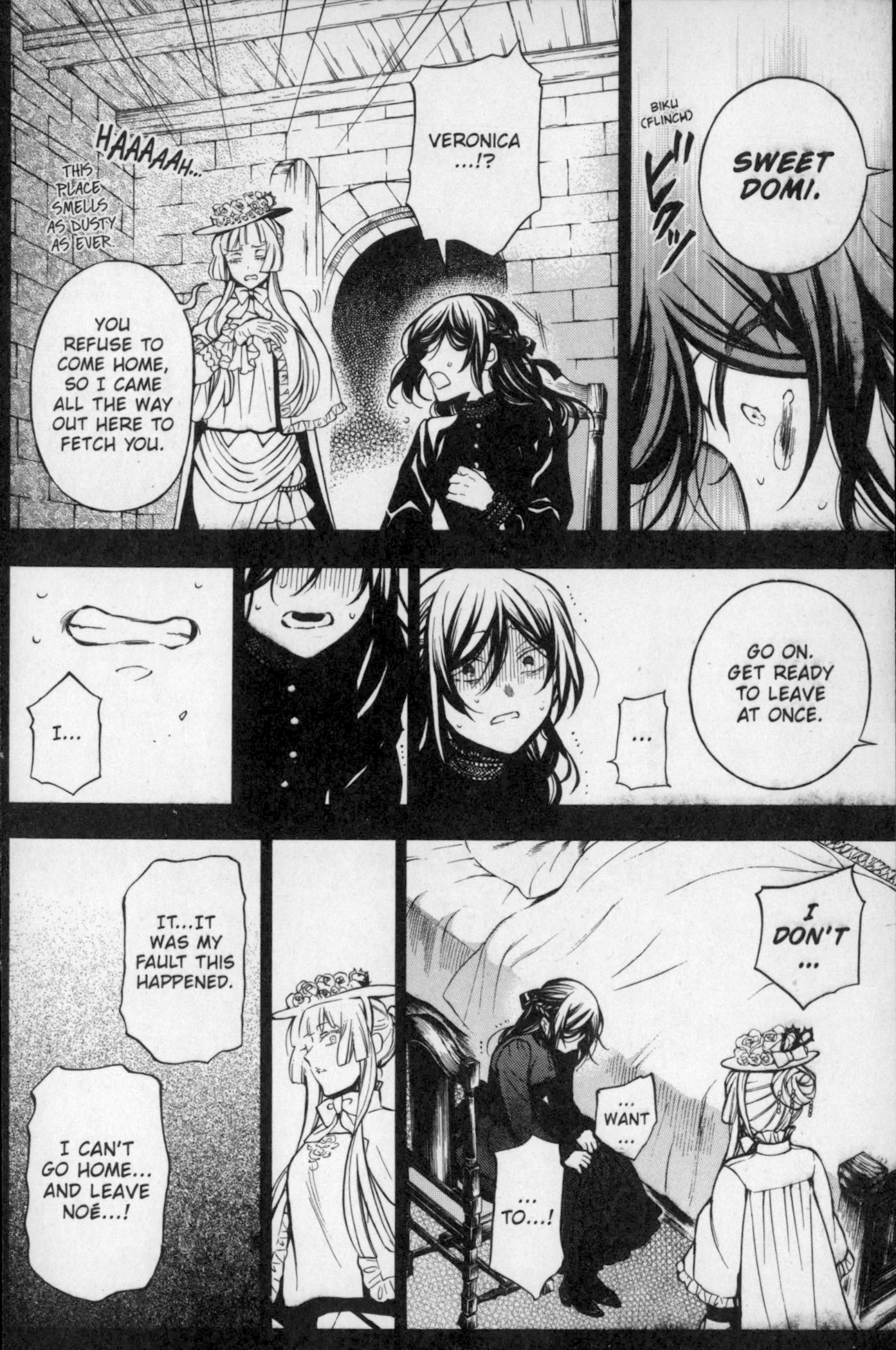
SWEET DOMI.
BIKU (FLINCH)
VERONICA ...!?
HAAAAAAH...
THIS PLACE SMELLS AS DUSTY AS EVER.
YOU REFUSE TO COME HOME, SO I CAME ALL THE WAY OUT HERE TO FETCH YOU.
GO ON. GET READY TO LEAVE AT ONCE.
...
I...
I DON'T ...
... WANT ...
... TO...!
IT...IT WAS MY FAULT THIS HAPPENED.
I CAN'T GO HOME... AND LEAVE NOÉ...!

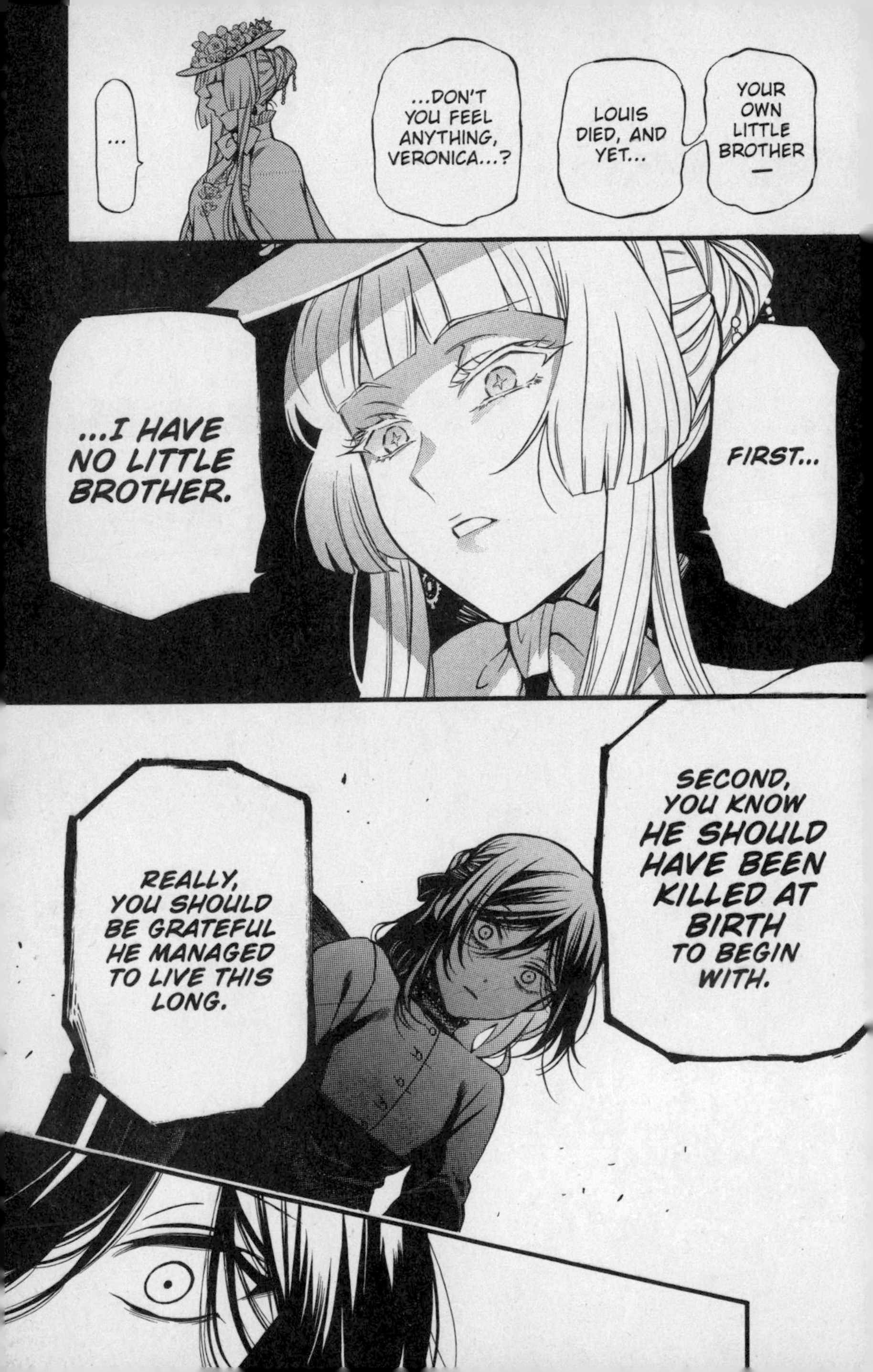
YOUR OWN LITTLE BROTHER —
LOUIS DIED, AND YET...
...DON'T YOU FEEL ANYTHING, VERONICA...?
...
FIRST...
...I HAVE NO LITTLE BROTHER.
SECOND, YOU KNOW HE SHOULD HAVE BEEN KILLED AT BIRTH TO BEGIN WITH.
REALLY, YOU SHOULD BE GRATEFUL HE MANAGED TO LIVE THIS LONG.

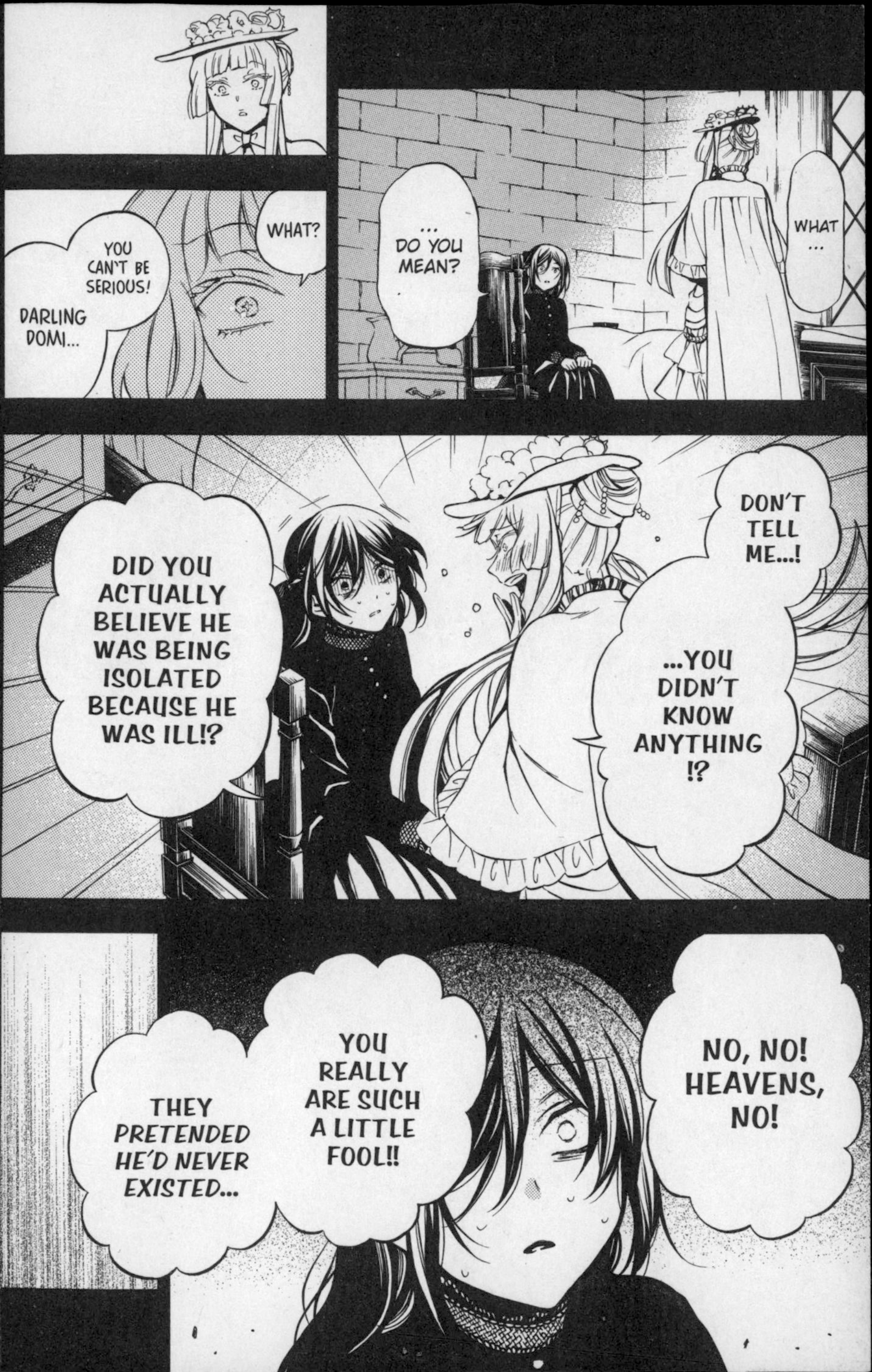
WHAT ...
... DO YOU MEAN?
WHAT?
YOU CAN'T BE SERIOUS!
DARLING DOMI...
DON'T TELL ME...!
...YOU DIDN'T KNOW ANYTHING !?
DID YOU ACTUALLY BELIEVE HE WAS BEING ISOLATED BECAUSE HE WAS ILL!?
NO, NO! HEAVENS, NO!
YOU REALLY ARE SUCH A LITTLE FOOL!!
THEY PRETENDED HE'D NEVER EXISTED...

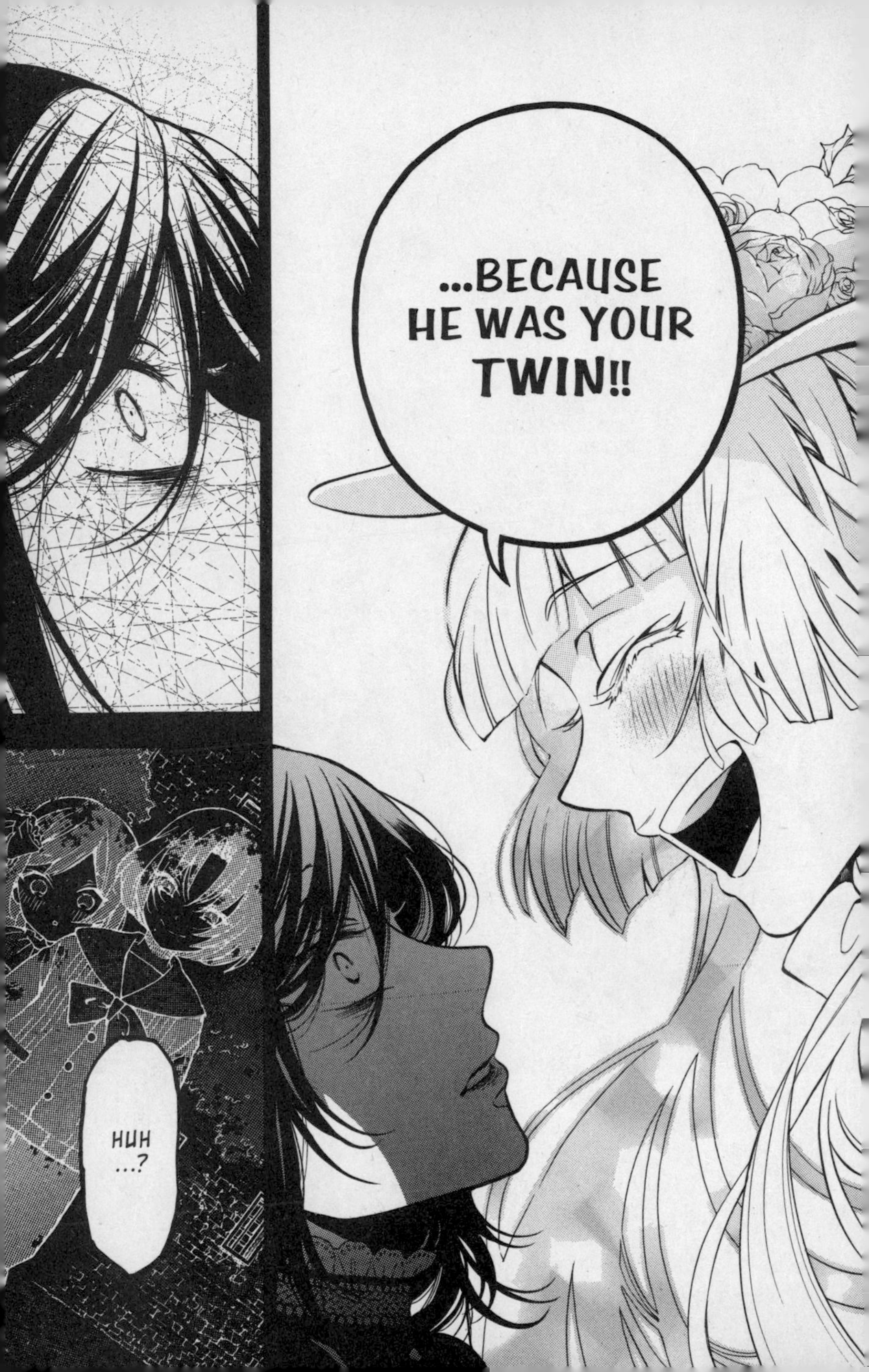
...BECAUSE HE WAS YOUR TWIN!!
HUH ...?

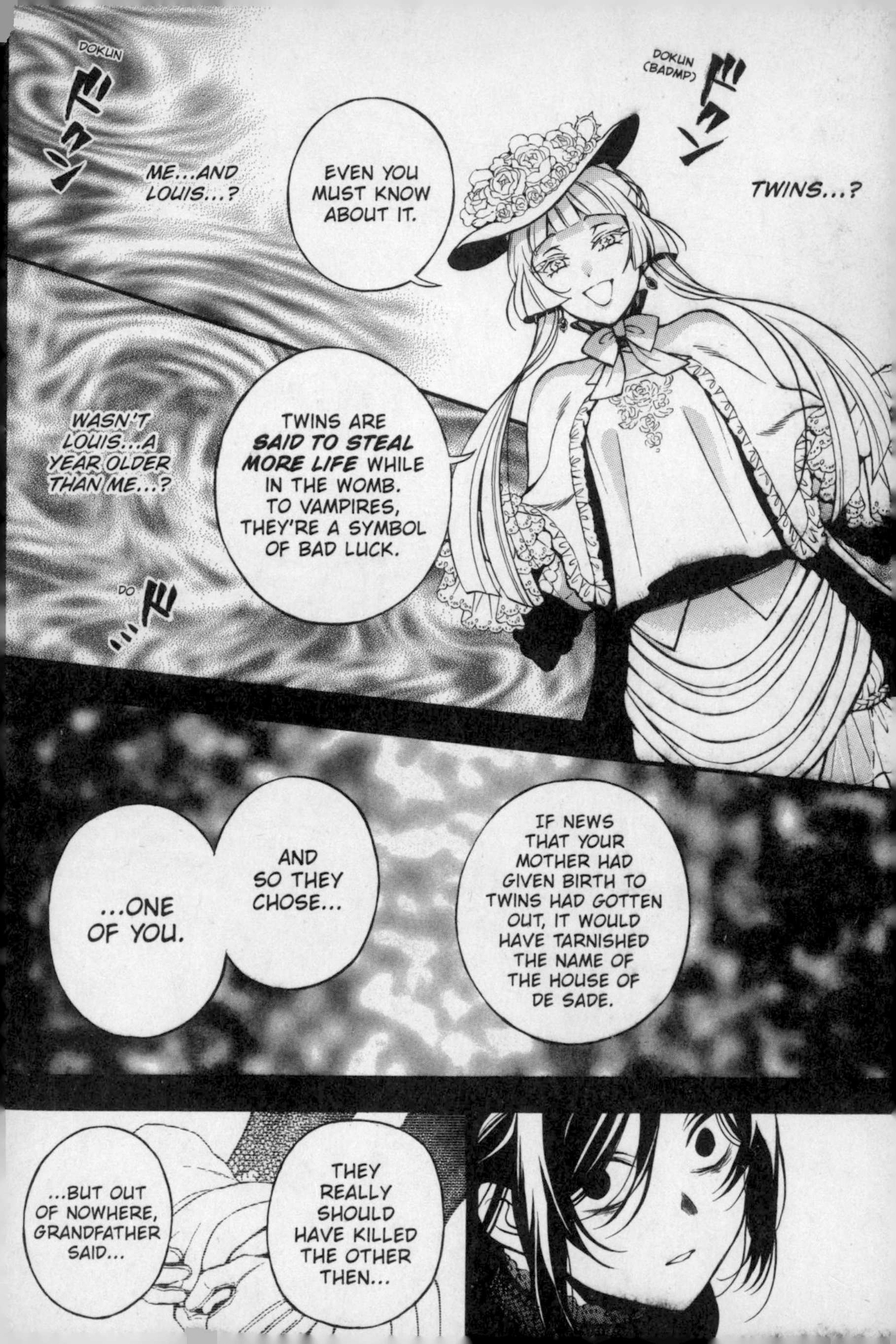
DOKUN (BADMP) ドクン
TWINS...?
EVEN YOU MUST KNOW ABOUT IT.
ME...AND LOUIS...?
DOKUN ドクン
TWINS ARE SAID TO STEAL MORE LIFE WHILE IN THE WOMB. TO VAMPIRES, THEY'RE A SYMBOL OF BAD LUCK.
WASN'T LOUIS...A YEAR OLDER THAN ME...?
DO ド...
IF NEWS THAT YOUR MOTHER HAD GIVEN BIRTH TO TWINS HAD GOTTEN OUT, IT WOULD HAVE TARNISHED THE NAME OF THE HOUSE OF DE SADE.
AND SO THEY CHOSE...
...ONE OF YOU.
THEY REALLY SHOULD HAVE KILLED THE OTHER THEN...
...BUT OUT OF NOWHERE, GRANDFATHER SAID...

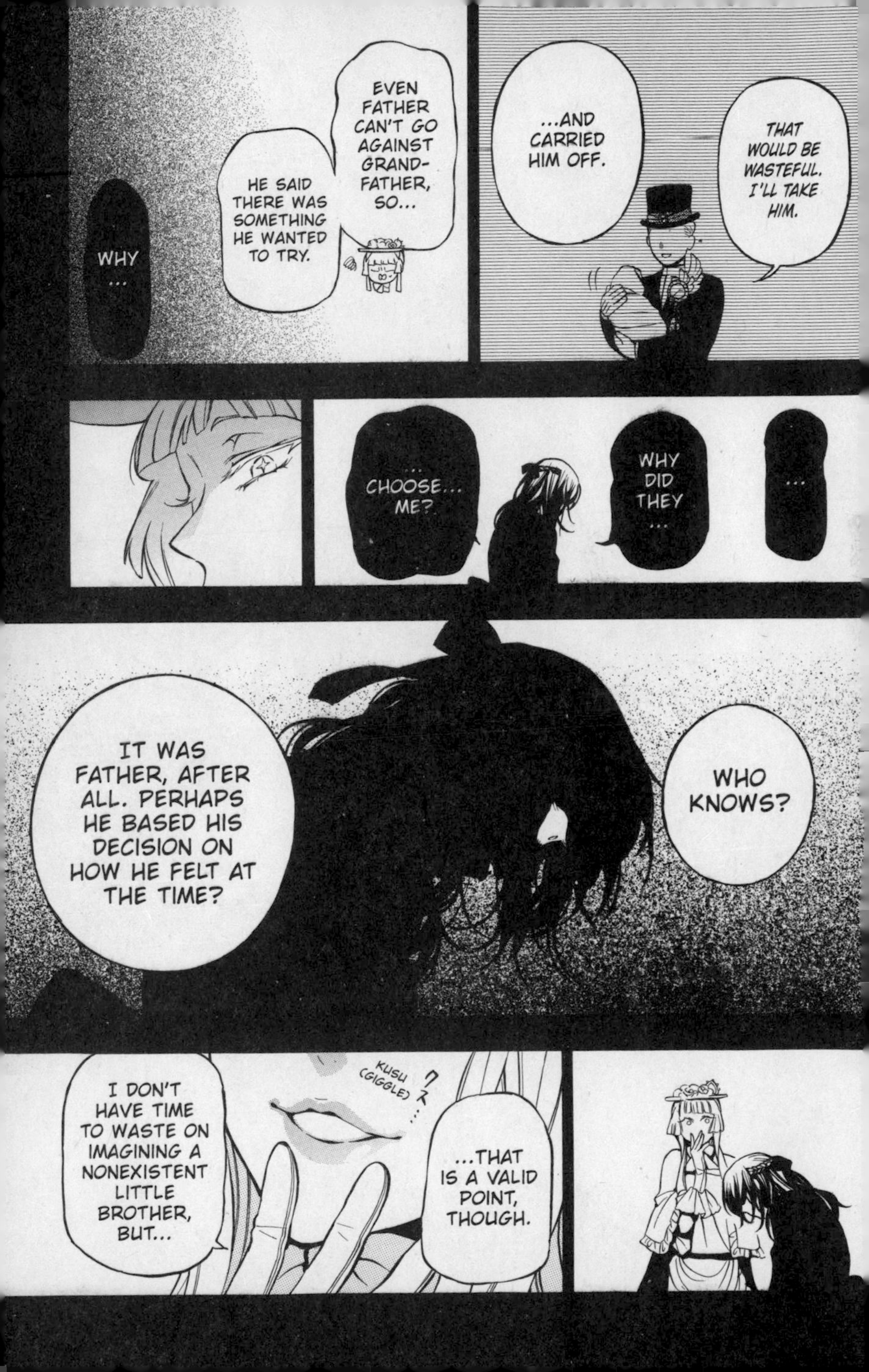
THAT WOULD BE WASTEFUL. I'LL TAKE HIM.
...AND CARRIED HIM OFF.
EVEN FATHER CAN'T GO AGAINST GRANDFATHER, SO...
HE SAID THERE WAS SOMETHING HE WANTED TO TRY.
WHY ...
...
WHY DID THEY ...
... CHOOSE... ME?
WHO KNOWS?
IT WAS FATHER, AFTER ALL. PERHAPS HE BASED HIS DECISION ON HOW HE FELT AT THE TIME?
KUSU (GIGGLE)
I DON'T HAVE TIME TO WASTE ON IMAGINING A NONEXISTENT LITTLE BROTHER, BUT...
...THAT IS A VALID POINT, THOUGH.

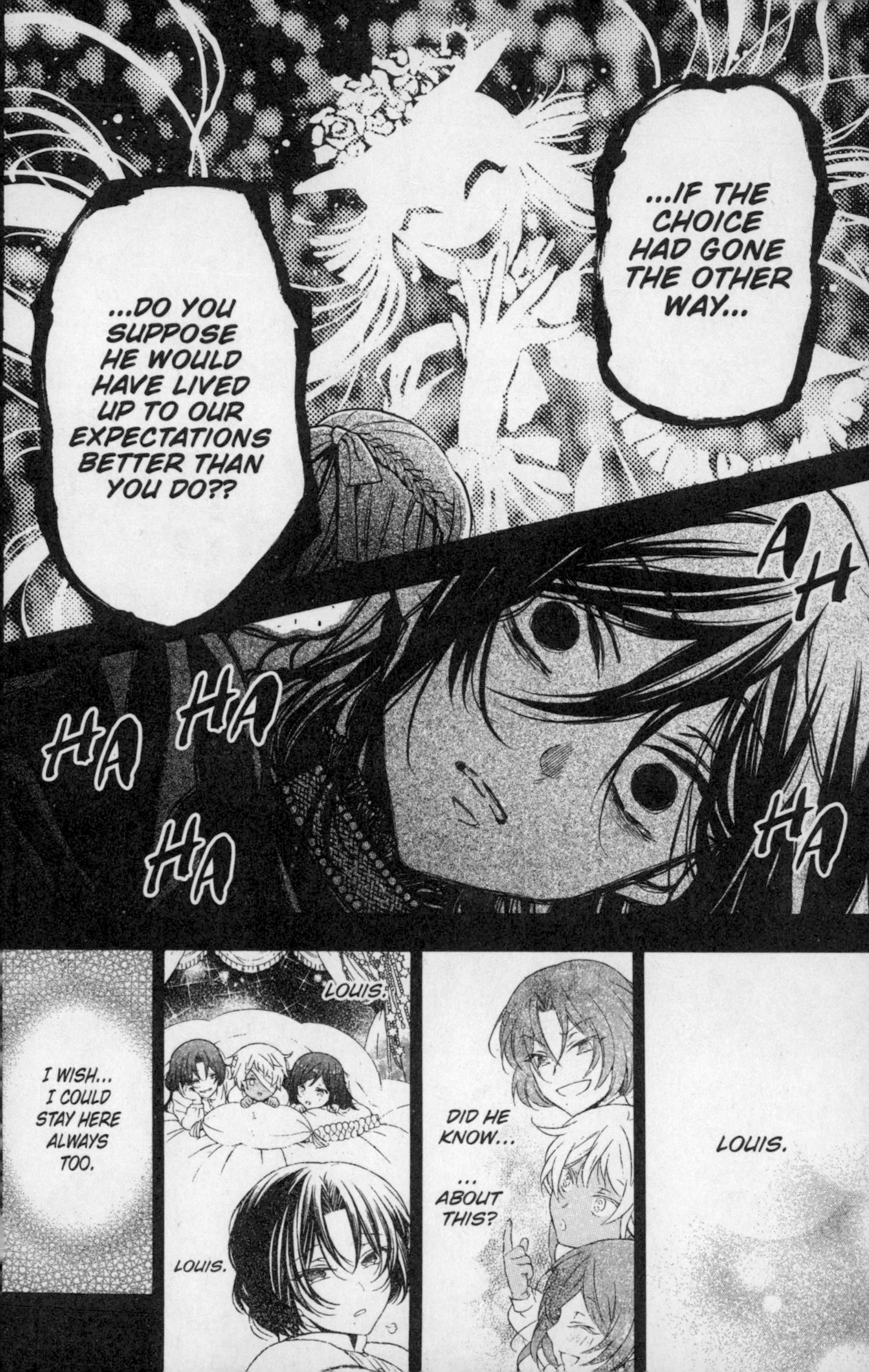
...IF THE CHOICE HAD GONE THE OTHER WAY...
...DO YOU SUPPOSE HE WOULD HAVE LIVED UP TO OUR EXPECTATIONS BETTER THAN YOU DO??
AH
HA
HA
HA
HA
LOUIS.
DID HE KNOW...
...ABOUT THIS?
LOUIS.
LOUIS.
I WISH... I COULD STAY HERE ALWAYS TOO.

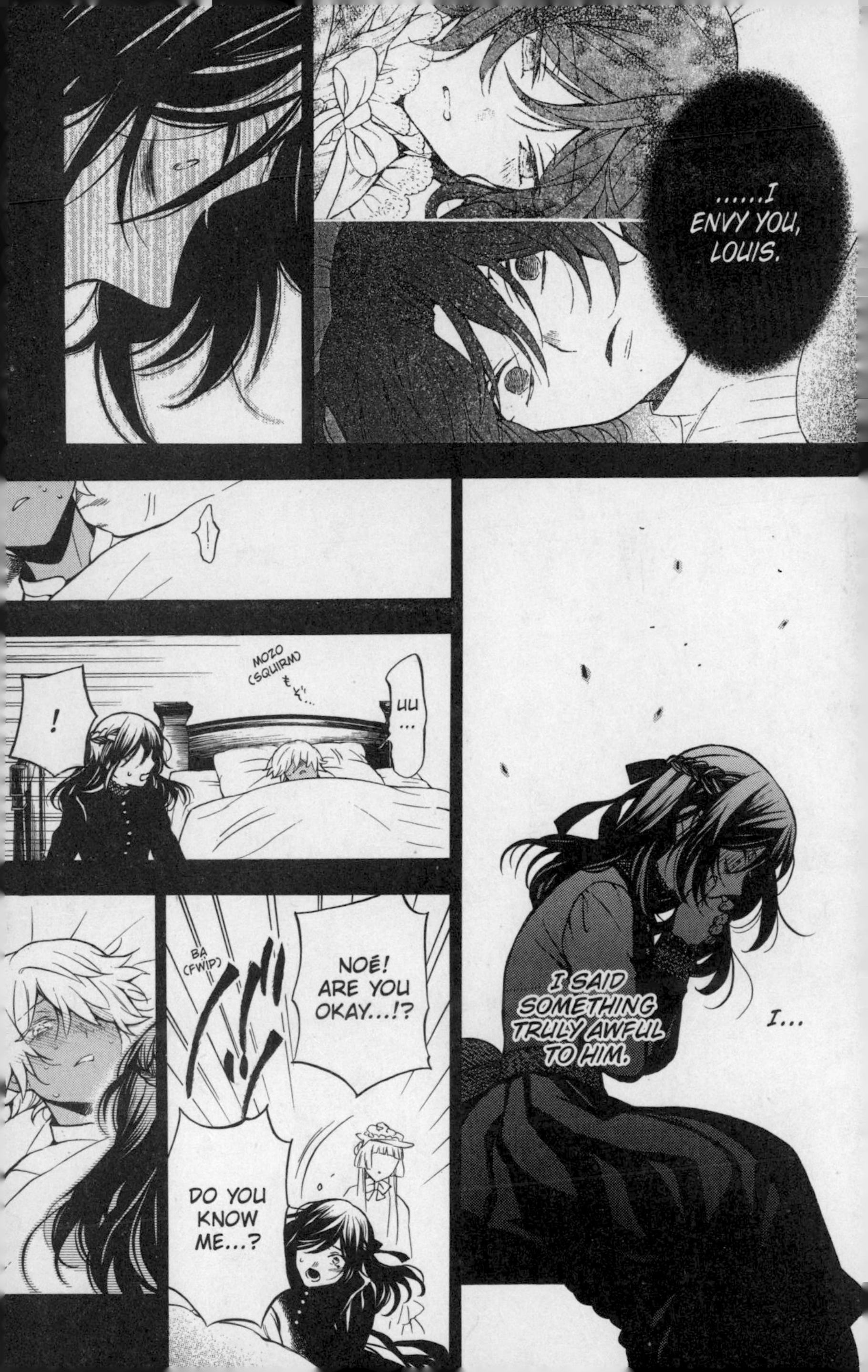
......I ENVY YOU, LOUIS.
I...
I SAID SOMETHING TRULY AWFUL TO HIM.
!
UU...
MOZO (SQUIRM)
!
NOÉ! ARE YOU OKAY...!?
BA (FWIP)
DO YOU KNOW ME...?

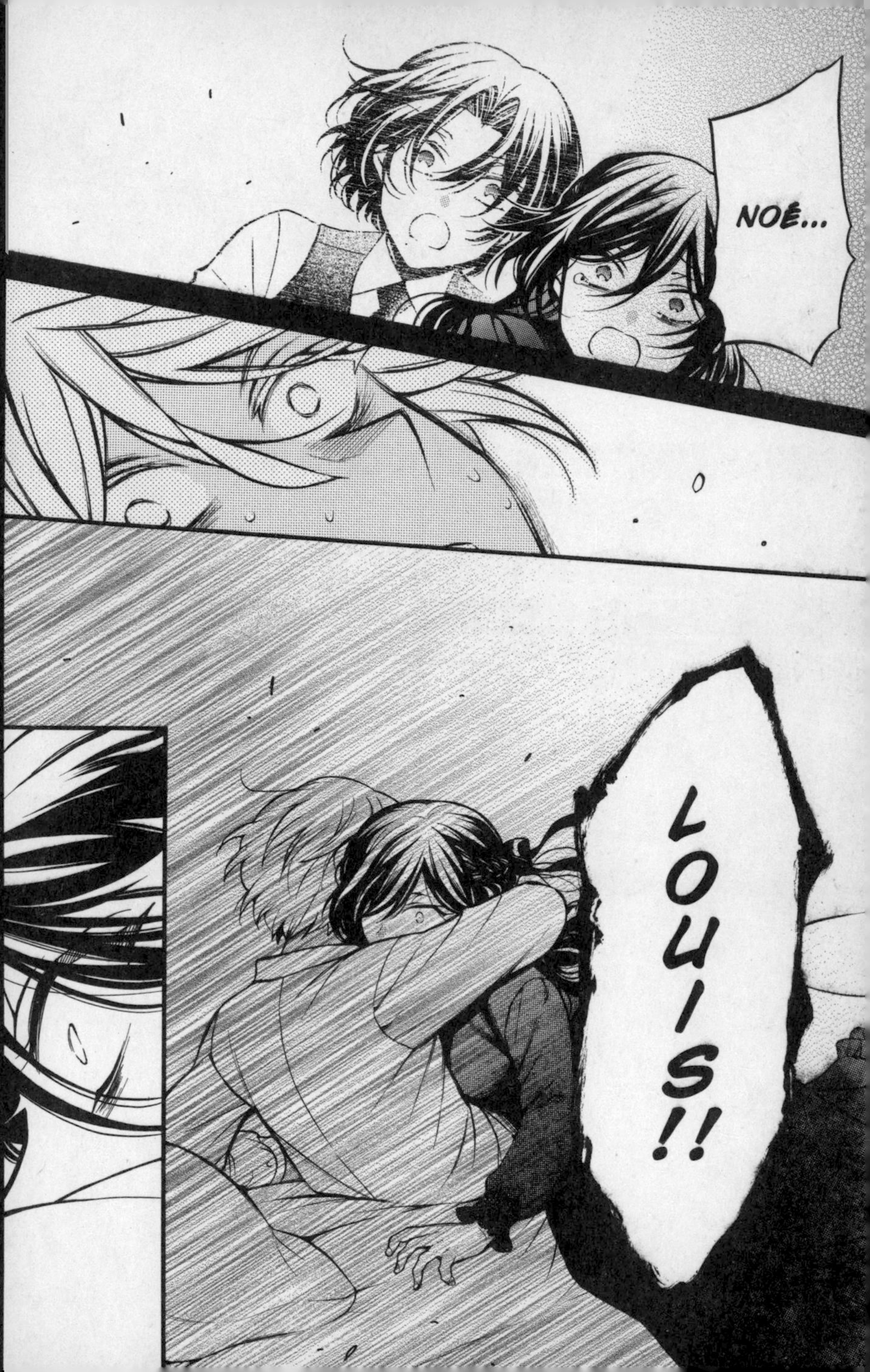
NOÉ...
LOUIS!!

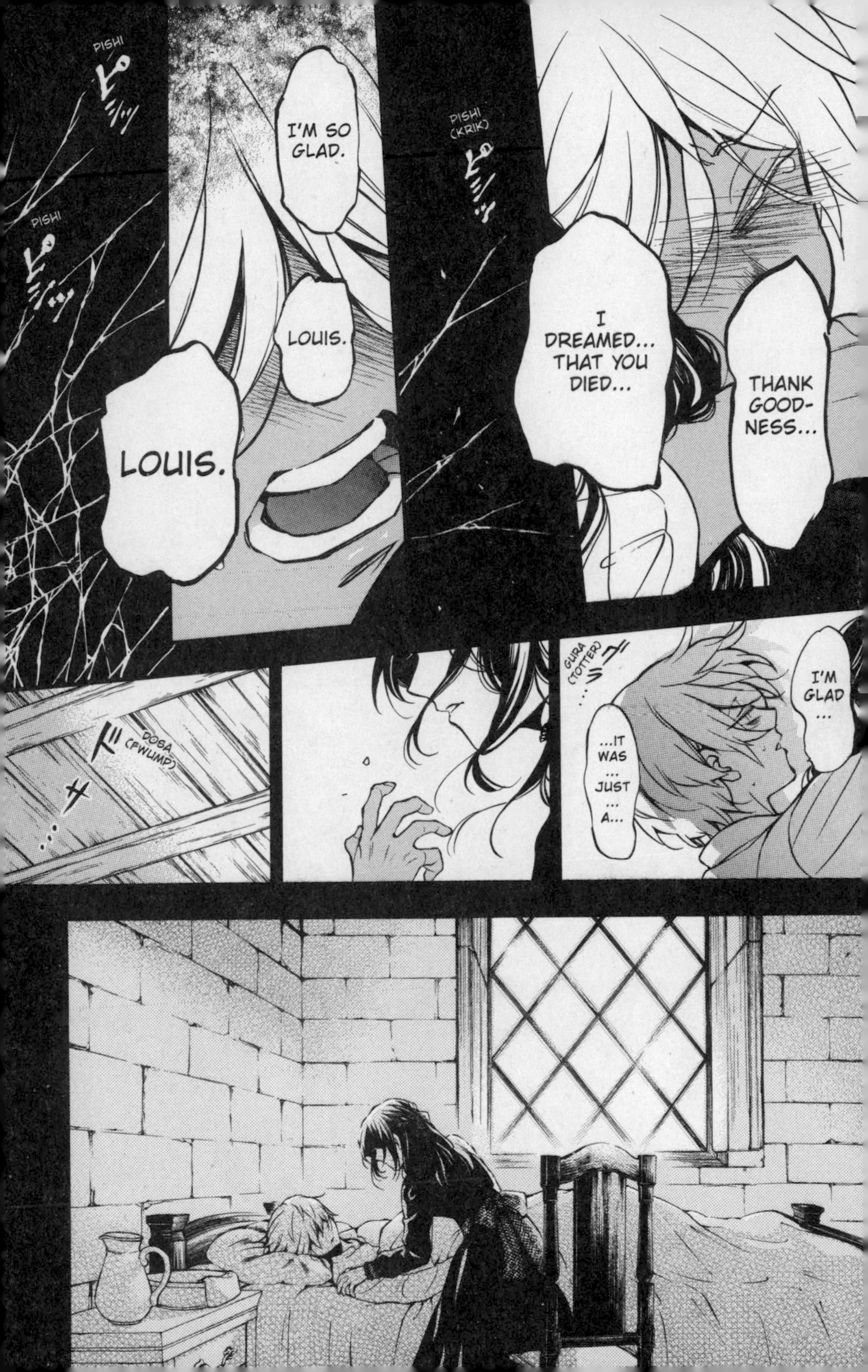
PISHI (KRIK)
I DREAMED... THAT YOU DIED...
THANK GOODNESS...
PISHI
I'M SO GLAD.
LOUIS.
PISHI
LOUIS.
I'M GLAD ...
...IT WAS ... JUST ... A...
GURA (TOTTER)
DOSA (PWUMP)

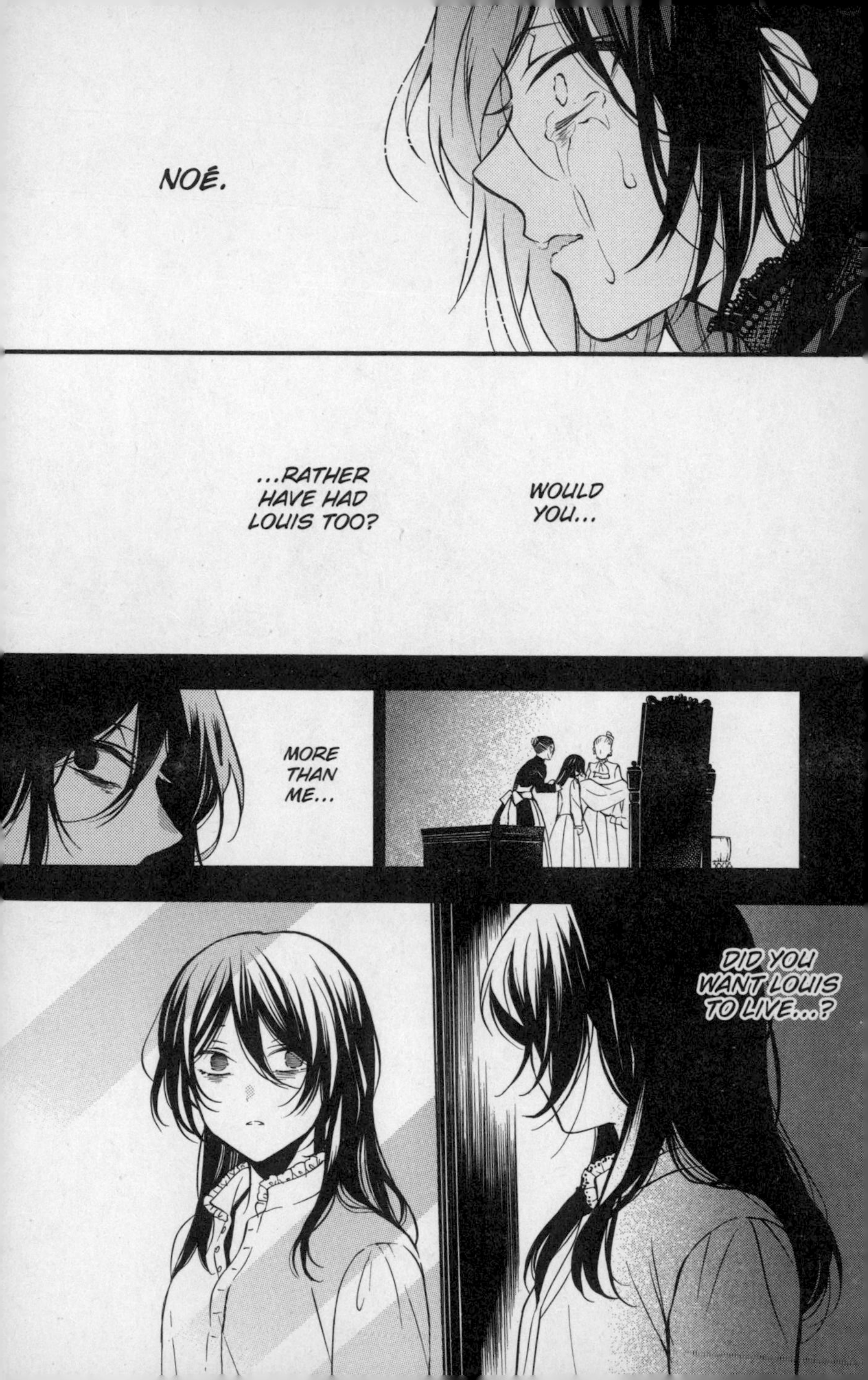
NOÉ.
WOULD YOU...
...RATHER HAVE HAD LOUIS TOO?
MORE THAN ME...
DID YOU WANT LOUIS TO LIVE...?

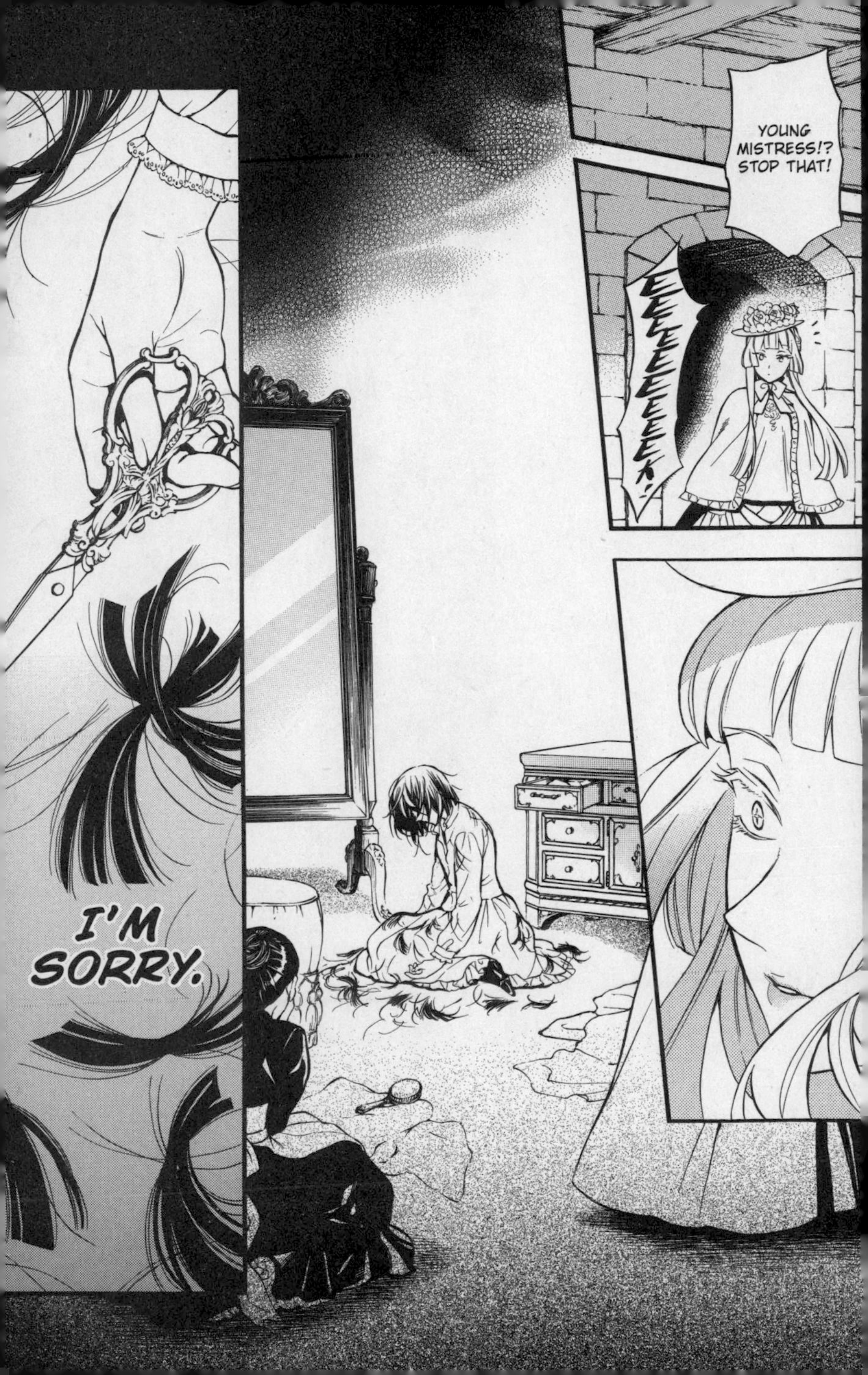
YOUNG MISTRESS!? STOP THAT!
EEEEEEEEEEK!!
I'M SORRY.

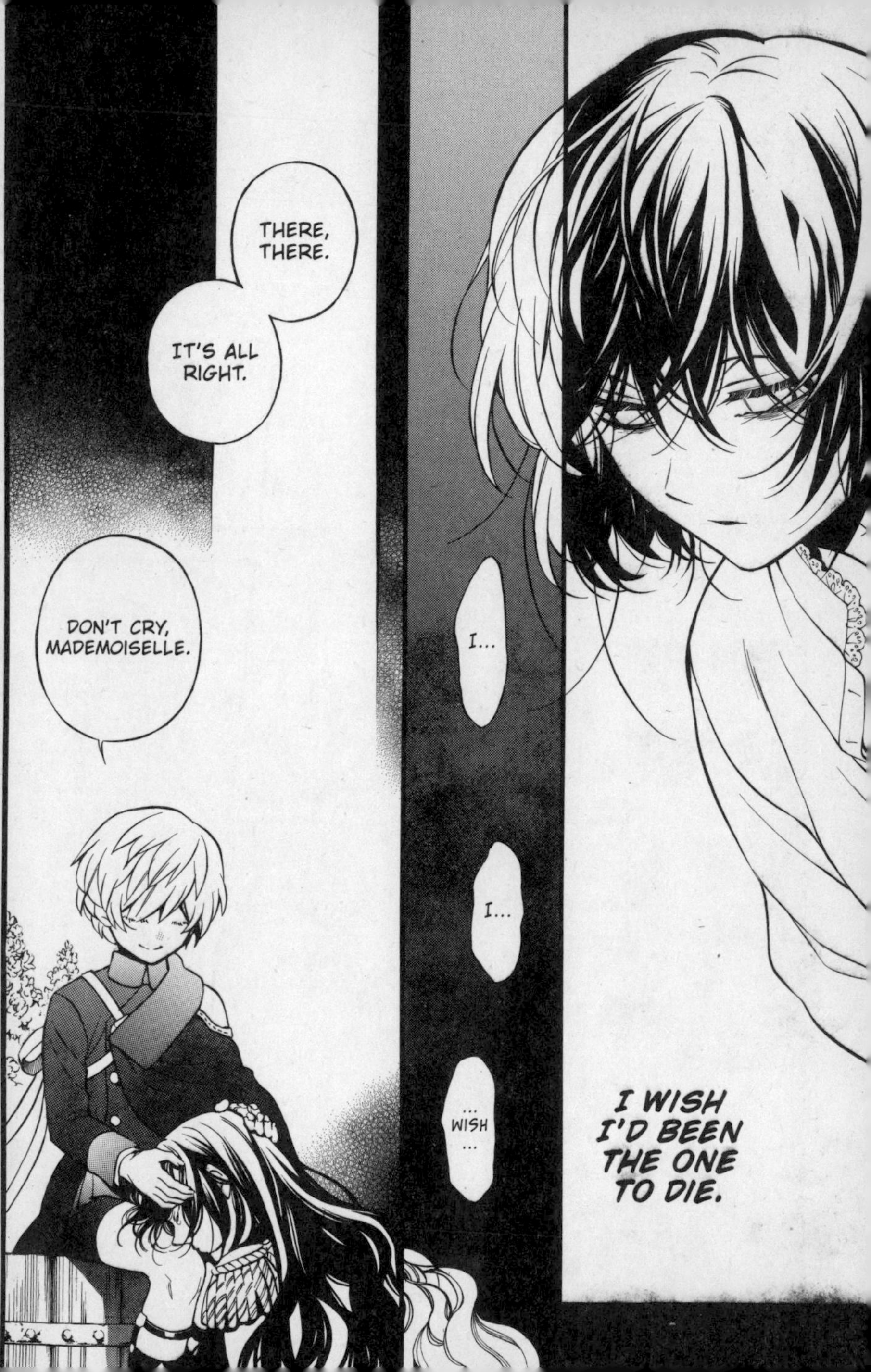
I...
I...
...WISH...
I WISH I'D BEEN THE ONE TO DIE.
THERE, THERE.
IT'S ALL RIGHT.
DON'T CRY, MADEMOISELLE.

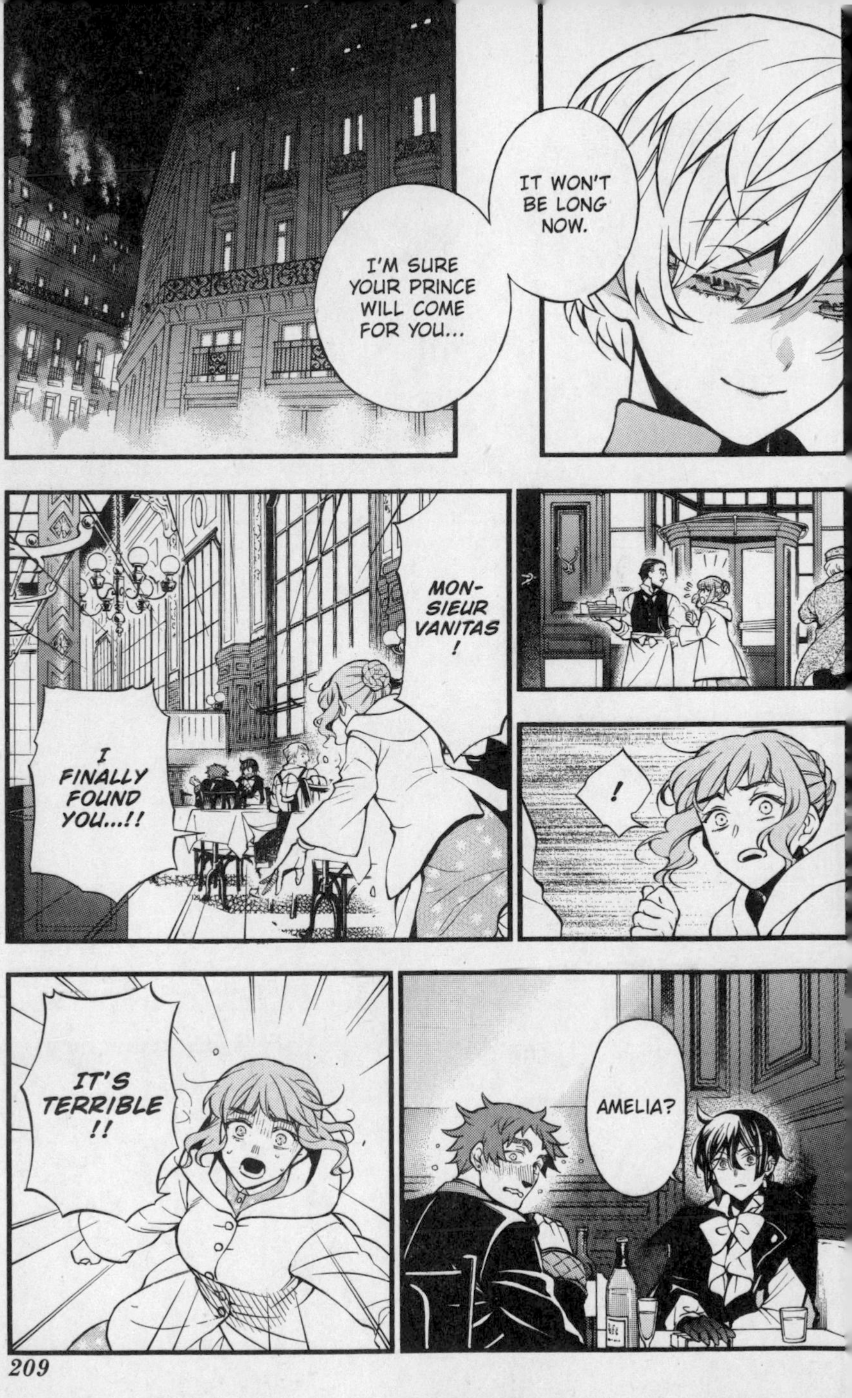

IT WON'T BE LONG NOW.
I'M SURE YOUR PRINCE WILL COME FOR YOU...
!
MON-SIEUR VANITAS!
I FINALLY FOUND YOU...!!
AMELIA?
IT'S TERRIBLE!!

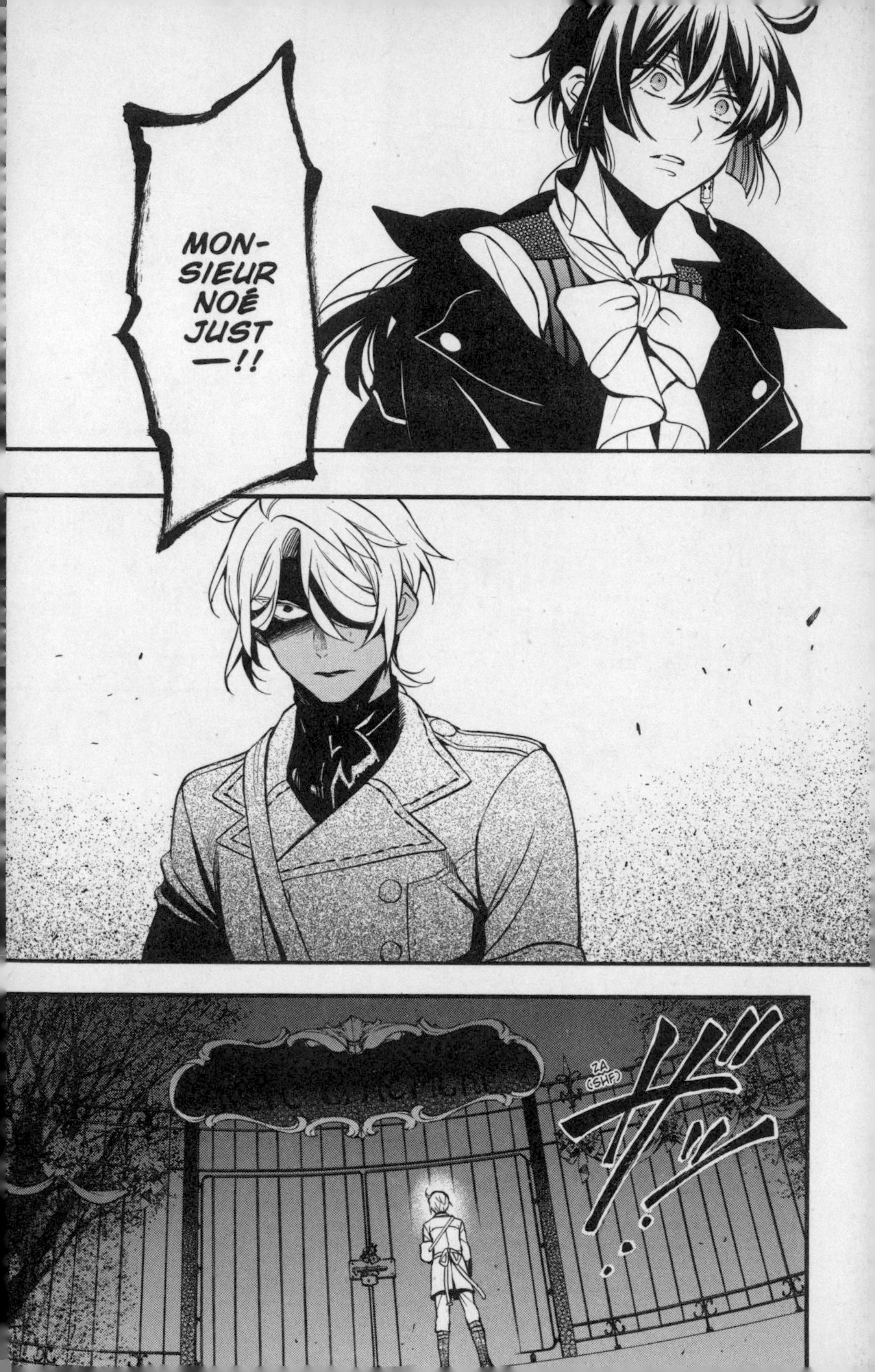
MON-
SIEUR
NOÉ
JUST
—!!
ZA
(SHF)

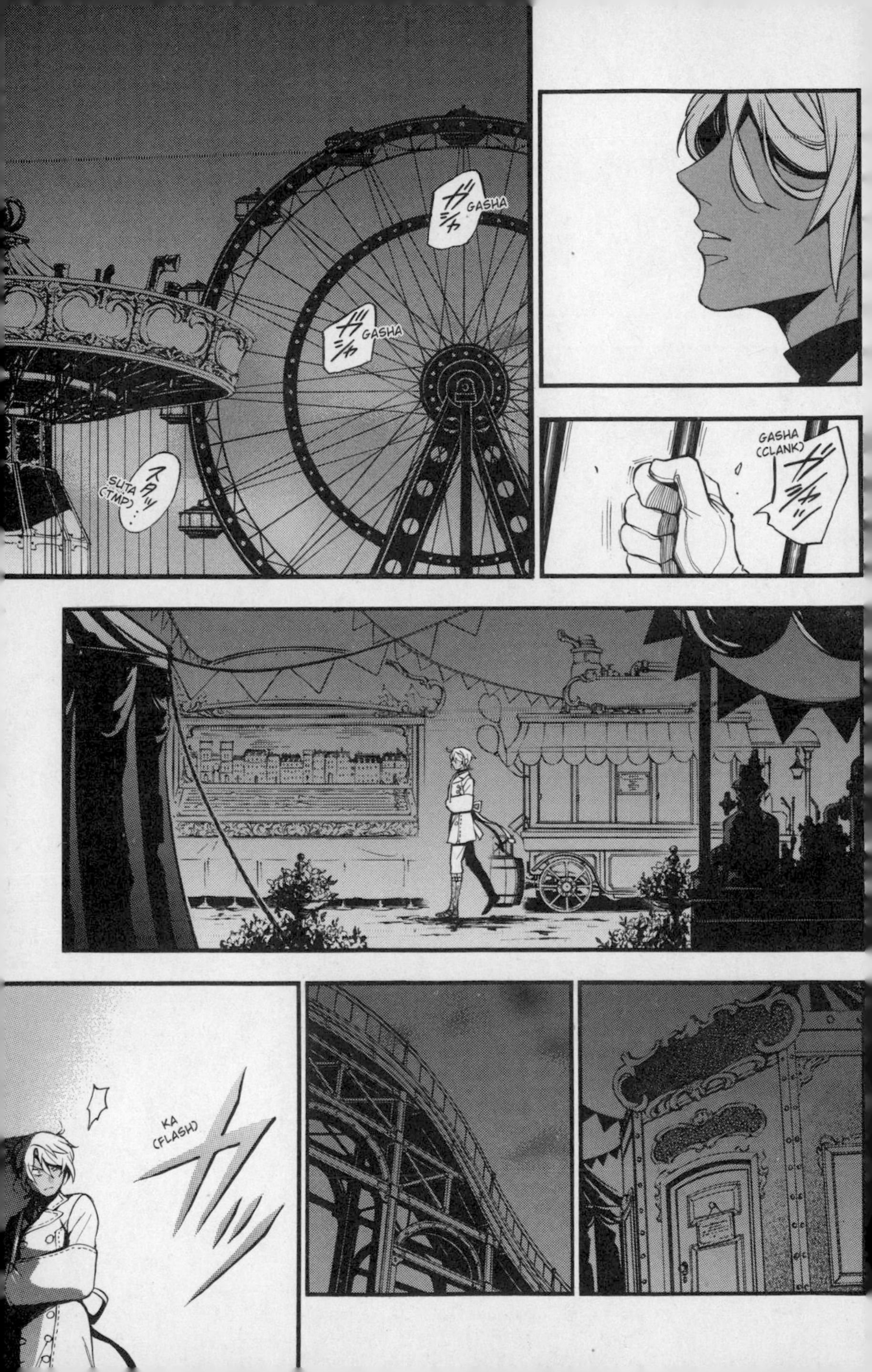
GASHA (CLANK)
ガシャッ
ガシャ
GASHA
ガシャ
GASHA
スタッ…
SUTA (TMP)
KA (FLASH)

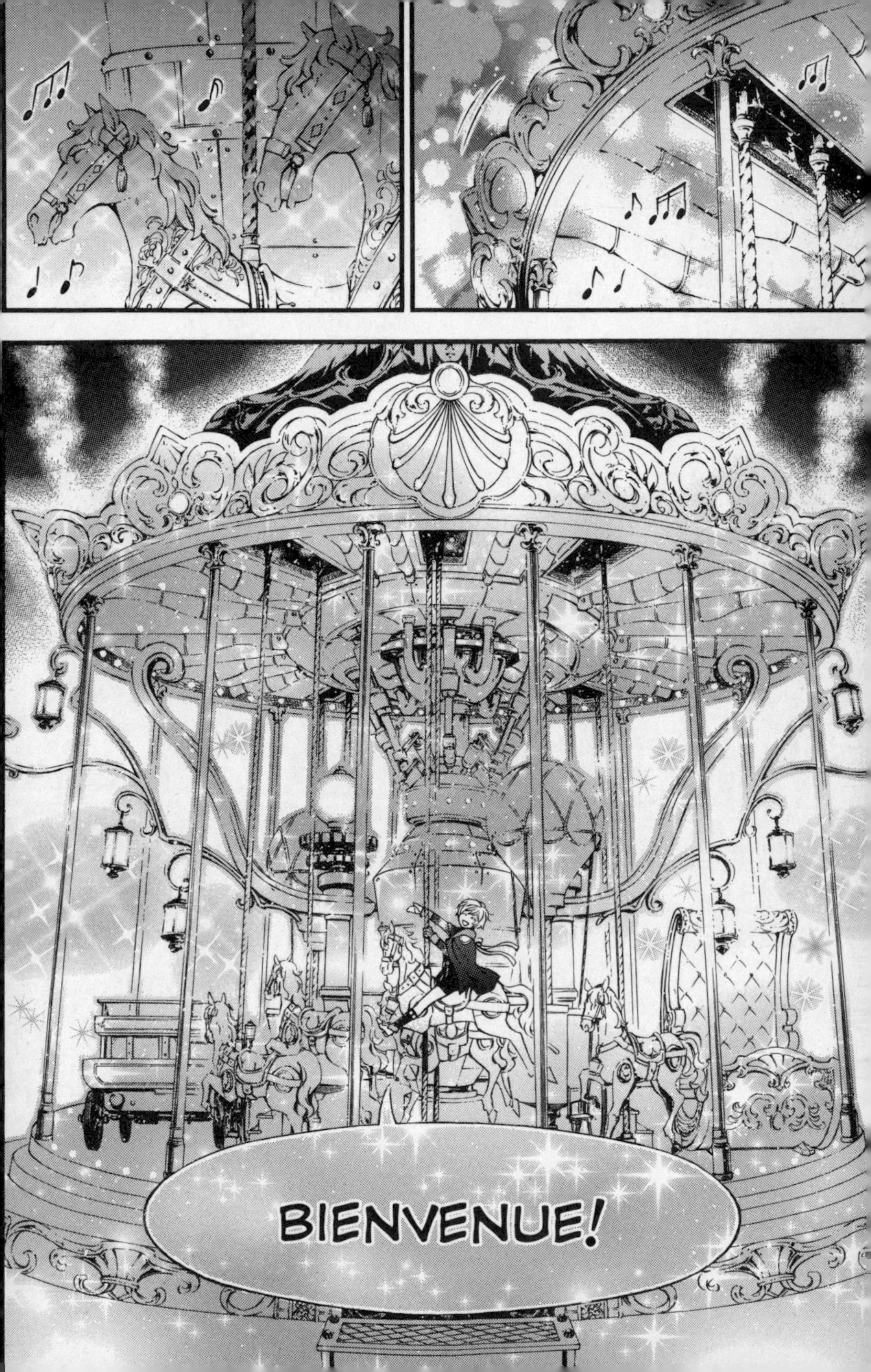
BIENVENUE!

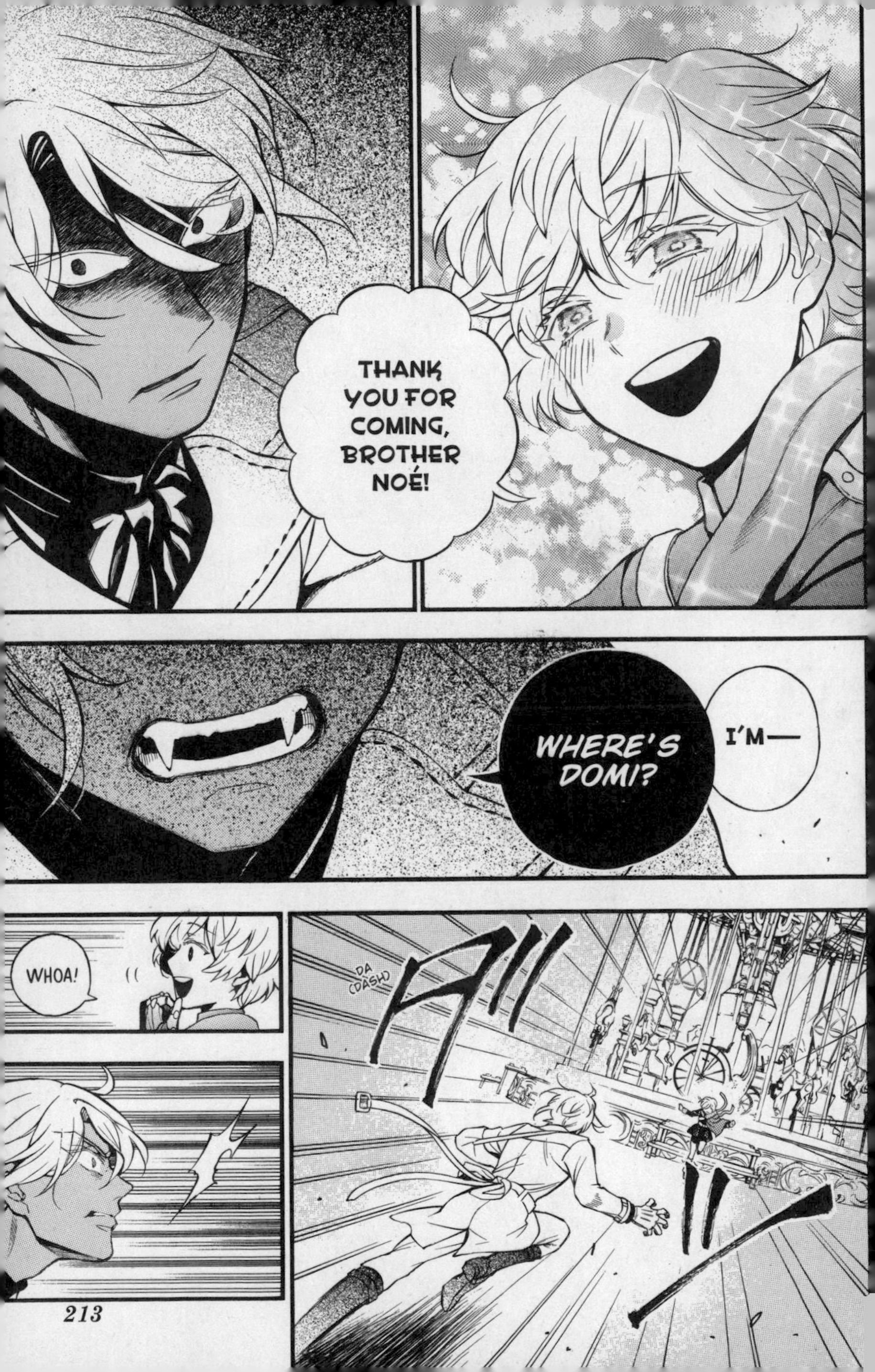
THANK YOU FOR COMING, BROTHER NOÉ!
I'M—
WHERE'S DOMI?
DA (DASH)
WHOA!

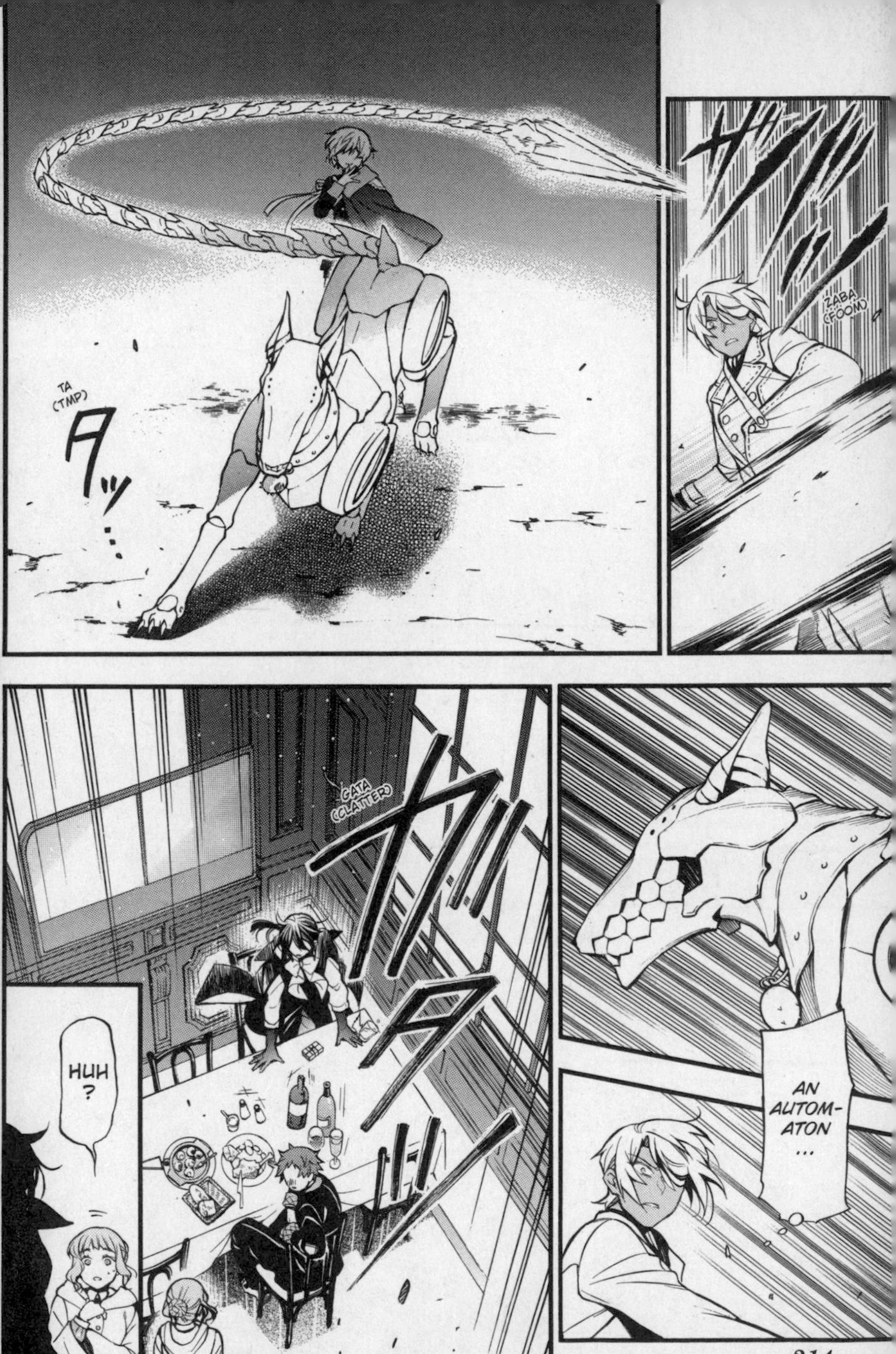
ZABA (FOOM)
TA (TMP)
AN AUTOMATON...
GATA (CLATTER)
HUH?

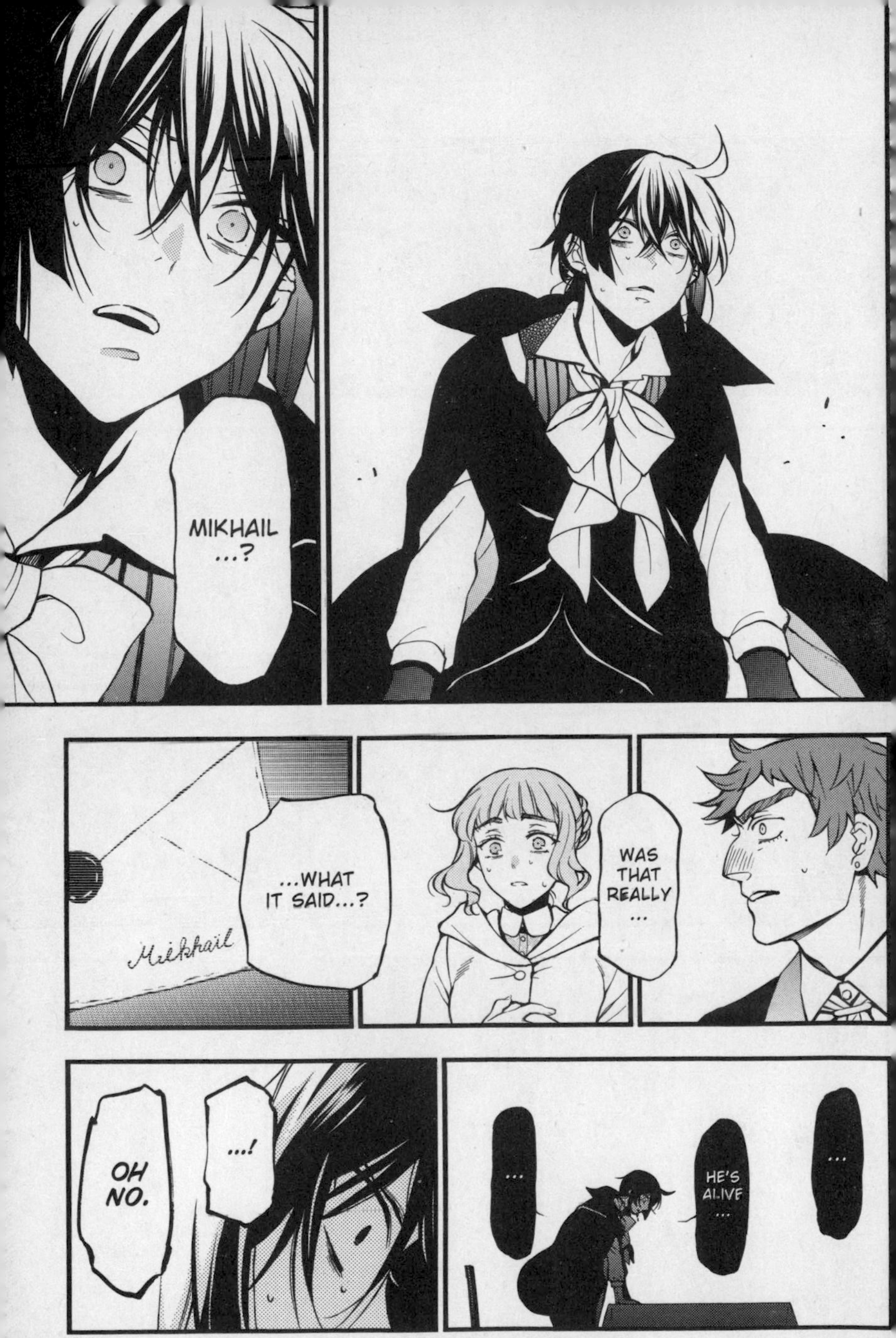
MIKHAIL ...?
WAS THAT REALLY ...
...WHAT IT SAID...?
Mikhail
...
HE'S ALIVE ...
...
...!
OH NO.

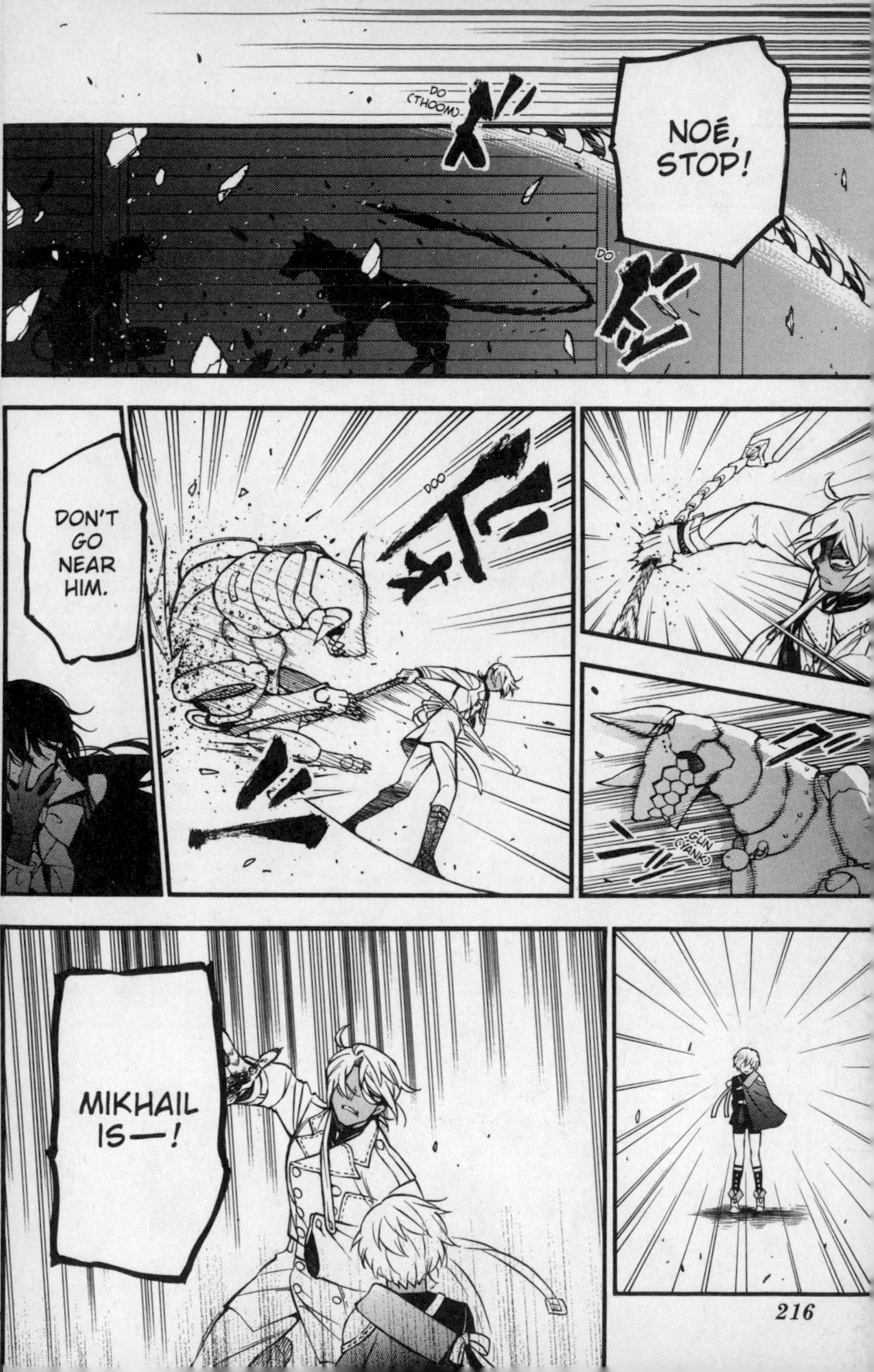
NOÉ, STOP!
DO
DO (THOOM)
GUN (YANK)
DOO
DON'T GO NEAR HIM.
MIKHAIL IS—!

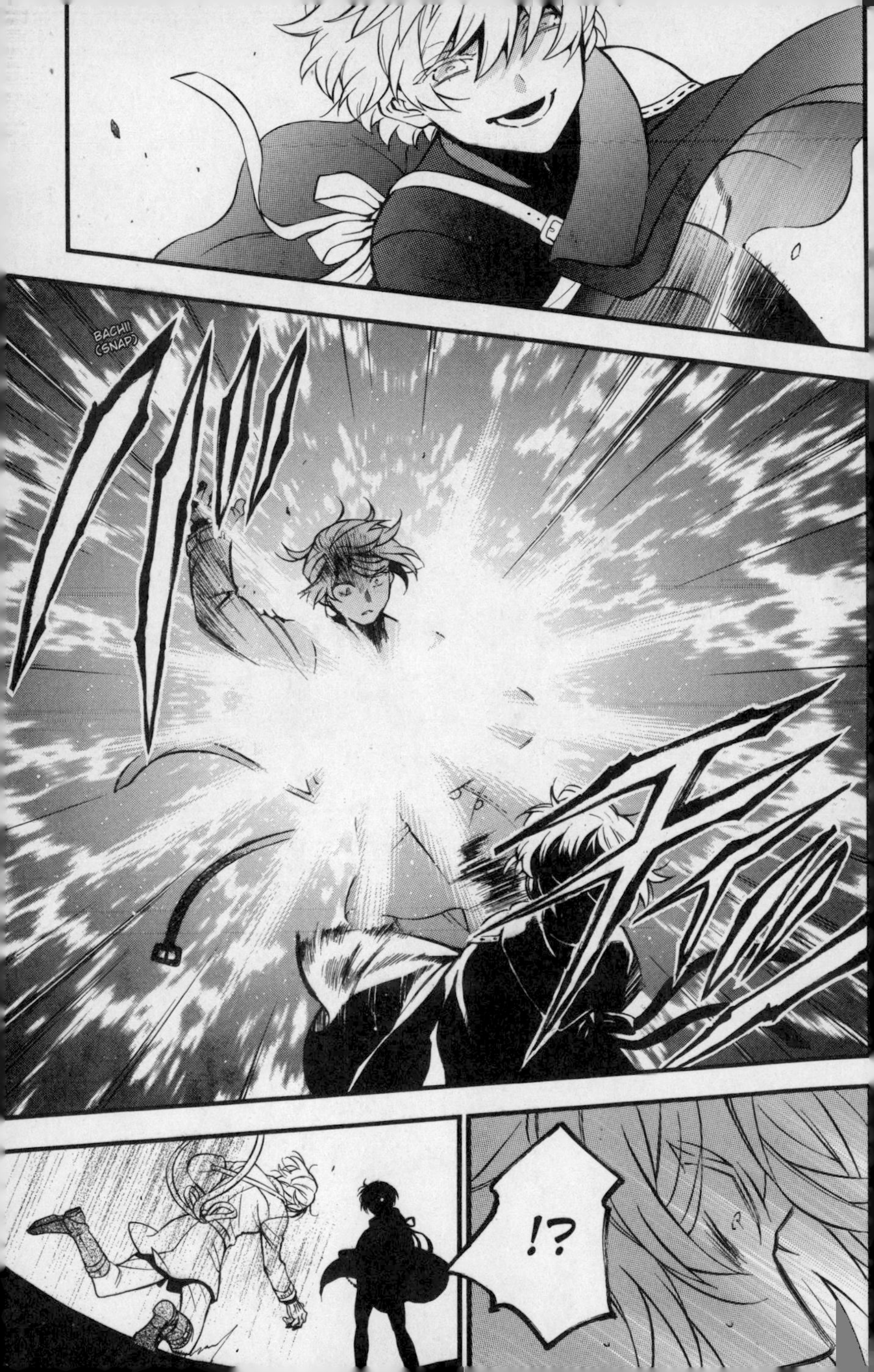
BACHI!
(SNAP)
!?

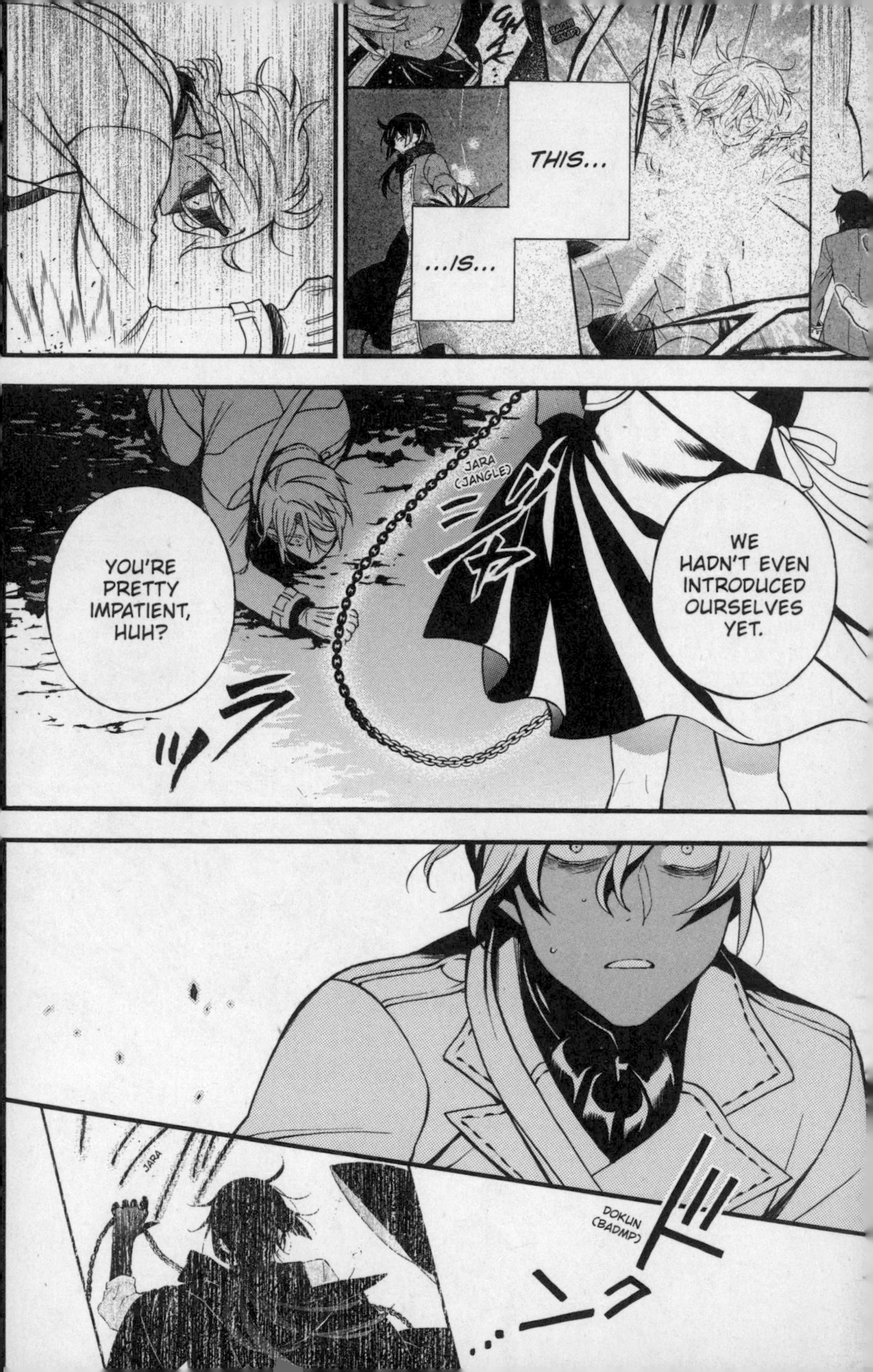
BACHI (SNAP)
GHAK...
THIS...
...IS...
WE HADN'T EVEN INTRODUCED OURSELVES YET.
JARA (JANGLE)
YOU'RE PRETTY IMPATIENT, HUH?
DOKUN (BADMP)
JARA

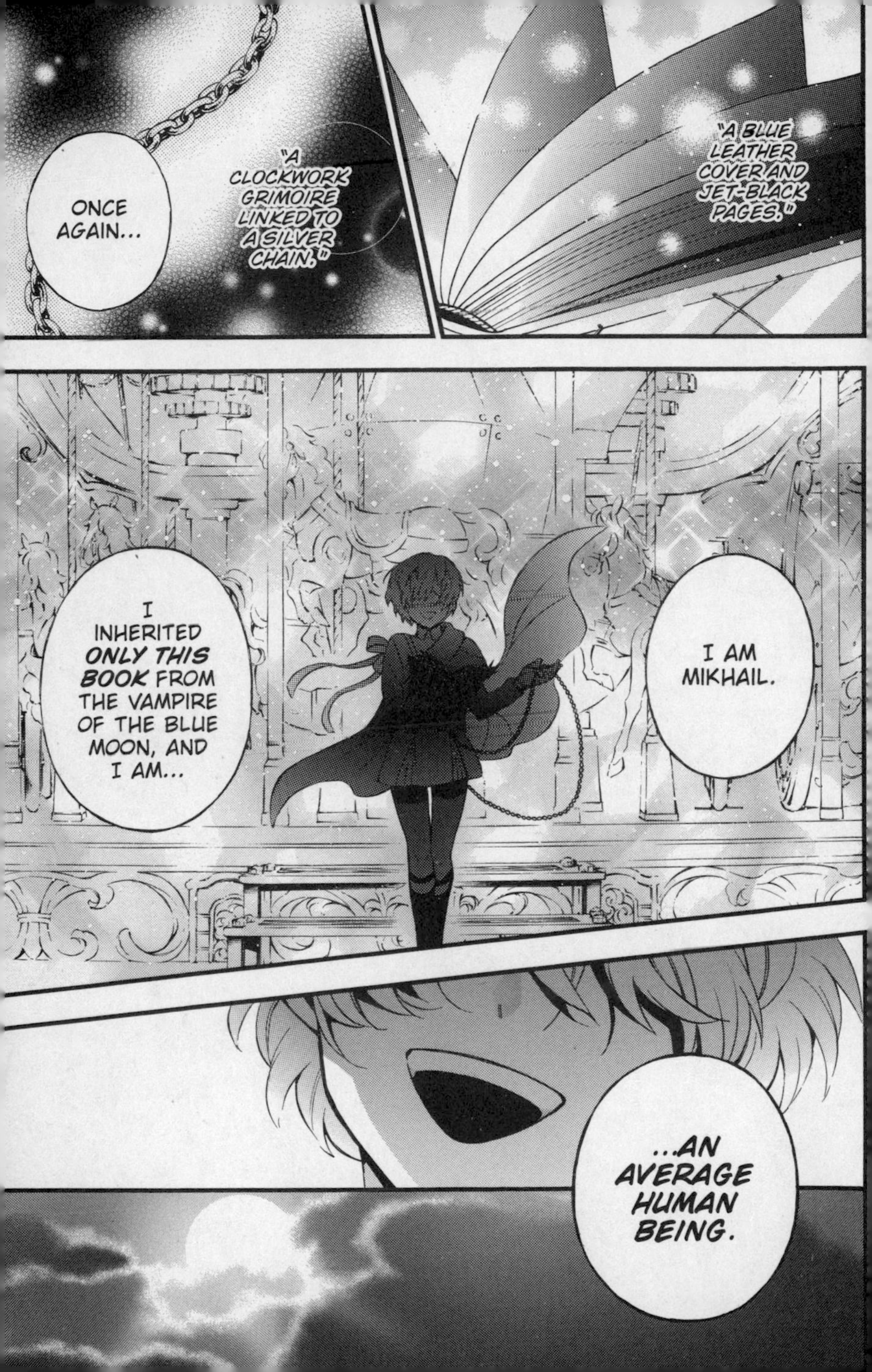
"A BLUE LEATHER COVER AND JET-BLACK PAGES."
"A CLOCKWORK GRIMOIRE LINKED TO A SILVER CHAIN."
ONCE AGAIN...
I AM MIKHAIL.
I INHERITED ONLY THIS BOOK FROM THE VAMPIRE OF THE BLUE MOON, AND I AM...
...AN AVERAGE HUMAN BEING.

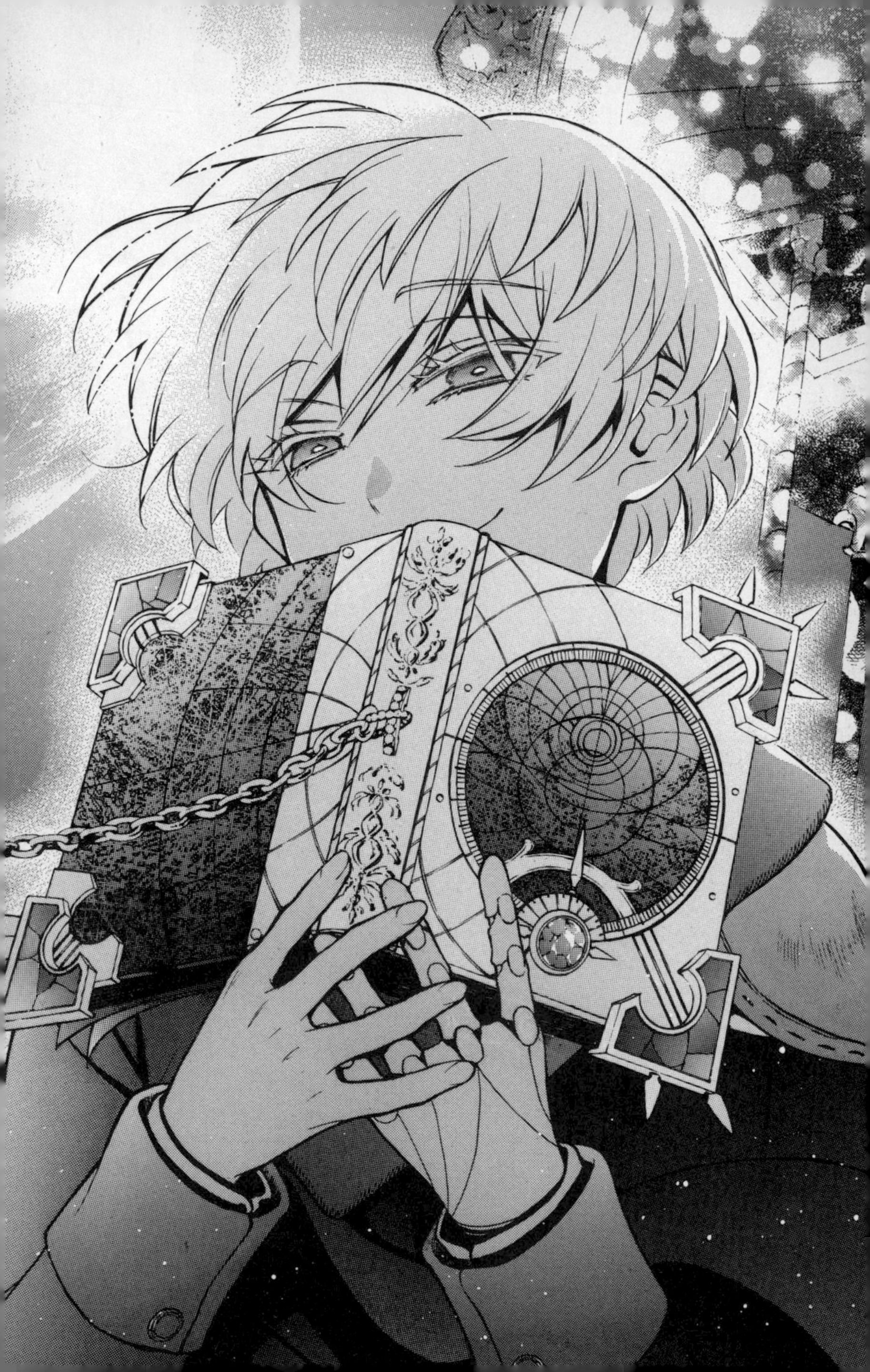

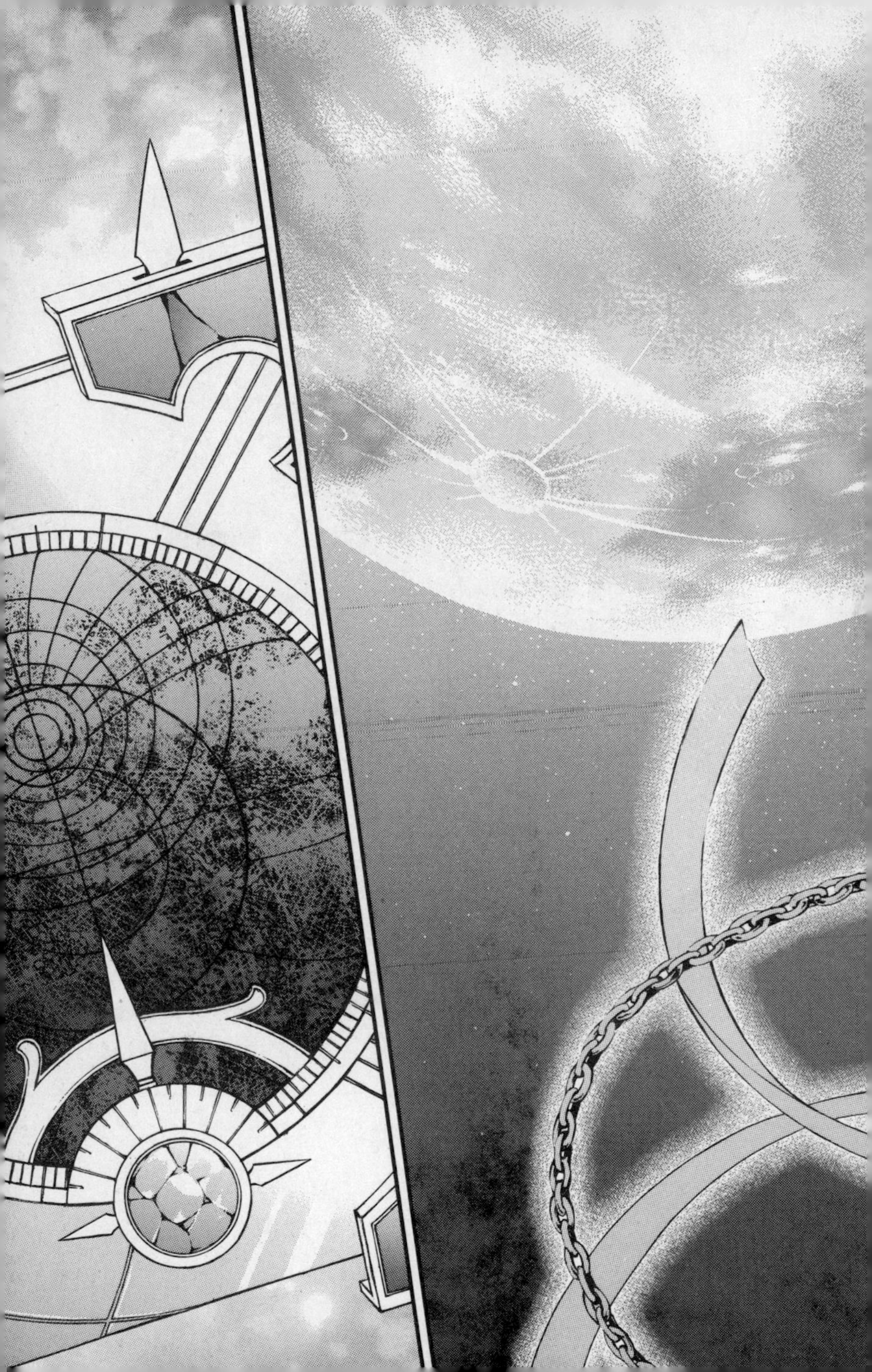

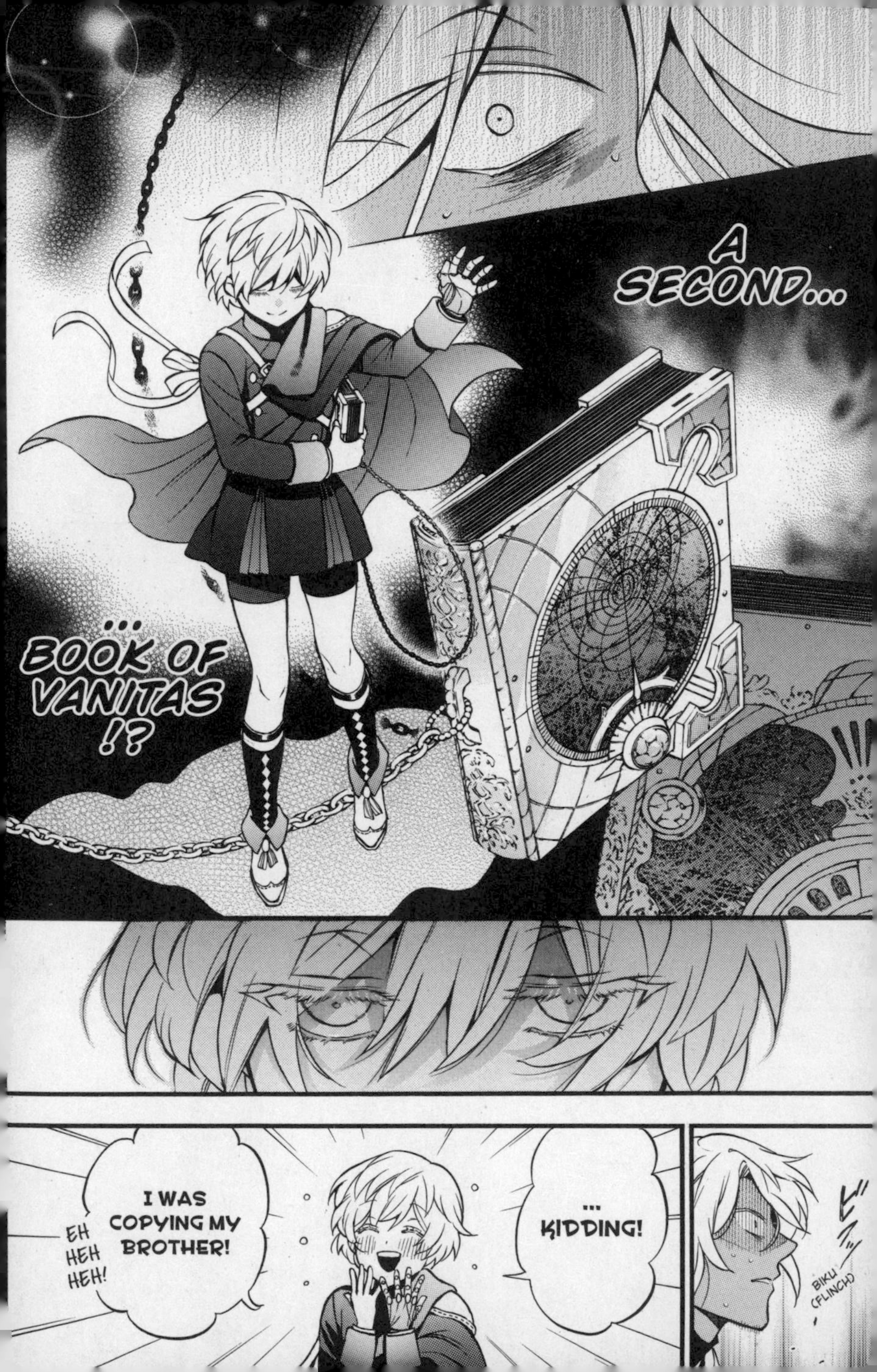
A SECOND...
...BOOK OF VANITAS !?
BIKU (FLINCH)
...KIDDING!
I WAS COPYING MY BROTHER!
EH HEH HEH!

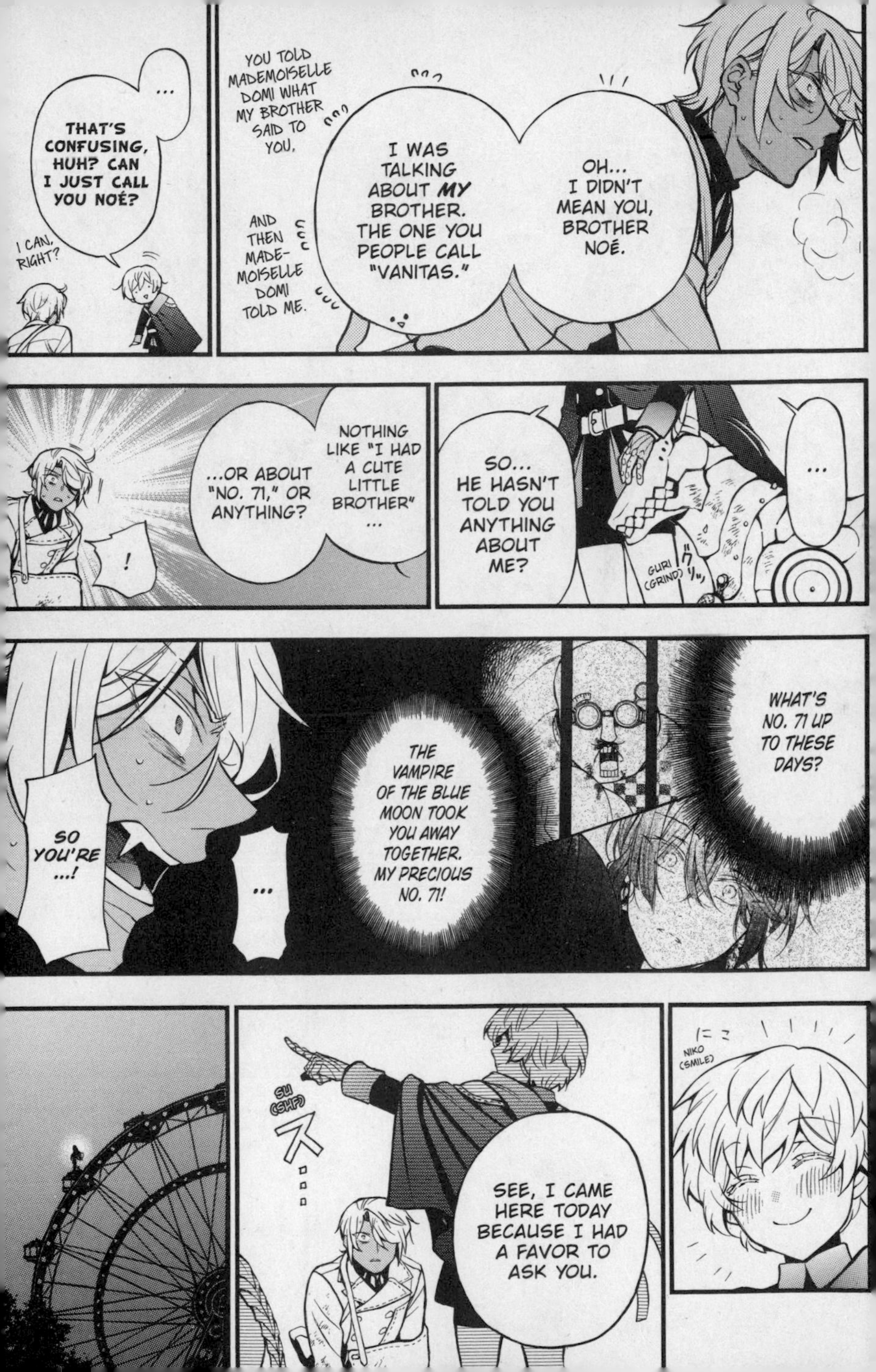
OH... I DIDN'T MEAN YOU, BROTHER NOÉ.
I WAS TALKING ABOUT MY BROTHER. THE ONE YOU PEOPLE CALL "VANITAS."
YOU TOLD MADEMOISELLE DOMI WHAT MY BROTHER SAID TO YOU.
AND THEN MADE-MOISELLE DOMI TOLD ME.
...
THAT'S CONFUSING, HUH? CAN I JUST CALL YOU NOÉ?
I CAN, RIGHT?
...
SO... HE HASN'T TOLD YOU ANYTHING ABOUT ME?
GURI (GRIND)
NOTHING LIKE "I HAD A CUTE LITTLE BROTHER"...
...OR ABOUT "NO. 71," OR ANYTHING?
!
WHAT'S NO. 71 UP TO THESE DAYS?
THE VAMPIRE OF THE BLUE MOON TOOK YOU AWAY TOGETHER. MY PRECIOUS NO. 71!
...
SO YOU'RE ...!
NIKO (SMILE)
SU (SHF)
SEE, I CAME HERE TODAY BECAUSE I HAD A FAVOR TO ASK YOU.

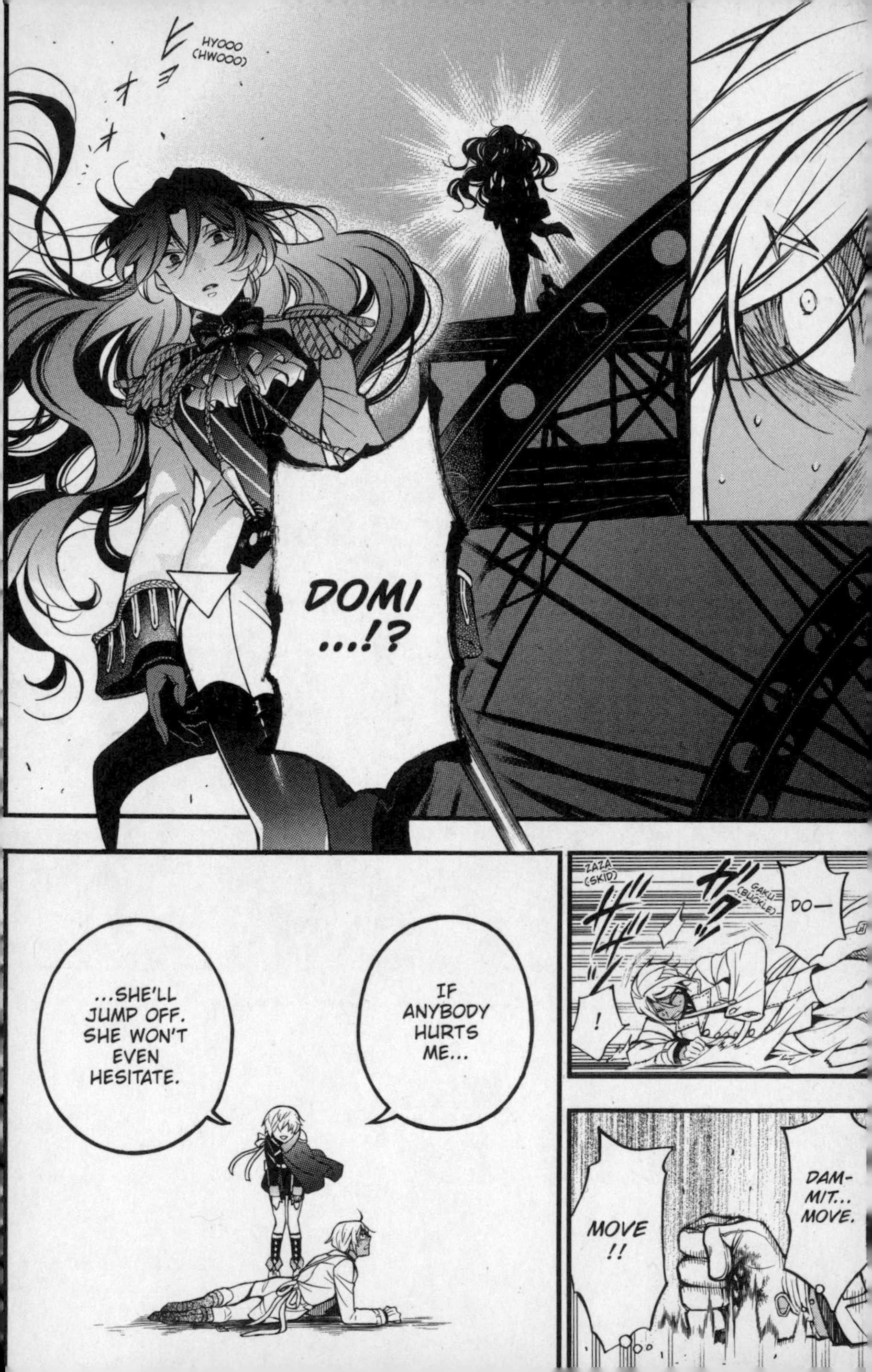
HYOOO (HWOOO)
DOMI ...!?
DO—
GAKU (BUCKLE)
ZAZA (SKID)
!
DAM-MIT... MOVE.
MOVE !!
IF ANYBODY HURTS ME...
...SHE'LL JUMP OFF. SHE WON'T EVEN HESITATE.

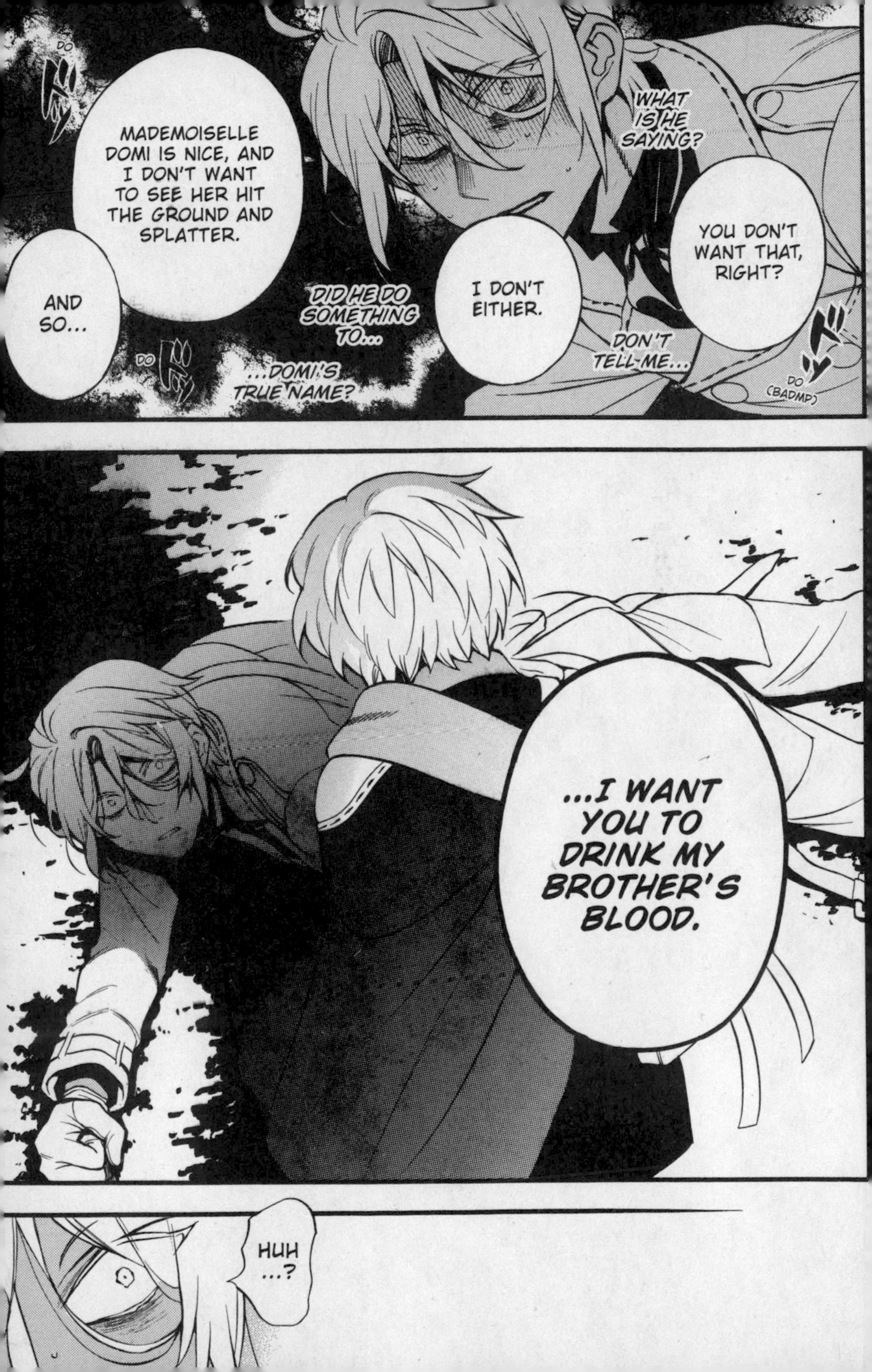

DO (BADMP)
WHAT IS HE SAYING?
YOU DON'T WANT THAT, RIGHT?
DON'T TELL ME...
I DON'T EITHER.
DID HE DO SOMETHING TO...
...DOMI'S TRUE NAME?
DO
MADEMOISELLE DOMI IS NICE, AND I DON'T WANT TO SEE HER HIT THE GROUND AND SPLATTER.
DO
AND SO...
...I WANT YOU TO DRINK MY BROTHER'S BLOOD.
HUH ...?

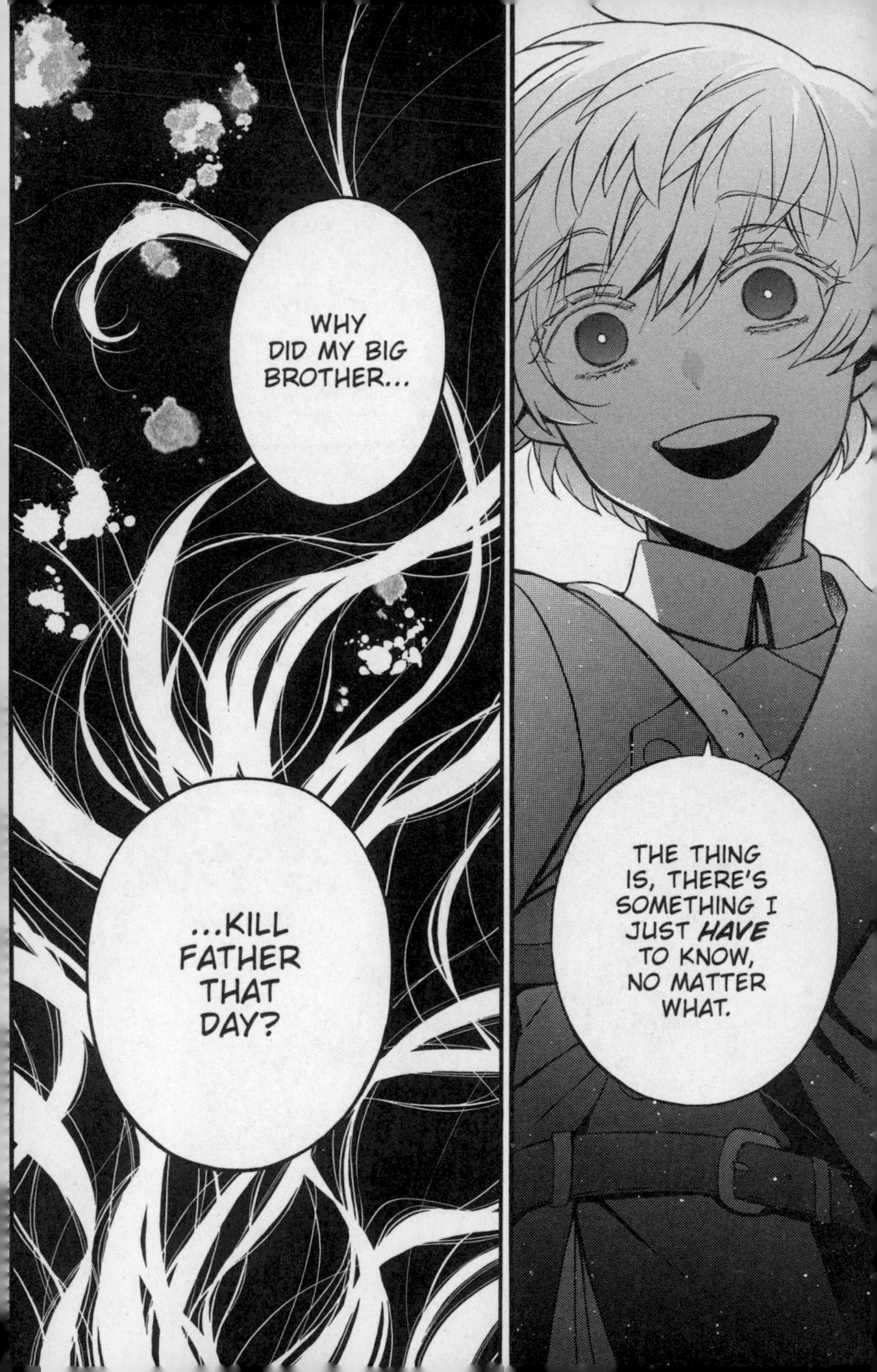
THE THING IS, THERE'S SOMETHING I JUST *HAVE* TO KNOW, NO MATTER WHAT.
WHY DID MY BIG BROTHER...
...KILL FATHER THAT DAY?

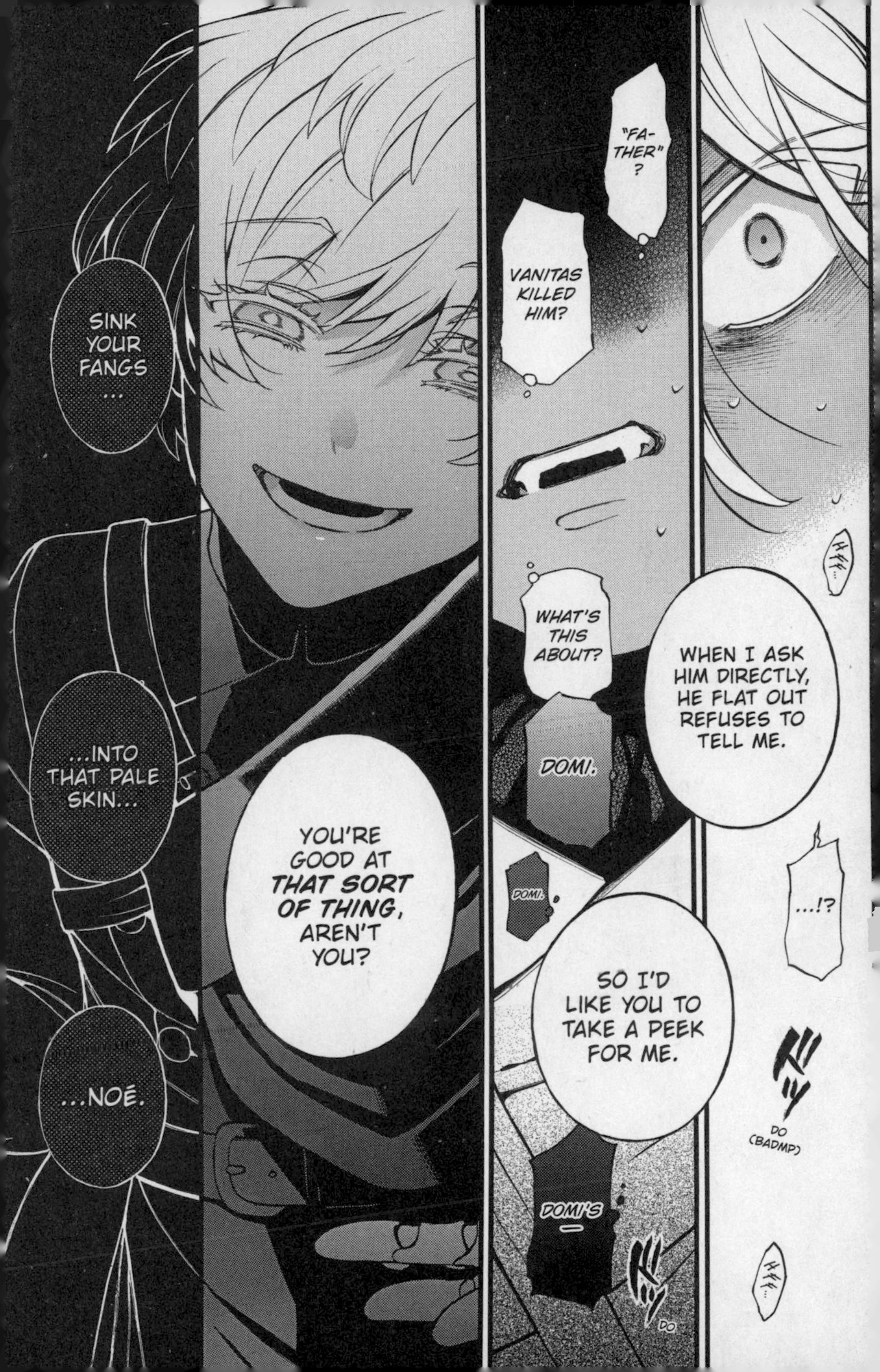
HFF...
"FA-THER"?
VANITAS KILLED HIM?
WHAT'S THIS ABOUT?
DOMI.
WHEN I ASK HIM DIRECTLY, HE FLAT OUT REFUSES TO TELL ME.
...!?
DOMI.
SO I'D LIKE YOU TO TAKE A PEEK FOR ME.
DO (BADMP)
DOMI'S—
DO
HFF...
YOU'RE GOOD AT THAT SORT OF THING, AREN'T YOU?
SINK YOUR FANGS...
...INTO THAT PALE SKIN...
...NOÉ.

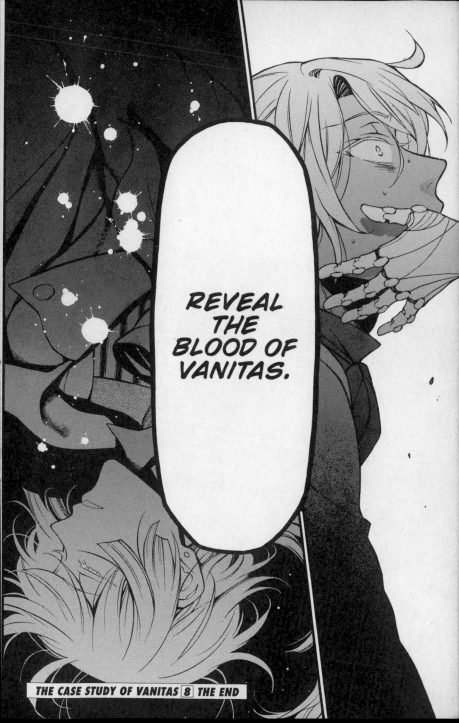

REVEAL THE BLOOD OF VANITAS.

THE CASE STUDY OF VANITAS [8] THE END

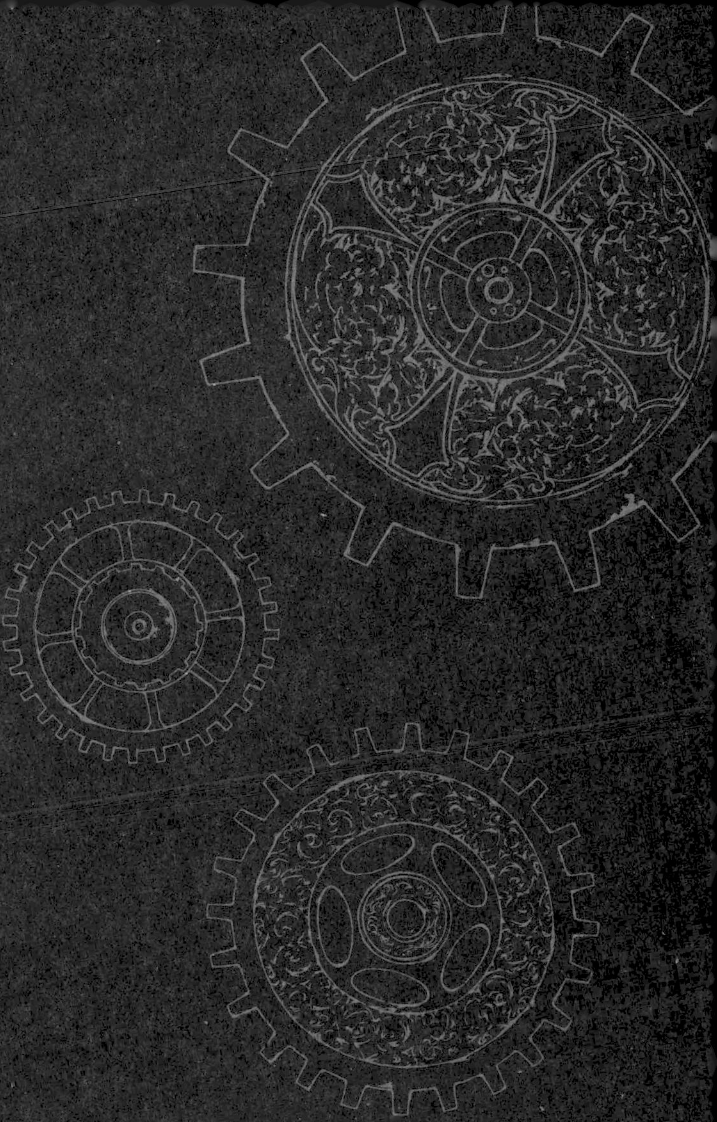

Mémoire 46 Un Autre SCAR

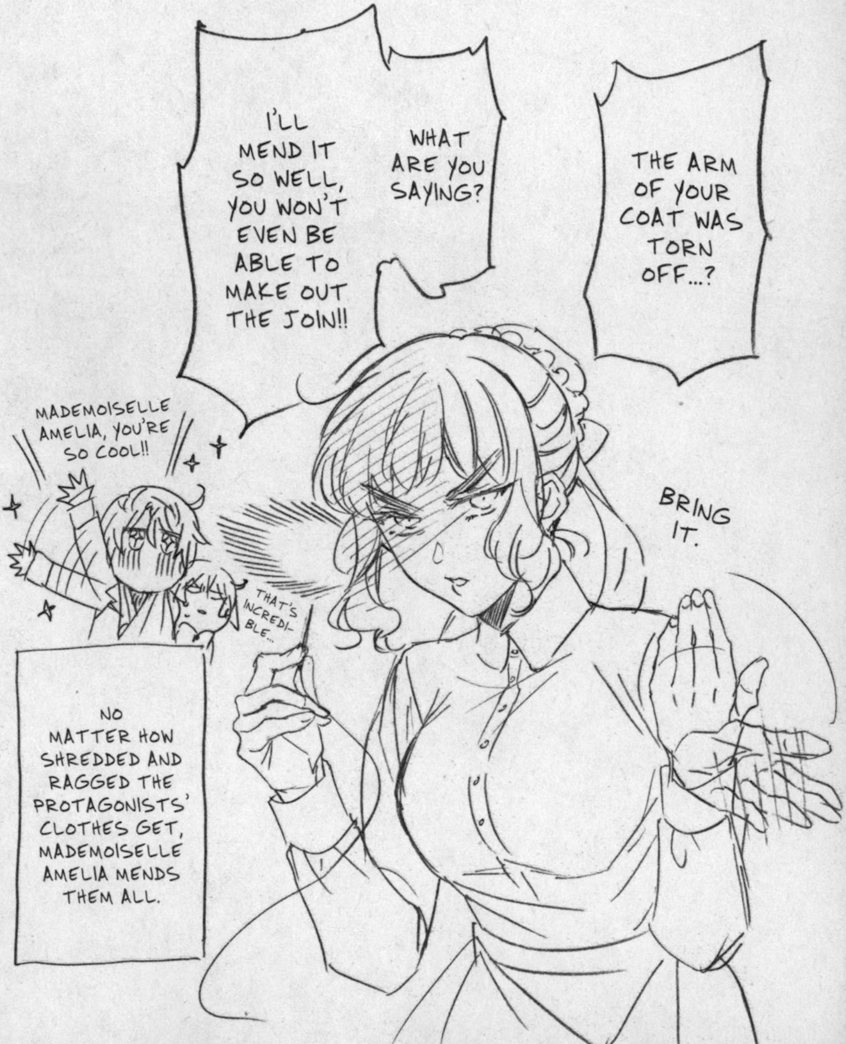
THE ARM OF YOUR COAT WAS TORN OFF...?
WHAT ARE YOU SAYING?
I'LL MEND IT SO WELL, YOU WON'T EVEN BE ABLE TO MAKE OUT THE JOIN!!
BRING IT.
MADEMOISELLE AMELIA, YOU'RE SO COOL!!
THAT'S INCREDIBLE...
NO MATTER HOW SHREDDED AND RAGGED THE PROTAGONISTS' CLOTHES GET, MADEMOISELLE AMELIA MENDS THEM ALL.

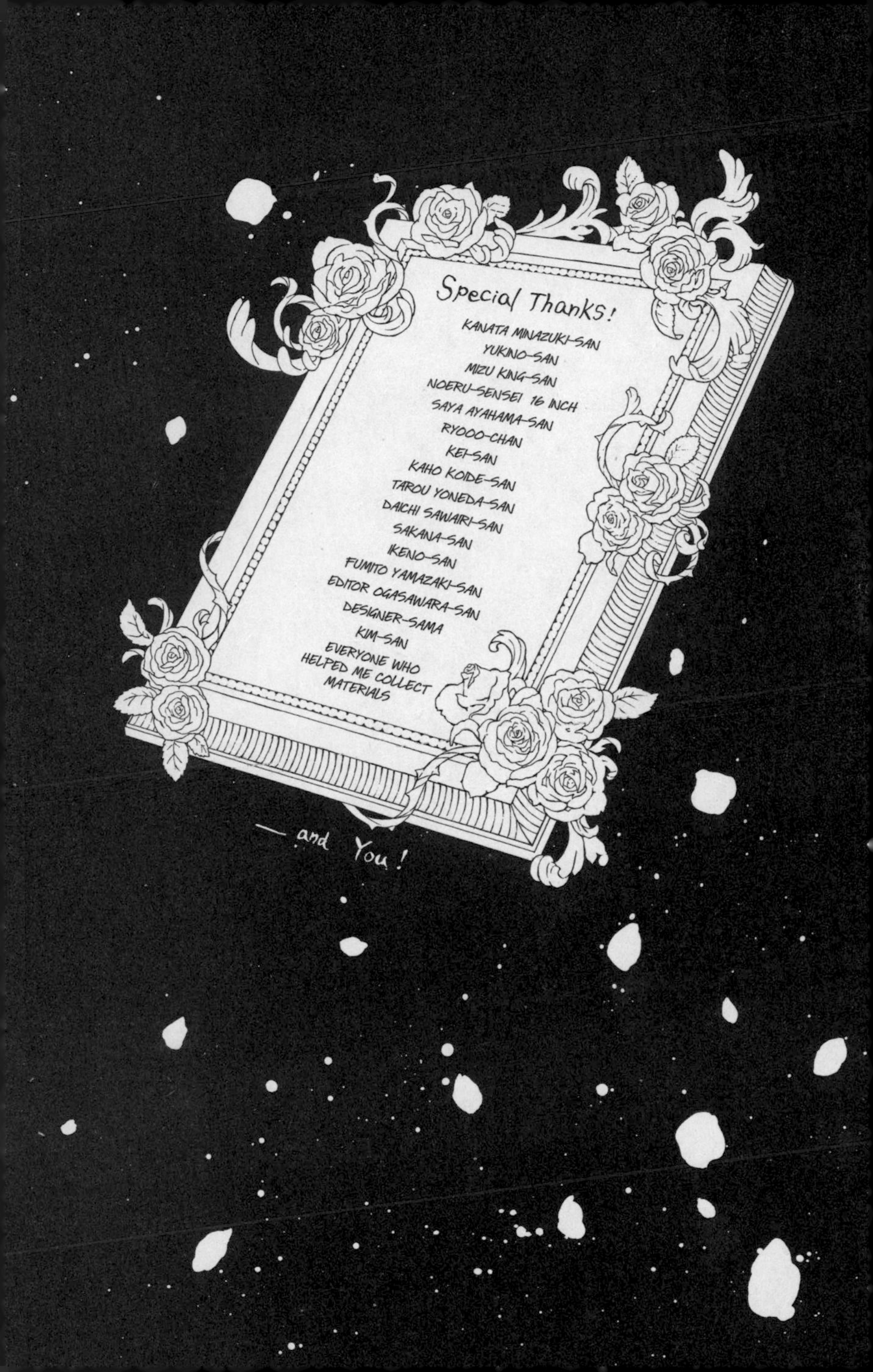
Special Thanks!
KANATA MINAZUKI-SAN
YUKINO-SAN
MIZU KING-SAN
NOERU-SENSEI 16 INCH
SAYA AYAHAMA-SAN
RYOOO-CHAN
KEI-SAN
KAHO KOIDE-SAN
TAROU YONEDA-SAN
DAICHI SAWAIRI-SAN
SAKANA-SAN
IKENO-SAN
FUMITO YAMAZAKI-SAN
EDITOR OGASAWARA-SAN
DESIGNER-SAMA
KIM-SAN
EVERYONE WHO HELPED ME COLLECT MATERIALS
—and You!

Next
Volume
Preview

A SECOND
BOOK OF VANITAS...

...HAS APPEARED.

HE WAS "VANITAS."

A VOLUME
LEFT BEHIND
BY A SHADOWY
ENIGMA...

...ONE THAT
BINDS TWO
BOYS TO
EACH OTHER.

The Case Study of Vanitas

VOLUME *9* COMING SOON

A TALE FROM BEFORE

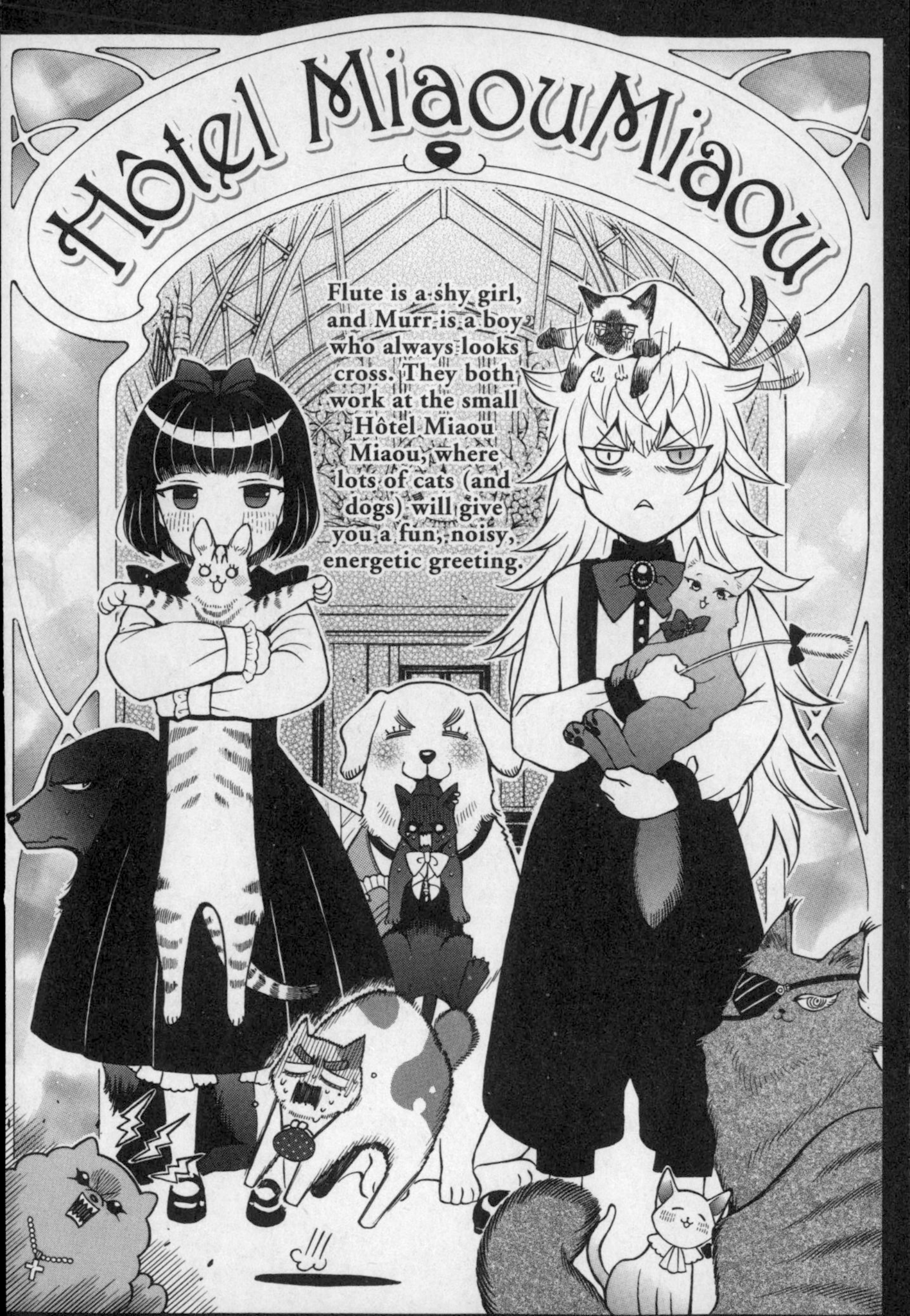
Hôtel MiaouMiaou
Flute is a shy girl, and Murr is a boy who always looks cross. They both work at the small Hôtel Miaou Miaou, where lots of cats (and dogs) will give you a fun, noisy, energetic greeting.

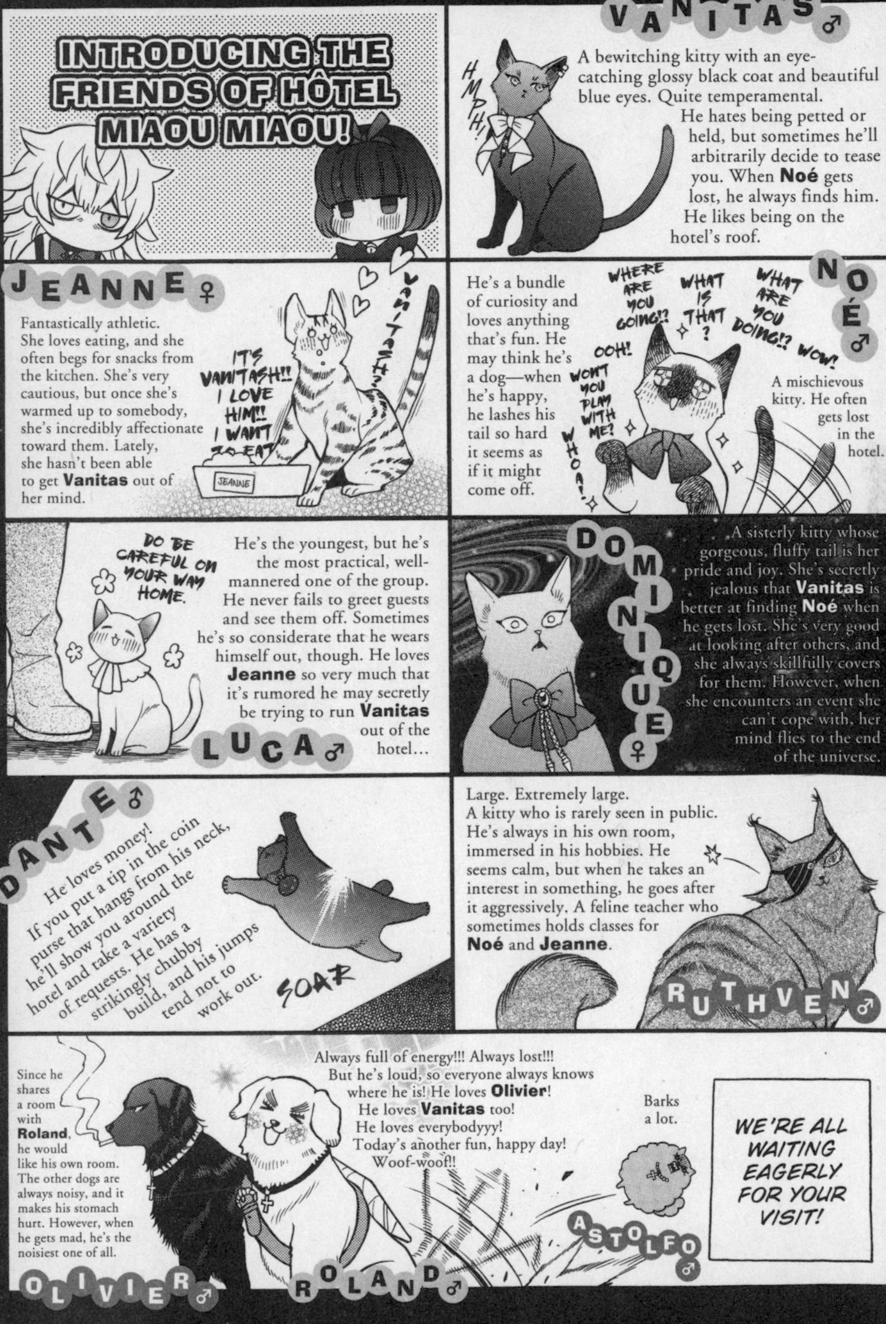
VANITAS ♂
A bewitching kitty with an eye-catching glossy black coat and beautiful blue eyes. Quite temperamental. He hates being petted or held, but sometimes he'll arbitrarily decide to tease you. When Noé gets lost, he always finds him. He likes being on the hotel's roof.
HMPH!
INTRODUCING THE FRIENDS OF HÔTEL MIAOU MIAOU!
NOÉ ♂
A mischievous kitty. He often gets lost in the hotel.
He's a bundle of curiosity and loves anything that's fun. He may think he's a dog—when he's happy, he lashes his tail so hard it seems as if it might come off.
WHAT ARE YOU DOING!? WOW!
WHAT IS THAT?
WHERE ARE YOU GOING!?
OOH!
WON'T YOU PLAY WITH ME?
WHOA!
JEANNE ♀
VANITASH?
IT'S VANITASH!! I LOVE HIM!! I WANT TO EAT
JEANNE
Fantastically athletic. She loves eating, and she often begs for snacks from the kitchen. She's very cautious, but once she's warmed up to somebody, she's incredibly affectionate toward them. Lately, she hasn't been able to get Vanitas out of her mind.
DOMINIQUE ♀
A sisterly kitty whose gorgeous, fluffy tail is her pride and joy. She's secretly jealous that Vanitas is better at finding Noé when he gets lost. She's very good at looking after others, and she always skillfully covers for them. However, when she encounters an event she can't cope with, her mind flies to the end of the universe.
He's the youngest, but he's the most practical, well-mannered one of the group. He never fails to greet guests and see them off. Sometimes he's so considerate that he wears himself out, though. He loves Jeanne so very much that it's rumored he may secretly be trying to run Vanitas out of the hotel...
DO BE CAREFUL ON YOUR WAY HOME.
LUCA ♂
Large. Extremely large. A kitty who is rarely seen in public. He's always in his own room, immersed in his hobbies. He seems calm, but when he takes an interest in something, he goes after it aggressively. A feline teacher who sometimes holds classes for Noé and Jeanne.
RUTHVEN ♂
DANTE ♂
He loves money! If you put a tip in the coin purse that hangs from his neck, he'll show you around the hotel and take a variety of requests. He has a strikingly chubby build, and his jumps tend not to work out.
SOAR
WE'RE ALL WAITING EAGERLY FOR YOUR VISIT!
Barks a lot.
ASTOLFO ♂
Always full of energy!!! Always lost!!! But he's loud, so everyone always knows where he is! He loves Olivier! He loves Vanitas too! He loves everybodyyy! Today's another fun, happy day! Woof-woof!!
ROLAND ♂
Since he shares a room with Roland, he would like his own room. The other dogs are always noisy, and it makes his stomach hurt. However, when he gets mad, he's the noisiest one of all.
OLIVIER ♂

I ENJOY READING
ESSAYS ABOUT
OVERSEAS
TRAVELS.

GORO
(ROLL)

GORO

Jun Mochizuki

AUTHOR'S NOTE

I'd like to grab
a backpack and
dash off on an
overseas trip.

Now read the latest chapters of BLACK BUTLER digitally at the same time as Japan and support the creator!

The Phantomhive family has a butler who's almost too good to be true...

...or maybe he's just too good to be human.

Black Butler

YANA TOBOSO

VOLUMES 1-29 IN STORES NOW!

HE DOES NOT LET ANYONE ROLL THE DICE.

A young Priestess joins her first adventuring party, but blind to the dangers, they almost immediately find themselves in trouble. It's Goblin Slayer who comes to their rescue—a man who has dedicated his life to the extermination of all goblins by any means necessary. A dangerous, dirty, and thankless job, but he does it better than anyone. And when rumors of his feats begin to circulate, there's no telling who might come calling next...

Light Novel V.1-11 Available Now!

Check out the simul-pub manga chapters every month!

Yen Press   YEN ON
www.yenpress.com

THE CASE STUDY OF VANITAS
VOLUME 8

JUN MOCHIZUKI

TRANSLATION: TAYLOR ENGEL
LETTERING: BIANCA PISTILLO

Vanitas no Carte Volume 8 ©2020 Jun Mochizuki/SQUARE ENIX CO., LTD.
First published in Japan in 2020 by SQUARE ENIX CO., LTD. English translation rights arranged with SQUARE ENIX CO., LTD. and Yen Press, LLC through Tuttle-Mori Agency, Inc., Tokyo.

English translation ©2021 by SQUARE ENIX CO., LTD.

Yen Press
150 West 30th Street, 19th Floor
New York, NY 10001

Visit us at yenpress.com
facebook.com/yenpress
twitter.com/yenpress
yenpress.tumblr.com
instagram.com/yenpress

First Yen Press Edition: May 2021

The chapters in this volume were originally published as ebooks by Yen Press.

Yen Press is an imprint of Yen Press, LLC.
The Yen Press name and logo are trademarks of Yen Press, LLC.

Library of Congress Control Number: 2016946115

ISBNs: 978-1-9753-2453-7 (paperback)
978-1-9753-2452-0 (ebook)

10 9 8 7 6 5 4 3 2 1

WOR

Printed in the United States of America